Industrial Relations and Health Services

Edited by AMARJIT SINGH SETHI
and STUART J. DIMMOCK

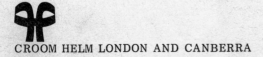

CROOM HELM LONDON AND CANBERRA

© 1982 Amarjit Singh Sethi and Stuart J. Dimmock
Croom Helm Ltd, 2-10 St John's Road, London SW11

British Library Cataloguing in Publication Data

Industrial relations and health services.
  1. Industrial relations - Addresses, essays, lectures
  2. Medical care - Addresses, essays, lectures
  I. Sethi, Amarjit Singh
  II. Dimmock, Stuart J.
  331'.0413621   HD6976.H/

ISBN 0-7099-0379-0

Reproduced from copy supplied
printed and bound in Great Britain
by Billing and Sons Limited
Guildford, London, Oxford, Worcester

CONTENTS

Acknowledgements

Preface

Part I: Labour and Health Care: Introduction 11

  1. Industrial Relations in the Health Sector 13
     A.S. Sethi and S.J. Dimmock
  2. Health Sector Labour Market: Canada, USA
     and UK 20
     M. Gunderson

Part II: Labour Movement 39

  Introduction 41
  3. The Labour Movement in Health Care: Canada 42
     R. Sykes and A.S. Sethi
  4. The Labour Movement in Health Care: USA 54
     C. Schoen
  5. The Labour Movement in the National Health
     Service (NHS): UK 74
     M. Carpenter

Part III: Legislation 91

  Introduction 93
  6. Legislation Governing Health Industrial Relations:
     Canada 94
     C. Steinberg
  7. Legislation Governing Health Industrial Relations:
     USA 113
     T.C. McKinney and M. Levine
  8. Legislation Governing Industrial Relations in the
     National Health Service: UK 139
     S.D. Anderman, J.H. Angel and R. Mailly

Contents

Part IV: Collective Bargaining Experience   169

Introduction   171
9. Structural Issue of Centralised Bargaining in
    Health Services: Canada, USA and UK   172
    G. Adams, D. Beatty and M. Gunderson
10. Collective Bargaining Among Nurses: Canada,
    USA and UK   190
    *A.S. Sethi, G. Rowsell, N. Solomon and
    M. Carpenter*
11. Collective Bargaining Among Non-professional
    and Allied Professional Employees in the Health
    Sector   208
    *A.S. Sethi, R.H. Stansel, N. Solomon and
    S.J. Dimmock*
12. Bargaining Strategies Among Physicians: Canada,
    USA and UK   233
    E.J. Moran, T.A. Barocci and S.J. Dimmock

Part V: Conflict Resolution   257

Introduction   259
13. Conflict Resolution: The Canadian Experience   260
    W.P. Kelly
14. Dispute Resolution Methods   269
    A.V. Subbarao
15. Role of Arbitration in Health Sector Dispute
    Settlement: Canada, USA and UK   287
    L. Harnden

Part VI: Policy   301

Introduction   303
16. Effect of Incomes Policy on Health Industrial
    Relations in Canada   304
    F. Reid
17. Incomes Policy and Health Services in the UK   325
    S.J. Dimmock
18. Effect of Incomes Policies on the Health Care
    Industrial Relations System in the USA   342
    R. Santos and I.B. Helburn
19. Health Industrial Relations: A Concluding
    Observation   358
    A.S. Sethi and S.J. Dimmock

Contributors   366

Index   368

Acknowledgements

We must pay thanks to the various contributors of this volume, without whom this book would not have become a reality. We thank Tim Hardwick of Croom Helm Ltd, London whose support and suggestions were critical in the development of this work. Thanks are due to the University of Ottawa who granted Professor A.S. Sethi the sabbatical leave to finish the study. Special thanks are given to Dr Norman Solomon, Dr Charles Steinberg, Mr Lynn Harnden and Dr Alton Craig for their advice and research assistance. Special thanks are due to Mrs Diane Fontaine for typing the manuscript.

Preface

This book has been written for all those interested in industrial relations in health services: health administrators and policy-makers, negotiators, physicians, nurses and students and researchers in health-care administration.

'Industrial Relations and Health Services' is a book of readings that covers a wide variety of issues affecting industrial relations in the health sector in Canada, USA and UK. Some of these issues covered in the book include health labour market trends, structure of the labour movements, the nature of state and federal labour legislation, collective bargaining strategies and techniques employed by the actors and their relative power status, dispute resolution methods, including mediation, conciliation and arbitration, effects of incomes policy, and structural and operational changes in both health-care delivery system and the industrial relations system.

The various contributors in this volume explore how the results of an industrial relations system are produced in three health-care delivery systems through the industrial relations processes. The overall framework that has been adopted is that of John Dunlop's concept of an industrial relations system. This has been applied to industrial relations in the three health sectors in order to identify the roles of the principal actors and the internal and external influences that affect their behaviour and values.

The book is divided into six parts. Part I identifies and discusses the conceptual framework of the book and deals with the health sector labour market in Canada, UK and USA. In Part II the structure of the labour movement as applicable to the health sector in each country is examined. Part III deals with the legislative framework of health industrial relations in Canada, USA and UK. In Part IV, the structural issue of centralised bargaining is analysed, and the comparative analyses in this part include the discussion of collective bargaining trends among hospital workers, nurses, physicians and allied professionals. In Part V conflict resolution techniques are examined, including a discussion of mediation and arbitration techniques. In Part VI, the authors assess the effect of incomes policy on health industrial relations in Canada, USA and UK, together with some concluding observations on industrial relations in the health sectors of Canada, USA and UK.

The approach in the text is comparative, in so far as this is possible. The purpose is to allow the reader in each country to look at similar or different labour problems in health care in countries other than their own to learn the complexity of each problem and how it has been tackled in that country. In this way it is hoped that lessons can be learnt from each other's experience and the book may provide a stimulus both to students and the practitioners in health industrial relations to profit from this comparative approach. The opinions of the authors, however, do not reflect value judgements of the editors.

Amarjit Singh Sethi, Ottawa, Canada.
S.J. Dimmock, Leeds, England.

PART I

LABOUR AND HEALTH CARE: INTRODUCTION

1. INDUSTRIAL RELATIONS IN THE HEALTH SECTOR

A.S. Sethi and S.J. Dimmock

This book examines a number of the major industrial relations issues, which have emerged with increasing force in the late 1960s and the 1970s, in the health sectors in Canada, the USA and the UK. It is hoped thereby to develop an understanding and sensitivity in the reader towards the complexities of the industrial relations systems within the respective health sectors. The concept of an industrial relations system was pioneered by John Dunlop, who posited that it could be viewed as an analytical subsystem of an industrial society on the same logical plane as the economic subsystem. These two subsystems are not coterminous, as in some respects they overlap and in other respects both have different scopes.[1] Blain and Gennard in discussing the work of Dunlop have argued that the industrial relations system overlaps with a further principal subsystem – the political subsystem.[2] Diagrammatically the situation can be represented as in Figure 1.1.

Figure 1.1: Relationship of the Industrial Relations System to Wider Society

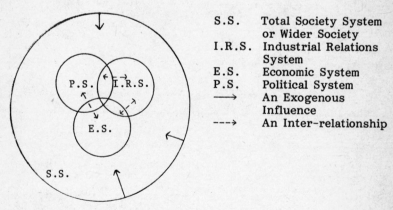

S.S.	Total Society System or Wider Society
I.R.S.	Industrial Relations System
E.S.	Economic System
P.S.	Political System
$\longrightarrow$	An Exogenous Influence
$--\rightarrow$	An Inter-relationship

For Dunlop the industrial relations system comprises three groups of actors: workers and their representative organisations; managers and their representative organisations; and governmental agencies concerned with the work place and work community.[3] The interactions of the three groups of actors produce a 'web of rules'. These rules can be broadly divided into three types: substantive rules which relate to the work place, e.g. the regulation of pay and conditions; procedural rules which govern the conduct of substantive rule-making, e.g. disputes procedures; and procedures for deciding the application of substantive rules to specific situations, e.g. arbitration and grievance settlement. The element which binds the industrial relations system together is a shared ideology. The essence of the common ideology is a reciprocal understanding and acceptance between the actors of the role and function of the others within the system. The industrial relations system is affected by three interrelated environments: the technology, the market or budgetary constraints and the power relations within the larger community. Figure 1.2 (based on the work of Eldridge[4]) is a diagrammatic representation of Dunlop's industrial relations system with its associated contextual features.

Figure 1.2: John T. Dunlop's Industrial Relations System

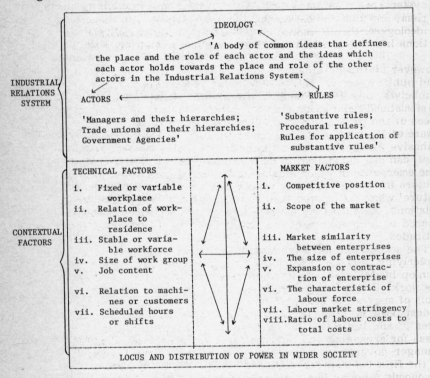

While the views of Dunlop have been subjected to a series of criticisms, it remains an influential view of industrial relations.

Indeed a great deal of subsequent work has been based upon it. In Britain, for example, Flanders[5] has also identified rules as the core of industrial relations, although he tended to focus on the relationship between rule-making and collective bargaining rather than the influences that emanate from the wider environment.[6]

In the context of examining industrial relations in the three separate health sectors it is necessary to identify and discuss, albeit briefly, two major criticisms of Dunlop. The first criticism stems from Dunlop's treatment of ideology, which is based on the structural-functionalist approach of the sociologist Talcott Parsons. In the view of radical theorists the usage of 'ideology' infers a basic conservatism within the industrial relations system. For example, Hyman when referring to Dunlop's view that '... these ideologies be sufficiently compatible and consistent so as to permit a common set of ideas which recognise an acceptable role for each actor',[7] makes the following observation:

> ... if it is part of the definition of an industrial relations system that it contains built-in tendencies towards equilibrium, and that radical conflict is excluded from the actors' ideologies, then it cannot be assumed that industrial relations in the real world constitutes a system at all.[8]

However as Dunlop indicates, hierarchies of managers, workers and public agencies tend to develop or adopt intellectuals, publicists, or other specialists concerned with articulating systematically and making some form of order out of the separate ideas of the principal actors. This suggests that Dunlop was aware of the problematic nature of the concept of ideology as an adhesive within the system.[9] Equally the notion of 'radical conflict' can also be subject to different degrees of interpretation. The emergence of major industrial disputes in the three health sectors in the 1970s clearly represents a conflict of a 'radical nature' when set against the established traditions of industrial relations. As such they have clearly had an impact on both the shared understandings of the actors and their discrete sets of attitudes.

The second and more fundamental criticism centres on the underlying purpose of Dunlop's industrial relations system. Dunlop himself claims to have provided different functions for his work: it is a '... general theory of industrial relations; ... tools of analysis to interpret and to gain understanding of the widest possible range of industrial relations facts and practices',[10] and lastly that it '... develops a systematic body of ideas for arranging and interpreting the known facts of worker-manager-government interaction'.[11] Many have been dismissive of the first two aspects of Dunlop's claim, while the latter taxonomic function has been more widely accepted. Bain and Clegg lend support to this view of Dunlop's achievement and argue that it is 'only permissible and useful to use the notion of a "system" as an heuristic device for structuring data'.[12]

The breadth of approach offered by the third function of Dunlop's industrial relations system has led to criticisms that as an heuristic device for ordering complex data it fails to capture the dynamic within the industrial relations system:[13] the ways in which the various elements within the system itself and the interrelated environments interact and the degree of significance that can be attached to these different interactions. Thus it has been argued that the system encourages descriptions of industrial relations rather than explanations.[14] By comparison it has been argued that if the industrial relations system is seen as a rule-making system, then it does provide a theoretical object: '... if it is accepted that the distinctiveness of Dunlop lies in the establishment of the *concept* of an industrial relations system, conceptual work of this type should be regarded as a required stage of theoretical analysis and theory building'.[15]

Industrial relations in the health sector has assumed new dimensions over the last ten or so years. The sheer speed of events has largely precluded systematic empirical investigations of the issues to be discussed in this book. Indeed until the last few years few academics in these countries have been seriously concerned with health sector industrial relations. Against this background the intention is to use Dunlop's approach according to its claimed third function: a means for arranging a systematic body of ideas for arranging and interpreting the known facts of worker-manager-government interactions within the field of health care. It is argued that approaches of this kind are a-theoretical and tend to present data of a largely descriptive and historical character. If this criticism is a legitimate objection to the approach of the book, then the objection is sustained. However, it should be borne in mind that some form of conceptual map is required before empirical expeditions can be successfully mounted. This book is an attempt to identify and examine some of the major elements of the landscape of industrial relations in these three health sectors. Moreover, the application of the concept of an industrial relations system to three different health sectors follows Dunlop's own interest in comparative national analysis.

THE FOCUS AND OUTLINE OF THE BOOK

As the health sectors in the three countries enter the 1980s they carry with them a history of labour conflicts which represent a deeper malaise. The developments in industrial relations over the preceding decade have often had the effect of disturbing or overturning traditional public expectations of the role of health workers - a deeply held and unchanging vocational commitment. Therefore, and perhaps not surprisingly, both the conflicts themselves and the issues they represent are frequently referred to as 'problems' by the groups of actors within the industrial

relations system and by the wider community. The characterisa-
tion of industrial conflict and related events as 'problems' may
often indicate a particular set of assumptions: a belief in the
basic equilibrium of the system in which conflicts emerge from
the inadequacies of existing structures. (Reference has already
been made to this by Hyman.) The concern to adopt a 'reformist
approach' to industrial relations, by the process of restructuring either the representative agencies of the actors, or by
changing the rules that govern the system, has been roundly
criticised by Goldthorpe.[16] Taking up his criticism it is important to note that, in terms of the size of the health sectors, the
numbers employed and the sheer complexities of the organisations for the delivery of health care, the incidence of industrial
conflict (often perceived by management and government as a
'problem') remains relatively low when compared with other
industrial sectors in the three countries. Thus while the term
'problem' is sometimes used in the text it is not the authors'
intention to take a categoric stance over the major issues; rather
it should be seen as an indication of the perceptions of the
actors within the industrial relations systems and the magnitude
which they themselves attach to them.

The roots of these issues are buried within the historical
development of the three respective health sectors. During the
last decade elements within the distinct contexts that form the
environment of the industrial relations system have shaped their
rapid emergence. In broad terms the major issues can be categorised as follows:

1. Health-care workers have become increasingly aware of the
    differences and seeming inequities in their pay levels and
    those of other occupational groups within society. Added to
    this has been the frustration and anger caused by the impact
    of inflation, incomes policy and subsequent 'earning lag' in
    their relatively low pay levels. In consequence large seg-
    ments of health workers, particularly in the hospital sector
    have redefined their values towards work. These changed
    attitudes have prompted them to ask for greater incomes
    and for a greater involvement in the management of health
    care institutions.

2. The long standing neglect of pay inequities and the changed
    attitudes have led to a number of strikes in the health sec-
    tors. Under the rules in the health sectors' industrial rela-
    tions systems in North America, many of these strikes have
    been illegal – a situation which federal and state govern-
    ments (who represent one of the actors within the system),
    find difficult to ignore. To patients and those awaiting
    hospitalisation the impact of these events is a personal exper-
    ience. In the mind of the public at large, strike activity and
    other forms of industrial action have established health sec-
    tor industrial relations as a 'problem'. In the UK successive
    governments have set up a series of independent committees

of inquiry to provide a means for the resolution of these disputes. While in North America consideration of re-instituting binding arbitration awards has also assumed the dimensions of a political problem. These two events indicate the overlap between the industrial relations and the political subsystems. Alternatively governments in the three countries face the unions' insistence that the right to strike is a fundamental right in a democratic society. Thus the legal frameworks governing industrial relations in the health sectors are confronted with the challenge of responding to the changing aspirations and expectations of the workers.

3.   Another remarkable development, particularly in North America, has been the emergence of collective bargaining or similar practices among physicians, who traditionally in the eyes of the public are among the highest paid profes-sionals in society. By comparison the medical profession in the UK has enjoyed independent reviews of earnings on a systematic basis since the early 1960s, although on occasions its principal representative body has engaged in collective bargaining. However, in both North America and the UK the medical profession shares a common wish to maintain their relatively high income. Moreover they regard it as essential that they should be consulted in any change of the health care delivery system. The resident interns ('junior doctors' in the UK) claim to be both low paid and overworked. In the UK this frustration has been an important element in the fragmentation of the profession's representation. Although the success of collective bargaining among doctors varies in each country, the demands of the profession (who repre-sent the most powerful 'workers' within one group of actors in the industrial relations system), are a predominant force in the respective health sectors and society more generally.

In the various parts of the book the authors seek to explore these issues against Dunlop's concept of an industrial relations system. In Part I, Gunderson's discussion of major characteris-tics of health labour markets sets the scene in terms of some of the major features within the 'market and budgetary constraints' context of the environment. In Part II the authors examine the labour movement within the respective health sectors to identify some of the principal issues which affect one of the actors within the industrial relations system - workers and their organisations. Part III then examines the role of government and its influence on the rule-making process through the law. Part IV addresses the process of rule-making between workers' organisations and management at hospital, state/provincial, and national/federal levels. Part V turns to one of the principal types of rule-making identified by Dunlop - arbitration and mediation in conflict resolution - which forms an important element in the rule-making process in the North American context. The interwoven relation-ship between government and management is an important feature

of health sector industrial relations in Canada and the UK.
Although the USA health care sector is more distanced from
government it nevertheless plays a critical role in pay determination through the operation of incomes policy. Thus in Part VI
the effect of incomes policy on rule-making over pay and conditions is analysed in detail in each of the three countries.

REFERENCES AND NOTES

1 Dunlop, John T., (1958), 'Industrial Relations Systems',
Holt.

2 Blain, A.N.J. and Gennard, J., (1970), Industrial Relations
Theory - A Critical Review, 'British Journal of Industrial
Relations', vol.VIII, no.3, pp.387-407.

3 Dunlop, John T., 'Industrial Relations System', p.382.

4 Eldridge, J.E.T., (1968), 'Industrial Disputes', Routledge
& Kegan Paul, pp.19-22.

5 Flanders, A., (1965), 'Industrial Relations: What is Wrong
with the System?', Faber and Faber, pp.7-10.

6 The importance of collective bargaining, within the industrial
relations system, as the mechanism for determining both
material and psychological rewards has been emphasised by
Alton Craig, A Model for the Analysis of Industrial Relations
Systems, in H.C. Jain (ed.), (1975), 'Canadian Labour and
Industrial Relations', McGraw Hill Ryerson, Toronto,
pp.1-12.

7 Dunlop, John T., 'Industrial Relations Systems', p.17.

8 Hyman, R., (1972), 'Strikes', Fontana, p.68.

9 Wood, S.J., Wagner, A., Armstrong, E.G.A., Goodman,
J.F.B., and Davis, J.E., (1975), The 'Industrial Relations
System' Concept as a Basis for Theory in Industrial Relations, 'British Journal of Industrial Relations', vol.XIII,
no.3, pp.291-308.

10 Dunlop, John T., 'Industrial Relations Systems', p.vii.

11 Ibid., p.380.

12 Bain, G.S., and Clegg, H.A., (1974), A Strategy for
Industrial Relations Research in Great Britain, 'British
Journal of Industrial Relations', vol.XII, no.1, p.92.

13 See for example, Somers, G.G., Bargaining Power and Industrial Relations Theory, in G.G. Somers (ed.), (1969),
'Essays in Industrial Relations Theory', Iowa State University Press.

14 Hill, S., and Thurley, K., (1974), Sociology and Industrial
Relations, 'British Journal of Industrial Relations', vol.XII,
no.2.

15 Wood, S.J. et al., 'The Industrial Relations System Concept',
p.294.

16 Goldthorpe, J.H., (1978), Industrial Relations in Great Britain: A Critique of Reformism, in Tom Clarke and Laurie
Clements, 'Trade Unions under Capitalism', Fontana.

2. HEALTH SECTOR LABOUR MARKET: CANADA, USA AND UK

M. Gunderson

INTRODUCTION

The health sector labour market forms a legitimate line of enquiry for a variety of reasons. It has implications for each of the three main actors -- labour, management and government -- in the industrial relations scene. In addition, the labour market environment in which the actors operate has implications for many of the other topics addressed in this book, notably the impact of such features as unions, legislation, collective bargaining by professionals and nonprofessionals, centralised bargaining, alternative dispute resolution procedures, incomes policy and interest arbitration. These factors both shape and are shaped by the peculiarities of the health sector labour market.

From the public interest perspective, knowledge of the health sector labour market is also essential. Because of its size, labour intensity and the essential nature of the service provided in the health sector, the cost, quality and very availability of health services can be affected by such labour market outcomes as wage settlements, strikes and labour relations in general. Clearly this makes the health sector important in its own right; however, an analysis of the health sector also forms part of a larger enquiry into the nature of labour markets in the large and growing noncompetitive not-for-profit sector in general.

Even within the health sector itself, the labour market merits scrutiny because labour is a resource that is different from other resources in the health sector. This is aptly illustrated by Mejia and Fulop:

Manpower requires the longest preparatory period of all the health resources and cannot be improvised. It is also subject to a certain inherent inertia, in that the rigidity of the health and education systems and the attitudes of health workers do not make for easy mobility or conduce to improving geographical and occupational distribution. Nor can manpower be stored or discarded. If it is to be available at the proper time, it has to be planned for in advance in the right amount and type -- no more and no less than is needed. Because they are subject to obsolescence, manpower abilities and skills also need to be maintained by means of permanent supervision and continuing education.[1]

Clearly these characteristics illustrate how labour is different
from other resources in the health sector, and this, coupled with
the peculiarities of the health sector labour market relative to
other labour markets, gives rise to some interesting implications
for the health sector in general.

The purpose of this chapter is to examine the health sector
labour market, both by itself and in the more general context of
it being in the not-for-profit sector, and to discuss the implications of its peculiar characteristics. Rather than attempting an
exhaustive description of the institutional features of the health
sector in Britain, Canada and the US, the focus is at the conceptual, analytical level, utilising specific examples from the
three countries to illustrate the more general points. After a
brief discussion of the meaning and dimension of the health
sector labour market, the characteristics of the health sector
labour market, and their implications, are discussed under
labour demand characteristics and labour supply characteristics.

MEANING AND DIMENSION OF HEALTH SECTOR LABOUR MARKETS

The health sector labour market has both an industrial and
occupational dimension. The industrial dimension refers simply
to the health industry while the occupation dimension refers to
health-care work in whatever industry it is conducted. To a
large extent the dimensions overlap; that is, most health-care
occupations are in the health industry with hospitals being the
dominant employer. Nevertheless, there can be differences. The
industry designation can include non health-care occupations
such as secretaries and maintenance staff. Conversely, many
persons in health occupations may be employed in industries
other than health care: a company nurse, for example, may be
in the manufacturing sector.

Thus, a broad definition of the health labour market would
include all persons of all occupations in the health industry as
well as all health occupations in nonhealth industries. A narrow
definition would include only those in health occupations in the
health industry. The appropriate definition, of course, depends
on the purposes of the analysis. It is not that one definition is
right or wrong; although it may be important to be explicit about
the concept that is utilised. In our analysis the broader concept
of the health labour market is utilised, although at times references are made to the more narrow dimensions.

Table 2.1 gives some basic figures on various dimensions of
the health sector labour market in Canada, the UK and the US.
They should be regarded as, at best, illustrative since international data comparisons are quite hazardous. The United Kingdom is lower than Canada and the US in total health expenditures
as a percent of Gross Domestic Product (GDP) and this is also
reflected in its lower numbers of nurses and physicians per

10 000 population. The importance of the private sector in the US (unlike Canada and especially the UK where the public sector dominates the health industry), is evidenced by the low ratio (3.0 per cent of health expenditures to GDP, and by the lower proportion of expenditures covered by hospital and medical insurance.

Two further observations stand out as anomalies in Table 2.1. They are the large growth between 1960 and 1970 in physicians in Canada and nurses in the UK (albeit the latter still had the lowest number of fully-qualified nurses by 1970), and the large number of nurses per 10 000 population in Canada by 1970 (in spite of it having the slowest growth in nursing personnel). These observations suggest health care can be achieved in quite dramatically different ways and with different changes in resources over time, even in countries that are considered advanced in their provision of health-care resources.

Unfortunately consistent international comparisons are not readily available on the size and growth of the health sector labour market, both absolutely and relative to the total labour force, in each of the three countries. However, Ginsberg[2] indicates that the health sector in 1974 was the second largest industry in the US employing approximately 4.5 million persons, or more than 5 per cent of the civilian labour force. Comparable estimates of the health sector employing slightly over 5 per cent of the labour force are found in Canada according to the 1971 Census, and in Britain according to the Royal College of Nursing.[3] Clearly a sector of this magnitude deserves careful analysis, especially given the essential nature of the service provided.

Table 2.1: Select Characteristics Relating to Health Sectors,
*   Canada, USA and UK*

Characteristic	Canada	United Kingdom	United States
Physicians per 10 000 population	15.1	12.7	15.4
% change in physicians 1960–70	+32.7	+17.1	+17.9
Nurses per 10 000 population, 1970[a]	45.9	30.7	35.3
% change in nurses 1960–70[a]	+20.2	+47.6	+26.5
Public health expenditure as % of GDP[b]	5.1	4.6	3.0
Total health expenditures as % of GDP[b]	6.8	5.2	7.4
% covered by insurance	Almost 100%	Almost 100%	85% hospital 65% regular med. 35% major med.

Notes:
a. Figures for nurses refer to fully-qualified nurses only. The UK refers to England and Wales only for the physician and nurses figures.
b. The relevant dates are Canada 1973, the UK 1975 and the US 1974. The overall OECD averages are 5.7% for total and 4.4% for public health expenditures.

Source: Maxwell, R., (1975), 'Health Care: The Growing Dilemma', 2nd edition, McKinsey and Co., Tables 12-19; Organisation for Economic Cooperation and Development (1977), 'Public Expenditure on Health', OECD, p.10; Canada Department of National Health and Welfare (1974), 'A New Perspective on the Health of Canadians', p.27.

Labour Demand Characteristics

Knowledge of the nature of the demand for health sector labour is important for a variety of reasons. Wages, salaries and even professional income can be affected by growth in the demand for particular types of labour and by what economists term the elasticity of demand for labour -- the change in the quantity of labour that results from a given change in its price. Demand elasticity in turn affects such things as the employment effect, and hence the availability of health resources, that can emanate from such factors as occupational licensing and wage fixing through unions, minimum wages, equal pay laws and arbitration awards. In essence, the cost and availability of health services, as well as the well-being and quality of health sector workers, are intricately tied to the characteristics of the demand for labour in that sector.

The demand for labour in the health sector, as in other sectors, is a derived demand, derived from the demand for the ultimate services produced by the health sector. Consequently, any enquiry into the demand for labour in the health sector must examine the characteristics of the product or service market where the labour is employed. In this vein, the public nature of the health sector, the characteristics of the health-care system itself, and the importance of professionals can be identified as primarily important factors. Each of these will be examined in turn.

Public and Essential Service Sector

Probably the overriding characteristic that affects the health sector labour market most profoundly is that it is largely in the public, or more generally, in the not-for-profit sector. Most, but not all, employment is in hospitals, the vast majority of which are not-for-profit institutions, especially in Britain and Canada. In such circumstances the employers' wage and employment decisions need not be constrained by the ultimate need to make profits to stay in business. Consequently the pressure to be cost conscious need not be as great as in the private sector, and as suggested by Feldstein[4], hospitals may even engage in

'philanthropic wage behaviour'. Wage cost increases may be
passed on to taxpayers without their reducing their demand for
the services, given the indirect nature of payment and the
essential nature of the service. This opens up the possibility --
and it is only a possibility -- that wages may be higher and/or
labour may be used inefficiently relative to what they would be
if hospitals were exclusively in the private sector.

This may be offset by other factors that emanate from the
public sector nature of the health sector. Presumably health
care is largely a public sector activity because of a belief that
it cannot be provided fully in the private sector. The essential
nature of the service combined with the consumer misinforma-
tion problem have resulted in public domination of the health
sector, especially in Britain and Canada. This very fact, however, also affects the health sector labour market. In particular,
workers in the health sector are under considerable public
pressure to provide the service no matter what the pay or working conditions, many may regard their activity as a public duty or
even a 'calling', they are often denied the right to strike, and
their wages and working conditions are often determined by
arbitration. Recent pressures to curb the growth of the public
sector in general, and health costs in particular, will also put a
demand-side constraint on the public health sector that may be
as binding as the profit constraint of the private sector. In
essence, the pay and working conditions of health sector personnel are affected in an indeterminant fashion by the fact that
health care is predominantly an essential service conducted
largely through the public sector.

Limited empirical evidence suggests that in the US, where
there are a substantial number of private hospitals, nurses'
wages are higher in the public than in the private hospitals.[5]
However, Canadian evidence suggests that the hospitals (mainly
public sector) pay their maintenance workers less than similar
maintenance workers in the private sector.[6] Clearly, until more
comprehensive empirical evidence is available it is not feasible
to make blanket statements about how the wages of health-care
workers in general are affected by the public-sector nature of
their jobs.

Characteristics of the Health-care System
The characteristics of the health-care system itself will also
affect the demand for health services and hence the derived
demand for labour in the health sector. Of particular interest
is how health services are paid for and how the health delivery
systems are organised.

Britain has a universal (available to all) health-care delivery
system, financed from general revenues, where comprehensive
coverage (all health needs) is provided free of charge to users
at the point of delivery through a national health service.
Physicians generally receive payment on a capitation basis; that
is, on the number of patients registered with them, whether

they see them or not. A basic salary is also provided to cover expenses, and supplements are given for special services. The patients are free to choose their physician and the physicians are free to limit their patients and to accept paying patients. Specialists are normally salaried and hospitals are government institutions with funds from government appropriations. In essence, the health-care delivery system in Britain is highly 'socialised' with universal free coverage provided under government control.

The United States on the other hand relies to a considerable degree on the private sector market mechanism for the delivery of health care. The US does not have a national health insurance programme, but rather the state limits its coverage to the aged through Medicare and the needy through Medicaid, both enacted in 1965. As of 1969 the costs of personal health care in the US were covered from the following sources: three-eighths through government agencies from general revenues or social security; three-eighths from private health insurance; and two-eights from private payments. Although the health sector is regulated or influenced by various federal, state and local laws and regulations, the delivery system is largely in the hands of physicians, health insurance plans (nonprofit and profit), voluntary and social agencies, and hospitals of which 54 per cent in 1969 were nonprofit, 32 per cent government owned and 14 per cent private.[7] In essence, in the US, health care is a mixed private-public undertaking, with the private market mechanism being relied upon to a considerable degree to extract payment for, and to ensure the delivery of, health services.

As with so many features of social and institutional life, Canada lies between Britain and the US with respect to the organisation of its health-care system. In Canada the different provinces have different medical and hospital care programmes with the federal government setting minimum requirements and providing grants, out of general revenues, to the provinces to cover about half the cost. The remaining 50 per cent is usually financed out of provincial revenues, and in some provinces partly through insurance premiums. Coverage is nearly universal and the degree of comprehensiveness varies by province, with some cost sharing between the patient and the provincial plan being common. Physicians are paid on a fee-for-service basis, most of which is ultimately paid by the insurance fund but a portion of which may be paid by the patient.

The varying characteristics of the health-care system in the three countries can have implications for the health sector labour markets in each. Most important there is the possibility that the less the market is used to allocate resources in the health sector (as is the case in all three countries but especially in Britain and to a lesser extent in Canada), the greater the potential for the inefficient utilisation of resources, including the various types of labour involved. As third parties (either the government or insurers) increasingly pay the user charge, the potential for over-use is obvious, especially when physicians are relied upon to tell the patient how much health care should be demanded. Capitation (as in Britain) can alleviate some of the potential over-use because payment is based on the number of patients listed in the doctor's care; however, there may be an incentive for the physician to minimise the number of visits and time spent since payment is forthcoming no matter how long or how often one sees the patient. In addition, capitation and the payment of salaries to hospital specialists could lead to some of the better, or at least more marketable, practitioners emigrating to countries where they can increase their income by charging a fee-for-service. A fee-for-service system where government insurance pays most of the cost runs the risk that physicians will engage in unnecessary referrals and return visits, knowing that the patient does not pay the cost. A largely private fee-for-service system (as in the US) runs the risk that adequate medical care may be denied to those who cannot afford the service. Clearly the dilemma for public policy is to strike the balance between the adequate provision of health care for all, while at the same time ensuring that the system is not over- or under-used and that resources are allocated efficiently. That all three countries are having both problems and successes with their health-care system suggests that there is not a unique answer to this fundamental problem of public policy.

Demographic Changes
Demographic factors, notably the age structure and location of the population, can also play an important role in the demand for health services and hence in the derived demand for health sector labour. As indicated by Denton and Spencer[8] health expenditures tend to be highest for the very young and the very old. This suggests that the well-known post-World War II baby boom may have increased demand at its inception and when the baby boom itself began to have children through the late 1960s and early 1970s. The more recent decline in the number of births, to the extent that it is permanent, may be reducing demand in recent years. When the baby boom reaches old age the demand increase again will be dramatic and a matter for social concern to the extent that the working age population that pays into public insurance funds or tax revenues will be small.

The demographic changes not only affect total demand for health care but also its composition. Just as individuals require different types of medical care as they age, so an aging population will require different medical services, with different labour requirements. From a public policy perspective it is imperative that the health-care system and the associated health sector labour market be able to adapt to these changing demands.

The location of the population can also affect the demand for health services. In particular, one of the potential problems facing the health sector labour market is to allocate health personnel to the sources of demand, especially to populations in remote regions or urban ghettos. This can be especially difficult if market mechanisms are thwarted from providing compensating wage or salary differentials for locating in such environments. When this occurs other incentive structures are often utilised such as rural practice supplements in Britain, loans to medical students that are forgiveable upon practice in designated regions, and the easing of immigration requirements for doctors who are willing to practise in remote regions.

Labour market activities of the population can also affect the demand for institutional health care. In particular, the increased labour force participation of married women that has gone on in all three countries, and the decline of the nuclear family, mean that some health care that traditionally may have been conducted within the family may now be conducted in the institutional health sector. This is especially the case for the health care of children and older persons.

Professionalism and Self-generating demand
The health sector, more than most sectors, is dominated by professional groups. Not only does this have implications for the supply side of the health labour market (to be developed more fully in the subsequent section), but it also has implications for the demand side. In particular, many health-care professionals -- notably doctors and dentists -- are in the position of determining the demand for their services.

This comes about because of the complex and essential nature of most of the services they provide. The consuming public generally does not have the required knowledge of how much of the particular health service to purchase; hence, the patient relies on the professional to make this determination. It is in fact this heavy reliance on the professional, because of the complex and essential nature of the service, that is the rationale for professional regulation and licensing. In such circumstances the professional is in the position of determining, or at least heavily influencing, how much professional services the patient should demand.

The problem is further complicated by the fact that physicians determine the demand not only for their own services, but also for a variety of related services. As pointed out by Evans: 'Since the physician decides admission to hospitals, duration of stay, use of diagnostic and therapeutic procedures, referrals and the pattern of further examination it has been estimated that costs attributable to physicians represent nearly eighty percent of total health costs.[19] This raises the possibility that an increase in the supply of physicians need not necessarily lead to a reduction in the price of physician services. To the extent that supply creates its own demand, salaries may be maintained and health-care costs will rise accordingly.

Implications for Labour Demand in Health Sector
These various factors -- the public sector dominance of the

health sector, the characteristics of the health-care system,
demographic factors and professionalisation -- all have implications for the demand side of the health sector labour market. In
particular much of the growth in the overall demand for health
personnel that has occurred in recent years may be explained
by such factors as the decrease in the 'user price' paid by consumers as governments and insurers pay a larger portion of the
cost, the disproportionate number of very young people (until
recently) in our population, the increased labour force participation of married women and the decline of the nuclear family.
These factors, coupled with the possible lack of constraints from
public sector employers and the ability of professionals to generate the demand for their own services (a temptation that may
not be resisted when third parties pay), may account for much
of the growth on the demand side. This growth in turn would
generate increases in the wages and employment possibilities of
health sector personnel. To the extent that many of these
factors currently are changing, or have reached a level that
can generate no more demand, then wage increases and employment possibilities in the health sector may dissipate.

In addition to influencing this growth in overall demand, the
various factors may also influence the elasticity of demand for
health-care personnel. There is the possibility that the employer's
demand for many types of health personnel may be fairly wage
inelastic; that is, the quantity of personnel demanded may not
be reduced much as wages increase. This would be the case if
public sector employers could pass wage cost increases to
taxpayers without having to worry about a reduction in the
demand for health care (in part because of its essential nature),
or if it were not possible to substitute other inputs for the
more expensive labour. To a certain extent these factors may
be offset, in part at least, by the fact that labour costs are a
large portion of total cost in the health sector and this will make
employment demands sensitive to wage changes.

Econometric evidence generally tends to find substantial
elasticity in the demand for health-care personnel indicating
that employers will reduce their employment as wages rise. Such
studies, based on US data, include Benham[10] for registered
nurses, Davis[11] for hospital employees, Intriligator and Kehrer[12]
for nurses, technical personnel and secretarial-clerical personnel in physicians' offices. Ehrenberg[13] also has the interesting
result that the employment reduction associated with a nurses'
wage increase is significant for all categories of private hospitals
but insignificant for all classes of state and local hospitals,
suggesting that private, but not public, hospitals will utilise
fewer nurses if they become relatively expensive.

The econometric evidence is buttressed by qualitative evidence
suggesting that it is feasible to substitute cheaper for more
expensive inputs in the health sector. Kohn and White[14] in their
international study of health care indicate that there is a wide
variation across countries in the resources, including health-

care personnel, that are utilised to provide health services.
There also appears to be considerable scope for the substitution
of processes in the provision of health care. Yett et al.,[15] for
example, give econometric evidence to indicate that outpatient
care is a good substitute for inpatient care, indicating that if
the labour cost of inpatient care becomes too great, patients can
substitute for the less labour intensive outpatient care.

Evidence also suggests that unions in the health sector do not
provide a barrier to the substitution of resources. As stated by
Miller, Becker and Krinsky in a US study:

> The traditional controls over work rules and job security
> often present in industrial labour-management situations are
> absent from health-care contracts. Very little restriction, if
> any, is placed on management in the way it uses hospital
> manpower. Hospitals can subcontract, use supervisors for
> work in the bargaining unit, unilaterally determine job con-
> tent, and assign whatever number of individuals it deems fit
> to task or machine.[16]

Their study also found that the union impact on wages was fairly
small in the health sector. Specifically, unions were found to
raise wages by approximately 5 per cent, a figure that is within
the range of 4 to 8 per cent found by Fottler in the US. However, unionism was also associated with reduced turnover cost
so that on net the union impact on average costs was approximately 2 to 4 per cent. Becker's[17] estimates, for example, indicate that unionisation can reduce turnover by as much as 50
per cent in hospitals. As he indicates, this increased employment stability provides support for the Bishop's[18] statement
that the hospital labour market may be in the transition from the
secondary to primary labour market. This small impact of unions
on hospital wages also adds support to the contention that the
demand for health sector labour may be fairly elastic so that
wage increases are tempered by the threat of employment reductions.

In summary, on the demand side, it appears that health sector
employers will substitute away from personnel that experience
rapid relative wage increases. This provides some check at least
to excessive cost increases emanating from wage increases. In
essence, there are market pressures operating on the demand
side, at least from some elements of the health sector.

Labour Supply Characteristics
On the supply side, the health sector labour market also has
characteristics that make it distinctive and that have implications for the cost and availability of health services. Prime
amongst these characteristics are professionalisation, international mobility, occupational licensing, monopsony and the
responsiveness of the labour supply of health-care personnel to
changes in their wages. Each of these will be examined in turn.

Professionalism and Its Attributes

As discussed earlier, the health sector labour market is characterised by a large number of professional and paraprofessional
groups. This in turn means that the health sector labour market
will be affected by the various characteristics of professionals --
long training period, specialised knowledge, independence,
allegiance to the profession and most important, a degree of
self-regulation. These attributes of professionals in turn can
affect their labour market behaviour.

The long training period, for example, that is incurred by
doctors, dentists and skilled nurses will obviously affect their
lifetime earnings profile, making it rise quite rapidly after the
training period to compensate for training costs including the
income foregone while in training. The high training costs may
also be a deterrent for lower-income people to enter into these
occupations. Other subtle changes in earnings can also result
from changes in training costs. For example, in the 1950s and
1960s in the US there was a shift from training nurses in hospitals where they often received 'company-specific' training peculiar
to their hospital, to the provision of more 'general' training in
educational institutions.[19] Such general training would be usable
in a variety of health-care institutions, not just in the hospital
providing the training. This shift in the provision of training
would make the lifetime earnings profile of nurses rise more
steeply; that is, they would receive no wage during most of
their general training programme, but upon graduation they
could command a competitive market wage because their training
would be usable in a variety of health-care institutions that
would bid for their services. This is in contrast to their former
earnings profile when hospitals provided the training. Such a
profile would be relatively 'flat' over their lifetime because
nurses would be paid a wage during their hospital training;
however, they would not receive a large wage increase after
training because the usefulness of the training is mainly in the
sponsoring hospital and therefore competition for the nurses'
service is reduced.

The implications of this changing wage profile could be quite
dramatic. Disadvantaged people may not be able to afford the
costly general training period unless loans are available that
could be paid out of their higher post-training wage. Mobility
of health-care personnel would increase as they move to the
highest bidder for their generally-usable training. Health care
will become more of a career since a lengthy post-training
period of employment is necessary to recoup the training costs.
Loyalty to a particular hospital may break down as it is no longer
trainer and employer. What appears to be dramatic wage cost
increases may actually simply be transfers of cost as hospital
training costs drop but their wage costs rise. In essence, some
of the increase in wage rates of health-care personnel in recent
years may simply be reimbursement for their bearing a greater
share of training costs. Markets, including labour markets, can

respond in subtle fashion.

Other professional characteristics can also have implications for the health sector labour market. Professional independence and their allegiance to the profession may at times conflict with the requirement of employers. Similarly their high level of skills, and the associated high remuneration, make them usually quite mobile across regions. In fact the international movement of skilled manpower has given rise to a particular problem -- the brain drain -- that plagues many countries.

International Mobility and the Brain Drain
The so-called 'brain drain' is a problem associated with the international mobility of many types of skilled manpower; however, it is particularly acute for health sector personnel, notably physicians. Mejia, for example, estimates that there were almost 300 000 expatriate physicians and nurses in 1972 and that the number of physicians migrating in 1970 equalled one-eighth of the world medical school output.[20] Over half go to the US. In the early 1970s foreign medical graduates accounted for approximately 25 per cent of all physicians in Canada and the UK and about 20 per cent in the United States, with more immigrating than graduating from US medical schools. While both Canada and the UK are net recipients of foreign medical graduates they also have a fairly high emigration of doctors, with many from the UK going to Canada and many from Canada going to the US.

The problem with the international migration of high-level health personnel is that they tend to go to wealthy countries that already have a well-developed health sector and they often come from poorer countries that are in urgent need of health services. In essence the labour market signals of higher remuneration in the recipient countries induce a movement away from the countries of greatest need (at least when need is measured by indicators of ill-health rather than willingness or ability-to-pay). The problem is compounded in situations where the donor country subsidises the education of its health manpower who then are able to go to other countries that pay the most.

Solutions to the so-called brain-drain problem have been suggested but most have associated problems. If the lengthy and expensive education process were not subsidised in the donor countries, then at least such countries would not lose that subsidy; however, the concern is that without the subsidy many would not be able to afford the education process, especially in poorer countries. The problem is compounded in countries that attempt to reduce income inequality by reducing the wage premium for skilled jobs, since the lack of a wage premium reduces the incentive to privately financed education. An exit-tax equal to the magnitude of the state subsidy would at least compensate the donor country, and it would appear fair since the higher remuneration in the recipient country would provide the means for the emigrating personnel to pay; however, exit taxes tend to be politically unpopular, often for reasons of human rights.

This is also the case with other policies designed to discourage emigration, such as the refusal to grant passports or the requirement of military service before leaving.

Much of the loss comes from students studying abroad and who do not return. Their return could be encouraged by sponsoring them only on the condition that they return for a fixed period, or encouraging their return by persuasion or information programmes. The indigenous training of such personnel, perhaps by importing teachers rather than exporting students, has been utilised. This may be particularly effective if the training can be 'country-specific', that is, usable mainly in the sponsoring country, since then the international marketability of the personnel is reduced. This is more feasible in less-developed countries where certain health problems may be unique or where training periods could be interspersed with long periods of practical experience so as to retain the personnel at least over the lengthy training experience period.

Clearly each of the policy options could help alleviate the brain-drain problem, although all have other negative effects. The problems occur because of the conflict inherent in such diverse objectives that include minimising the constraints placed on mobility, providing low-cost subsidised education, providing education that is internationally recognised, and being concerned over human rights. As with so many elements of public policy, trade-offs are involved.

Occupational Licensing

Because of the large number of so-called professional workers in the health sector, occupational licensing is a prominent characteristic of that sector. As discussed earlier, licensing is advocated to protect uninformed consumers in purchases that are usually complex, essential, infrequent and often irreversible. In such circumstances regulation is often advocated, usually in the form of licensing (with only licensed professionals having the exclusive right-to-practise) or certification (with only certified professionals having the right-of-title, but with others being allowed to practise). Because only the professional groups themselves are deemed to have the appropriate knowledge of licensing requirements, they themselves are given the right to govern their profession -- hence the term self-governing or self-regulating professionals.

Occupational licensing usually is associated with the ability to control entry into the profession by determining education, training and residency requirements and by controlling the output of schools and the use of substitute labour including paraprofessionals. Discriminatory practices, such as more stringent licensing requirements for foreigners, may also be used.[21] While such devices may be used to ensure a high quality of service (albeit at a higher price), they may also be used artificially to restrict entry into the profession to maintain high salaries. The potential for abuse is particularly prevalent to the extent that incumbent professionals can receive the artificially high salaries without bearing any of the cost of the entry restrictions. This could be achieved by having the entry restrictions apply only to *new* entrants (e.g. raising education qualifications), and by making existing practitioners exempt through 'grandfather' clauses.

The ability to restrict supply in their occupation, along with an ability to tell clients how much medical service to demand, puts high-level health-care personnel in a very powerful position to influence their own salaries and employment opportunities. This can affect the cost of health care directly through excessive salaries, as well as indirectly through consumers purchasing higher quality (and more expensive) care than they would purchase without stringent licensing requirements.

Monopsony

While some high-level health sector personnel can exert considerable influence on their labour market positions, others can be subject to monopsony power on the part of employers.[22] Monopsony occurs when the employer is so large relative to the size of the local labour market for the particular skill that the employer is a wage-setter not a wage-taker. The employer has to raise wages to attract additional workers; conversely, if the employer lowers wages, not all workers will leave. Monopsony is usually associated with such interrelated characteristics as a large and dominant employer, a small local labour market for the particular skills, labour immobility and specialised skills. In the UK monopsony may feature in the national labour market given the predominant role of publicly funded health care.

Some health sector occupations may be particularly susceptible to monopsony. Nurses, for example, have specialised skills that are usable mainly in the health sector, and in some communities one or a few hospitals are the dominant employer of nurses. Even when there are more than one hospital, they may behave collusively in their wage decisions or a single wage may be established through pattern bargaining, as smaller hospitals follow the pattern set by the largest hospital or as interest arbitrators follow other awards. The preponderance of females in nursing may also mean reduced mobility, a characteristic that is conducive to monopsony.

To the extent that some hospitals behave as monopsonists, or oligopsonists in the case of a few hospitals, some interesting implications follow. Monopsonists will employ less labour than they would if they behaved as competitive buyers of labour. This occurs because monopsonists are reluctant to hire additional labour because to do so means that they have to raise wages, and this in turn means that they have to raise the wages of their existing workforce in order to maintain internal equity. Because wages of the existing workforce have to be raised then the cost of hiring an additional worker is not only the higher wage but also the additional cost associated with the wage increase for the existing workforce. Clearly this would serve as a deterrent to hiring additional workers.

In addition the monopsonist pays a wage that is lower than it would have paid were it a competitive buyer of labour. This follows from the fact that the monopsonist hires less labour than if it were a competitive buyer; hence, it is able to hire the workers that were willing to work at the lower wage. Perhaps the most interesting implication of monopsony is that the monopsonist will report shortages of labour at the going wage but will do nothing to reduce these shortages -- they are what economists term 'equilibrium vacancies'. This seemingly paradoxical result of shortages or vacancies being in equilibrium occurs because at the going wage rate the employer would like to hire additional workers. However, by definition, the monopsonist cannot hire more at the going wage rate but rather has to raise wages. Because these higher wages also have to be paid to the existing workers, the monopsonist will not hire additional workers. Thus the monopsonist will report shortages of labour at the going wage but will not do what is required -- raise wages -- to reduce those shortages. This suggests that the concept of shortages that occurs so often in the health sector should be regarded with caution since at least some of those shortages may occur to the extent that some hospitals behave as monopsonists and hence would like to hire more labour at the going wage, but will not raise wages to reduce the shortage. As discussed, for example, in Altman[23], Sorkin[24], and Yett[25], there are many concepts of shortages and vacancies in the health sector and they need not imply any willingness-to-pay to reduce the shortage.

Empirical evidence does tend to suggest that many hospitals behave as monopsonists in their hiring of at least some types of personnel. Evidence of monopsony for nurses in the US is found in Cohen[26], Hurd[27], and Link and Landon.[28] On the other hand, Ehrenberg finds no evidence of monopsony power in hospitals.[29] Clearly the evidence on the extent of monopsony power of hospitals is by no means conclusive.

Responsiveness of Supply to Wage Changes
The supply of health-care personnel can be changed in a variety of ways. The quantity dimension is affected by the decision to participate in the labour force (as opposed to engaging in household, education or retirement activities), and by hours worked. Of particular importance is the responsiveness of supply to wage changes; that is, the wage elasticity of supply. Theoretical considerations suggest that labour supply in the health sector may be fairly responsive to wage changes, given the large number of female employees who have a fairly high degree of flexibility in their work decisions. On the other hand to the extent that there are few employment opportunities for health-care personnel in industries other than the health sector, and to the extent that labour markets are segmented into relatively

noncompeting groups, then labour supply may not be responsive to changes in relative wages. In addition, wage increases can have opposing effects on the labour supply decision of individuals. On the one hand, a wage increase would raise the return to labour market activities relative to nonlabour market activities and this would induce a substitution of labour market activities for nonlabour market activities. On the other hand, a wage increase means more income which could enable some to afford more nonlabour market activities perhaps in the form of early retirement, engaging in household activities or reducing hours of work. Clearly, theoretical considerations do not give unambiguous implications concerning the supply responsiveness of health sector labour to wage changes. Consequently it is necessary to appeal to the empirical evidence.

With respect to nurses, most studies find a small but positive increase in their labour supply associated with a wage increase. This is the case in Altman[30], Benham[31], Bishop[32], Bognanna, Hixson and Jeffers[33], and Link and Settle[34], with Sloan and Richupan[35] finding evidence of a substantial positive supply response. With respect to the individual labour supply decision of physicians the evidence as given in Feldstein[36], Sloan[37], and Vahovich[38] indicates no strong positive increase in the labour supply of physicians as their salaries increase. They either increase their labour supply only slightly, or in some instances reduce their work effort as salaries increase.

In summary, the empirical evidence tends to suggest that as their earnings increase, physicians do not increase their labour supply by much (and may actually reduce their supply). Nurses do increase their labour supply but probably by a fairly small amount, although there is not a consensus on this latter point.

Such knowledge of labour supply elasticities is important for a variety of policy purposes. To the extent that labour supply does not increase much as salaries rise -- and this appears to be the case for physicians and possibly nurses -- then demand increases will be associated with wage cost increases more than increases in the number of availability of personnel. On the other hand the fact that there is some positive response for nurses, suggests that salary increases will be associated with more nurses being available for employment. This raises the interesting policy question of whether it would be cheaper to try to increase the number of health-care personnel by training or education programmes or simply by increasing their wages. Sloan and Richupan[39] calculate that the latter is cheaper; however, their results depend upon their own high wage elasticities of supply. Manpower planners in the health sector clearly have to pay attention to how the quantity of health personnel depends upon wage changes as well as on the more traditional instruments used to affect manpower supply -- licensing and entrance requirements and the capacity of training institutions.[40]

CONCLUDING OBSERVATIONS

Clearly the whole operation of the health sector both affects, and is affected by, the health sector labour market. The adjustment mechanisms of the labour market may be subtle, as may be the way in which the labour market affects, and is affected by, the industrial relations system and the health-care delivery system. Nevertheless, adjustments will occur and their impacts will be felt. The crucial need for sensible policy decisions is to have both theoretical and empirical knowledge of how the health-care system interrelates with its component parts, of which the labour market is but one -- albeit an important -- part.

REFERENCES

1 Mejia, A., and Fulop, T., (1978), Health manpower planning: an overview, in 'Health Manpower Planning' by T. Hall and A. Mejia (eds), World Health Organisation, pp.12-13.

2 Ginsberg, E., (1974), The Health Services Industry: Realism in Social Control, 'Journal of Economic Issues', vol.8, June, pp.381-94.

3 Royal College of Nursing of the United Kingdom, (1977), 'Evidence to the Royal Commission on the National Health Service', Whitefriars Press, p.38.

4 Feldstein, M., (1971), 'The Rising Cost of Hospital Care', Information Resources Press, p.69.

5 King, S., (1974), Wage Differences Narrow Between Government and Private Hospitals, 'Monthly Labor Review', vol.97, April, pp.56-7; Fottler, M., (1977), The Union Impact on Hospital Wages, 'Industrial and Labor Relations Review', vol.36, April, pp.342-55.

6 Gunderson, M., (1978), Public-Private Wage and Non-Wage Differentials in Canada: Some Calculations from Published Tabulations, in D. Foot (ed.), 'Public Employment and Compensation in Canada: Myths and Realities', Butterworths, pp.145-8.

7 Kohn, R., and White, K., (1976), 'Health Care: An International Study', Oxford University Press, pp.420-1.

8 Denton, F., and Spencer, B., (1975), Health-Care Costs When the Population Changes, 'Canadian Journal of Economics', vol.12, February, pp.34-48.

9 Evans, J., (1976), Manpower Problems in the Medical Care System in Canada, in P. Kent (ed.), 'International Aspects of the Provision of Medical Care', Oriel Press, pp.55-68.

10 Benham, L., (1971), The Labour Market for Registered Nurses: A Three Equation Model, 'Review of Economics and Statistics', vol.53, August, pp.246-52.

11 Davis, K., (1974), The Role of Technology, Demand and Labour Markets, in M. Perlman (ed.), 'The Economics of

Health and Medical Care', Macmillan, p.298.
12 Intriligator, M., and Kehrer, B., (1974), Allied Health
   Personnel in Physician's Offices, in M. Perlman 'The
   Economics of Health and Medical Care', p.454.
13 Ehrenberg, R., (1974), Organisational Control and the
   Economic Efficiency of Hospitals, 'Journal of Human Resources', vol.9, winter, pp.21-32.
14 Kohn and White, 'Health Care', pp.108-12.
15 Yett, D., Drabek, L., Intriligator, M., and Kimbell, L.,
   (1974), Econometric Forecasts of Health Services and Health
   Manpower, in M. Perlman, 'The Economics of Health and
   Medical Care', p.463.
16 Miller, R., Becker, B., and Krinsky, E., (1977), Union
   Effects on Hospital Administration, 'Labor Law Journal',
   August, pp.512-19.
17 Ibid.
18 Bishop, C., (1977), Hospitals: From Secondary to Primary
   Labour Markets, 'Industrial Relations', vol.16, February,
   pp.26-34.
19 Altman, S., (1970), The Structure of Nursing Education
   and its Impact on Supply, in H. Klarman (ed.), 'Empirical
   Studies in Health Economics', John Hopkins Press,
   pp.335-52.
20 Mejia, A., International Migration of Professional Health
   Manpower, in T. Hall and A. Mejia (eds), 'Health Manpower
   Planning', pp.257-60.
21 Brown, M., (1975), Some Effects of Physician Licensing
   Requirements on Medical Manpower Flows in Canada, 'Relations Industrielles', vol.30, August, pp.436-49.
22 Gunderson, M., (1980), 'Labour Market Economics: Theory
   Evidence and Policy in Canada', McGraw-Hill, pp.165-84.
23 Altman, S., (1971), 'Present and Future Supply of Registered Nurses', US Department of Health, Education and
   Welfare.
24 Sorkin, A., (1977), 'Health Manpower', D.C. Heath.
25 Yett, D., (1976), The Chronic Shortage of Nurses: A Public
   Policy Dilemma, in H. Klarman (ed.), 'Empirical Studies in
   Health Economics', Johns Hopkins. Yett, (1975), 'An Economic Analysis of the Nurse Shortage', D.C. Heath.
26 Cohen, H., (1972), Monopsony and Discriminating Monopsony in the Nursing Market, 'Applied Economics', vol.4,
   March, pp.39-48.
27 Hurd, R., (1973), Equilibrium Vacancies in a Labour Market
   Dominated by Non-Profit Firms: The Shortage of Nurses,
   'Review of Economics and Statistics', vol.55, May, pp.234-40.
28 Link, C., and Landon, J., (1975), Monopsony and Union
   Power in the Market for Nurses, 'Southern Economic Journal',
   vol.41, April, pp.249-59; Link, C., and Landon, J.,
   (1976), Market Structure, Nonpecuniary Factors and Professional Salaries: Registered Nurses, 'Journal of Economics
   and Business', vol.28, winter, pp.151-5.

29 Ehrenberg, Organisation Control and the Economic Efficiency
   of Hospitals.
30 Altman, Present and Future Supply of Registered Nurses.
31 Benham, The Labour Market for Registered Nurses.
32 Bishop, C., (1973), Manpower Policy and the Supply of
   Nurses, 'Industrial Relations', vol.12, February, pp.86-94.
33 Bognanno, M., Hixson, J., and Jeffers, J., (1974), The
   Short-Run Supply of Nurses Time, 'Journal of Human
   Resources', vol.9, winter, pp.80-93.
34 Link, C., and Settle, R., (1979), Labour Supply Responses
   of Married Professional Nurses', 'Journal of Human Resources', vol.14, spring, pp.256-66; Maxwell, R., (1975),
   'Health Care: The Growing Dilemma', 2nd edition, McKinsey
   and Co.
35 Sloan, F., and Richupan, S., (1975), Short Run Supply
   Responses of Professional Nurses, 'Journal of Human
   Resources', vol.10, spring, pp.241-57.
36 Feldstein, M., (1970), The Rising Price of Physicians'
   Services, 'Review of Economics and Statistics', vol.52,
   May, pp.121-33.
37 Sloan, F., (1979), Physician Supply Behavior in the Short-
   Run, 'Industrial and Labor Relations Review', vol.28,
   July, pp.544-69.
38 Vahovich, S., (1977), Physicians' Supply Decision by
   Specialty, 'Industrial Relations', vol.16, February, pp.51-60.
39 Sloan and Richupan, Short-Run Supply: Responses of
   Professional Nurses, p.254.
40 Sorkin, Health Manpower, p.153.

PART II

LABOUR MOVEMENT

Introduction

The trade union movements in the health sectors in Canada, the USA and the UK are still in the process of growth. Within the last decade this has been fairly dramatic in all three countries. In each of these countries pressures inside and outside the area of health care have pushed health groups towards the development of a greater sense of the need for collective organisations to pursue improved pay and conditions. There are, however, a number of issues which present difficulties and obstructions to this development both within and between health-care occupations. Principal of these are the divisions which are created by the structure of the trade union movement itself, particularly the distinction between 'craft' and 'industrial' unionism. Whilst this distinction is less relevant to the UK where many trade unions have long since developed a 'general structure' through recruiting across industrial sectors, it experiences similar difficulties in the health sector in terms of the 'professional-trade union dichtomy'. In the health sector the commitment of some occupational groups to the ideals of professionalism underlines the distinction between different union types. In this context the ethos of professionalism and the principles and methods of trade unionism can be in direct conflict in each of the three countries.

The authors of the succeeding chapters examine this and other aspects within the respective labour movements in health care in Canada, the USA and the UK. Sykes and Sethi point out the degree and extent of fragmented trade union structure in Canada and the role of the Labour Relations Board and the effects of its policy. In Chapter 5 Schoen takes up the theme of union fragmentation and discusses the challenges presented by the requirement for trade union reorganisation. In the UK the unions and professional associations achieved significant penetration in the health sector in the 1970s. Carpenter examines the implications of this for both these types of organisations.

3. THE LABOUR MOVEMENT IN HEALTH CARE: CANADA

R. Sykes and A.S. Sethi

INTRODUCTION

The purpose of this chapter is to review the structure of the labour movement in Canada as a whole, outlining what exists in each of the different sectors within the health-care industry. The labour structure in each province is outlined involving different classes of health manpower. Some comparisons are made between and among the provinces, highlighting some of the major issues facing the unions and the employers within health industrial relations.

The health-care system in Canada is highly unionised. Although no percentage figures are published, it is estimated that in excess of 75 per cent of eligible health-care employees are now covered by collective agreements. In some provinces, for example New Brunswick and Saskatchewan, the percentage is very close to 100.

Most of the unionisation of health-care employees has taken place in the past fifteen years. Prior to that time, unionisation was essentially restricted to fairly large urban centres, and to the hospital sector. The last ten to fifteen years have seen steady progress in organising both the smaller, non-urban hospitals, as well as other sectors within the health-care system - homes for the aged, nursing homes, and health units. This trend toward organisation was no doubt facilitated by the development of province-wide bargaining structures in most provinces in the late 1960s and early 1970s. With the exception of the private nursing home sector, the vast majority of health-care institutions in Canada now have one or more groups represented by trade unions and associations.

Before examining the labour movement structure as it applies to the health sector, we will outline a brief summary of the Canadian structure of collective bargaining as it obtains in the health sector, as detailed discussion of this topic has been done in Part IV of this volume. The growth of trade unions in the health sector is directly linked with the structural developments of the collective bargaining system, of which the union is a crucial party, and at times becomes instrumental in changing the system itself.

THE STRUCTURE OF BARGAINING

There is no national structure of negotiations and bargaining
in Canada, like that of the Whitley system in the UK. There are
multiple structures and varying frameworks within which various
classes of health manpower negotiate to obtain their goals.

Out of a medley of arrangements that exist throughout Canada,
two broad structures may be categorised. The first is where
negotiations are carried on between individual hospitals and
individual unions within a given region or province. A variant
of this structure is where a group of hospitals in a region establish a bargaining committee and negotiate with various unions
(or a committee of these unions). The second type of structure
is 'province-wide', where negotiations are conducted on a provincial level by the representatives of hospitals, provincial
authorities, unions, and professional associations. The collective
agreements negotiated at this level apply uniformly to various
classes of health workers throughout a province. Such a system
prevails in all provinces except Ontario and Nova Scotia. The
negotiation structure is complex and varied – as the Canadian
collective agreements generally cover in detail a wide variety of
topics and situations.

Unions in the Health Sector

There are a number of unions involved in a single hospital in
Canada. On average there will be about four unions in one large
hospital (i.e. 400 plus beds) representing support/service staff,
nurses, paramedical personnel and administrative and clerical
staffs, and interns and residents. There is a trend in some provinces where a variety of paramedical and health sciences personnel form a single union.[1]

Insofar as the nature of health unions is concerned, unions
may be divided into three broad categories: unions affiliated
with the Canadian Labour Congress; unions affiliated with the
Confederation of National Trade Unions; and independent
unions.[2]

As health unionism centres on the two major labour federations
in Canada, it is pertinent briefly to review the origins and
structure of the Canadian Labor Congress (CLC) and the Confederation of National Trade Unions (CNTU). The CLC, formed
in 1956 after a merger of the existing two major labour federations at that time, brought an unprecedented degree of unity
to the organised labour movement in Canada. Most of the unions
representing support/service staff in provinces outside of Quebec are affiliated to the CLC. The CNTU, the central labour
congress in Quebec, was established in 1921 in Hull, Quebec.
The CNTU is an almost exclusively Quebec-based federation,
and is the major union on the staff side representing various
classes of health personnel in conducting negotiations in that
province. These two major federations have developed ideological
differences, although they both focus, particularly in hospitals,

on the improvement of wages and working conditions for workers.
The CLC is a loose, decentralised structure, consisting of a
large number of unions, many with overlapping or dual jurisdictions. The CNTU has a more central and easily directed structure
made up of fewer and larger unions. Hospital employees are
members of various unions which are either affiliated to the CLC
or the CNTU, or are in independent unions. Several of the
unions affiliated with the CLC are also international: the Service
Employees International Union (SEIU) for example has dual
affiliation with the CLC and with the US federation AFL-CIO,
and its headquarters are at Washington DC.

Characteristics of Health-care Unions
Three major types of unions have evolved in health care in
Canada. First, there are industrial unions which encompass
within them differing types of hospital workers. Secondly, there
are the pure craft unions which only organise and bargain for
a particular profession, or groups of related professions or
occupations. Thirdly, there are mixed 'craft-oriented' unions
which do organise occupations and classifications outside their
particular craft area.

An example of the first type of union -- the industrial union -
is the Canadian Union of Public Employees (CUPE). CUPE is
the dominant union in the health industry in Canada, encompassing over 55 000 employees in all ten provinces. Another industrial union is the international SEIU, and it has members in most
of the Canadian provinces, although its membership is small in
the Atlantic Region and in the provinces of British Columbia
and Alberta. CUPE and SEIU are the nationwide industrial
unions in the health-care field. However, there are some other
industrial-type unions in particular provinces. In Quebec the
Federation of Social Affairs, a branch of the CNTU, organises
most of the hospital occupational groups. In Manitoba the Institutional Employees Union (IEU) operates as an industrial union.
The Winnipeg based IEU grew from among the French-speaking
hospital employees in the St Boniface and those of other French-
speaking communities in Manitoba, and it has expanded to
include some 20 different health care bargaining units covering
about 3 000 employees in the province of Manitoba. By contrast,
in Nova Scotia the Canadian Brotherhood of Railway Transport
and General Workers (CBRT) organises hospital workers on an
industrial basis.

On the craft side, dealing with the professional staffs, there
are firstly the Nurses Associations in each province. These are
basically limited to organising nurses alone - Registered Nurses,
and in some cases graduate nurses as well. In a few provinces
the Registered Nurses' Associations also organise other nursing
related groups such as registered nursing assistants or licensed
practical nurses. However, in most provinces that particular
occupational group is represented by the industrial unions. A
major craft grouping is the laboratory and medical technologists.

In most provinces, this group is organised on a craft union
basis encompassing units of technologists only. In a few provinces some of them are included in the main industrial grouping
as well.

Another craft unit within the hospital or health-care industry
is the operating engineers. In most provinces, operating engineers are organised by the International Union of Operating
Engineers (IUOE) or the Canadian Union of Operating Engineers
(CUOE). There are a few exceptions to this rule and in some
provinces the operating engineers fall within the industrial
unions' purview. In Ontario, operating engineers in some hospitals are oganised by the (IUOE) or the (CUOE) while in other
hospitals, they fall within the main service or support bargaining unit - usually organised by CUPE or SEIU. The craft units
of operating engineers tend to consist of operating engineers,
although in some hospitals there are operating engineer craft
units which do include other maintenance trades, such as electricians and plumbers. In a few provinces there are other types
of craft units: provincial associations of interns and residents.
In Alberta the registered nursing assistants have organised into
separate bargaining units although in some hospitals, and in
most nursing homes and old age homes, the auxiliary nursing
group is organised by CUPE.

Structure of Health Labour Movement in each Province
A brief outline of the structure of the labour movement in each
province in Canada is given below.

British Columbia. There are three major unions involved in
the health-care field in this province. The first is the Registered
Nurses Association of British Columbia (RNABC) which bargains
on behalf of the nurses in the general hospitals in the province.
The second major union involved is the Hospital Employees Union
(HEU) Local 180, which was formerly a local of CUPE but went
independent in 1969 and has remained outside the mainstream
of the labour movement and it is not a member of the CLC. It
bargains for the support group in the hospitals, including all
of the general service workers, the clerical employees, as well
as the auxiliary nursing personnel and the operating engineers
in some hospitals. The third major group is the paramedical
staff which is represented by the Health Sciences Association of
British Columbia and includes laboratory and medical technologists. There are a number of hospitals which have carved out
craft units of operating engineers as well. However, the dominant pattern is to have three major groups in each hospital.
Each of these three groups -- the RNABC, the HEU and Health
Sciences Association-signs a province-wide master collective
agreement with the Health Labor Relations Association.

Alberta. In Alberta, registered nurses are represented by the
craft union of nurses - United Nurses of Alberta - which was

recently formed as an offshoot of the Alberta Association of
Registered Nurses. The auxiliary nursing group, consisting
of registered nursing assistants, orderlies, nurses aides and
operating room technicians, is recognised by the Labor Relations
Board to be a separate valid bargaining group, unlike most other
provinces. There are a few auxiliary nursing units which are
represented by CUPE and are included in the general support
group, which in Alberta also includes clerical employees. They
are represented for the most part by CUPE, although in hospitals
which are run directly by the provincial government, the support group is represented by the Alberta Union of Provincial
Employees, which is a civil service union. There are a few other
small unions involved in Alberta that represent support employees. The SEIU has one remaining local at the Edmonton General
Hospital, and an independent group called the Alberta Hospital
Employees Union represents the employees at Royal Alexandra
Hospital in Edmonton.

The paramedical group in Alberta is a separate craft grouping and is represented, as is the case with British Columbia, by
the Health Sciences Association -- the Health Sciences Association of Alberta. In addition to the paramedical technical group,
the Alberta Board of Industrial Relations also recognises a
further craft division as appropriate for bargaining - the professional paramedical group. This consists of pharmacists,
dieticians, medical social workers, physiotherapists, occupational
therapists, and medical record librarians.

Saskatchewan. In Saskatchewan, nurses are represented on a
province-wide basis by the Saskatchewan Union of Nurses (SUN).
The support employees in Saskatchewan are split between the
CUPE and the SEIU, with CUPE being larger in terms of numbers
of employees and the number of hospitals represented. These
two industrial unions also represent the clerical and the technical
employees in a number of hospitals, although technical employees
in some hospitals are represented by the Health Sciences Association.

Manitoba. In Manitoba there is a proliferation of unions in the
health-care field, probably more so than in any other province.
There seem to be three major bargaining units, which is the
general norm across the country - the nurses, the support
employees, and the paramedical or the technologist group. However, among the support group there are a wide variety of
different unions with members in the field. CUPE is the largest
single union in the support field, having 54 different bargaining units covering some 4600 employees. The Institutional
Employees Union has approximately 3000 members. In addition
to these two, the IUOE also organises the general support group.
They have a number of support bargaining units in Winnipeg
hospitals. The SEIU has a few bargaining groups and both the
United Steelworkers and the United Food and Commercial

Workers Union have units in the hospital field.

The nurses in Manitoba are represented by the professional group, the Manitoba Organisation of Nurses Associations (MONA). MONA also organises the Licensed Practical Nurses (RNAs) in the hospitals. Most of the paramedical employees fall under the technical group called the Manitoba Paramedical Association (MPA). MPA is the equivalent of the western Health Sciences Associations. They have about 20 bargaining units covering some 350 employees. CUPE also represents certain technical groups such as registered psychiatric nurses, X-ray technicians, EKG technicians and so on. In some hospitals the operating engineers are included in the general support group while in others there are carved out units of operating engineers represented by the IUOE.

Ontario. In Ontario most of the nurses are represented by the Ontario Nurses Association. There are a few hospitals where the nurses are represented by other unions, such as CUPE or SEIU. The support group is generally represented by either CUPE or by SEIU. In some cases the support group includes clerical employees as well. However, the Ontario Labor Relations Board does recognise clerical employees as a separate and appropriate group for collective bargaining purposes, so that in many cases the clerical group in a hospital is either not organised or else is organised into a separate bargaining unit from the support employees and may well bargain separately from the support employees. The technicians and technologists are primarily in the Ontario Public Service Employees Union. There is no health sciences or paramedical association in Ontario per se. In a few hospitals the paramedics are organised by CUPE or by SEIU.

As is the case with most other provinces, the operating engineers in Ontario are sometimes organised as separate craft units by either the IUOE or the CUOE, while in other hospitals they form part of the general support bargaining unit and fall within the CUPE or SEIU jurisdiction. The Ontario Labor Relations Board now no longer recognises operating engineers as separate craft units. The present ones have been allowed to remain but any new applications will not be considered as operating engineers are now to be part of the general support unit in Ontario.

Quebec. Quebec is different from all the other provinces because the collective bargaining in the health-care industry is centralised. The major union in the health-care field, is the CNTU -- the Confederation of National Trade Unions. The CNTU represents almost all hospital workers in any given hospital from the nurses to the clericals to the support staff and the technologists. They are by far the largest bargaining group in Quebec. However, there are a number of other unions with members in the health-care field in Quebec as well. In the

nursing area, the United Nurses Union seems to be heavily concentrated in the English language hospitals, particularly in the
Montreal area. The Société Professionnelle des Infirmiers et
Infirmières du Québec is an organisation of largely French-
speaking nurses centred in the Quebec City area. CUPE and
SEIU are also both involved in the health-care field in Quebec
although in a much smaller way than the CNTU. CUPE and
SEIU represent the traditional support unit primarily but they
also include clerical and some technical employees as well.

New Brunswick. In New Brunswick, collective bargaining is
also highly centralised. By law, under the Public Service Labor
Relations Act, only one union can represent employees in any
particular bargaining unit or group of bargaining units as set
out under the legislation. In New Brunswick the registered
nurses in general hospitals are all represented by the Nurses
Provincial Collective Bargaining Council, an offshoot of the
New Brunswick Association of Registered Nurses. The support
group, including clerical employees and operating engineers,
is exclusively represented in all hospitals by CUPE. The paramedical group in all hospitals is exclusively represented by the
New Brunswick Public Employees Association. Like Ontario, this
is another example of the provincial civil service union representing paramedical employees in hospitals. In summary, there
are three major bargaining units represented by three unions
and a province-wide collective agreement that covers all of the
hospitals in the province is signed in each case.

Prince Edward Island. Prince Edward Island is somewhat similar
to New Brunswick. The nurses are all represented by the Prince
Edward Island Nurses Provincial Joint Bargaining Council, similar
to New Brunswick. The support employees are represented by
the CUPE. Included in the support group are the RNAs (or
LNAs as they are called in Prince Edward Island). The paramedical and clerical personnel are represented by the Prince
Edward Island Hospital Staff Association, which is an independent
association representing basically those who fall outside into
either the nurses or the support bargaining unit. Each of the
three major groups bargains on a province-wide basis, and signs
a provincial collective agreement with the provincial Health
Negotiating Agency.

Nova Scotia. Unlike its neighbouring province of New Brunswick,
the Nova Scotia system seems relatively unregulated. There are
a number of different unions involved in the field and the bargaining groups are different from any of the other provinces.
The nurses are all represented by the Nova Scotia Nurses
Association. The general support units encompass the traditional
support employees. However, in some cases they also include
the clerical employees and the operating engineers. In some
hospitals, the operating engineers are organised separately.

The clerical employees are sometimes organised separately or else are combined with the technicians into a clerical and technical group. There is an auxiliary nursing group of certified nursing assistants and related classifications. While in some instances they are included in the main support bargaining unit, they may also form separate units, or be combined with technicians and clerical.

The Nova Scotia Labor Relations Board has a policy of considering four appropriate bargaining groups. First, the nurses' group, which consists of all registered and graduate nurses. The second is termed 'health-care employees', that is, all employees directly concerned with the treatment of patients. That would bear some correspondence to the auxiliary nursing group which is recognised in Alberta. Specifically the health-care group would include certified nursing assistants, nursing assistants and aides, and orderlies, but it also includes in Nova Scotia the technical group. Secondly, the technical group which consists of both the technical paramedical and the professional paramedical - lab technicians, technologists, dieticians, therapists, pharmacy clerks, and medical records librarians. The third group recognised by the Labor Relations Board consists of office employees. Outside Nova Scotia most provinces do not recognise office employees as a discrete unit -- separate and apart from the support group. The fourth group is termed the 'residual' unit (the support group) and includes housekeeping, dietary and laundry. Technicians are represented in some cases by CUPE and in some cases by the Nova Scotia Government Employees Association.

Newfoundland. Newfoundland generally recognises the traditional three major bargaining groups, namely, the nurses, the support and the paramedical. The nurses group is represented by the Newfoundland Nurses Union. The support group, which also includes clerical, registered nursing assistants and operating engineers, is represented by either CUPE or the Newfoundland Association of Public Employees (NAPE) (the civil service union). NAPE also represents the paramedical employees in hospitals as well.

Emerging Structural Issues

From this brief review of the situation which exists in each of the provinces, it is clear that the structure is quite different from province to province - from the very centralised scheme presently in force in New Brunswick for example, to a rather more fragmented and less precisely defined situation in Nova Scotia or Manitoba. The Labor Relations Board policy has significant effect on how bargaining units are structured in each province.[3] There is no standard definition on an inter-provincial basis of what constitutes an appropriate bargaining unit within the hospital field. However, there does seem to be a general model. That model would consist of the three major groups:

(1) the registered nurses or professional nursing groups;
(2) the support group, which would include RNAs, clericals
and operating engineers; and (3) the paramedical group.
Although this 'three unit model' seems to be the most common,
there are several variations of it. In particular the support
group is broken down in many provinces. The support group
sometimes includes RNAs, operating engineers and clerical
employees, while in certain provinces the RNAs and other auxiliary nursing personnel are carved out. The operating engineers
may be carved out and the clerical employees may also be a
separate unit.

The more fragmented the bargaining units are, the more difficult it is for the industrial unions to organise all the different
areas within the hospital. The craft unions are, of course,
constantly pushing for a breakdown in the units. It is in their
interest to make the hospital structure as fragmented as possible, whereas, it is in the industrial union's interest to make
the bargaining structure as broad and as unfragmented as
possible.

There are some hospitals in the country which have only one
main bargaining unit. That major bargaining unit would include
registered nurses, auxiliary nurses, all support, clerical and
paramedical personnel as well. The closest example would be the
Riverdale Hospital in Toronto, where CUPE represents virtually
all the employees in the hospital including registered nurses
and lab technologists, as well as the support and clerical
employees.

In most provinces, the employees of psychiatric hospitals and
mental retardation centres are represented by the civil service
union -- examples are the Ontario Public Service Employees
Union, or the British Columbia Government Employees Union,
or the Manitoba Government Employees Association. In those
hospitals, all employees are in one large union. Because they
are connected directly to the civil service they are structured
in a number of different bargaining units within the hospital,
but these bargaining units extend across the civil service
generally. For example, support employees within the hospital
may be part of a larger 'operational' category within the province and their terms and conditions may be set in conjunction
with operational employees who work in prisons or public
buildings. Similarly the nursing group also extends beyond the
hospital to other provincial institutions.

Federal hospital employees are divided into nationwide bargaining categories. The nurses, for example, are in a separate
bargaining category that includes all federal nurses, not just
those who work in hospitals. They are represented by the Professional Institute of Public Service. The support service
personnel in the hospitals are in the Hospital Services Group
of the Public Service Alliance of Canada. The clerical group is
represented by another bargaining group within the Public
Service Alliance, as are the operating engineers.

Size of Institution and the Bargaining Unit
The structure of the union movement is to a substantial degree
dependent on the size and type of the institution. The larger
the institution the more there is a tendency to proliferate bargaining units and have craft unions represent them. If there
are only one or two or a handful in any particular grouping in
a hospital, it makes little sense for the employees to be carved
up as a separate unit, particularly in terms of the operating
engineers for example. In a large hospital there may be twenty
operating engineers, thus forming potentially a viable bargaining
unit that the international union can become involved in. However, in a very small hospital there may only be three or four
people potentially within an operating engineers bargaining unit.
So from a public policy standpoint it makes little sense to have
that group carved out, nor is the craft union very anxious to
organise such a small group of employees. The same would hold
true with regard to clerical employees as well. There is a much
greater tendency to lump clerical and support employees together
in the smaller institutions. For example, in its guidelines for
hospital bargaining units, the Labor Relations Board of Nova
Scotia has said that in a small hospital or a nursing home the
Labor Relations Board might conclude that a broader unit or
even an all-employee unit is appropriate.

Areas of Conflict
Possibly the most highly disputed area within the hospital bargaining structure is that of the position of the Registered Nursing Assistant group, also called the auxiliary nursing group.
The RNA is in a particularly interesting position in the hospital
hierarchy. In most hospitals RNAs are treated as support service
employees. However, they do have a very strong identification
with the registered nurses in any given hospital because they
work very closely with registered nurses and have similar,
although not as extensive training. The RNAs, for these reasons,
sometimes look very sympathetically on representation by the
Registered Nurses' Associations. In Manitoba they are in fact
represented by the Registered Nurses' Association. In most
other provinces there are regular rumblings from the RNAs,
mainly through their provincial professional association, concerned with deserting the service unit and becoming a part of
the registered nurse bargaining unit. While these statements
are regularly made, there has never been, at least to this point
in time, a serious push to take the RNAs out of the service unit
and put them into a nurses unit in any of the other provinces.
    Another major area of contention involves the lab technologists.
On the one hand, unions such as CUPE and SEIU do organise
laboratory employees on a regular basis in competition with
units such as the Health Sciences Associations and the civil
service unions, as for example Ontario Public Service Employees
Union. Alternatively professional paramedicals such as dieticians,
therapists and medical social workers, are pushing for their

own union, to separate them from the so-called 'technical'
paramedicals.

The division within the paramedical group is openly recognised
in some provinces, such as Alberta. However, that situation does
not exist in most provinces. In Ontario, a recent decision at the
Stratford General Hospital concerned itself with the question of
carving out of a separate professional paramedical unit from the
overall technical paramedical unit. The Ontario Labor Relations
Board determined that it was appropriate to have one all-encompassing paramedical unit and not to recognise a separate professional group. The professional group at that time was
organised in a few hospitals under the Allied Health Professionals
of Ontario. The Stratford General decision almost completely
laid that organisation to rest because it is now encumbent upon
any union organising the technical group that they organise
the majority in the entire group, and it is not possible for them
to carve out a separate professional group.

Trend Towards Centralised Bargaining
In all provinces over the past ten years, there has been strong
move away from local hospital bargaining towards some form
of centralised or even province-wide bargaining. Full-scale
province-wide bargaining is a reality in most of the provinces
with the exceptions of Nova Scotia and Ontario. The move
towards province-wide bargaining has been having and is bound
to have further effect, leading towards the establishment of
broader based units. As the bargaining scene grows larger and
wider, smaller organisations, like the craft organisations which
represent a small number of employees, will probably become
increasingly less attractive to the workers.

SUMMARY

It seems that in Canada many employees within the health-care
industry have gravitated to a substantial degree towards craft
or professional type of units and have wanted to remain as
separate groups, apart from an all-inclusive or all-encompassing
unit. There are, however, many examples of bargaining groups
and unions which represent complete industrial units and
include all different types of personnel within hospitals and
other health-care facilities. The provincial government hospital
is one example.

There has to be recognition within the labour movement that
health-care workers of various kinds do have differing concerns -- arising out of their different backgrounds, education
levels and training. While industrial unionism has many clear
advantages it must ensure that their specialised needs are met;
otherwise they will face alienation by professional and skilled
groups and probably will not be able to make further progress
in organising and/or merging with such groups.

The evolution of a variety of union structures in the health sector suggests that three key variables are important in the shaping of a labour movement: the dynamic nature of the health-care occupations, the age of the bargaining relationship, and the job consciousness of the actors in the industrial relations system.[4] As Anderson has pointed out, 'bargaining may tend to move from a reliance on hard core tactics and political pressures to an emphasis on more rationalised and professional negotiations'.[5] The authors believe that the labour movement in the health sector in Canada will become increasingly rationalised through the creation and development of an organisational network manned by specialised personnel.[6]

REFERENCES

1 An example is that of the Health Sciences Association of British Columbia, which was certified as a trade union in June 1971 by the British Columbia Labour Relations Board, and currently holds a two-year contract with the BC Hospital Association covering 61 units. HSA member groups include physiotherapists, medical record librarians, dietitians, medical social workers, hospital pharmacists, occupational therapists, medical gymnasts, medical technicians, and radiological technicians.
2 The first category of unions, affiliated with CLC would include CUPE -- the largest hospital union. The second category would include another large union, National Federation of Social Affairs - the biggest hospital union in Quebec. The third category would include SEIU (AFL-CIO/CLC), or the IUOE. The last category represents a number of independent hospital unions, not affiliated to either of the parent trade union federations. These would include unions such as the Société Professionnelle des Infirmiers et Infirmières du Québec, Professional Association of Medical Technologists of Quebec, various Nurses Associations, or Medical Syndicates.
3 Kelleher, Stephen (1980), 'Canadian Labour Relations Board', Supply and Services, pp.77-81.
4 Perlman, S., (1949), 'A Theory of the Labor Movement', Kelley.
5 Anderson, John C., (1979), Bargaining Outcomes: An IR Systems Approach, *Industrial Relations*, vol.18, no.2, Spring, pp.142-3.
6 Barbash, Jack, Collective Bargaining as an Institution - A Long View, *Proceedings of the 29th Annual Meeting of the Industrial Relations Research Association*, Reprint no.208, pp.303-10.

4. THE LABOUR MOVEMENT IN HEALTH CARE: USA

C. Schoen

INTRODUCTION

The history and structure of the labour movement in the US health-care industry is markedly different from labour movements in other sectors of the US economy. In general, the movement to organise industrial workers into unions emerged during the Great Depression and reached its peak in 1954 with 25 per cent of the labour force organised, or 35 per cent of the employed, nonagricultural workforce.[1] Since then organising has generally failed to keep up with growth and changes in the US labour force resulting in a decline of organised labour to 20 per cent of the labour force, or 24 per cent of employed nonagricultural workers.[2]

In stark contrast to the stagnation of the US labour movement generally in the post-World War II era, unionisation in health care has exploded since the early 1960s when a negligible number of health-care facilities were organised (only 3 per cent of hospitals had collective bargaining contracts in 1961).[3] By 1978, roughly 24 per cent of hospital workers and 33 per cent of nursing home workers had joined unions or associations to bargain with employers over working conditions and for political action.[4]

This chapter presents an overview of what we perceive as the significant characteristics of the labour movement in health care and its structural differences from other US industries.

US HEALTH-CARE INDUSTRY

The United States' health-care system is unique among industrialised countries. Unlike Canada, Great Britain and all other industrialised countries (with the exception of South Africa), the US lacks a national health insurance or national health service system. Instead, a mixture of public programmes (federal, the 50 states and multiple local governments) and private funds (insurance and patient fees) finance health-care services. These services are produced by a similarly complex system in which, on the one hand, publicly owned facilities serve patients who cannot pay or who are inadequately insured while private facilities, on the other hand, compete with one another to attract well-insured patients. Table 4.1 illustrates the distribution of funds and ownership of major resources as of 1979.[5]

Table 4.1: Distribution of Financing Sources and Resource Ownership in the US Health-Care System

A. FINANCING: 1979 $Billions [a]

	TOTAL	PRIVATE			PUBLIC	
		FEE	INSURANCE	OTHER	FEDERAL	STATE AND LOCAL
TOTAL	$212.2	$60.0	$54.4	$6.4	$60.9	$30.5
ALL PERSONAL SERVICES	188.6	60.0	50.3	2.4	53.3	22.6
HOSPITAL	85.3	6.9	29.8	.9	34.9	12.8
NURSING HOME	17.8	7.5	.1	.1	5.5	4.6
OTHER						
ADMINISTRATION	7.7	–	4.1	.3	1.8	1.5
PUBLIC HEALTH	6.0	–	–	–	1.3	4.7
RESEARCH/ CONSTRUCTION	9.9	–	–	3.7	4.5	1.7

B. OWNERSHIP: Beds in 1000s [b]

	TOTAL	PRIVATE		PUBLIC	
		NONPROFIT	PROFIT	FEDERAL	STATE/LOCAL
Hospitals (beds) (1978)	1381.0	684.0	81.0	122.0	494.0
Nursing Homes (beds) (1977)	1402.0	296.0	971.0	–136.0–	

Sources
a. Gibson, Robert, (1980), National Health Expenditures, 1979, 'Health Care Financing Review', Summer, US Department of Health, Education and Welfare.

b. Hospitals: American Hospital Association, 'Hospital Statistics 1979 Edition', Chicago, IL.

Nursing Homes: National Center for Health Statistics, 'The National Nursing Home Survey: 1977 Summary for the United States', US DHEW, Pub. No. PH579-1794 July 1979.

In the industry discussion below, we do not attempt to compare the nature of health-care industries or their regulatory underpinnings across countries. We confine the discussion to the US health-care labour movement -- to critical characteristics and changes that have given rise to the relatively recent surge in health-care worker organising.

The Industry
Over the past 15 years, financing system reforms have fuelled dramatic growth in US health care. This rapid expansion has made the industry fertile ground for labour organising.

Following enactment of federal and state programmes for the poor, disabled and elderly in 1965, health care grew from a $42 billion industry consuming 6 per cent of GNP, to a $212 billion industry in 1979 consuming 9 per cent of GNP. The expansion has been particularly rapid among health-care institutions, where today five of seven health-care workers work. The hospital industry has grown to $85 billion in 1979 from $14 billion in 1965, nursing homes to $18 billion in 1979 from $2 billion in 1965.[6] Meanwhile, the health-care workforce has kept pace, growing from 4.2 million workers in 1970 to roughly 7 million in 1979. Again, workforce expansion has been largely in hospitals and nursing homes -- 4 million and 1 million respectively in 1979.[7]

In addition to the rapid growth of the industry in recent years and changed working conditions in health care, the composition of the workforce itself has contributed to the drive for worker organisation and collective action. Historically, the health-care workforce has comprised predominantly women (for example, 81 per cent of private sector hospital workers and 93 per cent of nursing home workers) and a relatively high proportion of minority workers (blacks constitute 19 per cent of private hospital workers and 20 per cent of nursing home workers compared to 11 per cent of all workers).[8] Over the years, hospital and nursing home managers could keep their labour costs down by hiring largely women and minority workers to exploit existing patterns of wage and job discrimination in the US as a whole.

Another factor that has more recently invited unions to organise health-care workers grows out of the jumbled and fragmented financing and ownership of health-care institutions. For while individual institutions continue to grow in size and require ever larger capital investment, the industry's sources of revenue are split between a variety of federal and state financing programmes as well as numerous private insurers; and the ownership of the institutions ranges from private for-profit corporations, including hospital and nursing home chains, to various forms of government control, to numerous nonprofit and charitable agencies. In short, the industry's multiple jurisdictions and occupations do not fit the sort of industry or craft definitions on which the larger American unions have

been built. Accordingly, numerous unions concerned with one
or several characteristics of health-care workers -- e.g., that
they are professionals, or service workers, or public employees,
etc. -- and drawn by the growing size of the workforce and
industry revenues at stake, have pushed vigorously to organise
'their share' of health care workers. (We are stressing here
the fragmented nature of financing and ownership in the industry as a factor inviting multiple union activity; we shall discuss later the nature and consequences of such union activity
on the structure of US labour movement in health care.)

Table 4.2: *Unionism in Hospitals, 1961-76*

Percent of Hospitals With One or More Union Contract

	Total	Federal	State/Local	Nonprofit	Profit
1961	3.0	0	1.0	4.3	4.3
1967	7.7	22.6	5.3	8.2	4.9
1970	14.7	52.0	14.1	12.4	8.0
1973	16.8	63.2	16.6	13.9	8.0
1976	23.1	80.7	22.4	19.7	10.8

Source: 1961-70, AHA Research Capsules - No.6, 'Hospitals
          JAHA', April 1, 1972, vol.46, p.217; 1973-1976
          Employee Relations and Training Department, 'AHA'.

Finally, national and state attempts in recent years to control
the rising costs of health care have added further impetus to
the labour movement. For workers are increasingly discovering
the need not only to negotiate effectively with management but
also with various government entities. While only eight states
had actually legislated hospital cost controls as of 1979, the
numerous federal and state proposals for cost containment have
put considerable pressure on hospital and nursing home
managers to cut costs.[10] Managers, in turn, have justified
placing the burden of cost containment efforts on workers by
reference to the state programmes or imminent legislation. Thus,
managers have increased work loads and intensity, while resisting workers' wage and welfare demands. Moreover, existing
state cost containment programmes often dictate wage and
working conditions from outside the confines of regular worker-
manager negotiations. As one labour leader observed, 'while
cost containment efforts make it easier to organise health care
workers, bargaining becomes more difficult'.[11]

Labour Movement Structure
The structure of the US health-care labour movement differs
from more established sectors of organised labour in three
key respects. First, the movement so far has not committed

itself to organising along one or the other traditional union line -- that is, either craft or industrial -- nor has it evolved some new combination. Second, the movement is fraught with vigorous inter-union competition that sometimes verges on predatory; this is in sharp contrast to the recognition of and the attempt to preserve established jurisdictions among unions in most other industries. Third, the movement has no model or blueprint yet for an internal union structure that combines centralised strength with local autonomy. Below, we consider first the prevailing structures in the US labour movement as a whole and then distinguish relevant aspects of the health-care labour movement.

First, the US labour movement has evolved from two distinct lines of worker organisation: early on the craft unions and more recently industrial unions. US industries tend to be organised along one line or the other. The construction industry, for instance, comprises plumbers, carpenters, electricians and other craft unions. In contrast, workers in the automobile, steel and mining industries constitute single industrial unions.

Second, the problems of organising multi-occupational workplaces have long plagued the US labour movement. For such workplaces continually pose the danger of erupting into hotly contested battlegrounds for aggressive unions asserting jurisdiction. In 1955 the US labour movement sought to abate these problems by merging the CIO (industrial unions) with the AFL (craft unions). The merger gave rise to an entity with a national, regional and local labour superstructure committed to resolving inter-union jurisdictional disputes and ending 'raids' by some unions on others' traditional constituencies.[12]

However, notwithstanding formation of the AFL-CIO, which currently presides over unions representing some 80 per cent of all organised workers in the US, the problems did not entirely abate. The AFL-CIO's superstructure, a loose confederation, has lacked the power to prescribe and enforce exclusive union jurisdictions in labour markets or industries that still remain to be organised. Thus, while workers in manufacturing industries and in crafts, with some exceptions still tend to be organised by single, established unions, workers in the rapidly growing service industries such as health care are often trapped between unions trying to assert jurisdiction.

Third, industrial unions in the US have, for the most part, evolved structures in which locals -- usually plant-based -- endow their national union with strong, central powers. The constitutions of the major US unions reflect this centralisation: Central Executive Boards have authority to grant and withdraw local charters, repeal non-conforming local by-laws, remove local officers and replace them with trustees, and levy per capita dues on the rank and file sufficient to support central strike, health and welfare, and administrative funds. The power to levy dues gives national union officers and their staffs substantial control over their unions' resources. In addition,

national officers may have considerable decision-making powers
in internal union matters. In industrial unions these decision-
making powers usually extend to strike actions, organising and
political activities, and bargaining strategies that affect all
member locals. Locals, for their part, carry out contract terms
and handle day to day labour-management conflicts. These
functions are generally conducted by shop stewards, business
agents and local officers.

Perhaps the major reason US trade unions have centralised
is their traditional emphasis on effective collective bargaining.
Industrial unions, in particular, have centralised their union
structures in order to bargain from a position of strength,
to establish uniform wage patterns throughout the industry
(including both industry-wide and patterned contract agreements), to co-ordinate timing of negotiations among different
employers, and, finally, to use union bargaining resources
efficiently rather than bargain on a plant by plant basis. Thus,
the locals of traditional US industrial unions rarely do their
own collective bargaining or have a plant-specific contract
which varies significantly from industry-wide patterns.

We can now compare the relevant characteristics of the labour
movement in health care. First, in contrast to manufacturing
industries with well-established craft and industrial union
jurisdictions, health-care facilities have been organised along
both craft (occupational) and industrial lines. For instance,
the workforce of one large public hospital in Chicago is divided
into at least seven bargaining units represented by different
national unions: service, maintenance workers, guards, technicians, practical nurses, registered nurses, and physician
housestaff. Yet, in a similarly large public hospital in New
York one public union represents all but the registered nurses.
Such variations occur facility by facility regardless of political
or geographical jurisdictions.

Second, the diversity of workforce composition has fostered
multiple jurisdictional claims and competitive free-for-alls
among unions seeking to organise health-care facilities. In 1977
the National Labor Relations Board recorded at least 44 national
unions competing to represent health-care workers in private
health-care facilities (the NLRB does not record election campaigns in public facilities).[13] In addition, at least 100 independent professional worker associations -- for example the
American Nurses Association -- organise health-care workers
and bargain on their behalf. Not surprisingly, the AFL-CIO has
denied petitions for exclusive jurisdiction, since little factual
support exists on which to grant them.

In some cases, local unions have tried to mitigate divisive
inter-union competition through formal and informal agreements
covering one or several nearby facilities. Such local inter-
union co-operation has been particularly productive in New
York, Buffalo and Chicago.[14] To date, however, such agreements have been rare and fragile -- none extend to national

unions and none cover all potential competitors. Meanwhile, each year yet another union, often with shrinking membership in its traditional realms of jurisdiction, enters the fray. Most recently, the powerful American Federation of Teachers (AFT) hired several registered nurses and mounted expensive campaigns to represent registered nurses across the country. The campaigns attempted both to woo nurses away from other unions and to organise yet unorganised health-care facilities.[15]

This internecine struggle among unions has rendered every unorganised health-care facility a potential battleground. Unions, to conserve their resources, have concentrated their organising drives around geographic areas in which they considered themselves well-established or at least where workers are receptive generally to unionisation. Accordingly, the bulk of the movement has been confined to traditional labour strongholds -- namely, to urban, manufacturing centres in the northeast, midwest and west. Table 4.3 displays the emerging, uneven pattern of the labour movement in hospitals and nursing homes across the country -- from the south and southwest, where workers in the majority of health-care facilities do not bargain collectively, to the northeast, where bargaining units have won contracts covering the majority of workers in over 95 per cent of public hospitals in some cities.[16]

Third, health-care unions' structures are considerably more decentralised than their counterparts in other industries. This decentralisation reflects several major factors: wide variation in the working conditions, size and range of services among US health-care facilities; highly fragmented ownership patterns, including a multitude of public, nonprofit private and profit-making private facilities; a multi-occupation work-force; and innumerable local health-care market variations within cities, from city to city, and from state to state.

A brief look at collective bargaining in health care shows the extent of decentralisation and gives some insight into the present state of health care unions' structures. In general, contract negotiations take place on a facility by facility basis, often with separate contracts for each bargaining unit. Where several unions co-exist in one facility, there often tends to be little formal co-ordination of the timing or bargaining demands in the separate negotiations.

This single employer bargaining pattern has major exceptions. In large industrialised cities with relatively long histories of health-care unionism, unions have succeeded in creating multi-employer contracts or, at least, patterned bargaining agreements (one contract sets the pattern for all others in the area). A 1976 report on bargaining in the private sector counted 20 formal multi-employer agreements.[17] The largest is one New York union's contract with 60 hospitals covering more than 35 000 workers. Other significant agreements include: Minneapolis-St Paul with up to 23 hospitals under one contract; San Francisco with three separate master contracts covering public hospitals, nonprofit private hospitals and the Kaiser hospital system (a private, prepaid group practice); and Seattle contracts for professional health-care workers. In the absence of multi-employer formal agreements, some unions have crafted informal agreements to foster uniform policies and working conditions across facilities in a given urban area.

Table 4.3: *Unionisation in Hospitals in Selected US Cities, September 1978*

% Of Workers In Hospitals With Majority Covered by Contracts

Area	Professional & Technical		Nonprofessional	
	Private	State/Local	Private	State/Local
Northeast				
Boston	5-9	80-84	--	95+
New York	5-9	95+	40-44	70-74
South				
Atlanta	--	--	10-14	--
Dallas/ Ft Worth	--	--	--	--
Miami	--	95+	--	90-94
North Central				
Chicago	0-4	95+	35-39	95+
Minneapolis	90-94	50-54	80-84	60-64
St Louis	0-4	85-89	0-4	85-89
West				
Denver	--	--	--	--
San Francisco	55-59	70-74	80-84	70-79
Seattle	65-69	95+	15-19	95+

Source: 'Industry Wage Survey: Hospitals and Nursing Homes, September 1978', Bureau of Labor Statistics, US Department of Labor.

By the end of the 1970s, however, collective bargaining and labour-management relations in general had still not been any further centralised than city-specific multi-employer agreements. Even within states considerable variation continues from city to city. This decentralised bargaining structure[18] is further complicated where states have enacted hospital cost control programmes. In these states (eight by 1980), public agencies determine prospective rate controls designed to slow inflation of hospital costs in the state. The programmes vary from

relatively tight controls affecting all hospitals and all hospital
revenues (Maryland) to relatively loose controls affecting only
a portion of hospital revenues (federal Medicare controls).[19] In
all cases, the cost control programmes place limits on the structure and content of labour-management negotiations.[20] Health-
care employers and labour leaders must bargain with these
regulatory agencies as well as one another. This cost control
structure forces unions in health care to bargain on two fronts.
To date this multi-lateral bargaining has consisted of a series
of two party negotiations rather than trilateral sessions.

Notwithstanding the general tendency for collective bargaining in health care to be decentralised, health-care union structures vary widely in their efforts to represent members interests
at industry-wide levels and, at the same time, allow local
independence to respond to individual workplace and market
conditions. The variety of internal structure exhibited by the
four leading US health-care unions (in terms of membership
size) illustrates the struggles of the health-care labour movement to evolve a structure compatible with the complexities
of the industry, that combines centralised strength with local
autonomy. The four unions, in order of our discussion below
are: the Service Employees International Union (SEIU), the
American Federation of State, County and Municipal Employees
(AFSCME), the National Union of Hospital and Health Care
Employees (1199), and the American Nurses Association (ANA).
In the private sector SEIU, 1199 and the ANA account for three
out of five negotiated contracts.[21] SEIU and AFSCME together
control the bulk of organised public sector health facilities.

Service Employees International Union (SEIU). SEIU, formerly
named Building Service Employees International Union, began
in the early 1920s as a craft union. Initially, SEIU claimed
jurisdiction over building service and maintenance workers
and concentrated its organising activities in New York City,
on the west coast and in midwest cities. During the 1930s SEIU
organised city hospital workers in San Francisco, thus gaining
the distinction of being first among the many unions now in
health care. After World War II, SEIU expanded its jurisdiction
into other service industries -- including government, recrea-
tion, hotel and office as well as health-care workers, across
major urban areas in the northeast, midwest and west coast
states. The union now counts roughly 250 000 health-care
workers, and a total membership of about 700 000 (only AFSCME,
with over 250 000, rivals SEIU as the largest union in health
care). The job skills of SEIU's health-care workers like those of
the union's other members, correspond to the broad range of
occupations in the industry, from relatively unskilled hospital
staff workers in maintenance, cleaning and food services to
highly trained health professionals.

While SEIU has been organising in recent years along industrial lines (service industries), the union's internal structure

still reflects its traditional craft union origins. Most significantly, SEIU's decision-making powers are widely decentralised -- its 330 local affiliates by and large make decisions on organising, collective bargaining, and general policy. Indeed, this decentralisation is part of the union's operating philosophy -- in the words of an SEIU 'Report':

> Local Unions are the heart of our organisation. They are free to elect their own officers, to adopt their own by-laws, to negotiate their own contracts, to set up their own dues structure, to conduct their own strike votes (if they choose to) and, generally, to function as an autonomous labor organisation.[22]

The locals themselves are complex entities. Many are quite large and cover a multiplicity of service industries and employers - e.g., one California local has over 27 000 members including 25 000 health-care workers with the remaining 2000 spread across offices, schools, apartment buildings, stores and amusement facilities.[23] Accordingly, SEIU health-care workers often find that the local officers who represent their bargaining units in contract negotiations may also represent building service workers, clerical workers, public employees, even perhaps racetrack employees.

Decentralisation entails obvious risks. In particular, the decentralised union structure renders health-care workers vulnerable against the current onslaught of federal, state, municipal and private industry-wide health cost containment policies, proposals and measures. Recognising these risks, SEIU has taken two steps toward centralising certain union functions. First, it has established Joint Councils in geographic areas where several member locals are active. Through the Joint Councils the locals can pool their financial, research, bargaining and political action resources to confront the issues that affect them jointly or at least affect more than one local or several bargaining units. However, to serve member needs across a variety of service industries, the Joint Council staffs have had to be 'generalists'. In only one instance, so far, has an area officially designated staff specialists strictly for health-care matters in a health-care division. Second, SEIU has expanded its international staff, hiring several industry specialists -- including health -- to co-ordinate research, policy and political action at the national level.

In general, these steps serve to limit some risks of decentralisation. Joint Councils have been particularly effective in cities where SEIU locals represent large concentrations of health-care workers. In those cities a minimum of resources has produced strong multi-employer contracts as well as substantial clout in local legislatures. With respect to steps taken at the national level, it is perhaps still too early to pass judgment.

American Federation of State, County and Municipal Employees
(*AFSCME*). AFSCME currently is one of the largest and fastest
growing unions in the AFL-CIO. With over 1 million workers
nationally, including an estimated 250 000-plus health-care
workers, AFSCME is a major union voice in the US generally
and a strong rival of SEIU for labour leadership in the health-
care industry. AFSCME competes with SEIU for more than
leadership. Both unions claim jurisdiction over public and
nonprofit workers in many service industries; they compete
particularly fiercely in organising health-care workers.[24] A
large part of AFSCME's organising objectives is defined by
state governments. In general, state labour laws determine
whether the city, county, state or other public employees in a
state may join unions and bargain collectively. Thus, as states
have reformed their laws to allow organising in the public sectors, AFSCME has begun organising drives to unionise entire
city, county or state workforces.

AFSCME's structure is considerably more centralised at every
level of union operations than SEIU's. AFSCME's national administration is located, like SEIU's, in Washington, DC. AFSCME
members pay per capita dues of $3.05 (compared with SEIU dues
of $1.80) to support a large central organisation with extensive
research, organising, collective bargaining, legal and legislative
departments. In many instances, this central staff is responsible
for organising and bargaining on behalf of members at the
various local levels.

AFSCME's Constitution divides its membership into 21 'legislative' districts.[25] These legislative districts in turn are divided
into Councils or District Councils (the terms seem somewhat
interchangeable). Councils comprise delegates from AFSCME
'locals' in specified geographic areas of the US and its territories.
Generally a Council's jurisdiction tends to depend on both the
concentration of AFSCME membership in the state or local area
and historic developments in the particular state's public
employee labour laws. Thus, Councils in some states cover the
entire state, including all county and municipal employees as
well as state government employees; yet, Councils in neighbouring states may be county specific or municipality specific. For
instance, New York State has three major legislative divisions
and three corresponding regional councils. In contrast, seven
other large states, such as Pennsylvania, Illinois and California
have one legislative jurisdiction, and a wide range of council
affiliations.

In general, the Council or District Council performs the bulk
of research, organising, collective bargaining and political
activities in its region. However, some smaller Councils look to
the International for these services. In any case, the Councils
or District Councils serve important centralising functions at
the state, county or local level.

'Locals' are subordinate bodies of the Councils or District
Councils. In general, the locals are organised to represent

individual bargaining units; these may range in membership
from a group of workers in a single institution to an entire class
of workers throughout a city, county or even state. Not all locals
are affiliated with Councils; some locals have a homogeneous and
large enough membership to justify their own research and collective bargaining staffs. In most cases, however, AFSCME
locals tend to perform only 'administrative' services for their
members, such as enforcing contracts and processing grievances.

The extent of AFSCME's centralisation is indicated by the
AFSCME Constitution which specifies that, on average, member
dues payments should be split 30-60-10 per cent among the
International, Councils (including District Councils), and locals,
respectively.

This dues structure enables AFSCME to negotiate with relatively centralised public administrations at the various levels
of government whether the issues pertain to health or other
public service programmes. In a sense AFSCME is organised as
if the public sector were one large industry, rather than multiple industries and services. Like SEIU, AFSCME has no
separate health care division to co-ordinate and direct health-
care industry labour policies. While individual locals may comprise nothing other than health-care workers, often even in a
single health-care facility, AFSCME's various Councils and the
International combine their resources and policy departments
with no regard to service or industry sectors. As a result,
AFSCME's appeal to health-care workers is not as a health-care
union per se, but its ability to provide effective representation
in negotiating contracts with government agencies as well as in
lobbying for government action on issues of general concern to
public employees.

Currently, AFSCME leaders are expressing concern that the
lack of a centralised health-care industry division in its internal
structure is hampering the union's ability to marshall resources
effectively on behalf of its health-care membership. The recent
US trend to close nonfederal public health institutions, because
of state and local fiscal problems, has pressured AFSCME to
centralise, at least, its health-care worker policy-making.
Consequently, AFSCME leaders have proposed a national health-
care advisory committee to advise leaders and set priorities for
the political, organising and bargaining activities of the International and Councils with large numbers of health-care workers.

National Union of Hospital and Health Care Employees (1199).
The National Union of Hospital and Health Care Employees (1199)
is more geographically concentrated than either AFSCME or SEIU.
With roughly 60 to 70 per cent of its total membership in the
New York metropolitan area, 1199 is in some respects more like
a large local or regional union than either AFSCME or SEIU.
Nevertheless, 1199 has 100 000 members in 23 different states
and the union's activism in the health-care labour movement has

won it national recognition.

1199 is a large, independent affiliate of the Retáil, Wholesale and Department Store Workers Union (RWDSU). Originally it was RWDSU's Local 1199 -- an industrial union with jurisdiction over drugstore workers. In the late 1950s, 1199 began to organise hospital workers; since then it has grown rapidly from a small local of 5000 drugstore workers to its current 100 000 members in hospitals, nursing homes and clinics in addition to independent drugstore workers.[26]

Throughout this rapid expansion in jurisdiction and size 1199 has retained its identity as an industrial union for all health-care workers. 1199's efforts to incorporate both the craft and industrial dimensions of the health-care workforce into its internal union structure are unique. Most significantly, 1199 divides its membership into four occupational divisions: a general hospital division; a Professional and Technical Guild; a Drug Division; and a Nurses Division. 1199 created these divisions to allow its health-care workers their several occupational identities; at the same time, 1199 can co-ordinate the four divisions' activities and policies by virtue of its single industrial union structure.

1199, in principle, maintains the occupational divisions both at the national level -- headquarters in New York City -- and in its seven geographic 'District' organisations. Yet, since the Districts range in size from less than 2000 members in Massachusetts District 1199 to over 60 000 in the New York Metropolitan Area District, official subdivisions by occupation are not always possible.

Each District comprises bargaining units organised into 'Chapters'. As a rule the Chapters are confined to individual health-care facilities; the occupational divisions occasionally necessitate the creation of more than one 1199 Chapter in a single facility. Chapter officers are responsible for contract administration and grievances. The bulk of organising, research, negotiating, political action resources and policy-making is concentrated at the national level, though the Districts perform certain of these functions in accordance with the size of their membership and their geographic proximity to the National Union staff.

In all but New York, contracts tend to be facility specific. In New York, 1199 has succeeded in negotiating a master contract for some 36 000 members working in the 60 nonprofit hospitals and nursing homes that participate in the League of Voluntary Hospitals and Homes.[27] Sixty additional hospitals tend to pattern their agreements after the League contract.

1199's organising and policy activities are more centralised than SEIU's and AFSCME's and more focused on the health-care industry. Moreover, the 1199 National has also adopted broader policy goals and responsibility for the welfare of individual members. The union has, for instance, made a point of tying civil rights issues to labour issues in its publicity and organising

drives, and it maintains and administers its own health and
welfare funds, training and 'upgrading' funds, and a cultural
foundation. 1199's emphasis on serving its members in ways
that go beyond traditional collective bargaining representation
has won 1199 a national reputation as an innovator in the labour
movement.[28]

Despite its innovative structure and reputation, 1199 is still
confined to a relatively narrow geographic area; it does not
yet seriously challenge SEIU or AFSCME nationwide. Even
within New York, 1199 shares the health-care industry with
AFSCME -- public, city hospitals -- and SEIU -- the profit-
making hospitals. Thus, the impact of 1199's innovations, its
blending craft and industrial union features, on the structure
of the health-care labour movement as a whole is still uncertain.

American Nurses Association (ANA). In contrast to SEIU,
AFSCME and 1199, the ANA is a professional association of
registered nurses and not a trade union. Although the ANA
increasingly seeks to represent nurses as workers as well as
professionals, it has yet to blend the two goals effectively into
one organisational structure.

Historically, the ANA and its state affiliates shunned collective work place action to improve the working conditions of
nurses. Instead, the ANA relied on its members' professional
status, licensure laws and on health-care employers' good will
to protect nurses as workers. In contrast to a trade union,
the ANA was primarily concerned with the public image and
prestige of its membership rather than their economic and social
welfare.

Nevertheless, US nurses' low wages and adverse working conditions forced the ANA to change. At first, the national association merely issued guidelines to state affiliates for developing
statewide economic security programmes for nurses. The guidelines pledged no strikes and disassociated nurses from the
labour disputes of other health-care workers. Moreover, the
ANA provided few resources and little policy support to member
nurses trying to organise themselves.

By the end of the 1960s, the competition of trade unions to
organise and represent nurses coupled with the demands of
nurses for assistance, forced the ANA to take more active measures. Accordingly, the National Commission on Economic and
General Welfare was given the responsibility of planning and
implementing an ANA collective bargaining programme, including guidelines, funds, research and staff assistance for state
affiliate programmes. In addition, the 1968 Convention rescinded
the no-strike policy, and the 1970 Convention recommended
support of other health-care labour organisations.[29] These
actions have made the ANA the largest union of nurses in the
US. By 1978, roughly one third of the ANA's 200 000 membership were organised and covered under contracts administered
by ANA state affiliates.[30]

In contrast to SEIU, AFSCME and 1199, the ANA makes no attempt to represent all health-care workers. It defines its jurisdiction 'narrowly', to the more than one million registered nurses in the US. Thus, the ANA has no difficulty with craft-industrial questions.

The ANA's internal structure, however, presents other, perhaps more significant, issues than those confronting the three trade unions. The national organisation is a federation of 53 autonomous state (and the US territories) nurses' associations. Each state association determines the extent to which it will become involved in collective bargaining and workplace issues concerning its membership. Across the country, state associations vary from strongly pro-collective action to strict policies against nurses' unions. Thus, ANA union strength varies significantly from area to area.

Local units form the core of all collective bargaining and workplace activities.[31] Yet, state associations are officially the certified bargaining agents and supply the local units with resources and bargaining expertise.

This structure for collective bargaining under the auspices of a statewide professional association, fuels internal conflicts and tensions within the ANA. In contrast to trade unions, the ANA as a professional association must cover all nurses, regardless of their supervisory status. Nevertheless, US labour laws prohibit supervisors from bargaining in the same organisational unit as nonsupervisory workers. Thus, the ANA's interests in maintaining its character as a professional association and active union are in conflict as long as it attempts to maintain a unified organisational structure. This strain has been aggravated by recent court suits that threaten to invalidate certain ANA subdivisions' rights to bargain on behalf of all their members.[32]

The conflict of purpose has given rise to several independent nurses' associations which exclude supervisors and focus all resources on workplace and collective bargaining issues. This development has weakened the pressure from within the ANA to alter its structure to fit the dual goals of collective action and professional representation. Similarly, successful competition from unions -- notably SEIU, AFSCME and 1199 -- undermines ANA resources and internal determination to resolve its conflicting goals. Recently, the competition and internal conflicts have led three state associations to forego their contracts and organising programme and in favor of a more single purpose professional association.[33]

In sum the apparent inability of the ANA to resolve the structural tension between its role as a professional association and as a union hinders its ability to meet either the local or central needs of nurses for representation as workers. Thus, the four labour organisations reviewed in this chapter, the ANA structure presents the most barriers to a stable and strong future role in the US health-care labour movement.

The 1980s: Future Directions and Unresolved Issues
In all instances, the pressures exerted by cost control programmes are pushing unions and management alike to centralise
policies and to increase uniformity of working conditions across
relevant geographic areas. Our review of the US health-care
industry and the current structure of its labour movement has
highlighted the extent to which organised labour has not yet
evolved corresponding structural solutions to the industry-wide
and facility-specific needs of the multi-occupational health-care
workforce. Increased cost controls also put pressure on the
labour movement to resolve inter-union jurisdiction disputes.

As illustrated by our discussion of the major health-care
unions, key unions in the labour movement are already in the
process of working towards internal structural solutions to the
demands of labour relations. Yet, the strong union rivalry to
represent an as yet largely unorganised labour force continues
to hinder both internal and external co-ordination of power,
policy and resources. The competition also tends to weaken the
national and state political power of the labour movement by
dividing unions into competing health industry interests --
e.g. public against private sector, professional against nonprofessionals.

In conclusion, in contrast to other major US industries the
US health-care labour movement is still in the midst of organising and evolving stable, effective labour structures. Whether or
not it can co-ordinate the activities of its many actors and present a united front to protect workers from industry-wide cost
control pressures, will largely determine the role organised
labour will play in speaking for health-care workers in the
1980s.

REFERENCES AND NOTES

1 Bureau of Labor Statistics, US Department of Labor (1979),
  'Handbook of Labor Statistics 1978', Bulletin 2000, June,
  Table 150, p.507.
2 AFL-CIO Department of Research (1980), 'Union Membership and Employment', 1959-1979, February, pp.1-11.
3 Hospital Unionism Statistics for the 1960s are published by
  the American Hospital Association (1972), AHA Research
  Capsules - No.6, 'Hospitals, JAHA 46', 1 April. The 1978
  figure was obtained by the author from the AHA Research
  Department.
4 Nursing Home Statistics are published by the US Bureau
  of Labor Statistics (1976), 'Industry Wage Survey: Nursing
  Homes and Related Facilities', May, US Department of Labor,
  Bulletin 1964, p.2.
5 Gibson, Robert M. (1980), National Health Expenditures,
  1979, Table 1, 'Health Care Financing Review Summer 1980',
  vol.2(1), US Department of Health and Human Services.

6 Gibson, National Health Expenditures, 1979, note 5.

7 Office of Health Research, Statistics and Technology, Public Health Service, US Department of Health Education and Welfare (1980), 'Health United States, 1979', Table 47, p.155, US Government Printing Office, DHEW Publication Number PHS80-1232.

8 Bureau of Labor Statistics, US Department of Labor (1979), 'Employment and Earnings, United States, 1909-1978', Bulletin No.1312-11, p.810 for women; US Department of Health, Education and Welfare (1979), 'Employees in Nursing Homes in the United States, 1973-1974', Series 14, No.20, DHEW Pub.No. (PHS) 79-1815, for minority workers.

9 For examples of US nurses move to challenge authority see, American Nurses Association (1978), 'Power, Nursing's Challenge for Change', Papers presented at the 51st Convention Honolulu, Hawaii, 9-14 June.

10 These states were: Connecticut, Maryland, Massachusetts, New Jersey, New York, Rhode Island, Washington, and Wisconsin. For an overview of the different programmes see: US Department of Health, Education and Welfare, Health Care Financing Administration (1978), 'Abstracts of State Legislated Hospital Cost Containment Program', (HCFA No.017 (5-78), May.

11 Hardy, George, President of SEIU 22 June 1980, 'Press Release from SEIU National Convention'.

12 For a short, general history of the US labour movement see, Bureau of Labor Statistics, US Department of Labor (1976), 'Brief History of the American Labor Movement', Bulletin 1000.

13 Dewey Tanner, Lucretia, Goldberg Weinstein, Harriet, and Ahmuty, Alice L., (1980), Collective Bargaining in the Health Care Industry, Research Summary, 'Monthly Labor Review', US Department of Labor, February, p.49 and Labor-Management Services Administration, 'Impact of the 1974 Health Care Admendments to the NLRB on Collective Bargaining in the Health Care Industry', note 18, p.64. On NLRB elections, see Miller and Becker, Patterns and Determinants of Union Growth in the Hospital Industry: Implications for Organising Service and Professional Workers in the 1980s, unpublished manuscript, University of Wisconsin, Madison, April 1980.

14 Labor Management Services Administration, pp.54-61.

15 For a news release on the AFT decision to organise health-care workers see, 'Health Labor Relations Reports', 11 December 1978. See also the involvement of the National Education Association involvement, 'Health Labor Relations Report', 4 February 1980.

16 Bureau of Labor Statistics, US Department of Labor (1980), 'Industry Wage Survey: Hospitals and Nursing Homes, September 1978', Bulletin 2069, November, pp.4-5.

17 Labor-Management Administration, Impact of the 1974

Health Care Amendments, note 18, pp.56-8.

18 For example, the Service Employees International Union's regional councils for the state of California have succeeded only in co-ordinating the union's legislative agenda; the bargaining structure remains highly decentralised.

19 See note 16.

20 Schramm, Carl J. (1977), 'Regulatory Attempts at Hospital Cost Control and Their Impact on Collective Bargaining', paper processed by the Johns Hopkins University. Also, Weinstein, Paul A. (9 April 1979), 'Impact of Hospital Cost Review on Industrial Relations', Paper for Industrial Relations Research Association, Program of Industrial Relations and Labor Studies, University of Maryland-College Park.

21 Tanner, et al., Collective Bargaining in the Health Care Industry, note 39.

22 Service Employees International Union (1980), 'A Report from Service Employees International Union', SEIU.

23 SEIU Research Department documents on local union membership.

24 SEIU sees public health-care workers as service employees-- part of its industrial jurisdiction. AFSCME claims nonprofit private facilities are actually 'quasi-public' institutions and therefore in its public sector jurisdiction.

25 American Federation of State, County and Municipal Employees, 'International Constitution, As amended at the 23rd Convention, Las Vegas, Nevada, June 26-30, 1978'. Article IV (legislative districts) and Article IX Subordinate Bodies.

26 For a concise history of 1199 see Labor-Management Services Administration, Impact of the 1974 Health Care Amendments, note 18, pp.78-88.

27 Statistics from League contract for 1978 with 1199.

28 Several articles have praised 1199's activities. See for example, 'Business Week', A Union Crusades for Rank- and-File Culture, January 1979; 'Pension and Welfare News', Unusual Benefit Programs at New York's Local 1199, September 1970, pp.44-50; Raskin, A.H. (1970), A Union with Soul, 'The New York Times Magazine', 22 March.

29 Labor-Management Administration. Impact of the 1974 Health Care Amendments, note 18, pp.88-97 for an over- view of the ANA history and structure.

30 Miller, Richard U. (1980), 'Hospital Labor Relations', Graduate School of Business, University of Wisconsin, Madison, Monograph No. 11, February, pp.13-16.

31 Each local makes all its own bargaining decisions including strike decisions. This differs from all three trade unions which require all locals to apply to the national union for strike authorisations.

32 Miller, Hospital Labor Relations, note 23.

33 Health Labor Relations Reports (1980), Connecticut

Nurses Association Decides to End Role in Collective
Bargaining, 'HLR Reports', 28 April. Wisconsin and Texas
nurses' associations made the same decision in 1979,
see 'HLR Reports', 2 April and 16 April 1979.

5. THE LABOUR MOVEMENT IN THE NATIONAL HEALTH SERVICE (NHS): UK

M. Carpenter

The rapid growth and assertiveness of health service trade
unions, was undoubtedly one of the most significant developments within the service during the 1970s. Yet if a 'new
unionism' emerged alongside a 'new managerialism', the roots
of both lay further back. Though this chapter is primarily concerned with the causes, features and consequences of the new
unionism in the health service, it can only be understood against
the background from which it emerged.

HEALTH SERVICE UNIONISM FROM 1948 TO THE 1960s

The British industrial relations culture is famed for its multi-
unionism, and the NHS is by far the most extreme example,
with more than 40 recognised organisations. Any organisation
which could claim members and was prepared to engage in
collective bargaining was granted seats on Whitley Councils in
1948, though it has proved very difficult for new organisations
since then, however, to push their way into the system. The
major reasons for multi-unionism were: the divided administrative structure before 1948 which created different recruitment
spheres; the scramble between newer and older Trades Union
Congress (TUC) affiliated organisations for one of the most
rapidly growing yet poorly organised sectors of employment;
and, above all, the fact that many groups of workers had a
fragmented occupational rather than 'class' consciousness, pre-
ferring to join professional associations, thereby distancing
themselves from the association with 'trade' and manual work
that seemed to go with trade unionism.

Trade unions therefore gained a recognised, but partial foot-
hold in the new service. They were compelled to share power
with professional associations on the national negotiating
machinery (in only two functional areas, ancillary staffs and
administrative and clerical, did they exercise a dominant
influence) and their strength of membership at local level was,
at best, patchy. Throughout the 1950s and into the 1960s,
unions were not salient in the working lives of many health
workers. They were for the most part remote organisations 'up
there', as remote as the Whitley Councils themselves. Only in a
few areas did unions at local level enjoy a significant presence.
Management took staff loyalty for granted. However, that loyalty
had been forged in a time when unemployment was widespread.

74

In the tight labour market conditions of the 1950s, this situation had been transformed. Discontent may have rarely expressed itself in trade union militancy; but it did show itself in very rapid rates of staff turnover. The pay and conditions of many grades of workers were slipping behind the general level and the rest of the public sector. The failure to act decisively at this point undoubtedly stored up problems which were bound, sooner or later, to result in militant responses by staff organisations.

During this period the central obsession at government level was to keep the escalating costs of the service down. Beveridge's original assumption, that the need for health services would wither away as doctors cleared the backlog of accumulated ill-health, was very rapidly shown to be simplistic. As costs began to rise, control of the overall wages bill became the prime form of containment. During a period of rising prices, negotiations on Whitley Councils became subject to notorious delays, with the influence of the Treasury clearly working behind the scenes. The conclusion of an investigation of NHS bargaining published in 1957 reached the ominous conclusion that:

> Amongst the many reasons for the differences in pay between the health service and the engineering or mining industries is that the employers in these industries fear the unions more than the management sides fear health service staff organisations.[1]

The Growth of the New Unionism

Few commentators doubted that this situation had been transformed by the 1970s. Trade unionism in the health service had changed beyond recognition from the hesitant and conservative organisations of the past. Though the 'new unionism' affected each organisation differently, there was nevertheless a basic unity to the process. The first main feature was simply the extraordinarily rapid growth of unions during this period. Table 5.1 shows the pattern of union representation on NHS Whitley Councils which, effectively, establishes the recruitment fields in which unions can hope to expand.

Table 5.1: Representation of TUC Affiliated Organisations on the Ten Functional Whitley Councils

	No. of Councils
Confederation of Health Service Employees	7
National Union of Public Employees	6
Association of Scientific, Technical and Managerial Staffs[a]	4
National and Local Government Officers Association	4
National Union of General and Municipal Workers (inc. White Collars section)	3

Table 5.1: Representation of TUC Affiliated Organisations on
the Ten Functional Whitley Councils

	No. of Councils
Health Visitors Association	1
Transport and General Workers Union	1
Union of Shop, Distributive and Allied Workers	1

a. excluding Medical Practitioners Union
Source: Lord McCarthy (1976), 'Making Whitley Work',
      DHSS, Appendix B.

The National Union of Public Employees (NUPE) and Confederation of Health Service Employees (COHSE) are represented on
more Councils than other organisations, those covering the
largest occupational groups of ancillary workers, nurses and
midwives, and administrative and clerical. NUPE is strongest
among ancillary workers in general hospitals, while COHSE's
base is among nurses, especially in psychiatric hospitals. The
Association of Scientific, Technical and Managerial Staffs
(ASMTS), on the other hand, is restricted to those Councils
catering for professional and technical workers where fewer
members are employed, and its Medical Practitioners Section is
handicapped by its lack of recognition in the direct salary
negotiations between the British Medical Association (BMA) and
the government. The National and Local Government Officers'
Association (NALGO), as a white collar union, is unrepresented
among ancillary workers, but has some membership among nurses and certain professional and technical grades. The National
Union of General and Municipal Workers' (NUGMW) main base
is among ancillary staffs (manual workers), with some membership in the nursing field, while the Transport and General
Workers Union (TGWU)'s involvement in the NHS is restricted
to ancillary workers. The Health Visitors Association (HVA)
is a single-occupation association, while the Union of Shop,
Distributive and Allied Trades (USDAW) has minimal representation in the retail opticians' field.

The 1970s were not only expansionist years for NHS unions.
In 1974, for the first time in history, union density increased
beyond 50 per cent of the UK labour force, with women, the
public sector, and professional, technical and white collar
workers leading the field. As a result the composition of the
labour movement was more representative of the labour force as
a whole than it had ever been.[2]

The phenomenal growth of most unions recruiting among health
service staff can be seen clearly in Table 5.2.

Table 5.2: The Growth of TUC Affiliated Unions Recruiting Significant Numbers of Health Workers

	1970	1979
ASTMS	123 800	471 000
MPU[a]	5 502	5 106
COHSE	77 808	215 033
Hospital Consultants and Specialists Association (HCSA)[b]	–	4 021
HVA	5 287	10 881
NALGO	397 069	729 405
NUGMW	803 653	964 836
NUPE	305 222	712 392
TGWU	1 531 607	2 072 818

a. The MPU amalgamated with ASTMS but still affiliates
   separately to the TUC
b. The HCSA did not affiliate to the TUC until 1979
Source: 'TUC Yearbook of Industry and Services 1979-80'.

With the exception of COHSE, not all of this growth was in the NHS. ASTMS is a union with the bulk of its membership in the private sector, which has grown both by recruiting previously unorganised workers and by absorbing existing organisations. In the health services its base is primarily among laboratory technicians (now known as scientific officers) but in recent years has made gains among radiographers, physiotherapists and other professional and technical workers disillusioned with the ability of small professional associations to promote their interests. ASTMS has absorbed a number of these since the Medical Practitioners Union (MPU) became a Section in 1970. Section status, enjoyed by doctors and pharmacists, with the power to elect a Section Committee, and to communicate separately through their own journal, served as important enticements.

COHSE was until very recently a relatively small union which had only grown moderately since its inception in 1946. A dramatic change in its fortunes occurred following the nurses' pay campaign of 1974 when, alone among staff side organisations, it initiated a programme of industrial action. By 1979 it was the twelfth largest union in the TUC – a remarkable achievement for a union recruiting in such a limited membership field crowded with competing organisations. An important consequence was that COHSE achieved a much greater coverage of membership among general nurses, and had become a serious rival to the non-TUC Royal College of Nursing (Rcn).

NALGO and NUPE are two public sector giants which by 1979 had become, respectively, the fourth and fifth largest unions in the TUC. Both complement each other as a white collar and, broadly speaking, a manual workers' union, recruiting throughout public services and the nationalised industries, with size-

able proportions of NHS workers in membership. In 1979 NUPE's
health service membership was approximately 250 000 while
NALGO's amounted to just over 84 500. In 1979, therefore, the
'big three' of COHSE, NUPE and NALGO claimed to have in
membership just over 50 per cent of the 1 million or so employees
of the NHS.

Women Workers and Health Service Unions
The most striking aspect of the recent growth of NHS trade
unionism is that much of the new membership is among women.
In part this is because the growth in NHS employment has come
about largely as a result of the expansion of low ranking, low
paid jobs in the nursing, ancillary and clerical sectors - in
precisely the kinds of areas where women predominate. Table
5.3 shows the changing sex distribution of the membership of
the leading NHS trade unions.

Table 5.3: *Growth of Female Membership as a Proportion of Total
in Major NHS Unions*

	% 1974	% 1978
ASTMS[a]	17.7	17.5
COHSE	70.4	75.4
NALGO	40.2	44.9
NUPE	63.3	66.0

a. excluding MPU
Source: Hunt, Judith, and Adams, Shelley (1980), 'Women Work
and Trade Union Organisation', Workers Educational
Association.

In all but one of these rapidly growing unions, the proportion
of women members increased. The exception is ASTMS, which
remains the most male oriented white-collar union, reflecting
the fact that its prime base was still among male technicians in
the engineering industry.

Other health service unions increased their female membership, but none more rapidly than COHSE. By 1978 only one
other TUC union exceeded its percentage of female members.
The growth in female membership holds profound implications
for health service unions, whose representative structures and
policy-making bodies are dominated by male members. For
example, though NUPE's membership in 1974 was 63.3 per cent
female, a survey conducted the same year showed that only
37 per cent of NUPE's NHS ancillary worker stewards were
women.[3] In COHSE, an internal survey in 1979 showed that
though threequarters of the membership were women, only
approximately a quarter of branch secretaries were women, many
in branches with a very high proportion of female members
(averaging 90 per cent), suggesting that 'women only come for-

ward to be branch secretaries when there is virtually no male
alternative to take on the job'.[4]

The obstacles to women participating in union affairs, rather
than passively swelling membership figures, are numerous. The
growth in part-time employment, in 1977 41 per cent of the UK's
total female workforce - higher than other EEC countries - is
the most important factor:

> By working early in the morning or late in the evening they
> (women) are able to combine work with childcare and house-
> work. The drawback, of course, is that there is not time for
> anything else.[5]

Workers' attitudes do play a part. For example a recent survey
showed that while women and men had broadly similar attitudes to
work, a third of both thought that men make better shop stewards.[6]
However, the NUPE stewards' survey showed that management
were more reluctant to allow part-timers time off for union
duties.[7]

Trade unions are responding to this situation, if in most
instances rather sluggishly. A lead has now been taken by the
TUC, which in 1979 produced a 10-point Charter, 'Equality for
Women within Trade Unions', ranging from recommendations to
affiliated organisations to take special measures to co-opt women
on to decision-making bodies, to the provision of childcare
facilities for out-of-working hours meetings.[8] The TUC has
done less about encouraging unions to press the interests of
part-time workers, the majority of them women. However, the
TUC Women's Advisory Committee have drawn up a list of
priorities to be incorporated in collective agreements.[9]

Prior to prodding from the TUC, some unions had begun to
take some initiatives. When NUPE reorganised its structure in
1975, 5 out of 20 seats on its Executive Council were reserved
for women as an 'interim' measure. At lower levels of NUPE's
structure, however, not much was done to promote wider participation of women in union affairs. COHSE has no system of
reserved seats for women. Creche facilities are provided at
annual conference and the National Executive Committee has set
up an Equal Opportunities Committee to develop policy in this
area. NALGO has developed a network of equal opportunities
committees at different levels of the union hierarchy, and issues
a special bulletin on equal opportunities. ASTMS has established
a National Women's Advisory Committee.

If unions have taken only tentative steps towards the wider
involvement of women, little specific seems to have been done to
involve ethnic minorities. Yet ethnic minorities form substantial
sections of the nursing, ancillary and medical labour markets.
Furthermore, they tend to predominate in the lowest echelons.[10]
Yet we know very little about their union activities or degree
of present involvement, except when they become visible in
health service disputes.

The Character of the New Unionism
Although the recent image of a strike-happy NHS is sometimes overdrawn[11] waves of staff discontent shook the NHS during the 1970s affecting nearly all staff groups. While much of the industrial action was taken in pursuit of national grievances, there was also a growing tendency for local disputes to flare up.

Another important feature of the new unionism was a greater involvement of members in union activities. Though this was uneven among different occupational groups and localities, and often intermittent, it was a real change from passive membership to growing activism. Though linked to industrial action, it developed independently, primarily as a result of the growth of local organisations, largely based on shop stewards. Hitherto, local organisations had primarily centred upon the branch secretary, who handled (usually infrequently) most of the issues with local management, but mostly served as a means of downwards communication from union head office. The growth in stewards led to a wider involvement of members at the grassroots, a 'challenge from below' which held profound implications for both management and unions.

NUPE reacted sooner to these events, and took the process further, than most public sector unions, linking it also to the need to respond to the management reorganisations of the NHS, local government and the water industry in the early 1970s. Their own internal reorganisation was the result of a specially commissioned investigation,[12] giving rise to a complex structure, woven from the variety of public services in which NUPE has an interest. Figure 5.1 only does NUPE's complexity rough justice.

The pivots of the whole structure are the local District Committees, divided by service, and on which union stewards sit. These form the constituency for branch election on to the Executive Council and service-based National Committees, and for district representation upon the regional seats of government in NUPE, the Divisional Councils. The General Secretary is appointed by the Executive Council, rather than elected by the membership as a whole.

NUPE has always had a reputation for being on the left of the trade union movement, politically and industrially. Nevertheless, it was in many respects a bureaucratic union. The revolt of lower paid workers from the late 1960s, many of them in public employment, created the favourable circumstances which made the 1975 reorganisation of the union possible. One important indication that power had shifted within NUPE came during the 'winter of discontent' in early 1979. Union negotiators, including Alan Fisher, NUPE's General Secretary, reached agreement on a pay deal to end industrial action by local government and NHS manual workers. However, this was repudiated by the Executive Council, under pressure from Area and National Committees.

Figure 5.1: Simplified Representation of NUPE's Structure

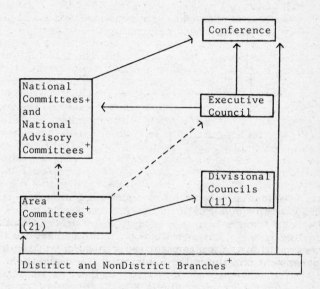

Legend: + By Service (in most cases)
——Direct Representation
---Indirect Representation by Branch Ballot

COHSE's structure is a good deal simpler than NUPE's, as can be seen in Figure 5.2. It has remained basically intact since COHSE's inception in 1946, and is based firmly upon the branches, who elect the delegates to Regional Council, which each in turn vote for two delegates on the National Executive Committee. Unlike NUPE, the General Secretary and the Assistant General Secretary are elected from a ballot of the whole membership.

While not reorganising its structure, COHSE has nevertheless shifted towards greater recognition of the part played by stewards. It has, in common with NUPE, issued a stewards' handbook and now mails directly out to them. However, branch secretaries remain in many instances key figures, especially in branches with low levels of membership activity. A special feature of COHSE are the existence since 1920 of officer and sub-officer branches, where nursing management members form their own separate branches. As with NUPE, there has been a growing tendency in recent years to ballot members over pay deals.

Figure 5.2: Simplified Representation of COHSE's Structure

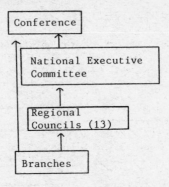

COHSE has undoubtedly become more militant in recent years. However, COHSE's generally cautious approach is largely determined by the conflicting pressures which arise from within, due to its status as an industrial union: from ancillary members who increasingly look to it to take a militant stance, and from nurses who more often expect it to have a 'professional' ethos and take service needs into account. It therefore casts one glance over the shoulder at NUPE and another at the Rcn.

NALGO's structure in some ways mirrors the complexity of NUPE's. In other respects however, it is much more firmly structured upon the branch than upon committees of stewards, as can be seen from Figure 5.3.

Throughout its history, branch autonomy has been the cornerstone of NALGO's structure and remains so today. It is still not affiliated to the Labour Party. Branches elect the 60-strong National Executive Council and other officers. National Service Conditions Committees (including one for the NHS) are an important means by which democracy manifests itself within the union, with provision also for Special Group Meetings to be convened in a particular service to instruct negotiators.

However, a factor which traditionally limited democracy within NALGO was the tendency for senior managers to become the Departmental Representatives who dominated Branch Committees and who, until recently, had no stewarding functions. However, growing rank and file militancy led the 1977 Conference to transform the role of Departmental Representatives to something closely resembling stewards.[13]

The New Unionism – Cause or Effect?
As has often been suggested trade unions are typically conservative organisations which respond to events already in train,

Figure 5.3: Simplified Representation of NALGO's Structure

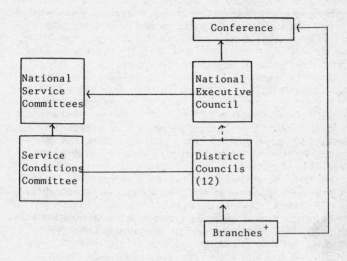

+ by service (in most cases)
—— Direct Representation
--- Indirect Representation by Branch Ballot

rather than initiate them. In many cases the new unionism can be traced to the intended and unintended consequences of actions taken by those in charge of the service, to which unions have only slowly responded. The most important of these stemmed from an intensification of policies designed to contain the wages bill, at a time of increasing economic stringency. Increasingly, however, these overall budgetary controls were combined with a complex and far-reaching restructuring of health care that began in the 1960s. First, health care became increasingly concentrated upon large district general hospitals, run upon impersonal bureaucratic lines. Just as trade unionism grew out of the industrial factories of the nineteenth century, so health service unionism grew out of the 'health factories' of the 1960s and 1970s. In the late 1960s came the first official encouragement for staff to join a union or professional association and it is clear that the impracticality for management to communicate individually with staff was a major factor. At around this same time there was also a series of attempts to restructure ancillary, nursing, scientific and technical, and administrative workforces, the end result of which was to create a mass of workers whose career mobility was blocked or limited, presided over by small occupational elites. Management was becoming increasingly modelled upon private industry.[14]

The processes involved - rationalisation, centralisation, and the economic and sparing use of skilled labour power - undoubtedly speeded the process of unionisation. This was especially the case with ancillary workers, who were in the forefront of the shopfloor unionism, which subsequently spread throughout the health service. The spur was undoubtedly the use of more sophisticated management techniques based on the identification of unit costs. The change was initiated in 1967 by the publication of the National Board for Prices and Incomes Report No.29 on manual workers in the NHS and local government, which recommended the introduction of 'interim' incentive bonus schemes, with some of the savings passed on to workers in higher earnings. It recognised in passing that such changes would mean that 'hospitals will have to develop relations with workers' representatives to a much greater extent than has been general hitherto'.[15] Progress was slow at first, but with further government prodding, schemes spread substantially and, alongside them, steward networks.

Industrial action undoubtedly spurred union organisation. Membership of NUPE soared after the campaign of selective strikes during the 1973 ancillary workers' pay campaign, and of COHSE after industrial action in 1974. Industrial action promoted local organisation as well as membership precisely because it often fell short of full strike action. Groups of workers met to plan who should be brought out and when. Management too were often keen to negotiate emergency cover, and to identify representatives who would make arrangements and ensure that a potentially explosive situation was contained.[16]

Indeed during the early 1970s all factors were working to create a favourable environment for the development of trade union organisation. Even the Conservative Government's Industrial Relations Act of 1971, with the ostensible aim of curtailing union power, probably assisted its development in the NHS. The requirements of the Code of Practice, forced local managements, often for the first time, to establish grievance procedures.[17]

The New Unionism and the Social Contract

The wave of industrial unrest which shook the service in the mid-1970s - in the latter period of the Conservative and early part of the Labour Government - was primarily economic in character. It was followed by a period in which advancing union organisation focused increasingly upon non-wage issues. In part this was due to 'spillover' effects of industrial action over wage issues, because, as we saw, these raised control issues. Ancillary workers and also psychiatric nurses' experience of involvement in determining the nature of emergency admissions, disturbed traditional relations of deference to consultants. Some ancillary workers had blacked private beds ('pay' beds) in

NHS hospitals during the 1973 dispute, and afterwards went on
to campaign for their elimination as a demand in its own right.[18]
Psychiatric nurses went on to seek a larger say in determining
admissions policy of 'difficult' patients. The nature of industrial action in the health service therefore tended to raise
control issues in ways that does not always happen in strike
situations in manufacturing industry.

From 1975 onwards, in return for TUC co-operation with the
Labour Government's pay policy as part of the Social Contract,
new employment legislation was passed, which in the NHS
extended bargaining frontiers over non-wage issues. The
Employment Protection Act 1975, the Trade Union and Labour
Relations Acts of 1974 and 1976, the Health Safety at Work Act
1974, and legislation against sex and race discrimination gave
new rights to local union activists, putting management on the
defensive.

As a result, competition between TUC and non-TUC professional associations intensified. With growing confidence, stewards
began to form local committees at local level which cut across
union boundaries and, in a number of areas, boycotted consultative committees and refused to sit down with professional
associations. This forced the associations to reorganise their
structures and (if they had not already done so) to introduce
systems of workplace representatives. To take advantage of the
new legislation they had to prove their 'independence'. Ironically, the fiercer competition from trade unions has probably
strengthened professional associations by forcing them to
become more efficient.

From 1976 job security also became an issue of concern for
health service trades unionists, due to the Labour Government's
programme of public expenditure cuts. These were combined
with a new system of budgetary controls – cash limits – in which
the amount spent is limited to a predetermined inflation allowance,
regardless of actual rates.

Public service unions were quick to organise protests at the
cutbacks in expenditure, though a steering committee of unions
was not joined by the NUGMW, a union traditionally loyal to the
Labour Party establishment. Some primarily private sector
unions, such as the 1.2 million strong Amalgamated Engineering Workers Union, actually wanted to see a redistribution of
expenditure away from public services towards the 'productive
base' of the economy.[19] At local level the fight against cuts
often centred upon the defence of small hospitals against closure,
which had, however, been taking place previously. Nevertheless the cuts accelerated closures. As powerful groups of
consultants sought to protect acute services more small hospitals,
often caring for the chronically ill or covering low-status
specialties were sacrificed. Spirited defence campaigns around
particular hospitals, such as the Elizabeth Garrett Anderson
Hospital and Bethnal Green Hospital (both in London) secured
partial victories or stays of execution. In the process new

alliances were often formed with groups of users in the wider
communities and notions of an alternative health-care system,
more responsive to people's needs, began to be articulated.[20]
Yet such campaigns, as activists realised, could not affect the
operation of cash limits at national level.

Of course, campaigns around non-economic issues are not
always entirely altruistic. For example, in the late 1970s, both
COHSE and the Rcn fought vigorously against a proposed reorganisation of mental handicap services which would have
caused a shift towards local authority, community-based services, with a declining role envisaged for hospital-based nurses.
COHSE and the Rcn alike were motivated mainly by concern
about the career prospects of their nurse members.[21]

The dilemmas facing unions - and professional associations - in
the long stay geriatric, psychiatric and mental handicap sectors,
are difficult ones. Members who pay subscriptions do so expecting their organisation to protect them if accusations of neglect
or ill-treatment are made. This can easily push organisations
into a purely defensive stance. However, COHSE members at
Normansfield mental handicap hospital in Middlesex went on
strike to call for the dismissal of Dr Lawlor, a consultant at the
hospital, dissatisfied with his treatment of patients and staff.
The official Report, though critical of the strike, confirmed
many of their accusations and, as a result, Dr Lawlor was
relieved of his post.[22]

The Conservative Backlash

As we have seen, from the end of the 1960s and through most
of the 1970s, trade unions in the NHS were riding on the crest
of a wave that seemed, with each new development, to rise
higher. Since the election in 1979 of the right-wing government
of Mrs Thatcher came to power partly as a result of the fact
that public sector workers in the NHS and local government had
rebelled against a further stage of incomes policy imposed by
the Labour Government of Mr Callaghan. The 'winter of discontent' 1978-9 brought many public service workers out on
strike against the government's 5 per cent policy.

Unlike previous occasions, they found very little media support for their actions. Public sector workers had since 1976
been the target of much criticism from monetarist economists
who claimed that featherbedded jobs in the public sector had
'crowded out' investment in Britain's 'productive base'. The
critical media attention given to the militant actions of public
service workers and the alleged affects on patients, flowed
naturally from the dominant view that these workers were in
any case a burden. The manipulation of these feelings helped
Mrs Thatcher to power, as industrial workers swung towards the
Conservatives.

The 'winter of discontent' had thus been portrayed as the
responsibility of unfeeling trades unionists in the NHS and
elsewhere, who thought nothing of putting patients' lives at risk.

After the election, a favourable atmosphere existed in which
to begin to dilute the strength of NHS unions. The government
found natural allies in many consultants, who had resented
the 'interference' of ancillary workers unions in their 'right'
to practise privately within the NHS, and local management
resentful at the loss of their prerogatives. They were also joined
by professional associations like the Rcn who seized the possibility of making significant membership gains by associating
with the new anti-union mood.

The result has been a much tougher management response to
a number of significant disputes that have occurred since 1979.
One of the most bitter was the highly publicised sacking of two
engineering workers at Charing Cross Hospital in London, for
refusing to carry out work they considered to belong to labourers. When their union, the AUEW, picketed heating oil deliveries
to the hospitals, it was defeated by unfavourable press publicity, local management and opposing demonstrations by groups
of nurses and doctors. There has been a rise in the number of
disciplinary cases against union activists and a number of
hospital work-ins against closure have been forcefully ended.
Two nurses have been disciplined by their professional body,
the General Nursing Council, for taking part in industrial action
during the 'winter of discontent'. Other professional bodies
have also warned that industrial action may lead to disciplinary
action.

The government's general approach is embodied in the Employment Act 1980 which, among other things, restricts picketing
to the immediate place of work and limits the numbers who can
take part to six, in an associated 'Code of Practice'. As far as
the NHS is concerned, the DHSS issued Circular HC(79)20 late
in 1979 which encourages local management to send staff home
who take industrial action short of a strike, or to reduce their
pay accordingly; and to make use of volunteers or agency staff
in order to break disputes. The circular produced a hostile
response from health service unions, who described it as 'pro-
vocative' and a 'scabs charter'. Since then the government has
further made it plain through a secret circular sent to Regional
Personnel Officers that workers in 'managerial' positions who
actively participate in union activities expose themselves to the
risk of disciplinary action.[23] Given the infinite gradations of
rank to be found in the health service, this would mean an
effective proscription against the majority of its staff.

While the government encourages a head-on attack against
trade unionists involved in disputes about wages, manning or
other issues primarily affecting the workers themselves, it has
shown itself capable of a more subtle approach in other situations. For example, though in the last resort it is prepared to
enforce management decisions to close hospitals it has preferred
to try to divert union-led campaigns into fund-raising rather
than oppositional activities, to keep services going or obtain new
facilities. In a number of instances these tactics have met with
some success.

The tide at the moment is turning against trade unions. There has been some loss of membership, COHSE in particular losing some nurses to the Rcn, whose recent growth has been quite dramatic. In 1976 membership of the Rcn was only 86 000, yet by the end of 1980 it had more than doubled to 177 500. Undoubtedly its opposition to industrial action was an important factor.

It would be hasty to conclude, however, that trade union numbers and influence are permanently on the wane. The industrial action of 1979 led through the Clegg Commission on Pay Comparability to large increases, at least for skilled and white collar workers. The gap between public and private sector earnings has again closed.[24] NALGO's health service membership has as a result continued to increase. Certainly the health service unions have not yet suffered the dramatic defeats and losses of some traditionally better organised groups, such as car workers, dockers and steel workers. Despite cuts and the growth of private health insurance schemes, the NHS is not yet in decline, though it is more than a little frayed at the edges. The growing numbers of elderly, and the health service's public popularity (which is still strong) to an extent protect it. There is no room for complacency however. The 'winter of discontent' perhaps showed the limits of fighting a traditional trade union campaign in a human service setting. If health service unions are to recover their strength, they will have to find ways of mobilising rather than alienating the support of working class people using the service. In taking public support for granted health service trade unionists have often failed to be sensitive to the negative as well as positive experiences that ordinary people have of the health service.[25] Trade unionists will have to be more self-critical about the role played by rank and file health workers in reproducing hierarchical relations with patients, and seek to overcome them to build new alliances between those who work for and those who use services.

REFERENCES AND NOTES

1 Clegg, H.A., and Chester, T.E. (1957), 'Wage Policy and the Health Service', Basil Blackwell, p.119.
2 For a more extensive discussion of the main post-war trends see R. Price and G.S. Bain (1976), Union Growth Revisited: 1948-1974 In Perspective, 'British Journal of Industrial Relations', vol.14, no.3, pp.339-55.
3 Fryer, R.H., Fairclough, A.J., and Manson, T.B. (1978), Facilities for Female Shop Stewards: the Employment Protection Act and Collective Agreements, 'British Journal of Industrial Relations', vol.16, no.2, pp.160-74.
4 'The Position of Women within COHSE', COHSE, 1979.
5 Sedley, Ann (1980), 'Part Time Workers Need Full Time Rights', National Council for Civil Liberties Rights

for Women Unit, p.7.

6 Coote, Anna, and Kellner, Peter (1980), Powerlessness - and How to Fight It, 'New Statesman', 7 Nov., pp.8-11.

7 Fryer et al., Facilities for Female Shop Stewards, p.170.

8 See Hunt and Adams, 'Women, Work and Trade Union Organisation', pp.16-17.

9 Sedley, 'Part Time Workers', pp.28-9. As Sedley points out, however, the guidelines are far from perfect, appearing to accept the principle that part-timers should be made redundant before full-time workers.

10 Doyal, Lesley et al., (1980), 'Migrant Workers in the National Health Service: Report of a Preliminary Survey', Department of Sociology, Polytechnic of North London.

11 For example, see Bosanquet, N., and Healy, G. (1979), Is the NHS Really Torn by Strife, 'New Society', 10 May, pp.328-9.

12 Fryer, Bob, Fairclough, Andy, and Manson, Tom (1974), 'Organisation and Change in the National Union of Public Employees', Department of Sociology University of Warwick.

13 Ayland, Tony (1980), 'Shop Stewards for NALGO? A Case Study of 4 Branches', MA Dissertation, University of Warwick. For a more accessible account of recent developments see Taylor, R. (1980), 'The Fifth Estate: Britain's Unions in the Modern World', Pan Books, pp.339-46.

14 See the separate articles by M. Carpenter and T. Manson in Stacey, M. et al., (1977), 'Health and the Division of Labour', Croom Helm, pp.165-93 and 196-214.

15 National Board for Prices and Incomes (NBPI) (1967), 'Report No.29', HMSO, para 97.

16 For example, see Management and Strikes, 'Hospital and Health Services Review', January, 1975, pp.3-4.

17 See Dimmock, S. (1977), Participation or Control? The Workers' Involvement in Management, in Barnard, K., and Lee, K. (eds) (1977), 'Conflicts in the National Health Service', Croom Helm, pp.121-44.

18 Widgery, D. (1979), 'Health in Danger: the Crisis in the National Health Service', Macmillan, Ch.7.

19 For a good account of nationally initiated union campaigns against the cuts and its contradictions, see Fryer, R.H. (1979), British Trade Unions and the Cuts, 'Capital and Class', Summer, pp.94-112.

20 See Politics of Health Group, 'Cuts and the NHS', POHG, London, 9 Poland Street, London W1, price 50 pence.

21 See Rolf Olsen, M. (1980), Take the Jay Train, 'New Society', 11 September, pp.508-9.

22 'Report of the Committee of Enquiry into Normansfield Hospital', HMSO, 1978.

23 'Health Services', December 1980.

24 Cairncross, Frances (1981), A Case of the Public Interest, 'Guardian', 3 January.

25 These issues are explored in more depth in London-
Edinburgh Weekend Return Group (1980), 'In and
Against the State', Pluto Press.

PART III

LEGISLATION

Introduction

Industrial relations in the health sector is governed by both
general and specific legal frameworks. In broad terms this
delineates the rights and responsibilities of union and management representatives, as well as individual employees. In some
respects the early history of the relationship between the law
and industrial relations, particularly in regard to its attitude
towards trade unions, bears some similiarity between the three
countries. However, the approach subsequently adopted towards
legal intervention and regulation of industrial relations in the
three countries was markedly different. In the USA a high
degree of legal involvement was favoured and legislation has
established, both at federal and state levels, relatively strict
statutory parameters for the conduct of industrial relations.
While Canada's legal framework is less regulative it nevertheless
reflects certain features of the USA's approach. By contrast
the UK has traditionally favoured a 'voluntaristic' approach
towards industrial relations, in which the law plays a much
reduced role in regulating the rights and responsibilities between employers, trade unions and employees.

From the 1960s in the USA and Canada the law became increasingly involved in the specific regulation of industrial relations
in the health sector. In the UK the movement in the 1970s
towards a more general, legal regulation of industrial relations
(in terms of both collective labour relations and individual
employment) also affected the health sector. The authors of
the following chapters examine these various developments in
the USA, Canada and the UK and discuss their impact on health
industrial relations.

6. LEGISLATION GOVERNING HEALTH INDUSTRIAL RELATIONS: CANADA

C. Steinberg

INTRODUCTION AND TERMS

This work reviews legislation governing labour-management relations in the Canadian health-care sector, which is taken to include hospitals, nursing homes, clinics and laboratories, the practices of the licensed professionals, and ambulance systems as the major sources of health-care delivery. Among these, their labour intensiveness and size have made Canadian hospitals the focal point of labour relations activity and problems. The study of legislation alone does not give a complete conception of the overall public policy framework, but it does provide an important first step in understanding the law of collective bargaining in health care.[1]

Some Problems Underlying Health-care Labour Legislation
Canadian labour legislation displayed early concern with guaranteeing the continuation of specific services deemed 'essential' to the public.[2] Here the law most heavily constrains labour-management relations in health care, which is more often than not considered an essential service. Yet essentially is difficult to define precisely, and does not by itself entirely explain the complexity of the health-care legislative framework.

Much of Canadian health care is delivered either directly by, or under the auspices of a senior government. Thus, the limiting attitudes and legal strictures on public sector collective bargaining also apply to a large portion of the health-care sector. First, bilateral negotiation of the terms and conditions of employment was early held to be a breach of 'sovereignty', an improper delegation of governmental responsibility. Second, taxing power in lieu of sale-for-profit as the source of governmental revenue creates problems. Continuing tension between unilateral civil service personnel procedures[3] and collective bargaining adds further distortion, and increased politicisation of bargaining.

Another part of the health-care sector is termed para-public since it is not-for-profit, but often dependent on governmental subsidy, introducing third party fiscal authority. That portion of health care clearly conducted for profit nevertheless carries the same public responsibilities of a life supportive service as the governmental and not-for-profit portions. Moreover, 'professionalism', and the extreme range of skill levels within the typical health-care delivery unit confound the orderly development of both union growth and bargaining structures, and create further legislative complexity. In sum, the health-care sector is vulnerable and prone to restrictive regulation.

The Range of the Law
These general problems also shape and weight a legislative framework whose parameters contain the same elements as those of the industrial sector including:[4]

The rights of free association to organisations of the employees' own choosing free of employer domination.
Certification of a majority organisation which thereby attains exclusive jurisdiction for a specified period.
Implied determination of the appropriate bargaining unit for such certification and exclusion of management.
Mandatory good-faith bargaining: required for both labour and management, and however determined.
Definition of and protection against unfair labour practices.
Written agreements having much of the status of civil contracts as the collective bargaining outcome.
Some independent, quasi-judicial administrative body, knowledgeable in labour matters, to oversee the orderly development of labour-management relations and to adjudicate in the first instance, problems arising therefrom.
Enforcement powers either vested in the overseeing agency or derived through its access to the courts.
The extent of the rights to strike and lockout, either tacitly present or their limitations outlined: any absolute limits; any required preliminary steps such as mandatory conciliation or mediation; any mandatory impasse resolution procedures in lieu of the strike.

Legislation covering labour relations in the health-care sector may go far beyond these elements, for example, into limiting bargainable items and determining which of these are to be set by fiat outside of the collective bargaining process but within the health-care sector, and which by general public regulation. Nevertheless, these concepts contain the underpinnings of Canadian labour relations legislation in general, and of health-care labour relations in particular.

The range of the law, and the focus of this review is the extent to which legislation covering labour-management relations in the health care sector includes, excludes, or remains silent about these basic elements of a collective bargaining system.

Despite the wide variety of detail and emphasis that emerges from the three-country context of this volume, these same elements appear in one form or another. Some are not emphasised but present, some are clearly defined by statute, some are ill-defined but accruing at common-law, some are emphasised as rights gained by bargaining precedent. Yet each element plays some role in the formation of a stable labour-management relations system in each of the three countries.

Canadian Context

More than 90 per cent of the organisable Canadian labour force is covered by provincial law, unlike the legislative jurisdictions of the US and UK which tend to be federal and national in scope. There are thus eleven Canadian bodies of labour legislation built on a common basis but increasingly diverse in approach as well as detail.

Understandably, Canadian and American labour laws have a common heritage in the English common law tradition. The post-Tudor conspiracy doctrine, that collective efforts by labour to determine the terms and conditions of employment constituted a conspiracy in restraint of trade, culminated in the British Combination Acts of 1799 and 1800.[5] Not even the American revolution freed labour from the power of the conspiracy doctrine as the Philadelphia Cordwainer Cases (1804-6) attest. In all three countries, the evolution of labour law was thus a gradual development towards the guarantees of collective bargaining.

Canadian law followed the British pattern even after confederation. The Trade Union Act of 1872 gave freedom from conspiracy to registered bona fide unions, but the Criminal Law Amendment Act of the same year and the many enactments thereafter circumscribed the activities of unions, and hedged the strike round with restrictions.

By 1900 the Parliament of Canada had created a Ministry of Labour, taken responsibility for labour standards, and experimented with conciliation legislation in a series of laws that matured in the Industrial Disputes Investigation Act of 1907, which contained a two-tiered, tripartite, mandatory conciliation process in specified sectors through which labour and management accrued strike and lockout rights. The IDI Act of 1907 became the Canadian shield behind which government intervention was built into the present system.

This almost complete federal title to regulation of labour matters, though not undisputed, held until 1925, when, in the so-called Snider Decision, federal intervention under the IDI Act into a dispute between the trolley carmen, and the Toronto Electric Street Railway Commissioners was escalated through court appeals to the Judicial Committee of the Privy Council in London, which upheld the Commissioners in voting that labour matters fell under the titles 'property' and 'civil rights', classes of subjects that were expressly ceded to the provinces by the British North America Act and therefore ultra vires the Parliament of Canada. The federal jurisdiction over labour matters vanished except for the relatively few subject areas allowed it by the BNA. Though unintended, and not used extensively during the next half dozen years, the provincial jurisdiction now existed.

The 1930s brought to Canada both the depression and the

demonstration effect of the US collective bargaining supports developed in the Railway Labour Act of 1926, generalised and subsumed in the Labour Codes of the National Industrial Recovery Act, lost in 1934 when the Act was struck down by the Supreme Court, regained in fuller form under the Wagner Act of 1935, and finally validated in a US Supreme Court decision of 1937.[6]

Several Canadian provincial experiments introduced aspects of the Wagner Act's encouragement of collective bargaining, mainly during the last half decade of the Thirties. The first overtly positive amendment of the federal Criminal Law, however, appeared in 1939, making it an offense for an employer to dismiss an employee for joining or encouraging unionism.

World War II restored federal responsibility for most of industry under two War Measures Acts. It also restored a uniform labour law by consensus with the provinces in the 1944 Privy Council Order 1003. This contained the Wagner Act principles, but incorporated also the mandatory two-tiered conciliation procedures of the IDI Act, with the additional provisions that strikes and lockouts were forbidden during the life of the collective agreement, and binding grievance arbitration was required. This general framework became the basis of the present Canadian legislative structure. After World War II the Parliament of Canada enacted PC 1003 with few changes as the Dominion Industrial Relations and Disputes Investigation Act (IRDI) of 1948, but limited in scope to its post-Snider decision jurisdiction. Several provinces opted (as after 1925) to cede authority to the federal government. Several enacted provincial IRDI Acts in a variety of legislative forms, yet containing essentially the same elements (with an important Saskatchewan exception). However, a 1950 Canadian Supreme Court decision (Attorney General of Canada v. Attorney General of Nova Scotia) sharply restricted such cession of jurisdiction among senior governments as not intended by the British North America Act. This guaranteed what, in fact, has happened in the three decades since; an increasing diversity in labour legislation among the eleven governmental jurisdictions, though most of the common IRDIA basis remains.

This review now treats the specific health-care sector legislation in each jurisdiction.

The Federal Jurisdiction[7]

The few existing federal hospitals and medical services are relegated to the federal public sector and do not fall under the Labour Code of Canada. The Industrial Relations and Disputes Investigation Act of 1948, which applied to Crown corporations but not to Crown employees, has a very small reference to the health sector. Nevertheless it excluded doctors from the uses of the Act (C.54).

The law thus placed the federal public servants in health care under the Civil Service Act which, in 1960-1, provided 'consultation' with the appropriate staff associations over salaries and other terms and conditions of employment (C.57). The procedures were typically unilateral, rather than those of collective bargaining.

In 1966-7 (C.71) the Public Service Employment Act reduced the powers of the Civil Service Commissioners essentially to staffing. This significant change was consistent with the introduction of the major Public Service Staff Relations Act (C.72) which extended full collective bargaining rights to Crown employees with no medical exceptions. The actual structure of the Act is well covered elsewhere but it should be noted that the Act specified (S. 56(2)) that the resulting collective agreement could not contain terms that would require change in legislation or regulations except for pay, thus substantially limiting the number of bargainable items and building the pre-existing civil service personnel system into the determination of the terms and conditions of employment.

Its dispute resolution procedures required the unions to choose *in advance* either binding interest arbitration (S. 60-67), or the IRDIA-like conciliation process prior to legalisation of the strike (S. 77-89), with required maintenance of 'essential services' by employer--'designated employees' (S.79), though the union might grieve over the designation. The Act also attempted to solve the duality of government-as-employer through tripartitism, with a powerful, independent Public Service Staff Relations Board Chairman appointed by the courts.

The federal health sector is small, and only incidentally covered by a Public Service Staff Relations Act (PSSRA) intended for the massive federal service, but its implications for the other Crown health sectors across Canada were substantial. Moreover, many of the 'underlying problems' cited above are now clearly visible and portable to each jurisdiction.

A remaining note on the federal health-care sector. The Canada Labour Code amendment of 1972 (C.18) removed the previous exclusion of doctors, and added professional employees in appropriately determined bargaining units so that the small non-public sector aspects of health care might be covered by the Canada Labour Code.

British Columbia.[8] This province made a remarkable legislative odyssey from little or no coverage to almost complete surveillance of the health-care sector in little over a decade. Initially, the private health care workers could seek coverage under the Labour Relations Act of 1954 which excluded doctors and dentists from the definition of employee and did not apply to Crown employees. While the large government hospital sector was active, despite civil service regulations, government employees in general did not have real access to joint consultation or collective bargaining until 1973, which ushered in a troika of laws: a new Labour Code, a new Public Service Labour Relations Act, and, a Public

Service Act conveying broad new coverage for collective bargaining in the health sector.

The new Labour Code again excluded chiropractors, doctors and dentists from the definition of 'employee' (C.122), made interest arbitration available, but only to firemen, hospitals and police at the election of the union (S.73) and also repealed the Mediation Commission Act of 1968.

The 1973 Public Service Labour Relations Act (C.144), administered by the Labour Relations Board, established three bargaining units: all nurses, licensed professionals, and the public service other than these (S.4). It provided for certification, designation of unfair labour practices, and decertification (S.5-7) and created industry-wide bargaining in effect by stipulating a master agreement with the bargaining unit, and subsidiary agreements with the occupational groups, while S.12 allowed the parties to negotiate the employees to be excluded from the bargaining unit with final decision by the Board, and listed criteria (management, confidential management policy, confidential industrial relations officers, as examples); non-negotiable items were treated in S.13. Dispute settlement was outlined (S.17) offering both mediation (1) and mutual submission to arbitration (3), but requiring a strike vote (7), and noting the timing and notice of strike required (10), or lockout (11-12) if mediation and arbitration are rejected. The complex problem of technological change in S.18-20, like its Canada Labour Code counterpart, made contract reopeners possible if substantial change was anticipated.

The 1973 Public Service Act (C.143) gave the Public Service Commission a mandate to negotiate on behalf of government (S.4), and established a grievance board for matters outside of the collective agreement (S.69), e.g., for civil service personnel matters, thus closing another loop-hole. The British Columbia health sector was now well covered by one or another form of legislation but the increasing labour activity shifted even greater attention to limiting the impact of strikes.

Each year brought additional problems and efforts to cope by legislation. Eight major enactments were made between 1973 and 1977[9] when the Essential Services Disputes Act (1977, C.83) repealed S.73 (1-6) of the Labour Code dealing with hospitals, policemen, firemen. The new Act (S.3) created an Essential Services Advisory Agency, provided that the union might elect binding arbitration (S.6(1)), determined in S.7 the criteria in arbitration of interests, and in S.8 defined and acted upon essential services giving the Lieutenant-Governor-in-Council the right to determine whether:

(a) immediate and serious danger to life, health or safety existed; or
(b) immediate and substantial threat to the economy and welfare of the province; whereupon,
(c) essential services could be designated;

(d) a 90-day cooling-off period with a list of requirements
    imposed; and
(e) a special mediator appointed.

Where an order was made under S.8 by the Lieutenant-Governor-
in-Council the union was given 14 days to exercise its option
to go to arbitration. Finally, this Act was applied to both the
private and public sectors, as implied in the definitions above.
In 1978,[10] a Miscellaneous Statutes Amendment (Bill 40) amended
the Public Service Act to make the Public Service Adjudication
Board sole arbiter of rights disputes arising within collective
agreements in the public service. Legislation seemed to breed
legislation.

Alberta.   This province was one of the few after PC 1003 to
develop a general labour code that included, with a collective
bargaining structure, the intervention machinery of the IRDI
Act, and provincial labour standards legislation all gathered in
the Alberta Labour Act of 1947. Yet it made no specific provisions relating to the health sector, nor was the government
or its agencies bound by the Act. Arbitration of interest disputes was included after a conciliation process (S.80), but the
parties were free to reject the 'award'. Private sector health-
care units might apply for coverage provided that the employees
involved were not excluded either by the definition of, or
specific exclusions to the term 'employee' in the Act, but Crown
employees could not.
Seven amendments relevant to the health sector followed over
the next three decades. Doctors and dentists were excluded,
arbitration boards were renamed as Conciliation Boards and the
Alberta Registered Nurses Association was named as bargaining
agent for the nurses. Most important among these, however,
was the expansion of emergency procedures which the Lieutenant-
Governor-in-Council could invoke, the formation of a Public
Emergency Tribunal giving the Minister the option to initiate
inquiry and mediation-arbitration while substantially expanding
the definition of 'emergency' over the years to include unreasonable third party hardship.
Seven enactments were also made for the public sector between
1959 and 1973 covering Crown employees and Crown agencies
separately, gradually integrating collective bargaining into
the joint consultation procedure of the civil service regulations
under the Public Service Act (PSA).
However, in 1977 a new Public Service Employee Relations
Act (PSERA) was passed (C.40). The powers of government
previously represented by the Public Service Commissioner, or
the Lieutenant-Governor-in-Council acting under the PSA, were
now made subject to collective agreements on the regulations
governing terms of employment and discipline. The Crown
Agencies Employment Relations Act (CAERA) was repealed, but
the new Act did not apply to professionals excluded from

bargaining by S.2. Consequently, the Act was applied to the Crown and its agencies (S.1 (0)), Crown employees formed a single bargaining unit (S.18), Crown agencies generally formed an exclusive unit (S.19), and the Public Service Labour Relations Board was empowered to determine the number of bargaining units in hospitals under the Act (S.20). Doctors and dentists, who were excluded unless the majority wished to stay (S.22-23), could opt out as well. Part 6 outlined dispute resolution procedures that called for a single mediator (S.46-47), an arbitration board (S.48-60), indicated non-arbitrable matters (S.48(2)), and the arbitration criteria (S.55). Under the catch-all 'other matters', S.93-94 precluded strikes or lockouts during the transitional period, and in S.99 the Alberta Union of Provincial Employees (previously the Association) was designated bargaining agent for the units it had represented under CAERA and the PSA. Finally, under S. 101 the Act covered professional employees not covered by S.22-23.

This consolidation of public sector legislation reduced total health sector application to the omnibus Public Service Employee Relations Act, and the Alberta Labour Act.

Saskatchewan. The early and single exception to the PC 1003 incorporation of IRDI Act with Wagner Act concepts was the Saskatchewan Trade Union Act of 1944 2nd session (C.69) which extended the right of collective bargaining to all employees in the province, with the standard management exception, and included employees of the Crown. In 1945, the province amended the Public Service Act (C.4) by incorporating collective bargaining into the Act (S.64, (a)) and making the terms of the collective agreement paramount.

A new Public Service Act of 1947 (C.4) excluded the classification and compensation plan from the scope of collective bargaining, otherwise the collective agreement prevailed for those within the bargaining unit. In 1949 (C.4) the PSA was again amended to remove some exclusion of the basic pay plan's negotiable items.[11]

This collective bargaining framework for both private and public sector stood until 1966, 2nd session, when the Essential Services Emergency Act (C.2) defined conditions under which the Lieutenant-Governor-in-Council might invoke the provisions of this Act to settle a labour dispute including hospital services by: establishment of compulsory arbitration of interests (S.4-6); prohibition of strikes and lockouts (S.7); decertification of trade unions for violation of the Act by union or members (S.10); and by making injunction available (S.14). In the Second Session of 1970 the Essential Services Emergency Act was amended (C.1) to define and add construction services (S.2); to include construction services in the definition of 'emergency situation' (S.3); and, at the discretion of the Lieutenant-Governor-in-Council to provide a multi-employer labour dispute arbitration board.

The legislation was not long-lived. In the 1971 second session the Essential Services Emergency Act was repealed (C.2). The Saskatchewan health care sector now certifies and bargains under the Trade Union Act with substantial latitude.

Manitoba. The legislative impact on health sector collective bargaining is essentially through the Labour Relations and the Civil Service Acts.

The Labour Relations Act of 1948 (S.M.C.27, Amended RSM 1954, C.134), modelled on the IRDI Act, excluded the medical and dental professions, and specifically excluded the Crown, and any board, commission, association, agency or similar body appointed by government act or by the Lieutenant-Governor-in-Council. Under S.39 (1) the Minister was given power to establish inquiries and in other ways promote industrial peace.

Three Labour Relations Act amendments between 1957 and 1971 added to the list of excluded professionals, brought some of the uncovered Crown agencies under the Act, established a non-mandatory mediation board process for them, and also an essential services procedure which, if declared, could make strikes and lockouts illegal, and placed the decision with the Lieutenant-Governor-in-Council.

The new Labour Relations Act of 1972 (C.75) removed the exclusion of doctors, dentists and dietetics, defined professional employees for purposes of developing an appropriate bargaining unit, and required a majority before such a unit could be placed in a unit with other employees (S.1 (t and k). The Crown was bound by the Act, but the Civil Service Act was declared to supersede the Labour Relations Act (S.3-4 (3)) for Crown employees. Thus, since Crown agencies were covered, the health sector was placed in good part under the jurisdiction of the Labour Act, except for provincial institutional employees.

The Civil Service Act was amended in ways relevant to the health sector in 1958, 1960, 1965, 1969, 1976 and 1978, gradually strengthening collective bargaining from joint consultation alone to recognising employee organisation and requiring collective bargaining of government representatives, but it also changed voluntary mediation to final and binding interest arbitration, and gave the Lieutenant-Governor-in-Council final authority.

The present collective bargaining system in health care, then, falls to a large extent under the Labour Relations Act for the private and crown agencies sector of Health Care, while provincial institutional employees bargain under the Civil Services Act.[12]

Ontario. Ontario relies not only on its Labour Relations Act and a public sector bargaining act to cover health sector labour relations, but on a broadly defined and powerful Hospital Labour Disputes Arbitration Act.

The 1950 Labour Relations Act (C.34) excluded doctors and

dentists from the definition of employee and typically was not applicable to the Crown or Crown agencies. It also allowed municipalities to opt out of the Act thus removing some municipal hospitals from collective bargaining.

The 1965 Hospital Labour Disputes Arbitration Act (HLDA) (C.48) defined a hospital by description of operation, whether or not publically funded, and whether or not operated for private gain (1 (a)), and S.2 (1) applied the Act to hospital employees covered by Labour Relations Act. Thus, the HLDA Act modification of the Labour Relations Act removed the ability of municipalities to declare themselves outside of the Labour Relations Act with respect to hospital employees, and (S.3) forced parties to resume collective bargaining in good faith where the Minister of Labour decided not to appoint a mediation board under S.16, LRA. When the report of a conciliation board or mediator (LRAS 74) has been released to the parties and no settlement is reached, the dispute goes to arbitration, (S.4) if unsettled within 35 days of the action by the Minister in S.3 above, who may extend the time limit. S.5 established an ad hoc arbitration board, and S.6 cites the board's authority to examine and decide on matters in dispute as well as other matters necessary to settlement, so long as the board does not infringe on the jurisdiction of the Labour Relations Board. No strikes or lockouts are allowed (S.8). S.9 places limitations for application of decertification and prohibits changes in working conditions, and also ordered employees on strike at time of enactment back to work, the dispute(s) to be resolved in accordance with the HLDA Act.[13]

The 1972 amendment to the Act (C.152) added that nursing homes, laundries operating exclusively for hospitals, and stationary power plants operated principally for one or more hospitals were all deemed to be 'hospitals' S. (13). Pre-arbitration dispute resolution (S.3) was limited to a conciliation officer; mediators and conciliation boards were no longer available. However, if both parties agreed, a single arbitrator may be appointed S. 4(a), and it was possible to combine several arbitrations (S.5(b)(1)), though the arbitration board has power to require additional bargaining (3). The last section of this amendment contained a back-to-work order dealing with a strike involving a power plant. The work stoppage was to be terminated, and the dispute resolved under the revised HLDA Act.

The Public Service Act was amended in 1962-3, 1966 and 1968 to cover Crown employees not previously included, establish a joint council and a civil service arbitration board with binding authority, broaden the powers of the Minister to appoint mediators in dispute resolution, and finally to subordinate Civil Service Commission pay recommendations to existing collective agreements.

An omnibus Crown Employees Collective Bargaining Act of 1972 (C.67) replaced the Public Service Act for all public

employees except the police. S.1(1) excluded doctors and
dentists and placed restrictions on organisations that may
represent employees. Certification was by the Ontario Public
Service Labour Relations Tribunal which outlined the negotiation of agreements and provided mediation while added arbitration was limited to negotiable items and the Act cited the criteria
for decision making. In S.13 no legislative changes are allowed
by collective agreement or arbitration award and the exclusive
functions of employers are non-negotiable. S.17 cedes arbitration of rights disputes to the Public Service Grievance Board,
and in great detail S.19-54 outlined the operation of collective
agreements, decertification, unfair practices, prohibition of
strikes or lockouts, cited enforcement, established a review
tribunal and the offenses under the Act; in all a detailed and
stringent piece of legislation.

Together with a 1972 Public Service Act amendment (C.96)
referring to police negotiations, but which made public service
collective agreements supersede regulations, a 1974 Crown
Employees Collective Bargaining Act amendment had broad
general implications (C.135) requiring, among a mass of details,
a grievance settlement board to handle all rights disputes arising from collective agreements in an effort to adjust the Act
from experience, and complete public sector coverage.

Quebec. This jurisdiction provides complex legislative control
of the health sector: heavy with legislative coverage; replete
with ad hoc legislation to deal with specific problems; unique in
establishing a labour court to adjudicate labour matters, and a
labour relations board essentially for administrative matters
within the Labour Relations Act; allows government to make
settlements for broad sectors by 'decree'; and centralises health
sector bargaining in the hands of the government.

The Labour Relations Act of 1944 (C.30) created the modern
labour relations framework contemplated in PC 1003. It excluded
doctors, dentists, and the professionals where the governing
body was created by statute, but was amended in 1946 to give
continuity to organisations formed under the Professional
Syndicates Act of 1924 which contained no similar exclusion. A
major labour code revision of 1964 (C.45) eliminated the medical
exclusion and broadly defined 'public services' to include most
of the health sector. It also gave wide powers to the Minister
of Labour to limit strikes by inquiry or injunction if public
health or safety were imperilled, and in effect subsumed much
of previous Public Services Disputes Act provisions except for
'functionairies' and police, for whom there was an absolute strike
prohibition, and mandatory interest arbitration.

The Civil Service Act of 1965 (C.14) accommodated collective
bargaining but forbade strikes unless essential services were
maintained or determined by the Labour Relations Board. These
public and private sector labour codes both encouraged unionisation and curbed strikes.

The 1971 Civil Service Act changes created the present
centralised governmental bargaining by covering any body
where government was party to the negotiation, changing 'public hospital' to 'public establishment', and elaborating the decree
settlement method by sectors. By 1974, private health sector
establishments were included in this public sector coverage.
A year later, a labour court judge was held to be a 'Commissioner of Essential Services'. The Act forbade strikes until
essential services could be agreed upon, but outlined negotiations, dispute resolution, and gave the right to strike if essential services were maintained.[14]

In 1977, C.48 amended the Health and Social Services Act
(1971, C.48) to include rehabilitation centres, and the regulation of health care was almost complete. The 1978 Act repealed
1974, C.8, and in substantial detail (C.14) elaborated the
methodology and structure of province-wide bargaining among
education, social affairs and government agencies, by designat-
ing local and regional as well as provincial bargaining, and
requiring determination prior to negotiation which matters were
to be dealt with at each level, with final decision in government
should negotiations on agenda and levels fail (S.2-5). S.10 and
11 required employer bargaining committees to be formed in
health and education, under direction from the Treasury Board
which would co-ordinate the negotiations. This Act completed
the centralisation process.

In 1978, C.52 brought the public sector back under the
Labour Code. S.97(a) amended the Labour Code to include
strikes in the public sector and prohibited the hiring of striking employees and strike breakers. A massive set of Special
Provisions applicable to the public and para-public sectors were
enacted (S.99-99.1). The Labour Code was to apply to public
and para-public sectors (S.99 (a)) with the exception of the
first agreement procedures in the private sector (S.81 (a)-81
(e)). Sections S.99 (a)-(h) indicated the employers contemplated, changed time for decertification application, established
public information as a function of the negotiating committee,
set time limits for determining matters to be discussed at provincial and local levels, with negotiations to begin 180 days
before expiry of agreement or decree; obligated unions to submit to each other written proposals 150 days before expiry date
for both levels of negotiation, and the employer to submit
counter-proposals 60 days after receipt of union proposals.
Applicable only to health-related services, the parties must
negotiate the level and maintenance of essential services. If
there is no agreement the union must submit a list that cannot
be amended except by agreement of both parties (which led to
the 'anti-strike'). The right to strike was available with two
days notice of the day the agreement or decree expires, subject
to S.99(1) which forbade a strike unless essential services were
settled, and noted that the Lieutenant-Governor-in-Council
could suspend the right to strike for up to thirty days where

a strike is or could be endangering public health or safety,
while the right to lockout was suspended if essential services
were maintained.[15]

New Brunswick. New Brunswick governs the health sector
under its Industrial Relations, Civil Service and Public Service
Labour Relations Acts.

The 1949 Industrial Relations Act excluded doctors and dentists from the uses of the Act (C.20, S.1(i)) nor did it apply
to the Crown or Crown agencies. Amended in 1951, 1953, 1959
and 1960-1 with health sector implications, municipalities were
successively, excluded with opting in, included with opting out,
and were finally included. Crown agencies might be included by
order of the Lieutenant-Governor-in-Council. Dietetics and
nurses were added to the origianl exclusion of doctors and dentists.

The 1964 Civil Service Act amendment (C.17 9.52) added collective bargaining to joint consultation but without the right to
strike.

Under the 1968 Public Service Labour Relations Act, C.88
included by list almost all hospitals, and this structure has held
to the present.

The 1971 Industrial Relations Act removed the exclusion of
doctors, dentists, nurses and dietetics from the definition of
employee. Under S.1(5) doctors, dentists, nurses and dietetics
were separately deemed to constitute appropriate bargaining
units. With professional exclusions repealed, however, such
professional groups could, if they chose by majority vote, be
included with other employees in bargaining units. New Brunswick has, therefore, a fairly centralised structure.

Nova Scotia. In the relatively decentralised Nova Scotia health
sector, collective bargaining is done either under the Trade
Union Act, or the Civil Service Collective Bargaining Act.

The 1974 Trade Union Act (C.3) excluded doctors and dentists,
and Crown employees and agencies from application of the Act.
The latter restriction against Crown agencies was settled in the
1972 changes in the Trade Union Act (C.19, S.3). The Crown
was not within the act; the Crown agencies were. S.1(2)(b)
continued the exclusion of doctors and dentists and upheld an
additional 30-day waiting period previously tacked on after the
conciliation process, before the Crown agency employees could
accrue strike rights.

For the public sector, the 1967 Civil Service Joint Council
Act implemented limited collective bargaining, outlined impasse
resolution procedures and budget implications, and noted that
the Civil Service Association was not to sanction, support or
encourage strikes by its members, though there were no penalties outlined and no absolute prohibition.

In 1978, the Civil Service Collective Bargaining Act (C.3)
both further strengthened, and limited the collective bargaining

process within the civil service. The Nova Scotia Government
Employees Association was recognised (in S.2(c) without certification procedures). S.3 established an Employee Relations
Board, and termed the Civil Service Commission the employer
(S.2(h)), but doctors and dentists were excluded here as well,
and though S.13 made the Civil Service Act supersede, it did
not with respect to regulations dealing with terms of employment
other than hiring, firing, classification and transfer. Compensation and employee suspension are not subject to collective
bargaining. A conciliation officer is provided (S.19-22), and
an arbitration board subject to a list of arbitrable items. Either
party may request arbitration (S.23-32) but the arbitration
board has the power to direct a return to negotiations (S.24).
The criteria for arbitration board decision are outlined in S.31
(2), and the collective agreement and arbitration awards do not
require legislation for implementation, though implementation
might wait until funds are available or until the next fiscal year
with retroactivity (S.33 (1-2). S.34-38 notes that grievances
may be individual or by association. S.39 is an absolute prohibition of strikes and lockouts with no time limits. S.41-42
considers unfair labour practices, and Schedule A subdivides
bargaining units into health services, technical and professional.
Bargaining is not centralised for those aspects of the health
sector covered by the Trade Union Act.

Prince Edward Island. The smallest province has perhaps the
most unusual legislative structure for collective bargaining
governed by four separate pieces of legislation.

The 1962 Industrial Relations Act (C.18) in replacing the
Trade Union Act excluded doctors, dentists and registered nurses from the definition of 'employee' (S.1(i)). Policemen, firemen and any person required for the maintenance of essential
hospital services (sic, nurses) were all denied the right to strike
or engage in work stoppage (S.44), though there was no similar
lockout prohibition for these areas, nor did the Act contain any
provision for determining what constituted essential hospital
services. However, S.57 gave the Lieutenant-Governor-in-
Council very broad powers to make regulations under the Act
and the Act did not apply to any Crown employees.

Amendments in 1966 and 1971 made hospitals subject to the
no-strike provision, and then required the Minister to appoint
an arbitration board if conciliation failed for employees under
the strike prohibition.

In 1972, with nurses still excluded from the definition of
'employee' under the Labour Act, the PEI Nurses Act (C.35)
repealed its forerunner, and in S.12 made the Association of
Nurses of PEI the bargaining agent for all nurses, except those
still excluded by regulation under the Nurses Act, for the purpose of consulting, negotiating and executing contracts regarding salary and working conditions.

In 1974 the Hospital and Diagnostic Services Insurance Act

(HSDSIA) (C.1) was amended (the original Act of 1959 created the Hospital Services Commission). S.5(2-5) required the Commission to nominate two members to the province-wide Health Negotiating Agency, bound by the Hospital Act to consult and negotiate, required to ensure fulfilment of the award, and bound by the contract.

In conjunction with the HSDIA amendment, the Hospitals Act was also amended (C.2) to add Part V, outlining the collective bargaining provisions in which S.42(g) included those hospital employees excluded from, and not organised under the Labour Act. S.43-47 defined consultation and the committees to be established for bargaining at the local and provincial levels (S.42(d)), but applied the Act only to public hospitals having 20 or more beds. S.43 set out the bargainable items applicable on both provincial and local levels (S.43 and 45 (2)). Regulations on approval of organisations are in S.47 (1-2). S.48 centralised hospital bargaining by requiring all negotiations to be through the Health Negotiating Agency as established by this section (1), and applied this centralised system to hospital employees covered by the Labour Act as well. S.49(1) required the Health Negotiating Agency to obtain approval from the Treasury Board before making offers with financial implications, and offered the option of arbitration or conciliation and arbitration. To complete the new arrangements, the 1974 PEI Nurses Act amendment (C.3) required that the nurses establish a provincial collective bargaining committee.

For the public sector a new Civil Service Act, 1971 (C.5) recognised the Public Service Association of PEI (S.2(2)) but the Civil Service Commission with the approval of the Lieutenant-Governor-in-Council was empowered to make regulations governing almost all aspects of working conditions. The pay plan was established by regulation of the Lieutenant-Governor-in-Council (S.17), and S.68 established the Joint Council with limited bargaining powers. Amendments in 1972 and 1973 gave bargaining rights and the 1975 amendment to the Civil Service Act (C.41, S.65 A (6)) appeared to make collective agreement terms prevail over regulations made by the Civil Service Commission, as a complement to the general extension of collective bargaining in the services.

The 1980 amendments to the PEI Labour Act (C.31) seemed to attempt some integration of the complex legislative structure in the first instance by removing the exclusion of the registered nurses from the definition of 'employee', thus making the Labour Act available to registered nurses.

No doubt further streamlining of the collective bargaining process in the health sector is intended. However, at this juncture hospital employees organised under the Labour Act are governed by the Hospitals Act with regard to its regulations on collective bargaining and the resolution of interest disputes. Both Acts forbid strikes and require arbitration; the Hospital Act certainly implies this and presumably prevails (cf. S.51(1)

(m)). Further, S.40 (5-6) does so for both hospital and nursing home employees. Meanwhile the nurses are controlled by
regulations under the Nurses Act, but S.51 (2) of the Hospitals
Act states that its regulations will not conflict with those made
under the Nurses Act without the express permission of the
Nurses Association.[16]

The nurses working for provincial hospitals fall under the
Civil Service Act (as above), if the regulations under the
Nurses Act are excluded.

This description of a legislative process grown complicated is
not to imply that health sector collective bargaining does not
function, or that there is undue friction in Prince Edward
Island.

Newfoundland.   This jurisdiction evolved a legislative process
that tended to centralise collective bargaining in the health
sector.

The 1944 Trade Disputes (Arbitration and Inquiry) Act (C.1)
covered private hospitals and other private health sector employees in providing a voluntary means of settlement, only government employees were excluded.

The new Labour Relations Act of 1950 applied to the private
sector as well as to Crown agencies and corporations; though by
order-in-council these might be individually excluded none were.
The Act excluded Crown employees, and doctors were excluded
from the definition of 'employee'.

Amended in 1963, the Labour Act allowed a declaration of
emergency (caused by an impending hospital work stoppage) and
required dispute resolution procedures (C.82, S.38 (a)).
Strikes and lockouts were prohibited after the declaration of
emergency (S.39 (a)a) and establishment of arbitration boards
required to examine the dispute de novo (S.3). The arbitration
award was binding (S.9), and further prohibitions outlined as
a result of the declaration (S.10).

The 1966-7 Hospital Employees (Employment) Act (C.11)
repealed S.39 of the Labour Relations Act above, and was applied
to all hospitals including public ones. S.5 prohibited strikes
and lockouts, and S.6-7 contained ad hoc back-to-work orders
aimed at a strike then in progress. It should be noted that
while this Act applied to government employees in government
hospitals these employees did not have the right to collective
bargaining (see below), nor did this Act provide interest dispute
resolution.

It was the 1970 Public Service (Collective Bargaining) Act
(C.85) that extended the right of collective bargaining to Crown
employees but governed the entire process by regulation (cf.
S.7 especially a, d, e, f, g, h, l, m, n, r, s). The Act requires
arbitration where the powers under S.7 (1) (1 to m) are exercised. S.4 (2) enabled the government to bargain with all employees covered by the act including the private hospitals, which
were allowed to opt out (S.4) though those private hospitals

doing so could have government funding reduced, or other
conditions attached by the Lieutenant-Governor-in-Council
(effectively, the Cabinet) (S.5). Thus, not only were government employees given bargaining rights but hospital bargaining
was effectively centralised.

The 1973 Public Service (Collective Bargaining) Act (C.123)
repealed the 1970 Act and brought certification of unions under
the Labour Relations Board (S.6). This Act included all hospital
employees (S.1(i)), and established the need for 'essential
employees' (S.10). If, however, a majority of employees in the
bargaining unit were declared essential, the bargaining agent
could choose to have all declared essential (S.5). Government
negotiations served for all employers (S.12), conciliation was
provided (S.16-22), and essential employees were denied the
right to strike (S.25 (c)). On declaration of an emergency all
employees in designated units could be prohibited from striking
(S.27). If an emergency declaration was made under S.27,
interest disputes would be adjudicated (S.29-34) or, if some
employees were declared 'essential' under S.10(5), the union
could opt for arbitration by a self-declaration of essentiality for
the bargaining unit. S.30 established the criteria for interest
arbitration board awards.

The 1977 Labour Act (C.64) closed some loop-holes by including all hospitals not covered by PS (CB) Act of 1973, removed
the doctors exclusion, and recognised professional employees
for purposes of creating an appropriate bargaining unit.[17]

Some Observations
A few broad generalisations may be made from this limited
review of the Canadian health care sector legislation.

The 'underlying problems' cited above are reflected in the
legislation of each Canadian jurisdiction.

Collective bargaining as a means of settling the terms and
conditions of employment is growing even among the professionals.

Collective bargaining is tending to override unilateral civil
service regulation of the public sector in each jurisdiction.

Centralisation of the bargaining structure by major bargaining unit, if not by the health sector itself, seems to be gaining
favour.

Maintenance of 'essential services', with attendant strike
rights, appears to be increasing in use in place of outright
strike prohibition.

Legislation seems increasingly to provide additional techniques
and greater flexibility in treating impasse resolution, as alternatives to the traditional IDI Act mandatory, two-tiered conciliation machinery.

Regulation seems to spawn regulation. The legislative structures grow more complex, efforts to codify more detailed,
diversity among jurisdictions greater, and reliance on legislative control seems to be increasing. Unfortunately, legislation

does not provide itself with a mirror.

REFERENCES AND NOTES

1 In his 'Labour Policy in Canada', 2nd edn., Macmillan, 1973, Ch.1, passim, Professor H.D. Woods notes that public policy governing labour-management relations in general includes the court decisions, arbitration precedents, labour contract terms, personnel rules and shop level bargaining effects, tempered by the power relations among Professor Dunlop's 'actors', and shaped also by an ever-present but difficult to measure public opinion. Health care sector labour legislation is similarly, perhaps even more strongly influenced. Precisely how these elements of public policy interact and are synthesised in the legislative framework is a dynamic and complex process, fascinating in itself, but a largely unexplored field in labour relations study. Yet see, Kochan, Thomas A. (1978), Correlates of State Public Employee Bargaining Laws, 'Industrial & Labour Relations Review', February, for an interesting attempt to capture the public policy effect on public employee bargaining.
2 Woods, H.D. (ed.), (1966), 'Task Force on Canadian Labour Relations', Supply & Services, cf. Introduction and Ch.I.
3 Historically rooted in efforts to supplant the patronage with a merit system in government employment.
4 These points are among those noted in Woods, H.D., Labour Policy, p.93, but derive from US policy sources noted below.
5 Woods, ibid., Chapters 2 and 3, contain a thorough review of the development to 1948, but see also, Steinberg, Charles (1974), The Legal Problems in Collective Bargaining by Canadian Sea Fishermen, 'Labour Law Journal'.
6 The Canadian version of these collective bargaining supports is cited above as 'The Range of the Law'.
7 This is to acknowledge the careful review of the federal and provincial revised statutes and the case law by Mr Brock Myles, who served as my research assistant in preparing the materials for this chapter.
8 Weiler, Paul (1980), 'Reconcilable Differences: New Directions in Canadian Labour Law', The Carswell Co. Ltd, is an excellent description of the BC experience written by the architect of its legislative structure.
9 It should be noted that 'professionals', in appropriate bargaining units, and nursing staff other than registered nurses were covered, and doctors were first included, then excluded from coverage during this period. In addition the various back-to-work and essential services remedies were enacted.
10 It is interesting that the Essential Services Disputes Act was also amended to bring schools under its purview (C.42): an interesting interpretation of 'essential'.

11 However, in 1947, C.4, the Public Service Commission was
given some power to make regulations inter alia, regarding
working conditions. The Commission was to submit the
proposed regulations to trade unions representing affected
employees only for perusal and comment. Only wages had
been specifically excluded from the Commission's powers
with regard to the employees in bargaining units. However,
regulation 23.4/74 erased the contradiction, and presently
provides that terms of collective agreements supersede the
regulations.

12 In 1970, the Hospital Act (RSM C.H120) stipulated that to
be licensed for operation a hospital must establish by-laws,
regulations or rules, and duties of officers and employees
with a prescribed wage and salary scale, in effect, a classification and compensation plan, which established the
possibility of a somewhat decentralised, unilateral hospital
labour relations system in principle, but not in practice.

13 A 1970 Labour Relations Act amendment (C.85) protected
under the unfair labour practices section those employees
excluded by definition.

14 Nevertheless, the 1976 nurses' strike brought back-to-work
legislation (C.29). Applicable only to the nurses of designated establishments, the bill nullified the mass resignations from the Quebec Order of Nurses (S.1, 2-7 and 5).
The conditions of employment were established by Sessional
Paper #151 tabled in the National Assembly (S.8), while
S.9-20 outlined a wide variety of penalties. The Act was
repealed in 1976, C.38, S.27.

15 The 1979 Act respecting 'Proposals to Employees' (Bill 62)
was an effort to pursuade negotiators and their memberships
to settle. The government tabled latest proposals made to
education, social affairs and civil service employees by
21 November 1979, and prohibited strikes and lockout
between 13 November and 29 November 1979, with associations to refer government proposals to members for ratification by 29 November 1979, an interesting form of 'negotiation
by legislation'.

16 See Simmons, G.C. (1978), 'Collective Bargaining in the
Public Sector of PEI. To 1976', Government of PEI.

17 'Royal Commission on Labour Legislation in Newfoundland',
1972, Dr Maxwell Cohen, Chairman.

7. LEGISLATION GOVERNING HEALTH INDUSTRIAL RELATIONS: USA

T.C. McKinney and M. Levine*

Industrial relations in health care, like other industries, is governed by a specific legal framework which delineates the rights and responsibilities of union and management representatives, as well as individual employees. This chapter will examine the background and recent legislative developments in US labour law and their impact on health industrial relations in the United States, and where relevant, comparisons will be drawn between the US experience and that in Canada and the United Kingdom.

BACKGROUND

The Wagner Act

The turbulent economic, social and political climate of the 1930s was primarily responsible for the passage of the Wagner Act (the National Labor Relations Act of 1935). Legally, the Wagner Act is based upon the constitutional power of the federal government to regulate interstate commerce. The Act establishes workers' rights to collective bargaining. Substantive rights of employees are postulated in Section 7, buttressed by specific practices declared in Section 8 to be employer unfair labour practices. Section 7 provides that:

> Employees shall have the right to self organisation, to form, join, or assist labour organisations, to bargain collectively through representatives of their own choosing, and to engage in concerted activities, for the purpose of collective bargaining or other mutual aid or protection.

In Section 8 the Act delineates five employer unfair labour practices:

Section 8(1). It is an unfair labour practice for an employer to interfere with, restrain or coerce employees in the exercise of their rights guaranteed in Section 7.

Section 8(2). It is an unfair labour practice for an employer to dominate or interfere with the formation or administration of any labour organisation or contribute financial or other support to it. However, an employer is not prohibited from permitting

---

* Section I (Background) is written by McKinney. Section II (Legislative Trends: an overview), and Section III (Comparative Analysis) are authored by Levine.

employees to confer with him during working hours without loss of time or pay.

Section 8(3). It is an unfair labour practice for an employer by discrimination in regard to hire and tenure of employment or any term or condition of employment to encourage or discourage membership in any labour organisation. Employers may, however, discriminate with regard to hire or discharge or employees based upon a valid union shop agreement between the employer and the authorised representative of employees.

Section 8(4). It is an unfair labour practice for an employer to discharge or otherwise discriminate against an employee because he has filed charges or given testimony under the Act.

Section 8(5). It is an unfair labour practice for an employer to refuse to bargain collectively with the representatives of his employees.

Applicability of the Act to Hospitals   When one examines Section 2(2) and Section 2(3) wherein the terms 'employer' and 'employee' are defined, it is not possible to conclude that voluntary hospitals are covered by the Act. The issue concerning the applicability of the Wagner Act to hospitals was one which the National Labor Relations Board and the courts had to resolve.

In 1944 the National Labor Relations Board petitioned the United States Court of Appeals for the enforcement of its order requiring the Central Dispensary and Emergency Hospital to bargain collectively with the Building Service Employees' International Union which had been certified by the Board as the exclusive representative of the hospital's employees.

Representatives for the hospital argued that the order should not be enforced because:

(1) It was a nonprofit institution not engaged in trade, traffic, commerce or transportation within the meaning of the National Labor Relations Act;

(2) The Board's certification was improper because it was based upon an election in which out of 251 eligible voters only 108 cast ballots and of this number only 75 were for the union;

(3) By reason of changed conditions the court should not order the hospital to bargain with the union.[1]

These arguments were rejected by the court. It seemed clear to the court that the hospital was engaged in activities of 'trade, traffic, commerce, transportation, or communication' as defined by the National Labor Relations Act. Its activities involved the sale of medical services and supplies for which it received about $600 000 per year. It purchased from commercial houses material of the value of about $240 000 annually. It employed about 230 persons for nonprofessional services and maintenance work and 120 technical and professional employees. The fact that the hospital as a charitable institution engaged in such activities was immaterial to the question at issue. It remained a 'business activity' within the meaning of the law.

On this question of law, the Court of Appeals preferred to

follow the opinions of the Minnesota and Wisconsin Supreme
Courts as opposed to that of the Pennsylvania Court. In the
interpretation of its state Labor Relations Act, the Pennsylvania
Court held that the legislature did not intend to apply the Act
to hospitals. In contrast, Minnesota and Wisconsin Supreme
Courts held that charitable hospitals and their nonprofessional
employees are subject to the labour relations laws of their
respective states. In a telling comment, the Court of Appeals
rejected the notion of noncoverage of hospital employees by
stating: 'We cannot understand what considerations of public
policy deprive hospital employees of the privilege granted to
the employees of other institutions.'

The court viewed the election of the union by a minority of
its members as valid and representative. The election in this
case was carried by a majority of a minority, and the representative of the hospital contended that the Board's certification was
improper because only 108 persons voted out of 251 eligible
voters. Relying upon a 1937 Supreme Court decision, the court
ruled that 'Election laws providing for approval of a proposal
by a specified majority of an electorate have been generally
construed as requiring only the consent of the specified majority
of those participating in the election.'[2]

The third argument advanced by the responding representative of the hospital in opposition to the Board's order was that
by reason of changed conditions more than two years after the
election was held, the court should not order the hospital to
bargain with the union. In support of this contention, the
responding representative of the hospital filed a motion for
leave to adduce additional evidence showing that out of a total
of 251 employees who were eligible to vote in the election only
43 remained.

The court considered this type of evidence irrelevant. It
pointed out that the certification of the union which contained
the finding that at that time the union was representative was
issued by the Board in December 1942. Six months later the
Board issued an order to cease and desist from refusing to
bargain collectively. At that time the respondent had the right
to appeal to the court. The court also pointed out that the
respondent could have petitioned the Board at that time for a
hearing on whether the six months' delay in issuing the order
had created a change in the representative character of the
union. The respondent did not avail itself of either option. While
it is true that the Board delayed over a year in bringing the
case before the court for enforcement, the court would not allow
the respondent hospital to take advantage of that fact because
during the entire period it lay within its own power to seek
relief.

The Central Dispensary and Emergency Hospital case represented prevailing federal policy concerning the applicability of
labour law to hospitals prior to the enactment of the Taft-Hartley
Act of 1947. As has been noted, federal policy at that time in

history was compatible with state laws in Minnesota and
Wisconsin, but incompatible with Pennsylvania state law. It
became apparent that prevailing public opinion was in opposition
to the views expressed in Central Dispensary; it became
apparent that many jurists at the state level felt that it was
not in the public interest to make community hospitals subject
to the provisions of the Wagner Act.

Wagner Act
The Wagner Act achieved its purpose by restoring industrial
peace; and because of the protective benefits it brought to
employees and the organised labour movement, the ranks of
organised labour grew rapidly. The labour movement was given
an especially favourable jolt when the Supreme Court upheld
the constitutionality of the Act in the Jones and Laughlin
decision.[3]

Notwithstanding the benefits to labour and society in general
which are attributed to the passage of the Wagner Act, the
Wagner Act years (1935-47) were filled with controversy.
Employers arged that the Act, its interpretation by the courts,
and its administration by governmental agencies had produced
an unreasonable bias in favour of labour. Myers provides a
summary of the major criticisms of the Act:

1. The National Labor Relations Board was biased in favour of
   labour.
2. The constitutional free speech right of employers was severely
   limited by adverse interpretation of the Act.
3. The Act proscribed only employer unfair practices, leaving
   union unfair labour practices untouched.
4. The Act permitted all forms of union security, including the
   closed shop.
5. The Act left helpless the employer, caught in the midst of
   organisational or jurisdictional disputes, causing him damage
   on a matter in which he had no interest and over which he
   had no control.
6. Interpretation of the Act gave supervisors the right to form
   and assist supervisory labour organisations, along with
   prescribing for the employer the duty of bargaining with
   supervisors' unions, while holding that supervisors were
   management agents.[4]

A seventh criticism should be noted which is of particular
interest with reference to the status of voluntary hospitals:
interpretation of the Wagner Act provided protection to employees of voluntary hospitals who wished to participate in union
activities.

Congress had these major criticisms in mind when it passed
the 1947 Taft-Hartley Act. It seemed safe to say that public
opinion supported the new law which is a revision of the Wagner
Act (Title I) with additional provisions for unfair union

practices.

Very significantly, union unfair labour practices are provided in the new law. Thus, the law provides that it shall be an unfair labour practice for a labour organisation or its agents (a) to restrain or coerce employees in the exercise of the rights guaranteed to them in Section 7. However, the right of a labour organisation to prescribe its own rules with respect to the acquisition or retention of members is not impaired. Neither is the right of an employer impaired in the selection of his representatives for the purpose of collective bargaining or the adjustment of grievances. (b) It is an unfair practice for a labour organisation to cause or attempt to cause an employer to discriminate against an employee with respect to whom membership in the labour organisation has been denied or terminated on some ground other than his failure to tender periodic dues and the initiation fees. (c) It is an unfair labour practice for a union to refuse to bargain collectively with an employer, provided it is the representative of his employees, having been designated or selected for the purpose of collective bargaining by the majority of the employees in an appropriate bargaining unit. (d) It is an unfair labour practice for a labour organisation to engage in certain secondary activities such as strikes and boycotts. (e) It is an unfair labour practice for a labour organisation to require of employees covered by a union shop agreement the payment, as a condition precedent to becoming a member of such organisation, of a fee in an amount which the National Labour Relations Board finds excessive or discriminatory. And finally, (f) it is an unfair labour practice for a labour organisation or its agents to cause or attempt to cause an employer to pay or deliver or agree to pay or delivery any money or other thing of value, in the nature of an exaction, for services which are not performed or not to be performed. This last unfair labour practice is often labelled the anti-featherbedding clause.

The National Labor Relations Board which was created by the 1935 law continues as an agency under the provisions of Taft-Hartley, except that the Board members are increased from three to five.

In recognising the need to give greater protection to the rights of employees as individuals, Taft-Hartley gives employees the right to refrain, as well as to engage in, collective bargaining activities.

Employers are given greater freedom to speak out concerning the whole question of union relations. The law provides that the expressing of any views, argument or opinion, or the dissemination thereof, whether in written, printed, graphic or visual form, shall not constitute or be evidence of an unfair labour practice under any of the provisions of the Act, if such expression contains no threat of reprisal or force or promise of benefit.

Whenever, in the opinion of the President of the United States, a threatened or actual strike or lockout affects an entire

industry or a substantial part thereof in such a way as to imperil
the national health and safety, he is empowered to take appropriate action which may lead to the settlement of the dispute.
This may include an 80-day injunction which allows the parties
to settle their differences.

The Taft-Hartley Act

The Taft-Hartley Act was far more controversial than the Wagner
Act, and its real impact even more elusive. Proponents of the
law contended that it had, indeed, balanced the scales in collective bargaining by placing limitations on union conduct. Did
the law make unions more legally and financially responsible
for their actions? Did it reduce the monopolistic position of
unions? Was the public interest served by an attempt by the
federal government to control strikes? Management groups
answered those questions in the affirmative.

Organised labour denounced Taft-Hartley as a 'slave labor
law'. It was argued that organisational efforts were made more
difficult; that the right of labour to strike was curtailed; and
that the institution of free collective bargaining was seriously
threatened.

Perhaps both sides exaggerated their positions in assessing
the merits of the situation. To be sure, the law did not prove
to be a 'slave labour' law. Dulles reports that in the years
immediately after Taft-Hartley was enacted into law, there was
'...no interruption in the continued improvement of the wage
earners' status in American society. While the unions could not
sustain the rapid pace of their growth in the late 1930s and
early 1940s, membership expanded to an approximate eighteen
million and the proportion of workers whose terms of employment were covered by collective bargaining agreements was
steadily increasing.[5]

The original Wagner Act had as its purpose to facilitate the
organisation of unions and the establishment of collective bargaining. It was not concerned, except incidentally, with the
content and process of collective bargaining.[6] An important
influence of Taft-Hartley was to facilitate, perhaps even initiate,
the shift of the federal government's attention from more organisational problems to details in the management of personnel
and labour relations.

The Landrum-Griffin Act

The 1959 Landrum-Griffin Act accelerated the federal government's efforts to regulate personnel and labour relations. Unlike
the Taft-Hartley Act, which explicitly exempted voluntary
hospitals from its coverage, labour unions who deal with voluntary hospitals are covered by the Landrum-Griffin Act.

The declared purpose of Congress when it enacted the
Landrum-Griffin Act was to '... eliminate or prevent improper
practices on the part of labour organisations, employers, labour
relations consultants, and their officers and representatives

which distort and defeat the policies of the Labor Management
Relations Act, 1947...'.[7]

For some years after 1947, unions had argued for the outright repeal of Taft-Hartley. When President Truman won the
presidential election in 1948, he expected to seek repeal on a
two-sided basis, that is, with support from both labour and
management.[8] The drive to seek repeal of the law finally settled
into a continuous controversy surrounding reform of some of
its provisions. Title VII of the 1959 law addresses several controversial issues, while the first six titles deal mainly with the
internal control of union affairs.

Impact of the Landrum-Griffin Act. By far the most significant
influence of the Landrum-Griffin Act was the accelerated pace
of governmental regulation of the internal affairs of unions and
their relations with management. A labour organisation is a
private organisation which, traditionally, in the eyes of the
common law, has been regarded in the same manner as a church,
club, fraternity, professional organisation, private college or
university.[9] The activities of private organisations are directed
toward the achievement of their goals and objectives. Except in
the most unusual circumstances, their internal affairs are not
subject to direction and review by the courts and/or government agencies. It is assumed that private organisations are free
to select and retain their members, consistent with their constitutions and by-laws. Whenever a member of such an organisation appeals to the courts upon contending unfair treatment,
the courts are reluctant to review the substantive issues of the
case. Since the organisation would be considered private and
voluntary, the courts would content themselves with a review of
issues pertaining to procedure. Questions may be raised concerning whether or not the organisation maintained an internal
grievance procedure; if so, whether or not the procedure was
made available for use in the particular case. The courts would
rarely review the merits of the case except from a procedural
viewpoint.[10]

As emphasised, the Landrum-Griffin Act regulates the internal
affairs of unions, a trend that commenced at least with the Taft-
Hartley Act; but, it was greatly accelerated by passage of the
Landrum-Griffin Act. Substantive and procedural matters
became the object of review by the courts and were mandated
by law. The accelerated pace of government interaction into the
internal affairs of unions does not imply that unions and the
union movement were weakened by the 1959 law. Basic legal
rights established in the Wagner Act were not impaired. The
safeguards erected against irresponsible or corrupt union
leadership and the protection accorded union democracy were in
the interest of labour, management and the public.[11]

The 1974 Amendment to the Taft-Hartley Act. The health
services industry joins construction and the apparel and

clothing industries in receiving special consideration under US
labour relations laws.[12] The 1947 Taft-Hartley exemption for
private not-for-profit hospitals was removed by the 1974 amendment; but, not without special considerations being given to
the uniqueness of the industry.

Hearings on the Amendment.   Before the passage of the new law,
extensive hearings were conducted on H.R. 11357 on 16 August
and 6 September 1972. The Subcommittee on Labor of the Committee on Labor and Welfare of the Senate accepted testimony
from organisations and persons, including labour unions, state
hospital associations, the National Right to Work Committee,
national hospital groups and others.[13]

The President of the Service Employees International Union,
AFLC10, Mr George Hardy, testified that the bill would eliminate
the major cause for strikes in hospitals, namely, the failure of
hospital management to grant recognition to employees.[14] He
urged that coverage under the provisions of the National Labor
Relations Act would provide a peaceful method for employees
to obtain recognition from their employers. The statements
given by Ms Mary Munger, Vice Chairman of the Commission on
Economic and General Welfare of the American Nurses Association, also urged the adoption of the proposed measure. The
ANA, she reported, '...believes that the protection of the right
to organise and bargain should be extended to all health care
employees, professionals, and nonprofessionals... The ANA
supports collective bargaining as the means by which professionals as well as nonprofessionals will be able to influence not
only the standard of employment where they work, but also to
participate in the discussions about nursing practice standards.'[15]

As we would expect, persons who represented employee
organisations supported the measure. Perhaps typical of the
point of view of those opposed to H.R. 11357 was the testimony
of the representative of the Ohio Hospital Association, Mr James
D. Newcomer, who supported the position of the American
Hospital Association as expressed before the Committee on 16
August 1972.[16] The central idea behind his argument was that
the removal of the exemption would lead to interrupted health
services. The representative of the American Hospital Association in earlier remarks had contended that the basic elements
in the collective bargaining process under the National Labor
Relations Act -- that is, strikes, picketing and work stoppages -- should not be inflicted on health-care institutions via
the passage of the bill.

The Senate Report.   The Senate Committee on Labor and Public
Welfare, recommended that the bill be passed.[17] The Senate
report outlined the basic features of the Act. The new bill
repealed the exemption for private nonprofit hospitals. It also
established new procedures governing labour relations in

health-care institutions and erected a new definition of health-care institutions to include hospitals, nursing homes, health maintenance organisations, extended care facilities, health and medical clinics and similar facilities caring for the sick, infirm or aged.

Special provisions designed to facilitate collective bargaining settlements and to provide advance notice of strikes and picketing involving health-care facilities were incorporated into the bill. These included the following:

1. The requirement for notice of termination or expiration of a contract in 90 days.
2. The Federal Mediation and Conciliation Service must be given 60 days notice of such termination or expiration.
3. In initial contract negotiations a 30-day notice of a dispute to the Federal Mediation and Conciliation Service is required.
4. The health-care institution and the labour organisation are required to participate in mediation at the direction of the Federal Mediation and Conciliation Service.
5. The health-care institution must be given a 10-day notice by a labour organisation before any picketing or strike (whether or not related to bargaining) can take place.

The Senate Report favoured the removal of the 1947 Taft-Hartley exemption in section 2(2) and extended protection to the same degree as was applicable to employees in nursing homes and proprietary hospitals.

Between 1947 and 1974 approximately one and a half million employees of private nonprofit hospitals were not protected by the Taft-Hartley Act. This meant, of course, that more than one half of all hospital employees were unprotected by the Act. From the point of view of the Senate committee, there were no good reasons why this state of affairs should continue. It seemed reasonable that health-care employees in private nonprofit hospitals should have the same protection as that given proprietary hospital and nursing home employees.

Recognition is given to the argument that the needs of patients in health-care facilities require special consideration in any law that would remove the exemption for voluntary hospitals. It is for this reason that the Committee's report contains recommendations that require hospitals to have adequate notice of any strike or picketing to permit appropriate arrangements to be made for the noninterruption of vital patient care in the event of a strike. The recommended legislation's special notice and conciliation procedures designed to facilitate settlements without work stoppages apply to proprietary as well as voluntary hospitals and to all other health-care institutions, defined as including health maintenance organisations, clinics, nursing homes, extended care facilities, or other institutions devoted to the care of the sick, infirm or aged. The employees of federal, state and local government health-care facilities would not be covered. The legislation that the Senate committee recommends provides the same special protection for all health-care facilities with the exception of government institutions.

The Bargaining Unit Question. The American Hospital Association, in its testimony on the exemption bill, specifically requested that legislation provide for not more than four broad bargaining units in health-care facilities - units for professional, technical, clerical and service and maintenance employees. The Committee's report, while not endorsing this specific recommendation, favours broad as opposed to narrow bargaining units. The National Labor Relations Board is advised that due consideration should be given to the prevention of proliferation of bargaining units.

The bargaining unit question represents another area wherein public policy would dictate a different arrangement for health-care facilities compared with practice and policy in industry generally. At least this is true to a certain extent. While the National Labor Relations Board has generally favoured broad bargaining units, an approach which favours industrial unionism as opposed to craft unionism, the Congress has attempted to make it easier for craft unions to sever from large industrial unions.

The Labor Management Relations Act of 1947 affects the discretion of the parties in determining the structural basis of their bargaining relationship in two ways. First, the Act prohibits the National Labor Relations Board from deciding that any craft unit is inappropriate on the ground that a different unit has been established by a prior Board determination, unless a majority of employees in the proposed craft unit have voted against separate representation; secondly, certain occupational classifications are restricted in the manner by which bargaining units may be formed.[18] Professional employees and plant guards are singled out for special treatment.

The Board may not include professional employees in a bargaining unit with nonprofessional employees unless a majority of the professional employees vote for inclusion in such unit.

Health Industry Experience with Bargaining Units. In broad terms, the trend has been to prevent the proliferation of bargaining units in the health-care industry. In deliberations concerning the 1974 amendment, this fact was noted with approval. Specific reference was made to the Board's findings in three cases - Extendicare of West Virginia (1973),[19] Woodland Park Hospital (1973)[20] and Four Seasons Nursing Center (1974).[21]

In the Extendicare of West Virginia case, Local 1199, West Virginia, National Union of Hospital and Nursing Home Employees, desired to represent three separate units of employees at the health-care facility. The units would be comprised of licensed practical nurses, technical employees and service and maintenance employees. The employer contended that only one unit was appropriate, an all-employee unit encompassing office clerical as well as the workers sought by the union.

It was the decision of the Board that the 23 licensed practical nurses (LPNs) would constitute an appropriate unit and another unit would be composed of the four X-ray technicians, two laboratory technicians, an inhalation therapist and 62 service and maintenance employees, including nurses aides, orderlies, housekeepers, dietary employees and maintenance personnel.

It was noted in the Board's rationale that the licensed practical nurses worked in the nursing department and were supervised by registered nurses. They requisitioned and administered medicines and drugs, charted patients and conferred with doctors. Their duties were not performed by any of the nurses aides and orderlies included in the service and maintenance classification. Although LPNs received an hourly wage, their pay was 40 per cent more than that of aides and orderlies. The educational requirements for LPNs were a high school diploma plus a year of formal training. In addition, they had to be licensed by the state. They enjoyed a substantial community of interest separate from those of other employees.

It was the belief of the Board that technical employees and service and maintenance personnel should be in a single unit because of their substantial community of interest and the low number of technical employees. A finding of two separate units for these employees would create unwarranted unit fragmentation. The union had expressed a willingness to represent these employees in a single unit as an alternative to the three units requested. The seven technical employees -- four X-ray technicians, two laboratory technicians, and an inhalation therapist -- worked under conditions substantially similar to those of service and maintenance employees. They were all paid on an hourly basis, punched a timeclock, and shared common fringe benefits.

A similar rationale was presented in the Woodland Park Hospital case in which the Board decided in favour of a broad unit of hospital employees. The X-ray technicians, through the Oregon Society of Radiologic Technologists, petitioned for a separate unit. Because these employees did not, in the opinion of the Board, have a community of interest that was any more separately identifiable than that of other employees in other technical departments, the petition was denied. To establish a separate unit for X-ray technicians would lead to severe fragmentation of units. The request of two employees in the maintenance department for a separate bargaining unit at the Four Seasons Nursing Center also resulted in a finding supportive of a broad bargaining unit.

The structure of collective bargaining units in health-care institutions has clearly emerged. This structure is shaped by congressional mandate that the proliferation of bargaining units in the health-care industry is to be avoided and from the pattern which is derived from cases. These factors are obviously

related in that the congressional mandate often serves as an
important justification for Board decisions.

The National Labor Relations Board generally finds five
collective bargaining units appropriate: (1) service and maintenance employees; (2) clerical employees; (3) technical;
(4) registered nurses; and (5) professional employees (exclusive of physicians who would constitute a sixth category).
These categories are not rigid. A Board decision may combine
technical and service and maintenance employees. It is not
unusual for several clerical employees to be placed in the same
bargaining unit with service and maintenance employees. This
is especially true in the case of ward clerks who have greater
community of interest with service and maintenance employees
than with business office clericals.

Ten-day Strike Notice. One of the special provisions of the
1974 Taft-Hartley amendment provides that a health-care institution be given a 10-day notice by a labour organisation before
any picketing or strike (whether or not related to bargaining)
can take place. This 10-day notice requirement, in a recent
Board decision, is being interpreted literally so as to cover
sympathy strikes.

The National Union of Hospital and Health Care Employees'
case[22] involved a union with no unit at the institution which sent
four officers to join a picket line that had been lawfully established by another union. The four officers joined the picket
line for one and one-half hours. The Board concluded that
Section 8(g) is clear in prohibiting *any* strike or picketing
without the 10-day notice. The law is void of any modifying
language respecting the character of the picketings, its objectives or the type of pressures generated. Under these circumstances, a union engaged in a sympathy strike cannot rely upon
the earlier notice given by another labour organisation as a
basis for fulfilling its own statutory obligation.

The text of the Board's decision reveals that the literal interpretation of 8(g) is mandated by its legislative history and
policy considerations which promoted the enactment of the 1974
amendment. During the Senate debate, Senator Taft noted that
the particular subsection in question applied not only to bargaining strikes of pickets, but also, as stated in the statute,
to 'any picket or strike', including recognition strikes, jurisdictional strikes, and the like. The phrase, 'and the like',
included sympathy strikes and picketing.

A union would not stand in violation of the National Labor
Relations Act if it threatened to strike a health-care institution without giving the 10-day notice. This is consistent with
the literal interpretation of 8(g). A threat to strike a health-
care institution is not a violation since the law specifically states
that 'engaging' in a strike is prohibited unless the institution
and the Mediation and Conciliation Service have been previously
notified not less than 10 days prior to the strike. The Board's

rationale would probably be that in the absence of a prohibition in the Act against threats to strike health-care institutions, it must be concluded that Congress did not desire to cover threats to strike. Apparently, this was a deliberate omission, since, at the time 8(g) was enacted, Congress was aware of examples wherein threats to strike as well as strikes were outlawed. Legislative history seems to indicate that Congress did not intend to prohibit such threats.

Further evidence is provided in the record which indicates the intent of Congress. While the legislation containing Section 8(g) was pending before the Conference Committee of the Congress, General Counsel Peter Nash of the National Labor Relations Board delivered an address in which he presented an interpretation of the pending amendment. His interpretation was that a threat to strike or picket a health-care institution within the 10-day period would in itself constitute a violation of Section 8(g). General Counsel Nash's interpretation was based upon the fact that failure to provide proper notice is remediable under Section 10(j) of the National Labor Relations Act as amended. Presumably, the 10-day notice would provide the National Labor Relations Board with the opportunity to determine the legality of the anticipated picketing or strike activity before it occurred. Senate and House Committee reports provided the basis of the General Counsel's interpretation of the Act.

When the legislation amending the Taft-Hartley Act cleared Conference Committee and came up for passage by the Senate and the House, senators and representatives who sponsored the measure rejected the interpretation given to Section 8(g) by General Counsel Nash. It is apparent that the Congress, indeed, did not intend to make 'threats' to picket or strike unlawful. It was not the wish of Congress to create a new unfair labour practice. While a 'threat' to violate Section 8(b)(4) is a violation of the Act, a 'threat' to violate 8(g) does not constitute a violation.

The Lein-steenburg case[23] is interesting because the question is raised as to whether or not the 8(g) provision applies to non-health care employees. A non-union contractor was engaged to work on a hospital renovation project. Members of the plumbers' local union began picketing the contractor. No interruption of hospital services ensued and hospital employees continued to work in spite of the picketing.

The union did not give 10-day notice to the hospital or the Federal Mediation and Conciliation Service. The National Labor Relations Board held that notices were required because the picketing took place at the health-care institution, even though the union members were not employed by the hospital. The District of Columbia Court of Appeals refused to enforce the Board's order. The picketing of a health-care facility by non-employees when services are not interrupted at the facility does not violate the 8(g) provision.

Table 7.1: Cases Filed and Elections Held in the Health Services Industry, 1975-8

	Cases Filed			Elections	
Year	ULP	Rep.	Held	Won	Per cent Won
1975	1423	1451	579	346	59.8
1976	1721	1138	710	416	58.6
1977	1750	1110	746	408	54.7
1978	1755	938	596	324	54.4

Source: Statistical Service Staff, Division of Administration, NLRB Washington, DC.

The number of elections held over the four years peaked in 1977; elections declined to the approximate 1975 level in 1978. The percentage of elections won by unions remained relatively stable over the four-year period.

It is interesting to note that union activities have expanded rapidly in the nursing home sector of the health-care industry. Table 7.2 indicates a dramatic increase in the number of NLRB cases involving hospitals as well as nursing homes immediately after the 1974 amendment was passed. Union activities in the nursing home sector, an area already subject to the Taft-Hartley Act prior to the 1974 amendment, were apparently influenced by increased union activity in private not-for-profit hospitals.

Table 7.2: NLRB Cases Involving Hospitals and Nursing Homes

Year	Cases	Nursing Homes	Hospitals	Total
1973	REP.	149	90	239
	ULP	200	91	291
	Total	349	181	530
1974	REP.	228	105	333
	ULP	248	131	379
	Total	476	236	712
1975	REP.	583	731	1314
	ULP	528	658	1186
	Total	1111	1389	2500

Table 7.2: NLRB Cases Involving Hospitals and Nursing Homes

Year	Cases	Nursing Homes	Hospitals	Total
1976	REP.	456	701	1157
	ULP	622	965	1587
	Total	1078	1666	2744
1977	REP.	451	687	1138
	ULP	719	929	1648
	Total	1170	1616	1786
1978	REP.	324	554	878
	ULP	211	354	565
	Total	535	908	1443

Source: Division of Operations, NLRB, Washington, DC.

The burst of union activity which was experienced immediately following the passage of the 1974 amendment has not been sustained. This is not to say that the strength of unionism in health services has declined. Neither should it be concluded that the impact of the amendment has been minimal.

A 1979 report from the Office of Research of the Federal Mediation and Conciliation Service notes a number of impacts resulting from the 1974 amendment.[24] It is observed that unions have responded to the amendment by placing new emphasis on educational and training activities for their members, and modifying their internal structures with the addition of committees, constitutional amendments and special staff to focus on health-care industry problems. Although bargaining issues and contract language in the health-care industry closely resemble those in other industries, the FMCS reports that contracts are generally shorter and more frequently contain provisions on issues relating to patient care standards and institutional policies and procedures. Issues involving union security and checkoff are more prevalent in contracts in the health service industry than in all other industries.

Legislative intent to promote early negotiations, as provided by the 90- and 60-day notices prior to the contract expiration date, has not altered the bargaining process which relies on 'eleventh hour' negotiations and a crisis atmosphere, so concludes the FMCS. It observes also that the Board of Inquiry procedure (Section 213 of the Amendment) is required to become operative too early in the bargaining process. The decision by the FMCS on whether to appoint a Board of Inquiry, if made at a time closer to contract expiration, would be based on a better understanding of the likelihood of a work stoppage. Useful recommendations are often difficult for a Board to make.

LEGISLATIVE TRENDS: AN OVERVIEW

An overview of legislative trends in US health services can best
be accomplished by describing the regulation of labour-management relations in three discrete arenas: federal government
health-care facilities; state and local government facilities; and
private proprietary and nonprofit institutions.[25] Chronological
developments in each jurisdiction describe the legal treatment
accorded collective relationships in US health services and also
allow for intra-sector comparisons.

The Federal Sector

Prior to 1978, federal hospital employees, numbering approximately 200 000, were covered by two presidential executive
orders governing labour-management relations in the federal
service. EO 10988, promulgated by President John J. Kennedy
in 1962, granted federal employees the rights to unionise and
bargain collectively over a limited number of topics, excluding
monetary items. Several types of union representation were
established, depending upon the proportion of union members
in the bargaining unit.[26] Union complaints of management bias,
particularly in dispute settlement procedures, led President
Lyndon B. Johnson to appoint a task force to recommend changes
to correct inadequacies in the programme. Many of the task
force recommendations were incorporated in Executive Order
11491, issued by President Richard Nixon in 1970. Substantive
changes included the creation of a three-member Federal Labor
Relations Council to administer the order, the establishment of
the Federal Services Impasses Panel to resolve contractual disputes, and the handling of recognition issues by the US Labor
Department. Neither executive order allowed strikes. In fact,
EO 11491 imposes heavy penalties upon striking federal workers,
including discharge, loss of civil service status, and ineligibility
for re-employment by the federal government for at least three
years. Furthermore, unions which initiate or support strikes
are deemed to commit an unfair labour practice.[27]

Executive orders, although not statutes, have the force of
law and can be rescinded only by the action of successor president or by the passage of legislation by Congress. Consequently, the enactment of the Civil Service Reform Act of 1978 nullified the two executive orders just discussed, and for the first
time, provided a statutory basis for federal labour-management
relations. Representation cases, unfair labour practice complaints and grievance arbitration cases, formerly handled by
the Federal Labor Relations Council and the Assistant Secretary
of Labor for Labor-Management Relations, now come under the
jurisdiction of a four-member Federal Labor Relations Authority.
The US Civil Service Commission is abolished and replaced by
two agencies: an Office of Personnel Management to direct personnel matters and a Merit Systems Protection Board with a
special counsel to handle employee appeals in disciplinary actions

and to ensure that politics does not enter into the selection of
career employees. The Act expands the scope of matters subject
to negotiated grievance and arbitration procedures to include
for the first time such adverse actions as discharges, demotions
and long-term suspensions. Departments and agencies which
issue government-wide personnel regulations must consult over
substantive changes with unions that have achieved national
recognition. Management has the authority to make decisions
and take actions which are not subject to the bargaining process, and the law excludes bargaining on federal pay and benefits. Strikes are still prohibited and constitute an unfair labour
practice on the part of labour organisations.

The State and Local Government Sector
Until the end of the 1950s, state and local governments resisted
the extension of organisational and bargaining rights to public
employees, citing the doctrine of sovereignty which holds that
public jurisdictions would incur a dilution of their sovereignty if
collective bargaining rights would be granted to public employees. Thus, in the absence of enabling legislation, public
employees are denied the right of collective action. The legislative vacuum that existed can be seen in the fact that until 1959,
when Wisconsin enacted the first statute regulating labour-
management relations in public employment, few state or local
government employees were covered by labour agreements, and
there were no state laws authorising unionisation, collective
bargaining or strike action. As a result, only 1 per cent of
state and local government hospital workers were covered by
collective agreements.[28]
Legislative action intensified greatly during the 1960s so that
at the end of the decade 36 states had enacted statutes regulating public sector labour relations. Some laws are comprehensive
in scope, covering all public employees while others are more
selective, applying only to specific occupational categories,
i.e., nurses, teachers, police or firemen. Nine states have these
restrictive laws so that in only slightly more than half of the
states (27) are health service employees granted organising and
bargaining rights. Moreover, as late as 1977, there were 14
states without any direct legal framework for public employees;[29]
yet the legal framework that had developed resulted in the
unionisation of approximately 1 out of every 5 hospital employees.
The state statutes and local ordinances included five major
components; organisational rights, the right to 'meet and confer'
with management concerning employment terms, collective bargaining rights, the establishment of dispute settlement procedures and the legal status of strikes. Thirty-six states have
legislated in one or more of these areas, with 12 jurisdictions
providing for 'meet and confer' arrangements where union representatives may discuss employment conditions with public managers but the latter are not committed to take any specific
action. In the states where full bargaining rights are granted,

union and management representatives jointly negotiate wages,
hours and working conditions. In 34 states, public employee
strikes or work stoppages are prohibited while only 8 states
allow strike action under specific restraints. Mediation, fact
finding, and compulsory arbitration are the usual types of dispute settlement mechanisms in 19 states.[30]

Since each state is a sovereign jurisdiction, with its statutes
having a binding character only within its geographical boundaries, diversity characterises the legal framework, as might be
expected. There are differences even between the legislative
treatment accorded state and local government workers. For
example, in Wisconsin state employees are covered by a State
Employee Relations Act which grants organisational and bargaining rights, statewide bargaining units but there is no right to
strike and the arbitration of interest disputes is forbidden.[31] In
contrast, a local government bargaining statute authorises the
unionisation and bargaining rights for employees of local jurisdictions, provides for limited strike action but does not deal
with bargaining unit structure or coverage.[32] Other states, such
as Washington, New York and California have similarly complex
laws so that little legislative uniformity exists on a national
basis.

The Private Sector Prior to the 1974 Amendment
Confusion and uncertainty regarding the labour relations status
of private, proprietary and nonprofit hospitals and health-care
institutions was guaranteed by the omission of any coverage in
the National Labor Relations Act of 1935, the federal labour
statute regulating labour-management relations in almost all
industries involved in interstate commerce. It remained for the
National Labor Relations Board and the courts to determine their
status, with the assumption that private hospitals were covered.
However, the NLRB usually declined to take jurisdiction in
cases involving private, nonprofit health-care facilities.[33]

The legal status of private, nonprofit health-care facilities
was resolved in 1947 with the passage of the Taft-Hartley Act
which exempted such institutions through the language of
Section 2(2) which did not cover 'any corporation or association
operating a hospital, if no part of the net earnings insures to
the benefit of any private shareholder or individual'.[34]

In the absence of federal legislative treatment for employees
of private, nonprofit hospitals, 12 highly unionised states
enacted statutes covering health-care facilities in order to minimise recognitional strikes and to provide special dispute settlement procedures to resolve negotiation impasses. In the other
38 states where collective bargaining for health-care employees
was not assured by law, collective bargaining relationships were
established either by recognitional picketing, striking or the
threat of such activity. State law determined whether such conduct could be enjoined. In Illinois, where there is no statute,
the state Supreme Court ruled that strikes against nonprofit

hospitals could not be enjoined pursuant to a state law prohibiting the issuance of labour injunctions.[35] As a result, collective bargaining relationships between such hospitals and
employees were typically based on commitments, contained in
recognition agreements, not to strike and to resolve all negotiation disputes by interest arbitration.

By the early 1970s legislative coverage apparently diminished
because only eight states, Connecticut, Massachusetts, Michigan,
Minnesota, Montana, New York, Oregon and Pennsylvania, had
laws which covered some or all hospital employees. In Idaho,
New Jersey and Wisconsin coverage was implied. A brief review
of the state laws follows in order to provide a current perspective.

Minnesota. The Minnesota Labor Relations Act of 1939 apparently
covered private, nonprofit hospitals, according to a judicial
decision holding that a charitable hospital qualified as an employer under the statute.[36] In 1947, the Charitable Hospital Act was
passed, outlawing strikes and requiring mediation and then
compulsory arbitration of interest disputes. The scope of bargaining was limited to disagreements over 'maximum hours of
work and minimum hourly wages'. Subsequently, in Fairview
Hospital Association v. Public Building Service Union, 241 Minn.
523, 64 N.W. 2d 16 (1954), the Minnesota Supreme Court further
excluded the union shop, union security and the internal
management of the hospital from joint determination.

New York. Nonprofit hospitals were specifically exempt from
the State Labor Relations Act but, in 1963, the state adopted
special amendments to cover workers in hospitals and nursing
homes in New York City and in 1965 the same provisions were
applied to the entire state. Every collective bargaining contract
between employees of a nonprofit hospital and the hospital was
required to contain final and binding arbitration for disputes
arising in negotiations. State law provided for fact-finding
commissions and the submission of disputes to final and binding
arbitration.

Pennsylvania. The Pennsylvania Supreme Court ruled in 1941
that the state's labour statute did not apply to private, nonprofit hospitals and nearly three decades passed until 1979 when
a law covering state, local and nonprofit health-care institutions
was passed. Mediation and fact-finding procedures for peaceful
settlement of disputes were provided, as well as the right to
strike. However, no strikes were permitted if a clear and present danger to the health, safety and welfare of the public was
found to exist.

Wisconsin. Wisconsin's Employment Peace Act of 1939 was
extended to cover employees of private, nonprofit hospitals in
1942. Mediation was required to resolve bargaining deadlocks

but strikes, lockouts and other types of concerted action were permitted under a unique state statute,[37] which made no distinction between hospitals and other private employers.

Massachusetts. In 1947, Massachusetts passed an Emergency Labor Disputes Act which covered food, fuel, electric light and power, and gas services. The law also covered medical services and profit-making hospitals. The statute empowered the Governor to establish procedures for dealing with labour disputes in these essential service areas.[38] However, public and private nonprofit health service institutions were not covered by legislation until 1964. Largely due to intensive lobbying efforts by registered nurses and licensed practical nurses, the 1964 statute covered these two occupational categories and provided dispute settlement procedures, including arbitration at the request of the parties.[39] By 1968, state law had been liberalised to cover all non-professional health-care employees.

Michigan. Proprietary and voluntary nonprofit hospitals were covered by the Michigan Labor Mediation Act of 1949, which required that no strike would be allowed unless the union or employer served a Notice of Dispute to the State Labor Mediation Board and on the other party no less than 30 days before the strike or lockout was to become effective. If the dispute was not settled by mediation within 30 days, the matter was brought before the Governor who then appointed a three-person commission to conduct hearings and prepare nonbinding recommendations within 30 days after appointment. After the report was issued, the parties were then directed to continue bargaining for at least ten days and, if no settlement was reached, the Mediation Board could supervise a strike vote.[40] Hence, Michigan and Wisconsin were the only states permitting strike action by hospital employees.

Connecticut. Although the Connecticut General Assembly had considered legislation previously in order to limit labour strikes in the health-care industry, a relevant statute was not enacted until 1967, including a strike prohibition and fact-finding with recommendations, provisions identical to those contained in the New York law.[41]

Oregon. Licensed practical nurses and registered nurses were accorded bargaining rights by statute in 1961. Strikes were defined as unfair labour practices and mediation and fact-finding without recommendations were the types of dispute settlement provided by the law.[42]

Montana. Registered and licensed practical nurses are the only occupational classifications covered by legislation passed in 1967, in large part due to the successful lobbying efforts of the Montana Nurses Association. Strikes are permitted if no

other hospital strike occurs within a 150-mile radius, and the
employer must receive notice 30 days in advance regarding the
exact date of the commencement of the strike. Unfair labour
practices are defined and the parties are encouraged to utilise
conciliation and/or mediation in the event of bargaining impasses.[43]

The 1974 Taft-Hartley Amendments

In 1974, the Taft-Hartley Act was amended by Congress to
provide comprehensive coverage for nonprofit health-care units
including hospitals, nursing homes and related health-care
facilities. The amendments covered approximately 1.4 million
employees who were brought within federal jurisdiction on 26
August 1974.

The amendments grant the National Labor Relations Board
jurisdiction over a broad range of nonprofit health-care institutions. Exempted from the law's coverage are: (1) federal, state
or municipal government health-care facilities; (2) purely local
health-care organisations which have no impact upon interstate
commerce; (3) facilities where the employer is not in fact a
health-care institution; and (4) situations where the employees
asserting rights do not fall within the NLRB's definition of
employee; e.g., interns and residents.[44]

The basic changes introduced by the amendments include the
following provisions:

(1) Section 8(d) (A) extended the notice a party desiring to
    terminate or modify a labour agreement must give to the other
    party from 60 to 90 days prior to the contract expiration date
    (60 days is the requirement in other industries).
(2) Also, under this section the Federal Mediation and Concilia-
    tion Service and appropriate state mediation agencies must be
    notified 60 days prior to the contract expiration date, instead
    of 30 days in other industries.
(3) Section 8(g) required that a labour organisation serve notice
    upon an employer 10 days in advance of instituting any picket-
    ing or work stoppage.
(4) Section 8(d) (B) covers initial contract situations by requir-
    ing the union to give at least a 30-day notice of the existence
    of a dispute to the FMCS and to appropriate state agencies.
    Consequently, including the 10-day strike notice, a minimum
    of 40 days notice is required before a strike or picketing can
    take place.
(5) Section 8(d) (C) mandates mediation efforts by the FMCS
    and is unique to health care in contrast to other industries
    where mediation is voluntary.
(6) Section 213 creates a fact-finding procedure: the Board of
    Inquiry, which is convened by the Director of the FMCS, if
    in his opinion a strike or lockout will 'substantially interrupt
    the delivery of health care in a locality concerned'. The
    impartial Board is to investigate disputed issues and submit

a non-binding report with its recommendations within 15 days after its appointment. The parties are then required to continue bargaining efforts for an additional 15 days, after which a strike or lockout is permitted provided the proper notification has been given.[45]

Prior to the amendments, most of the collective bargaining in the US health-care industry occurred in proprietary hospitals, nursing homes and nonprofit hospitals which voluntarily recognised unions as the collective bargaining agents of their employees or which were covered by state law. The 1974 amendments dramatically changed the legal framework of hospital collective bargaining in all states, not only those which did not have labour relations acts covering hospital workers. The Taft-Hartley changes superseded all state laws and brought all non-federal health-care institutions, proprietary and nonprofit, under the comprehensive coverage of one federal law. Employees of federal, state and municipal health-care facilities are excluded from coverage.

The 1974 legislation balanced the legislative desire to extend coverage to nonprofit, nonpublic hospital employees with the belief that the importance of maintaining continuity in the delivery of health-care services required a comprehensive programme designed to afford health-care institutions protections otherwise not available.

COMPARATIVE ANALYSIS

Three distinct legal frameworks regulate health care labour-management relations in the United States. Federal government health-care facilities, formerly governed by the provisions of two executive orders, now are covered by the Title VII of the Civil Service Reform Act of 1978, which prohibits strikes, defines unfair labour practices, prescribes dispute settlement mechanisms, and handles representation cases. State and local government health-care institutions can unionise and bargain collectively in slightly more than half of the states whose statutes follow no uniform pattern. In 14 states, public employees are not covered by legislation. Although private, nonprofit hospitals comprised nearly half of the health-care industry and two-thirds of the employees, they were specifically exempted from statutory coverage prior to the Taft-Hartley amendments in 1974 and were controlled by legislation in less than a dozen states. The state laws varied widely; only Wisconsin and Michigan allowed health-care workers to strike; most states accepted collective bargaining but prohibited strike action and dispute settlement techniques followed a less than uniform pattern. The 1974 Taft-Hartley amendments added stability and industrial peace to one of the fastest growing areas of the US economy by covering all private health-care facilities, proprietary and

nonprofit. The National Labor Relations Board now has full
authority to determine bargaining units and regulate the conduct between hospital management and labour organisations
under the Board's unfair labour practice authority. Framers of
the legislation intended to promote collective bargaining in the
health-care industry and provided procedures to promote the
peaceful resolution of disputes. Congress compromised on the
strike issue. While specificially rejecting the contention that
health-care employees were not entitled to strike rights, Congress did recognise the special nature of the health-care industry and thus enacted certain minimal safeguards for employers
in the event a strike should occur.

In Canada, there are certain parallels to the US experience
in that health care labour-management relations also is regulated
by three distinct legislative frameworks. Municipal employees
are treated by statutes in the provinces in similar fashion as
private sector workers, with the right to unionise and bargain
collectively. Strikes are permitted although enforceable dispute
settlement procedures modelled after the US Wagner Act seek to
minimise conflict. The 1967 Public Service Staff Relations Act is
the Canadian legislative counterpart to the US Civil Service
Reform Act of 1978 in its coverage of federal health-care institutions. It prescribes representation, bargaining rights and dispute settlement procedures, but Canadian federal employees
have considerably more latitude in exercising the right to strike
than do federal health-care workers in the United States.
Diversity marks the provincial statutes, on the other hand, in
the legislative treatment of public health-care institutions.
Strikes are prohibited in two provinces, while in the remainder
work stoppages are permitted only after efforts to resolve differences have been attempted.

The experience in the United Kingdom is quite different from
that of the United States and Canada where health services are
concerned. All employees are covered by the provisions of the
Whitley Councils and other bodies who co-ordinate the collective
bargaining process between labour and management and the primary dispute settlement tactic has been arbitration before the
Industrial Court. Over the last ten years the preferred tactic
has been ad hoc inquiries. However, due to the emphasis on
voluntarism in industrial relations generally, health service
employees may strike with greater impunity than in the United
States and Canada. If one were to construct a continuum describing the legal frameworks regulating labour-management
relations in the health services in the United States, Canada
and the United Kingdom, in terms of statutory efforts to minimise conflict the US system would be at one extreme, the United
Kingdom structure would be positioned at the other pole, and
the Canadian model would be located somewhere in the middle.
The same relative positions would obtain concerning the regulation of organisational and collective bargaining rights. All in
all, labour-management relations in the health-care field in

the United States is subject to considerably greater legal regulation than in either Canada or the United Kingdom.

REFERENCES AND NOTES

1 National Labor Relations Board v. Central Dispensary and Emergency Hospital, 145 F.2d 852.
2 Virginian Railway Co. v. System Federation, No.40, 57 S.Ct. 592.
3 National Labor Relations Board v. Jones and Laughlin Steel Corporation, 301 US 1 (1937).
4 Myers, A. Howard (1968), 'Labor Law and Legislation', fourth edition, South-Western Publishing Company, pp.450-1.
5 Dulles, Foster Rhea (1960), 'Labor in America', second revised edition, Thomas Y. Crowell Company, p.377.
6 Cox, Archibald, and Dunlop, John T. (1950), Regulation of Collective Bargaining by the National Labor Relations Board, 'Harvard Law Review', January, p.389.
7 Public Law 86-257 -- 87th Congress, S. 1555, 14 September 1959.
8 Fleming, R.W. (1949), Taft-Hartley Law to Date, 'Wisconsin Law Review', January, p.98.
9 Tripp, L. Reed (1961), 'Labor Problems and Processes: A Survey', Harper and Row, p.240.
10 Ibid., p.240.
11 Dulles, 'Labor in America', p.401.
12 'Hot cargo' agreements are unlawful except in construction agreements and in the apparel and clothing industry. The prehire contract coupled with the seven-day union shop in construction approximates the closed shop which is unlawful in industry generally.
13 Hearings before the Subcommittee on Labor of the Committee on Labor and Public Welfare, United States Senate, Ninety-Second Congress, Second Session on H.R. 11357, 16 August and 6 September 1972, US Government Printing Office, Washington, 1972.
14 Ibid., p.3.
15 Ibid., p.11.
16 Ibid., p.210.
17 Senate Report, Coverage of Nonprofit Hospitals Under the National Labor Relations Act, 93d Congress, 2d Session, Report No. 93-766, 2 April 1974.
18 Davey, Harold W. (1959), 'Contemporary Collective Bargaining', second edition, Prentice Hall, p.59.
19 Extendicare of West Virginia, Inc., 203 NLRB No. 170, 1973.
20 Woodlawn Park Hospital, Inc., 205 NLRB No. 144, 1973.
21 Four Seasons Nursing Center of Joliet, Ill., 208 NLRB No. 50, 1974.
22 District 1199, National Union of Hospital and Healthcare

Employees, 222 National Labor Relations Board No. 15
(1976).
23 219 NLRB 837 (1975).
24 US Federal Mediation and Conciliation Service (1979), 'Impact
of the 1974 Health Care Amendments to the NLRA on Collective Bargaining in the Health Care Industry', pp.432-7.
25 Miller, Richard U. (1980), Hospitals, in Gerald G. Somers
(ed.), 'Collective Bargaining: Contemporary American
Experience', Industrial Relations Research Association
Series: University of Wisconsin, p.381.
26 Ibid.
27 Ibid.
28 AHA Research Capsules-No. 6, 'Hospitals, JAHA', vol.46,
1 April 1972, p.217.
29 American Bar Association (1977), 'Report of the Committee
on State Law', in Bureau of National Affairs, Inc., 'Government Employee Relations Report', RF, 19 September, p.148.
30 Metzger, Norman, and Pointer, Dennis D. (1972), 'Labor-
Management Relations in the Health Services Industry:
Theory and Practice', Science and Health Publications,
Inc., pp.76-7.
31 State Employment Relations Act, WIS 111.80-111,97, Laws
of Wisconsin, 1971.
32 Municipal Employment Relations Act, 111.70 Wisconsin
Statutes, as amended 1 January 1979.
33 Farkas, Emil C. (1978), The National Labor Relations Act:
The Health Care Amendments, 'Labor Law Journal', p.263.
34 Labor Management Relations Act, Public Law 101, 80th
Congress, 1947.
35 Peters v. South Chicago Community Hospital, 44 I11, 2d
22, 253 N.E. 2d 375 (1969).
36 Northwestern Hospital of Minneapolis, Minnesota v. Public
Building Services Union, 208 N.W. 215, 1940.
37 Miller, Ronald L. (1969), Collective Bargaining in Non-
Profit Hospitals, unpublished PhD thesis, University of
Pennsylvania, pp.254-5.
38 Shultz, George P. (1957), The Massachusetts Choice of
Procedures Approach to Emergency Disputes, 'Industrial
and Labor Relations Review', vol.10, April, pp.359-74.
39 Gamm, Sara (1968), 'Toward Collective Bargaining in Non-
Profit Hospitals: Impact of New York Law', Bulletin 60,
State School of Industrial and Labor Relations, Appendix B.
40 Parker, Hyman (1961), The Laws Governing Labor-Management Relations in Michigan Hospitals, 'Labor Law Journal',
October, pp.972-90.
41 Gershenfeld, Walter J. (1968), Emerging Sectors of Collective Labor Relations in Hospitals, mimeograph,
28 March, p.5.
42 Collective Bargaining Law for Nurses Passed by Oregon
State Legislature, 'The Modern Hospital', vol.97, October
1961, p.162.

43 Kleingartner, Archie (1967), Nurses, Collective Bargaining and Labor Legislation, 'Labor Law Journal', April, pp.240-1.
44 Shepard, Ira M. (1978), Health Care Institution Labor Law: Case Law Developments, 1974-1978, 'American Journal of Law and Medicine', Spring, pp.1-14.
45 Labor Management Relations Act, as amended by Public Laws 86-257, 1959 and 93-360, 1974.

8. LEGISLATION GOVERNING INDUSTRIAL RELATIONS IN THE NATIONAL HEALTH SERVICE: UK

S.D. Anderman, J.H. Angel and R. Mailly

INTRODUCTION: THE GENERAL LEGAL FRAMEWORK

The most striking feature of British labour law by comparison with that of the USA and Canada is the degree of autonomy it leaves to trade unions and employers and to the collective bargaining process. In Britain, under the Trade Union and Labour Relations Act 1974, as amended, collective bargaining agreements are not normally legally enforceable. The use of labour injunctions or equivalent administrative sanctions against trade unions is strictly limited by legislation where strikes and other industrial action are taken in contemplation of furtherance of a trade dispute. Moreover, any legal actions for damages against trade union organisations for the industrial action of their members or even their officials are curtailed by law. These immunities have been reduced in recent years by the Conservative Government's Employment Act 1980 in respect of secondary picketing and certain types of secondary industrial action, but they still underpin a relatively wide freedom to organise strikes. Furthermore the actual regulation of trade union internal affairs is minimal and there is no legal duty placed upon trade unions to represent their members. Finally, arbitration, as well as mediation and conciliation are 'voluntary' rather than legally binding. In these respects, at least the British legal framework is 'non-interventionist' in character.

This non-interventionist thread running through British labour laws is attributable in large measure to the early success of British trade unions in obtaining recognition and collective bargaining by their own efforts. This, together with their bitter experience with the British judiciary, made the unions reluctant to ask for the help of the law where positive legal support might entail a reciprocal legal responsibility for disciplining their members. During the interwar period when the unions were weak, there was a wide social acceptance of unregulated collective bargaining. In the early 1960s however when the wider social acceptance of non-interventionism broke down in the face of strong workshop bargaining and 'unconstitutional' and 'unofficial' strikes, the overall importance of trade union opposition to legal regulation of collective bargaining manifested itself more clearly.

Both the efforts of the Labour Government in the 1968-70 period to introduce legal regulation at certain 'sore points' of collective bargaining and the efforts of the Conservative

Government from 1971-4 to introduce a comprehensive system of legal regulation of collective bargaining were ineffective in achieving their aims. The Labour Government's White Paper 'In Place of Strife' was never enacted. The Conservative Government's legislation, the Industrial Relations Act 1971, was ultimately repealed by the Labour Government when it returned to office in 1974, but long before its repeal it had demonstrated its inability to achieve its objective of applying a viable new legal framework of law to British collective bargaining. During this period British trade unions quite dramatically demonstrated their capacity to resist by industrial means parliamentary efforts to bring collective bargaining within the web of legislative regulation where the trade unions considered that such laws threatened their existence as institutions. Moreover, during the 1971-4 period there was strong evidence of tacit support from employers to prevent legal intervention into collective bargaining.

From 1974-9 however the trade unions became more intimately associated with the formulation of legislation as part of their participation in a 'social contract' which has involved certain restraints on pay increases. The Labour Government enacted the Employment Protection Act 1975 which for the first time provided positive legal rights for trade union organisations against employers on collective bargaining issues. That Act also increased the number of statutory employment protections for individual employees which were later all consolidated into the Employment Protection (Consolidation) Act 1978. Today individual employees regardless of trade union membership are given statutory protection in their relationship with their employers in respect of dismissals, redundancy payments and in various issues that arise during employment including guarantee payments and maternity rights. Moreover there are separate statutes regulating health and safety, sex and race discrimination (see Part III). The new positive statutory rights for trade unions now include rights to disclosure of information, time off for trade union activities, rights to consultation before redundancy decisions are taken, consultation on health and safety issues and on pension schemes which contract out of the state system. There was also a right to recognition (ss 11-16) and a right to unilateral arbitration over groups of workers whose pay fell below norms established by collective bargaining (Schedule 11) in the EPA 1975 but this was repealed in the EA 1980 (see Part II). Looking at this web of legal regulation it seems inaccurate to describe the industrial relations system as 'voluntaristic' or the legal framework as 'non-interventionist'.

Yet it would be a mistake to see in the extensive legal regulation created by the 1975 Act the basis of an erosion of the non-interventionist system. The individual employment laws are not regarded as a substitute for collective bargaining. They are intended to provide a safety net for groups who are not covered by collective bargaining and they are pitched at levels which do not effectively compete with the gains of collective bargaining.

Nor are the trade union rights of a type to undermine the autonomy of collective bargaining. In Britain, unlike the USA, the positive trade union rights have been grafted on to a trade union movement with a high density of membership in the work-force and a well established system of collective bargaining. These laws are marginal to rather than structurally interwoven with collective bargaining. This can be seen in part in the weak-ness of the remedies provided for the trade union rights. There are no court orders or cease and desist orders against employers who fail to meet their obligations. Instead the legislation pro-vides an enforcement mechanism that consists of arbitration awards which may be incorporated into the terms of the contracts of employment of individual members. Hence the duty to bargain, to disclose information, or to consult trade unions before lay-offs have not had the type of influence over collective bargain-ing that has characterised, for example, the duty to bargain in good faith in the USA. Indeed the overall impact of the statutory trade union rights has been slight.

The voluntarism remaining in the system is further indicated by the fact that the statutory rights made available to the trade unions do not entail a corresponding legal responsibility by the unions to refrain from taking industrial action or to prevent members from taking industrial action whilst making use of the legal machinery. There are several reasons for this, only one of which is the recognition of the limited capacity of the highly decentralised trade union movement to assume a legal respon-sibility for the actions of its members at plant and workshop level. Whatever the underlying motivation, this feature of the legal framework is evidence of a significant degree of non-intervention.

One major consequence of this new legislative framework is that it introduces legislation which creates legal responsibilities for the employer whilst omitting to create a legal basis for trade union responsibility for members' actions. Hence in matters of the administration of collective agreements as well as their nego-tiation, employers must develop joint machinery without an underpinning of legal sanctions against the unions themselves, though the law does provide support for the disciplinary powers of the employer directly against his own employees. Nevertheless British employers have long functioned in this voluntaristic industrial relations culture and have found that the absence of a legal basis does not mean an absence of trade union responsibil-ity in the collective bargaining process.

PART I: COLLECTIVE LABOUR LAW AND INDUSTRIAL ACTION: RELEVANCE TO THE NATIONAL HEALTH SERVICE

In contrast with many other Western countries, there is very little specialist legislation curtailing the right to strike by employees in the public sector in Great Britain. What legislation

there is, is very limited in its scope. The police do not have
the right to strike and there are restrictions on the right to
strike of postal employees (Post Office Act 1953). In the more
general area of public employment the Conspiracy and Protection
of Property Act 1875 (CPPA) allowed criminal sanctions to be
imposed against persons breaking contracts for the supply of
gas or water. This limb of the Act was repealed by the Industrial
Relations Act 1971 (IRA). A more important provision for the
NHS, which is still in existence, is section 5 of the Act, which
allows for a fine of £20 or a prison sentence of up to 3 months
to be imposed: 'Where any person willfully and maliciously
breaks a contract of service or of hiring, knowing or having
reasonable cause to believe that the probable consequences of
so doing, either alone or in combination or with others, will be
to endanger human life, or cause serious bodily injury, or to
expose valuable property ... to destruction or serious injury.'

This provision, which obviously has relevance to the National
Health Service, has not been used in modern times, although
much of the recent industrial action in the Health Service has
involved employees in unlawfully breaking their contracts of
employment.[1] However, two relevant Acts which have been used
recently are the Emergency Powers Act 1920 and the Emergency
Powers Act 1964. Both give extensive powers to the government
(in the case of the 1964 Act without consulting Parliament) to
use the military in industrial disputes where 'events occur which
might deprive the community of any substantial portion of the
community of the essentials of life'. During the 1979 ambulancemen's dispute the army were called in to man ambulances and
to provide emergency services.

With the exception of the limitations mentioned above, trade
unions in the National Health Service enjoy the same immunity
as private sector trade unions. Before 1974 there was some doubt
whether this was so because NHS employees are Crown employees[2] and the Trade Disputes Act (1906 and 1965) did not expressly bind the Crown. TULRA (s.30) states specifically that its
provisions bind the Crown, so this area of doubt has now been
cleared up. A further doubt about the extent of immunity of
trade unions in the public sector still exists however because
of the uncertainty in the legal definition of 'trade dispute'[3]
whilst TULRA widened the definition of a trade dispute in 1974,
it did not extend it to include a 'political dispute'. Recent
judicial decisions have suggested that industrial action by public
sector employees would be legitimate if perceived for a purpose
connected with collective bargaining even if it also related to
other matters such as government policy,[4] but they do not
preclude the possibility that a trade dispute in the public sector
could be defined as essentially a 'political dispute' and this could
affect industrial action in the NHS.

To the extent that a dispute in the NHS is within the definition of a 'trade dispute' as defined by statute, how wide are
trade union immunities in 1980? Before 1980, as has been stated,

industrial action gained immunity from actions in tort as long as it was taken 'in contemplation or furtherance of a trade dispute'. This immunity covered all forms of industrial action including picketing as long as it was peaceful. The courts between 1976 and 1980 attempted to curtail this immunity by giving an objective, restrictive definition of the 'Golden Formula'. This line of reasoning was finally brought to a halt in the cases of Daily Express v. McShane[5] and Duport Steel Ltd v. Sirs[6] where the House of Lords finally decided that the approach to the 'Golden Formula' should be a subjective one, the courts asking themselves whether the trade union officials honestly believed that their action would further the trade dispute. The scope of trade union immunity was restored to what it had been thought to be in 1976 when the TULRA (Amendment) Act was passed, namely that if contracts of employment or commercial contracts were threatened, interfered with or breached, there was no course of action in law for employers as long as the industrial action came within the 'Golden Formula'. Hence most forms of secondary industrial action were lawful. The Employment Act 1980 (EA) changed the state of trade union immunities quite substantially. The Act curtails trade union immunities in two main areas, secondary industrial action (blacking or secondary strikes) and picketing. The Act limits immunity for peaceful picketing (Section 16) to the employee's place of work except for trade union officials (lay or full-time) who must be representative of members who are on the picket line.[7] Section 17 limits immunity for breaches of commercial contracts by trade unions to breaches undertaken during secondary action which interferes with the supply of goods or services between the primary employer and the employer to whom the secondary action relates. Action taken to disrupt the supply of goods or services which are being produced by an 'associated employer' of the employer involved in the dispute in substitution for the primary employer is also given immunity. In both cases the immunity is subject to the objective test to be applied by the courts that the action is 'likely to achieve that purpose'.

How will this affect the industrial action in the Health Service? It could, if used, curb industrial action in a number of ways. First, limiting legal picketing to the place of work of the employee means that employees of a health authority who join a picket line outside a hospital that is threatened with closure will not be 'licensed' if they are not employed by the particular hospital. This means that management could take them to court by naming them in a civil action. Secondly, if, for example, members of the National Union of Public Employees (NUPE) withdraw their labour at the general infirmary over some local dispute and NUPE members at other hospitals in the area join them in sympathy, then the workers at the other hospitals would not gain immunity for any commercial contracts they might breach. This is because the principal purpose of the secondary action is certainly unlikely to be the disruption of goods or services between the two hospitals and therefore would not gain immunity under the new Act.

However, it is a fact that, even during the increasing incidence of industrial action in the NHS during the 1970s, full strike action was the exception rather than the rule due to the unique nature of the work done in the NHS. More usually action short of a strike is taken, such as a work to rule, go-slow, overtime ban or the provision of emergency services only. In this situation the sanctions management have at their disposal against the indidivual become far more important than any collective sanctions. The ability to use these sanctions results from the fact that while taking industrial action of this sort, an individual is usually in breach of his own contract of employment from which he has no immunity in the statutory provisions. The ultimate sanction is dismissal and management cannot be challenged on the fairness of dismissal in an Industrial Tribunal if the dismissals take place during industrial action and management does not discriminate between employees, either in dismissing them or in re-engaging them after the industrial action is over (s. 62 EPCA).

Obviously, this is a last resort and is not used with great frequency in the Health Service. However, there are actions short of dismissal which management can take if it can be shown that an individual is committing a fundamental breach of contract.

After the high level of industrial action during the 'winter of discontent' in 1979, the government issued a circular entitled 'If Industrial Relations Break Down' (HC(79)20), setting out those options in the following extract.

Restricted Performance of Duties
Where staff report for duty normally but refuse to carry out their normal duties by means of working to rule, 'blacking' certain areas of work, by selecting those duties they will carry out, or by deliberately restricting production, they are usually in breach of contract. An employee is not entitled to his remuneration for any pay period unless he can prove substantial performance of his contractual obligations during that pay period. Appropriate forms of management response where there has been a breach of contract will depend on local circumstances but will usually consist of one of the following courses of action:-
i if less than the full range of duties is acceptable to management in the sense that it is willing to accept specific but limited services the staff concerned should at the outset of the action be given notice (say 24 or 48 hours in advance of the sanctions being applied) that while they refuse to undertake normal working they are in breach of contract and are not entitled to full contractual pay. Terms which would then be offered might be one of the following. Terms (a) would be for staff to be offered such proportion of normal

payments as the Authority considers reasonable for the proportion of normal duties performed. Management should be careful to ensure that there has been a clear and valid directions to the employee to perform his full duties and that any payments should not be taken as an acceptance of or acquiescence in the employee's action. It is not necessary for authorities to devise complicated formulae for assessment purposes and a standard proportion of normal wages for groups of staff would usually be appropriate. It is sufficient that the Authority should offer a payment which they consider reasonable. The offer should be expressed to be ex gratia and should not be the subject of negotiation. In very exceptional circumstances, Authorities may consider that it is justifiable to continue full pay for partial working, but this should not be the normal course of action. Terms (b) would be to make clear that pay will be stopped while the industrial action continues but that management are prepared to pay (on a full-time basis) that number of staff required to maintain the level of service offered;

ii if less than full service is NOT acceptable to management and the Authority can establish that the duties not being undertaken or are being undertaken in an improper manner are among those which the employee has a contractual obligation to do, this could justify the sending home of the staff concerned without pay, as a serious and material breach of contract. In such a case, the appropriate staff side representative should be informed of management's intention to send home those staff who are not prepared to perform in a proper manner their full range of duties from an operative date. A warning notice should also be issued in writing to each of the staff concerned. The exact form of notice sent will depend upon the circumstances of the case and should be the subject of legal advice. Each of the staff concerned should be asked to acknowledge receipt of the notice by signing a copy of it. Where after such notice an employee does not agree to perform in a proper manner the full range of his duties, a further letter should be issued formally suspending him from duty without pay but inviting him to resume the normal range of duties appropriate to his grade. Again, a receipt should be asked for. The operative date for the action should normally be the date of receipt of the second letter and there should be at least 2 clear working days between the issue of the first and second letters. In all cases it should be made clear that this action does not amount to termination of employment and is not being applied as a disciplinary measure within the terms of Section XXXIV of the General Whitley Council Handbook.

The advice in the circular and in the annex is linked with a government policy which attempts to give local management more autonomy in dealing with disputes, and allow the government to

be seen to be withdrawing. The likelihood of disputes being
purely locally based in the future is not great however. Nor
will local managements have any significant power to settle.
Whilst the tactical benefits of using these sanctions will obviously
vary greatly depending upon the situation, there is a considerable risk that management through exercising these sanctions
may escalate a dispute without resolving it, so increasing the
likelihood of patients and public suffering harm. The advice in
the circular reveals the wide powers management have in taking
action against individuals, rather than unions, during industrial
disputes. If used, these sanctions could have a far greater
deterrant affect on employees taking industrial action in the
future than a criminal sanction (s.5 CPPA).

PART II: THE LAW AND COLLECTIVE BARGAINING

The lack of a positive right to strike in Great Britain is balanced
by the fact that legal sanctions cannot be used against a strike
purely because it is in breach of a collective agreement or an
agreement to go to arbitration. In this second part to the chapter we look at the law surrounding arbitration/conciliation and
its importance in the NHS. We then go on to look at the new
legal rights, which are only available to trade unions and trade
unionists, supporting collective bargaining. It is also important
to note that the use of strike action in place of using the new
legal machinery, for example on redundancy, does not in itself
allow the application of legal sanctions.

Arbitration and Conciliation
Arbitration and conciliation in Britain are voluntary processes
in two senses: first, they require the consent of both parties
and secondly, arbitration awards are not normally legally binding as between the collective parties. The Industrial Courts Act
(1919) established a permanent arbitration body, the Industrial
Court and also empowered the Minister of State to appoint single
arbitrators. Access to the court was limited: unions and employers had to refer the dispute to the Secretary of State who had
to see that two conditions were fulfilled before he referred the
dispute to the Court – one, the consent of the parties must be
obtained and, secondly, their own domestic machinery exhausted. A full analysis of the court's work from 1958–66 has been
published,[8] but does not give a breakdown of either the public sector's use of the court or of its use by the NHS. However, in a breakdown of the Court's awards 1967–9, Hepple and
O'Higgins[9] show that out of 38 references to the Court, 7 were
concerned with public employees of which 2 were from unions
in the NHS. One was concerned with payment of allowances to
radiographers for emergency duties and the other concerned
the grading of an individual administrative post. The outcome of
these references is not given. Between 1948 and 1966, some 158
general claims were referred to arbitration (which includes

references to the Industrial Disputes Tribunal, see below) from
the Health Services.[10] Some analysis of arbitration awards in the
NHS between 1948 and 1955 is given by Clegg and Chester.[11] Of
the 53 major settlements in the NHS in those years 26 were the
result of arbitration. Over half of these claims were made under
the Industrial Courts Act, but a large proportion were referred
unilaterally to the Industrial Disputes Tribunal (IDT). Two of
these references were made by management, the rest by the
staff side, of these 16 could be said to be 'won' by the staff
side, in that the award was more than the last offer by management. A total of 8 of the awards could be said to have been 'lost'
by the staff side.

The nature of the claims varied tremendously, in particular
references to the IDT (or as it was before 1951, the National
Arbitration Tribunal) varied from a number of claims for a 44-
hour week by the Ancillary Staffs Council, to attempts to obtain
improved wage settlements for general wage claims. Others (a
considerable number) concerned individuals, and in particular,
disputes over the correct grading of administrative and clerical
officers under the regrading agreement of 1951. The awards of
the Industrial Court (consisting of an independent permanent
Chairman and representatives of employers and employees,
usually one of each) were not legally binding, however those of
the IDT were.

The history of the IDT dates back to 1940, when Order 1305
established the National Arbitration Tribunal, the object being
to deal with the problems of wage adjustment without recourse
to strikes and lockouts. After the government prosecuted strikers
under the Order in 1950, the unions campaigned for its repeal
and it was replaced in 1951 by Order 1376. Under the new Order,
the power to prosecute strikers disappeared and the NAT was
replaced by the IDT. However, the procedure for unilateral
arbitration remained the same, either side being able to refer a
dispute to the Tribunal once internal procedures had been
exhausted. The awards of the IDT became legally binding in
that they became an implied term in the individual's contract of
employment. Out of 1277 awards made by the IDT between 1951
and 1959, 105 were made to unions in the NHS.[12] An analysis of
some of the results of the awards is given above. In 1959 the
IDT was dissolved. The main reason given for its dissolution
was that during peacetime it was 'out of keeping' with the
British system of industrial relations for 'one party to be coerced
by law'.[13] The NHS came third in a breakdown of applications
to the IDT by industry[14] and although it was used by well-
organised industries to an extent, it is apparent that the IDT
was predominately used by weakly organised sections of industry
or by unions who could not pose a credible strike threat.

It is clear by looking at references to both the Industrial Court
and the IDT, that NHS unions resorted to arbitration far more
frequently than many other sections of industry. A number of
reasons for this could be given, but two main ones stand out.

First, from the little analysis of statistics that has been done, it can be seen that more often than not the staff side achieved something by going to arbitration. Secondly, the low level of unionisation in the NHS before the early 1970s, and the difficulties in organising strike action meant that the staff side lacked any effective sanctions to impose upon management. One other reason is connected with the dissolution of the IDT itself. Management in the NHS was often under pressure not to give in to wage demands which were thought excessive by a government who were trying to hold down wages in the public sector. Management, therefore, often either agreed to arbitration or were forced unilaterally by the staff side to go before the IDT. Although the trade union movement generally is said to be in favour of a policy of 'non-intervention' by the law in industrial relations, the TUC favoured the reintroduction of unilateral arbitration on its evidence to the Donovan Commission.

One vestige of unilateral arbitration remained however after 1959. This was Section 8 of the Terms and Conditions of Employment Act. This section dealt with 'recognised' terms and conditions, allowing representative organisations from both sides of industry to claim that the recognised terms and conditions prevailing in that particular industry were not being observed. The Industrial Court could make an award which again became an implied term in the individual's contract of employment. However, employees in the NHS were excluded from this provision because there is 'statutory machinery for the settlement of remuneration' for NHS employees (namely the NHS/Remuneration and Conditions of Service/Regulations 1951). So since 1959 there has been no form of compulsory (to the extent of being unilateral) arbitration which applied to the NHS. In 1975 the Employment Protection Act replaced Section 8 with a wider provision, Schedule II. This allowed claims under a 'general level of terms and conditions' provision where there were no recognised terms and conditions operating in an industry. However, the Act had the proviso in Schedule II (3) that no claim could be reported by workers whose 'remuneration or terms and conditions, or minimum remuneration or terms and conditions, is or are fixed... in pursuance of any enactment'. In a case which reached the High Court[15] a group of ambulancemen from the north-western region claimed they were not being paid the 'general level of terms and conditions' of other ambulancemen in the country. The employers (North West Regional Health Authority) claimed Schedule II (3) barred the Central Arbitration Committee (CAC) from hearing the claim. The CAC decided to hear the claim because in reality the ambulancemen's wages were not 'fixed' by the Secretary of State directly. The High Court quashed their decision, saying that CAC had taken too narrow a view of the Schedule II (3). Thus all NHS employees were excluded from using Schedule II.

The use of independent arbitration by the NHS has been, until 1980 on an ad hoc basis. Clause 17 of the Whitley Council for the Health Services handbook says:

> every effort shall be made to accommodate differences of
> opinion between the two sides of the Council in order to
> reach an agreed decision. Where it is impossible to accom-
> plish this, it shall be given to the management or staff
> association concerned to seek arbitration in accordance with
> the terms of an arbitration agreement to be determined by
> the Council.

However, no national agreement on arbitration or on a dispute
procedure generally was agreed until 1980.[16] One reason given
is that some unions, after the dissolution of the IDT, wanted the
ability to opt for unilateral arbitration, while management wanted
a reserve power allowing the government to refuse to implement awards for policy reasons. However, the new agreement,
after making provision for conciliation by an independent chairman in parts 5, 6 and 7, in part 8 states that the dispute may
be referred to ACAS

(a) by either party to the dispute for conciliation or
(b) by joint agreement of the parties to the dispute for
     arbitration.

The ACAS (Advisory, Conciliation and Arbitration Service)
is an independent body, given statutory basis in the Employment
Protection Act (1975) where it was charged with the general
duty of 'promoting the improvement of industrial relations and
in particular of encouraging the extension of collective bargaining and its development, and where necessary, reform of collective machinery'. It consists of a 10-man council with an
independent chairman and 3 members nominated by the Confederation of British Industry (CBI), 3 from the Trades Union
Congress (TUC) and 3 independent members. Its powers in the
field of arbitration are, with the consent of both parties, to
appoint an arbitrator from outside, arrange for arbitration from
the staff of the Service or appoint a board of arbitration. Alternatively, cases can be referred to the Central Arbitration Committee. The CAC replaces the Industrial Court and consists of
an independent chairman, a representative from the employers
and a trade union representative. The ACAS most important
role, perhaps, has been in the field of conciliation. The history
of conciliation dates back to 1896, where under the Conciliation
Act the Secretary of State was empowered to 'inquire into the
causes and circumstances of a difference' between employers
and workmen. He could appoint a single person or a committee of
inquiry or investigation. This service was generally carried
out by employees in the Department of Employment where the
industrial relations service was supplied on both a central and
regional basis. In 1975 this was given a statutory basis with
the formation of ACAS.

The service does not break down references to it on an industrial basis, so it is difficult to say how frequently ACAS has offered its services or been used during disputes in the NHS. However, it can be said that ACAS has been used on an ad hoc basis until 1980, at least nationally with some local disputes procedures making explicit allowance for recourse to ACAS.

In conclusion it seems that arbitration has not performed the function it did in the 1950s or early 1960s in the NHS in recent years. During those years arbitration, whether unilateral or joint, served a purpose for both management and unions. To the unions it was a continuation of collective bargaining which quite often achieved results. In a situation where there was low unionisation, the lack of organisation necessary to pose a credible strike threat (nor the right climate of opinion perhaps)[17] and heavily centralised bargaining, arbitration and many advantages; especially unilateral arbitration. To management it was quite often an easy way of passing responsibility, when the government were putting pressure on them to keep wage awards low. The 1970s, on the other hand, have been a period of incomes policies whether statutory or non-statutory which have been more severe. This means that the use of arbitration is not going to achieve the same results, especially in a period when bargaining has become more localised for many workers, in the wake of the introduction of incentive bonus schemes.[18] The period has also seen a massive increase in unionisation in the NHS, low-paid ancillary workers have come to realise their power and have resorted to industrial action rather than arbitration. The ACAS has often been brought into a dispute after industrial action has been taken which was unheard of in the 1950s.

The ACAS's role is not confined to arbitration or conciliation but includes advice, and in 1979 they submitted their evidence to the Royal Commission on the National Health Service.[19] The report criticised heavily the state of industrial relations in the NHS and recommended some reforms. It was given enough weight by the Commission to be included as an appendix to the Report. In its evidence ACAS states that it has become increasingly involved in giving advice in the NHS. It also states that this was usually at the joint request of the parties and mostly at district level and below. The advice fell into three categories - eight Advisory Projects, nine 'Diagnostic Surveys' (medium-term studies designed to identify most causes of industrial problems), and one Inquiry.[20] It is important to note that the location of independent conciliation and advice has moved to the local level, where industrial relations problems now occur more often than at the centre.

Legal Support For Collective Bargaining

Trade Union Recognition. The Employment Protection Act (EPA) established a statutory recognition procedure which was predominately voluntary. The ACAS has the power to inquire into and issue a report on a union recognition dispute. If the report recommended recognition of a particular union(s) and an employer refused to follow that recommendation then the union concerned could opt for arbitration by the CAC, unilaterally. The CAC as an ultimate sanction, could make an award on terms and conditions which became an implied term in the individual's contract of employment. This provision (ss 11-17 EPA), has been repealed by the Employment Act 1980. There is now no separate statutory machinery for conciliation or arbitration in trade union recognition disputes. The machinery for certification of 'independent' trade unions introduced in the EPA, however, is still in existence.

TULRA introduced the category of an independent trade union; which is a trade union not under the domination or control of an employer or an employer's association, and 'not liable to interference by an employer...or association...tending towards such control'. Nearly all the new rights which the EPA gave to unions were limited to independent trade unions, and a Certification Officer was appointed to issue certificates of independence to a union that he 'determined' was independent. The General Council of the TUC had wished to deny certain rights which were in the EPA to those unions which were not affiliated to the Congress, or recognised by Congress as bone fide.[21] However, the Certification Officer has issued certificates to 'staff associations' and other professional associations which meet the definition of independence but are in competition with affiliated unions. This has importance in the NHS where many certified unions/associations are not affiliated to the TUC yet have full negotiating rights on Whitley Councils such as the Royal College of Nursing and the British Medical Association. This is a cause of some conflict in the NHS at the moment; some unions affiliated to the TUC will not sit with non-TUC affiliates during negotiations.

There are also a significant number of employee organisations who are recognised for bargaining purposes by NHS management but who do not have a certificate of independence. Such associations as the Association of Hospital and Residential Care Officers, the Society of Remedial Gymnasts and the British Dietetic Association are given similar rights as certified unions under Whitley Council agreements but they do not have a statutory right to them. There are ten such organisations in the NHS at the present time.

Legal Rights Of Trade Unions. The EPA gave a number of rights to certified, independent trade unions. At the present time some of these rights have had a more important impact on

NHS industrial relations than others. We will take those rights which have had a lesser impact first, going on to look at those rights which have had a bigger impact in more detail later.

Sections 17-21 of the Act gave trade unions a limited right to disclosure of information. The Act imposed a duty on employers to disclose any information in his possession which is both:

(a) 'information without which the trade union representative would be to a material extent impeded in carrying on with him such collective bargaining' and

(b) 'information which it would be in accordance with good industrial relations practice that he should disclose to them for the purposes of collective bargaining'. However, there are exceptions to this rule, for example, employers are not under a duty to divulge any information which would be against the 'interests of national security'. A union may complain to the CAC that an employer is not disclosing information which he is required to do. Disclosure of information has not been made an issue of in the NHS at this point and no case has reached the CAC.

Under Section 99 of the Act an employer is under a duty to consult with representatives of an independent trade union where an employer is preparing to dismiss as redundant 100 or more employees at least 90 days before the dismissals take place. Where an employer is preparing to dismiss as redundant 10 or more employees, he must consult at least 30 days before the first dismissals take effect. This provision, for the very reason that mass redundancies are rare in the NHS, has not had a great impact on health service industrial relations.

A provision which has had an important impact in the NHS is the right of a trade union official to be paid time off to perform trade union 'duties' and the right to time off for trade union 'activities'. The legislation (now Sections 27 and 28 Employment Protection (Consolidation) Act) has its history in the Report of the Donovan Commission which encouraged the formalisation of the shop steward's role. The Report[22] specifically encouraged employers 'to conclude with unions representative of their employees agreements regulating the position of shop stewards in matters such as...facilities to meet with other stewards, the responsibilities of the chief steward (if any), pay while functioning as a steward in working hours; day release with pay for training'. The EPA put this into statutory form by allowing trade union officials 'reasonable' time off with pay to perform their duties. The Act does not define what is 'reasonable', nor does it give any detailed definition of what are trade union 'duties'. This is left to the ACAS Code of Practice[23] on the subject, which came into effect along with Sections 27 and 28 on 18 April 1978. As with other Codes of Practice issued by ACAS, it does not have the force of law but is to be taken into account in any proceedings before a Tribunal. Employees can appeal

to an Industrial Tribunal after they think that they have been
unreasonably refused time off, or refused payment for time off.
  The provision has been important in the NHS for a number of
reasons; not least is the fact that before the early 1970s shop
stewards were very rare animals in the NHS. The growth and
expansion of the functions of the shop steward in the NHS during the 1970s caused problems for management attempting to
define his/her role and limit his/her functions. It also caused
problems for the unions in attempting to train stewards and
obtain enough facilities for them to do their job properly. The
statutory right to time off introduced in 1978, therefore was
important. It was especially important in an organisation where
the availability of staff to perform their function as servants of
the public in the provision of health care is of prime importance.
The legislation precipitated agreements locally on time off and
facilities for trade unions, as well as national agreement giving
general guidelines on arrangements for time off.[24]
  An official's duties are defined in the ACAS Code (para 13)
as 'those duties pertaining to his/her role in the jointly agreed
procedures or customary arrangements for consultation, collective bargaining and grievance handling where such matters
concern the employer and any associated employer and their
employees'. In listing what duties might come under this definition the ACAS Code includes (c) 'meetings with other lay officials
or with full-time union officers on matters concerned with industrial relations between his or her employer and any associated
employer and their employees'. However, the General Whitley
Council agreement on facilities for staff organisations gives a
somewhat narrower definition of an official's duties:

> 6. The functions of an accredited representative for the pur-
> poses of this agreement, shall be to represent the members of
> the staff organisation concerned who are employed by the
> employing authority; to investigate any complaint or difficult
> by those members; to make representation on such matters to
> the management of the authority and co-operate with manage-
> ment to ensure that agreements of the Whitley Councils are
> observed. In this respect accredited representatives shall
> have due regard to the rules of their organisation.

The definition of trade union 'duties' is where many of the
disputes have arisen in connection with this legislation. Although
the TUC pamphlet on facilities for trade union representatives
envisaged the legislation being used as a bargaining tool, unions
have resorted to legislation to enforce what they see as their
rights. This has occurred in the NHS, where a number of tribunal decisions, following the lead given by the Employment
Appeal Tribunal[25] (EAT) have limited the definition of trade union
'duties'. It has been held in one case[26] that quarterly meetings
of NUPE Area Committee fell within the definition 'activities'
(s.28) rather than S.27. A regional council meeting of the

Confederation of Health Service Employees (COHSE) did not come within the definition of trade union duties according to an industrial tribunal.[27] The tribunal looked at the minutes of the meeting and held it was exclusively concerned with the organisation and administration of unions. In another case[28] a Royal College of Nursing steward who attended a number of national committee meetings was held not to be entitled to paid time off. The cases reveal that the tribunals are interpreting the legislation on the basis that it was not meant to allow trade union officials to become better representatives or inform themselves on union matters. The legislation's 'raison d'être' was to promote 'orderly' collective bargaining and 'good' industrial relations.

Another consequence of the legislation has been the further consolidation of the phenomenon of workplace bargaining in the NHS. The fact that shop stewards now have what in effect is statutory recognition, means that a 'de facto' recognition (grudgingly given in many cases) of stewards by NHS management, has been converted into a 'de jure' recognition of the role of the steward.

A second enactment seriously affecting the NHS is the Health and Safety at Work Act (HASAWA). This Act emphasised the importance of management responsibility for safety and for developing employee co-operation through consultation rather than by use of legal sanctions in solving health and safety problems. It legislated for a system of health and safety representatives and of health and safety committees - originally based on all employees but converted by subsequent legislation into a system based upon trade union appointed or elected representates. Health and safety prior to the Act had a very low priority within the NHS, partly because little legislation applied prior to HASAWA. The Health and Safety Executive (HSE) in 1978 carried out a pilot study of health and safety within the NHS[29] which showed that NHS buildings could be dangerous places for workers and for patients, and that the hazards in hospitals were diverse and complex. This created a clear challenge to the newly appointed health and safety representatives and health and safety committees. Trade union safety representatives enjoy quite wide powers under the legislation. They include the right to consult with the employer on health and safety issues; to investigate potential hazards; to investigate complaints by an employee he represents relating to a health and safety issue and to liaise with the HSE. Safety representatives are entitled to reasonable time off with pay, both to perform their functions and for training. An employing authority is required to establish a safety committee within three months of receiving a request in writing from two or more safety representatives.

The most important facet of these provisions in relation to industrial relations in the NHS, is that they are all based upon local, workplace representation. A safety representative is appointed to represent his members on a local basis and consult with management on a local basis. Quite often amongst unions in the NHS, it is the shop steward who is appointed as safety representative, so performing a dual function and therefore spending an increasing amount of time on trade union matters. Safety committees are appointed at a 'workplace' level. A workplace is defined as 'any place or places where the group or groups of employees' which a safety representative is appointed to represent 'are likely to frequent in the course of their employment or incidentally to it'. The consequence is, again, a further consolidation of workplace bargaining in contrast to the formal, centralised Whitley system of bargaining, the two systems working alongside (and sometimes in conflict) with each other.

In the NHS the consultative aspect of the health and safety legislation is important because as Crown employees, health authorities are exempt from some of the legal consequences of the legislation. HAWASA makes provision for the issuing of improvement notices (requiring a fault to be remedied within a specific time) and prohibition notices (where there is a risk of serious personal injury) by an inspector who discovers a contravention of the Act. However, health authorities are exempt from these notices. The Health and Safety Commission (HSC), empowered to develop policy on health and safety issues, is pressing for the removal of Crown immunity. In the meantime the HSE have been instructed to implement a 'Crown notice procedure'. This means that in circumstances which would normally lead to the issue of a prohibition or improvement notice, except for the immunity of the Crown, inspectors will issue a 'Crown enforcement notice'. However, the only sanction if an authority fails to comply, is for the issue to be taken up by the Department and the Executive. NHS officers, however, are personally responsible for health and safety and theoretically could be prosecuted under the Act.

Union Security. Union security is an issue which has aroused immense controversy in recent years; primarily because it is concerned with arguments about collective 'strength versus individual liberty'. In Britain a closed shop can either be pre-entry (requiring a specified union card as a condition of obtaining a job) or post-entry (requiring that the employee join one of a number of specified number of unions within a short period after commencing employment). In the first comprehensive survey carried out on the extent of the closed shop in Britain, McCarthy[30] discovered that at least one in every six workers was in a closed shop. Since then, the extent of the closed shop has spread and its form changed. Negotiated, formal arrangements between management and unions (Union Membership Agreements or UMAs) are the rule rather than the exception at the present time. In the most recent survey carried out[31] it was estimated that at least 5.2 million of the 22 million employees in Great Britain or 23 per cent of the workforce are covered by closed shop arrangements.

Prior to 1971 there was no legal protection for anyone who was

dismissed or who had action taken against him/her short of
dismissal for not being a union member in a closed shop situation. The 1971 Industrial Relations Act (IRA) created a 'right'
not to belong to a trade union; a parallel right to belong to a
trade union of one's own choosing was also created. It became
an 'unfair industrial practice' for an employer to prevent a
worker exercising the right. The Act also outlawed the pre-
entry closed shops and provided strict limits on what was in
effect a legalised closed shop, the 'agency shop'. The Act did
not eradicate the closed shop, however, many still continued
to exist, although it became difficult to negotiate new UMAs.

In 1974 TULRA repealed the IRA and with the Amendment
Act 1976 made it automatically 'fair' for an employer to dismiss
someone who refused to become a member of a trade union (or
who was expelled from a union) where a legally correct UMA
was in operation. The one exception was where an employee
objected on 'religious grounds' to joining a trade union.

The closed shop continued to spread during this period, and
more UMAs were negotiated. Union membership in the NHS
increased dramatically during the 1970s, from about one-third
of the workforce before 1970 to about two-thirds by 1980. In
some health authorities, union membership amongst manual
workers is over 90 per cent. In at least three health authorities
UMAs have been negotiated with manual workers, the agreements allowing for religious objections and excluding non-
members. There is the possibility of two UMAs being negotiated
in the near future. However, the Employment Act 1980 will make
the negotiation of new UMAs very unlikely in the NHS and elsewhere.

The Act widens the 'conscience clause' by which employees
can refuse to join a trade union on the grounds of a 'deeply
held personal conviction' and the objection can apply to a particular union or any trade union whatsoever.

Any limits to be placed on these very wide grounds for objection will have to be introduced by the courts. Secondly, any new
agreement negotiated must gain a majority of 80 per cent of those
entitled to vote in a secret ballot.[32] The Act also introduces the
right not to have action short of dismissal taken against an
employee for reasons of not being a member of a trade union. A
novel provision in British labour law is the right of action
against a trade union for unfair expulsion or refusal of admission introduced in the Act. This will give the right to an individual who thinks he has been unfairly expelled or refused
admission to a union, to appeal to an Industrial Tribunal. The
Tribunal will decide on the fairness of the refusal or expulsion
on the equity and general merits of the case, overruling a
trade union rule if necessary. The Tribunal can issue a declaration that a person be taken back into a union, if the union
refuses to take a person back, then an additional award of
compensation can be made.

These changes will only be relevant to a small number of

Authorities in the Health Service, particularly where there has
been some pressure for negotiation of closed shop agreements.

PART III: INDIVIDUAL EMPLOYMENT LAW

Prior to the introduction of the Contracts of Employment Act
1963 (CEA), employees in Great Britain enjoyed very little
statutory protection. Individual employment law centred around
the contract of employment the common law treating the employer
and employee (or as thon referred to 'master and servant') as
free and equal contracting parties, ignoring the obvious dis-
crepancy in their bargaining power.

Since 1963 (and particularly since 1971) there has been a
spate of legislation providing the individual with protection
mainly during and at the termination of the contract of employment, which has led to a measure of job security for the employee. Since the CEA (which was viewed by both sides of industry
at the time as a major break from the tradition of 'voluntarism')
the legislation has included the Redundancy Payments Act 1965,
which established the statutory right to a severance payment
calculated according to length of service. The IRA which established the right for an employee not to be unfairly dismissed
and the EPA which gave rights in relation to maternity leave and
guaranteed payment for employees laid off work. The Race
Discrimination Act 1976 (RRA) and Sex Discrimination Act 1975
(SDA) which made discrimination on the basis of sex and race
unlawful particularly in the field of employment and the Equal
Pay Act 1970 (EqPA) which attempted to introduce equal pay
for women employed on 'like' or 'equivalent' work to men. Most
of this legislation can be enforced through an Industrial Tribunal.

This legislation has attempted to give employment protection
to employees which it could be said collective bargaining had
failed to do. It has provided a statutory 'floor' of rights for the
individual, which could be said to have created a 'property
right' for the employee in his job. Some would argue that this
has been at the expense of the employer's right to recruit and
manage his workforce. What follows is an examination of these
considerations in relation to the NHS as the law stands in
October 1980.

Position Of Crown Employees
One of the leading commentators on English law has said 'The
Crown is not bound by statute unless expressly named or bound
by necessary implications'.[33]

The courts have held that NHS employees are Crown servants.[34]
The position is complicated however by the fact that for the
purposes of some employment legislation NHS employees are not
Crown employees (e.g. s.121 (5) EPA), whereas in other statutes the Crown is specifically covered (e.g. TULRA), or

special provision is made for NHS employees (e.g. ss 111 and
112 EPCA).

The CEA which required (inter alia) employers to give their
employees minimum periods of notice to terminate employment
did not apply to the Crown and therefore to the NHS. However,
a circular (HM(64)69) was sent to authorities in the NHS
instructing them to follow the terms of the Act. But the position
is still far from satisfactory and unnecessarily complicated.

The Contract of Employment

Many of the statutory rights resolve around the existence of a
contract of employment and its terms. There is no statutory
requirement in relation to the form of the contract other than
that a written statement specifying some of the terms of employment must be given to the employee within 13 weeks of the
commencement of employment.[35] These terms and conditions
include:

1. the scale or rate of remuneration;
2. intervals at which remuneration is to be paid;
3. the title of the job which the employee is employed to do;
4. any disciplinary rules applicable to the employee or reference
   to a document which is accessible to the employee and which
   specifies these rules;
5. the specification of a person to whom the employee can apply
   for the purpose of seeking redress of any grievance relating
   to employment and also a person to whom he can apply if he
   is dissatisfied with any disciplinary decision relating to him.

The written statement is *not* the contract of employment as
such but provides evidence of some of the more important terms
and conditions of the contract.

The contract consists of a variety of terms express or implied.
An important source of terms, especially in the NHS, is the
provision of collective agreements negotiated by recognised
trade unions. In the NHS the incorporation of such terms is
usually by express reference in the employee's written statement
to the Whitley Council Agreements, and any alterations or modifications therein. Once referred to in this way the relevant
provisions of a collective agreement become legally binding as
between the employer and employee, despite the fact none of
these provisions are usually enforceable by the parties to the
collective agreement as against themselves.

Excluded Class of Employee

Each statutory right has its own qualification requirements and
if these cannot be met then the employee does not have the
benefit of the particular statutory protection. For example, an
employee has to be continuously employed for 52 weeks before
he or she can claim unfair dismissal, and two years for redundancy payments and maternity rights. This requirement has

caused particular difficulty for NHS employees because of the traditional mobility of labour between authorities. The transfer of an employee from one employer to another has the effect of breaking the continuity of employment, unless the second employer is an 'associated employer'. It has recently been held by the Court of Appeal[36] that an organisation like a health authority is not associated with another authority even though part of the same region for the purposes of the continuous service requirement. Obviously, this causes great difficulty for some groups of NHS employees whose only way of achieving promotion is through movement between authorities. Despite this restriction on statutory rights however, contractual rights have been negotiated through the Whitley Council procedure to give continuity of employment between authorities for the purposes of sick pay, redundancy, maternity and pension rights.

Another qualification requirement which particularly effects NHS employees is that requiring a minimum number of hours to be worked each week before an employee can be eligible to claim some of the statutory rights. For example, before an employee can claim unfair dismissal, he or she must normally work at least 16 hours a week or 8 hours a week after five years' continuous service. This requirement excludes a large proportion of part-time employees. Around 30 per cent of all NHS employees work part-time.[37] Out of 355 760 nursing and midwifery staff employed in 1977, 132 156 were part-timers. Although the definition of part-time worker for the purposes of these statistics is not the same as the legal definition, it is estimated that at least two thirds of these employees do not work the requisite amount of hours and so are excluded from statutory protection. A large proportion of part-time employees are women (90 per cent).

Unfair Dismissal
It was not until 1971, following the recommendations of the Donovan Commission, that the IRA introduced a statutory right for an employee not to be unfairly dismissed, the primary purpose of which was to provide to individual employees a form of protection against arbitrary termination of employment. The Act listed a number of potentially fair reasons for dismissal; namely lack of capability, misconduct, redundancy, where continued employment would be a breach of a statutory enactment, and finally some other substantial reason such as a reorganisation for economic necessity. Later legislation amended the unfair dismissal provisions so that a number of automatically unfair reasons for dismissal were created relating to discrimination on grounds of sex, race, trade union membership and activities and pregnancy.

Once the employer has shown that he dismissed for a permitted reason the Industrial Tribunal then has to be satisfied that:

in the circumstances (including the size and administrative resources of the employer's undertaking) the employer acted

reasonably or unreasonably in treating it as a sufficient
reason for dismissing the employee; and that question shall
be determined in accordance with equity and the substantial
merits of the case. (s57(3) EPCA as amended)

The main issue in most unfair dismissal claims is that connected with the determination of fairness arising from this test.
Not surprisingly it has provided a stimulus to the parties to
collective bargaining to develop and improve their own voluntary
procedures to deal with dismissal disputes. The legislation has
been supplemented by the issuing of a Code of Practice on
'Disciplinary Practice and Procedures in Employment' by ACAS.
Although the Code does not itself have the force of law it is
admissible in evidence before a Tribunal and any of its provisions must be taken into account in the Tribunal decision.
Therefore it is not surprising to find that the negotiation of
disciplinary procedures has been an integral part of the impact
of the legislation and the NHS has not been immune from this
process. At national NHS level a disciplinary procedure was
agreed in 1975 although it was acknowledged at the time that
the procedure was only interim and that a more detailed procedure should be negotiated.[38] However, since then Authorities
have negotiated their own detailed disciplinary procedures and
it would now appear unnecessary to attempt to negotiate a
detailed procedure at national level.

Once management have adopted a fair procedure, provided
they follow that procedure, Tribunals tend to be satisfied that
employers have acted reasonably. This is because when applying the fairness test Tribunals are concerned to see whether the
employer in question acted reasonably and not whether they
would have formed the same opinion as the employer. In other
words, they cannot substitute their own decision for that of the
employer. However, what has come out of the case law is that
disciplinary procedures are not relevant to every type of dismissal. Therefore, if applied in an inappropriate case this
could result in the dismissal being unfair. For example, one of
the requirements of the fair disciplinary procedure is that a
warning or several warnings should be given indicating the
consequences of further misconduct. Tribunals have held that
to give a warning to a person in relation to their ill health is
inappropriate and would not necessarily satisfy the fairness
test.[39] As a result the courts and tribunals have recognised the
necessity for adopting different procedures for the different
permitted reasons for dismissal. For example, the procedure to
be adopted in a case of poor performance should be different
to that adopted when selecting someone for redundancy. As yet
very few authorities have adopted any procedures other than
a disciplinary procedure and therefore are at risk of not satisfying the fairness test.

In relation to all these procedures, however, Tribunals have
begun to ignore procedural irregularities where it would make

'no difference' to the ultimate decision to dismiss. For example, the NHS has been through some major reorganisations and is at present going through another reorganisation. As a result it will no doubt become necessary to make certain employees redundant. Others will be dismissed despite their positions not being redundant, because for good sound business reasons the reorganisation is necessary. Before dismissing someone in this situation the tribunals have laid down a procedure requiring consultation with the employee.[40] The rationale being that by discussing the matter with the employee that may influence the way the employer carries out his reorganisation. However, where it can be shown that such consultation would make no difference, then such a procedural fault will not be fatal to the employer's case particularly where the procedural fault is technical rather than substantive.[41]

Redundancy

As mentioned above the statutory redundancy provisions do not relate to the NHS. The EPCA however make special provisions for Crown employees, but before considering these let us examine the meaning of the word 'redundancy'. An employee is taken to be dismissed by reason of redundancy if the dismissal is attributable wholly or mainly to

1. total cessation, either actual or prospective, of the business, either entirely or in the place of employment
2. cessation of diminution of a particular kind of work, actual or prospective, generally or in the place of employment.

Where a redundancy exists the legislation compensates the employee for loss of the value of the job. There is a formulated scale of compensation which is based on the length of service and the age of the employee. Where an employer offers a redundant employee suitable alternative employment then if the employee unreasonably refuses that offer, he or she will lose the right to a redundancy payment. An employer is entitled to be reimbursed 41 per cent of the payment from the Secretary of State for Employment who maintains a Redundancy Fund for this purpose.

Returning to the special provisions for Crown employees, where the Secretary of State is of the opinion that but for being Crown employees they would be entitled to a redundancy payment then he may make arrangements for reimbursement to the particular health authority involved on a similar scale to the statutory provisions. He is entitled, however, to make 'appropriate modifications' to the statutory provisions. In the case of the NHS he has approved a scheme which modifies the statutory provisions in particular in relation to whether a post is to be regarded as suitable alternative employment and whether it was unreasonably refused. The modifications relate to the 'place' and to the 'capacity' in which the employee would be employed.

a. *Place* - a post is normally suitable in place if it involves
no additional travelling expenses or is within 6 miles of
the employee's home. If the new post is at a greater distance, the fact that assistance normally outweigh any
added difficulties in travel, but exceptionally an employee's
special personal circumstances will be considered in comparison with the travel undertaken by other employees in
comparable grades. If the post is too far for daily travel,
it will be reasonable, since removal expenses will be payable, to require staff (other than those who can be expected
to seek employment in their neighbourhood) to move home
unless they can adduce special circumstances such as age.

b. *Capacity* - suitable alternative employment may not necessarily be in the same grade; the employment should be
judged in the light of the employee's qualifications and
ability to perform the duties. Nor need it be at exactly the
same pay. A post carrying salary protection for the employee should on that fact alone be treated as suitable in capacity.[42]

This modification would appear severely to restrict a Tribunal's
discretion in deciding whether an employee in the NHS has
'unreasonably' refused suitable alternative employment.

Maternity Rights
Whitley Council Agreements have provided maternity rights for
NHS employees for some time, even prior to the introduction of
statutory rights in this respect. The current agreement is in
part more generous, in others more restrictive than the statutory provision. (Where it is more restrictive the statutory provisions will prevail.) For example, in relation to maternity pay,
a women has the right to receive such pay provided she has
been employed for at least 12 months prior to her application for
maternity leave. This right is not lost where there is a transfer
of employment between authorities. In contrast there is only a
statutory entitlement to maternity pay where a woman has been
employed by the same or an associated employer for two continuous years immediately before the beginning of the eleventh
week before the expected week of confinement. However, the
present Whitley agreement imposes restrictions upon the right
to maternity leave itself. Notification of the expected confinement shall be made to the employing authority not less than
three months before the expected week of confinement and the
employee must declare in writing her intention to continue in
service for a minimum of three months after the expiry of the
leave. The statute makes no provision as to the right to maternity leave, but there are certain requirements a woman must
fulfil before she has a right to maternity pay if she does absent
herself from work. She must inform her employer (in writing if
he so requests) at least three weeks before her absence begins
or, if that is not reasonably practicable, as soon as is reason-

ably practicable, that she will be (or is) absent from work wholly or partly because of pregnancy or confinement.

Under the Whitley Council arrangements the amount of maternity pay depends on an actual return to work. In contrast the statutory entitlement is all received during the confinement, and it is irrelevant that a woman does not return to work. Needless to say the Whitley entitlement is greater than that provided for by the law.

In addition to a right to maternity pay, a woman is also entitled to return to work after a period of confinement provided certain qualifications and notification requirements are fulfilled. The necessary qualifications are similar to the statutory qualifications for eligibility to maternity pay. However, the notification requirements are somewhat complicated. (The Whitley agreement makes no provision for a right to return to work.) Briefly, a woman must inform her employer in writing that she wishes to return to work at least 21 days before her absence begins (or as soon as reasonably practicable thereafter) specifying her expected week of confinement, or if confinement has occurred, the date of confinement. The employer can request a medical certificate stating the expected week of confinement, which it is the practice of most authorities to do.

Not earlier than 49 days after the expected week of confinement, the employer may make a written request for confirmation of the woman's intention to return to work. This request must explain the consequences of failing to reply in time, because the woman must give written confirmation within 14 days of receiving the request (or, if that is not reasonably practicable, as soon as is reasonably practicable thereafter). The woman must then give 21 days written notice of the date of her return, provided this is within 29 weeks of the week of the actual confinement. A woman who fulfils all these qualifications and notification requirements must be given back the job which she was employed to do under her original contract, except where

1. it is not practicable for reasons of redundancy
2. it is not reasonably practicable for other reasons but an offer of suitable alternative employment is made which the woman unreasonably refuses.

This latter provision, which has just been introduced by the EA (s.12), is somewhat similar to that contained in the redundancy provisions, and in view of the size and administrative resources of the NHS it is likely to be interpreted strictly by Tribunals.

A new provision allowing paid time off for antenatal care to an employee after her first visit to a clinic, has been introduced by the EA (s.13). An employee shall 'have the right not to be unreasonably refused time-off during her working hours to enable her to keep the appointment'. The word 'unreasonably' is not defined and an employee must show either a certificate from a registered midwife or an appointment card showing that the appointment has been made. If an employee claims that she has been unreasonably refused paid time off then she can make a claim to an Industrial Tribunal.

These provisions are very important in the NHS where a large proportion of women are employed. However, the newly negotiated Whitley agreement will perhaps have more actual bearing on what happens in practice than the more stringent statutory provisions.

Discrimination In Employment
Two important statutes have attempted to tackle discrimination in employment. The SDA and RRA recognises three forms of discrimination; direct discrimination; indirect discrimination; and discrimination by victimisation. These make it unlawful to discriminate in offering employment, in affording access to opportunities for promotion and other facilities during employment and in the termination of employment.

Direct discrimination is where an employer treats an employee 'less favourably' than he treats other employees on grounds of sex or marital status or racial grounds. The legislation also recognises that women, married persons and blacks suffer from a legacy of past discrimination which in many cases prevents direct comparison with men, single persons and whites respectively. For this reason the statutes seek to cover conduct which may be said to have a discriminatory effect on an underprivileged group, although the discriminator has no intention to discriminate. The concepts of indirect or effects discrimination in the British legislation bears a close resemblance and may owe its origin to the interpretation by the United States Supreme Court of Title VII of the US Civil Rights Act 1964. Therefore it is not surprising to find that in order to establish indirect discrimination under British law a complainant must establish:

(1) the employer applied a 'requirement or condition' which he applies or would apply equally to members of the other sex, or to single persons, or to persons of another racial group as the case may be;
(2) the proportion of the complainant's sex, or of married persons, or racial group is considerably smaller than the proportion of persons of the other sex, or of single persons or of persons not of that racial group, as the case may be, who can comply with it;
(3) the requirement or condition is to the complainant's detriment because he or she cannot comply with it.

It is then for the employer to prove that the requirement or condition is 'justifiable' irrespective of the sex of the person to whom it is applied or irrespective of marital status or irrespective of colour, race, nationality or ethnic or national origins, as the case may be. The only exception to this is where the employer can show a 'genuine occupational qualification' which requires the employment of someone, say, of a particular sex or race.

At the same time as the SDA came into force the EqPA also became law. This Act implied an 'equality clause' into every contract of employment where a woman is employed on 'like work' or equivalent work (where a job evaluation scheme has been carried out and a man and woman's job have been rated as equivalent) to a man.

Persons who bring proceedings, give evidence or information, allege a contravention or otherwise act under the discrimination legislation are protected from victimisation unless the allegation is false and not made in good faith. The criterion for protection is that the person victimised must have been treated less favourably by the discriminator than in those circumstances he treats or would treat other persons.

The legislation is not affording in practice the protection it was set up to achieve. This is mainly because the burden of proving discrimination is placed on the complainant and the restrictive way the courts and tribunals permit evidence of discrimination to be presented before them. Also the enforcement agencies, the Equal Opportunities Commission and Commission for Racial Equality, have had little impact in practice.

Health authorities, who employ a large proportion of women and blacks compared with other employers, are particularly sensitive to the legislation. However, because of the large number of part-time women employees there is inevitably some indirect discrimination which is not regarded as unlawful under British law, although it may be unlawful under EEC law.

Other Rights

There are various other additional rights such as the right to have time off for public duties, and to be paid while suspended on medical grounds, which provide the statutory floor of rights referred to at the commencement of this section. Their effect on individual employment protection in the NHS has been significant, despite a rather restrictive interpretation of the legislation by courts and tribunals.

REFERENCES AND NOTES

1 See Dworkin, G. (1978), 'Industrial Relations and Contracts', Health Services Manpower Review, University of Keele, November, who argues that the legislation was used to bolster up a convention that certain classes of employee, although free to take industrial action, did not do so and that the convention has now gone.
2 See Pfizer Corporation v. Minister of Health (1963).
3 Express Newspapers Ltd and another v. Keys and others (1980) IRLR 247.

4 NWL Ltd v. Woods (1979) IRLR 478.

5 McShane and Ashton v. Express Newspapers Ltd (1980) IRLR 35.

6 Duport Steel Ltd and others v. Sirs and others (1980) IRLR 116.

7 The Employment Act also allows Codes of Practice to be published by the Secretary of State for Employment.

8 Wedderburn, K.W., and Davies, P.L. (1969), 'Employment Grievances and Disputes Procedures in Britain', Berkeley and Los Angeles.

9 Hepple, B.A., and O'Higgins, Paul (1971), 'Public Employee Trade Unions in the UK: The Legal Framework', Institute of Labour and Industrial Relations, p.200.

10 Ibid., p.205.

11 Clegg, H., and Chester, T.E. (1957), 'Wage Policy and the Health Service', Blackwell.

12 McCarthy, W.E.J. (1968), 'Compulsory Arbitration in Britain: The Work of the Industrial Disputes Tribunal' (Royal Commission on Trade Unions and Employers Associations) Research Paper no.8, HMSO, p.36.

13 Ibid., p.33.

14 Ibid., p.36.

15 R v. Central Arbitration Committee ex parte North Western Regional Health Authority (1978) IRLR 405.

16 Now part XXXV of the General Whitley Council Handbook (GWCH).

17 Clegg and Chester talk about an 'outburst of public indignation' rather than public sympathy being aroused if the strike weapon was used by NHS workers.

18 National Board for Prices and Incomes Report No.29. Pay and Conditions of Manual Workers in Local Authorities, NHS, Gas and Water supply.

19 Royal Commission on National Health Service (Chairman Sir Alec Merrison) Report (cmnd 7615 July 1979).

20 This is the in-depth work ACAS has been involved with in the NHS. Short-term advisory visits rose from 110 in 1976 to 142 in 1977 and the number of applications for collective conciliation from 36 in 1976 to 62 in 1977.

21 Which roughly means organisations which do not compete with affiliated unions and which observe other principles of what the General Council regards as 'good trade union behaviour'.

22 Royal Commission on Trade Unions and Employers' Associations (1968).

23 ACAS Code of Practice no.3, Time off for Trade Union Duties and Activities.

24 See Department of Health and Social Security Advance Letter (GC) 2/76 'Facilities for Staff Organisations', to replace Section XXIII of General Whitley Council Handbook, Conditions of Service.

25 See Sood v. GEC Elliot Process Automation Ltd (1979)

IRLR 416; Young v. Carr Fastners Ltd (1979) IRLR 420; and RHP Bearings Ltd v. Brookes (1979) IRLR 453.

26 Freebon v. Devon AHA/COIT 1979.

27 Smith v. Kent AHA/COIT 1979.

28 Wells v. North Yorkshire AHA/COIT 1979.

29 Health and Safety Executive Pilot Study: Working Conditions in the Medical Service, London HSE 1978.

30 McCarthy, W.E.J. (1964), 'The Closed Shop in Britain', Blackwell.

31 London School of Economics - Gennard, Dunn and Wright. Early results published in Department of Employment (1980), 'Gazette', HMSO.

32 This in effect means UMAs negotiated before the Act's provisions take effect are subject to the wider conscience clause and any dismissal will be judged to be fair or unfair according to that clause. Agreements negotiated after the Act will also be subject to the 80 per cent ballot rule and any dismissal in a closed shop situation when the agreement has not been approved in such a ballot will be unfair.

33 Halsbury's Laws of England, vol.7 (Constitutional Law, para. S36).

34 Pfizer v. Ministry of Health (1963) A11ER 779; Woods v. Leeds AHA (1974) IRLR 204.

35 Now S.1 EPCA.

36 Gardiner v. London Borough of Merton (1980) IRLR 472, overruling Hillingdon AHA v. Kauders (1979) IRLR 197.

37 Health and Social Services Statistics (1978).

38 The procedure is part XXXIV of the GWC Handbook and allows for appeal to an Appeal Committee of a health authority both against a formal warning and dismissal. Appeal is also possible to the Regional Health Authority.

39 See Spencer v. Paragon Wallpapers Ltd (1976) 373; and Liverpool AHA (Teaching) Central and Southern District v. Edwards (1977) 471.

40 Hollister v. National Farmer's Union (1979) IRLR 238 and see Genower v. Ealing, Hammersmith v. Hounslow AHA (1980) IRLR 297.

41 Pillinger v. Manchester AHA (1979) IRLR 430 and Banerjee v. City and East London AHA (1978) IRLR 147.

42 Section XXV of the GWC Handbook.

PART IV

COLLECTIVE BARGAINING EXPERIENCE

Introduction

In this part, the structural issue of centralised bargaining in health services in Canada, USA and the UK is discussed and analysed by George Adams, David Beatty and Morley Gunderson. Taking the experience of the UK's highly centralised bargaining structure, the authors sound a cautionary note against the establishment of a similar degree of centralisation in Canada and the USA. Overcentralisation can act to obscure local needs and feelings for autonomy. Moreover this of itself can produce strains within the bargaining structure as, in the example of the UK, management and unions at hospital level enter into bargaining, in an attempt to accommodate local pressures in working practices and behaviour. The UK's experience shows that increased unionisation of health workers not only may lead to greater pressures locally, but provides more muscle for their collective organisations in centralised bargaining. In consequence the authors argue that in North America public policy should take more account of the structural considerations appropriate to collective bargaining in the health sector.

Chapters 10, 11 and 12 examine the collective bargaining experience of nurses, allied and nonprofessional workers and physicians in health care in the three countries. As their authors point out, the design of the distinctive bargaining structures in Canada, the USA and the UK for health manpower have been subject to changes, particularly over recent years. The changes have been the result of shifts in environmental influences and in the perceptions of the actors, especially the unions, in the industrial relations system of the health sector. These chapters seek to demonstrate the issues that have emerged within the centralisation-decentralisation dichotomy and the way in which they have evolved. For example in the UK, although the Whitley system with its consensus orientation was adopted as the system for the resolution of industrial relations issues, alternative mechanisms, which operated outside the Whitley Councils, have increasingly been used. In Canada and the USA a wide variety of bargaining models emerged in response to increased unionisation. Finally the authors point to the internal and external pressures on bargaining; the bargaining strategies employed by collective organisations; and the incidence of inter-union competition among the various classes of health manpower in each country.

9. STRUCTURAL ISSUE OF CENTRALISED BARGAINING IN HEALTH SERVICES: CANADA, USA AND UK

G. Adams, D. Beatty and M. Gunderson*

INTRODUCTION

Interest in the structural issue of centralised bargaining in the health sector must be seen as part of the evolution of collective bargaining generally in the three countries under review. The degree of centralisation under which collective bargaining is conducted is but one of the many inputs that has shaped, and has been shaped by, the outcomes and the other inputs of collective bargainings. This is true in all industries; the health sector is no exception.

The term 'centralisation' can have a variety of meanings with respect to bargaining structure. It can refer to vertical centralisation across occupations or bargaining units. And it can refer to horizontal centralisation across various dimensions such as companies, industries or regions. In our analysis we use the term centralisation in its regional dimension which also involves, of course, more than one plant or hospital. Alternative terms include industry-wide, wider-based or multi-employer bargaining.

The health sector is made up of a variety of services ranging from hospitals and nursing home care situations to clinical laboratories, dental services, and paramedical and related services. Many of these services centre on small individual or group practices with only a relatively small number of persons being employed. For the most part their activities would be conducted on a classic individual employee-employer basis. Accordingly, our analysis is limited to bargaining structures in hospitals, nursing homes, sanitariums and infirmaries in the three jurisdictions to be studied with the emphasis being on hospitals. These areas of the health industry are where the bulk of persons are employed and where collective bargaining is most prevalent. Focusing on the larger institutions also permits a better understanding of the implications of bargaining structures for public policy.

All parties -- labour, management and the public -- have an interest to ensure that collective bargaining operates within a bargaining structure that accommodates their legitimate needs. Labour would like a degree of centralisation that enables them

* We are grateful to Mr S.J. Dimmock, Lecturer in Industrial Relations, University of Leeds, Leeds, England for updating the UK portion.

to improve their wages and working conditions in a manner that is administratively simple and that pays attention to their relevant intra-union trade-offs as well as inter-union concerns. Management would like a degree of centralisation that enables them to deliver health services in a cost-effective fashion, and with a reasonable degree of autonomy. The public has a clear interest in the quality and sustained availability of this essential service in a cost-effective fashion. Given the interests of all parties in the degree of centralisation of bargaining, then the potential for conflict is obvious; hence the importance of how varying degrees of centralised bargaining may affect the power relations. However, there also may be a potential for mutual gain. In such circumstances, the role of public policy is to enable labour and management to move towards the degree of centralisation that is in their mutual interest, consistent with the public interest.

Comparisons between Canada, the USA and Britain are particularly illuminating in spite of the different legal-political-institutional environments and the fact that they started off with vastly different degrees of centralisation, they appear to be moving towards a similar pattern of bargaining. In North America bargaining in health began in a decentralised fashion and is gradually evolving towards more centralisation. In Britain, on the other hand, bargaining started off with a high degree of centralisation and the pressures are towards more decentralisation. While the trends are in the opposite direction, this reflects their opposite starting points; all three countries appear to be moving towards a similar state of fairly centralised bargaining, with considerable decentralisation for purely local matters. The evolution reflects the common problems in the health sector that any structure of collective bargaining must accommodate. And it suggests that no matter what the starting point that is imposed upon the parties, the structure of bargaining will have to adjust to accommodate these common problems.

The purpose of this chapter is to document the evolution of centralised bargaining in the health sectors in Canada, the USA and Britain and to discuss the appropriate role of public policy in this evolution. The chapter begins with a documentation of the specific bargaining structures pertaining to the degree of centralisation in the health sectors in each of Canada, the US and UK. It then moves to a more general discussion of the reasons for the particular evolution of each structure, and of the pros and cons of centralisation. The chapter concludes with a discussion of some of the main public policy issues.

SPECIFIC BARGAINING STRUCTURES IN THE HEALTH SECTORS: EXPERIENCE IN CANADA, US AND UK

Canada

The principle underlying collective bargaining in the public hospital sector is that each hospital is an autonomous unit responsible for signing and complying with the terms of the collective agreement. For the purpose of certification, labour boards have therefore certified on an individual hospital basis and have recognised all or most of the following groups of employees as appropriate for certification: office; operating engineers; professional employees; service employees including cleaners, cooks and registered nursing assistants; and para-medicals (sometimes subdivided into technical and paraprofes-sional or professional); including medical laboratory and X-ray technicians, physiotherapists, dieticians and pharmacists.

There is not an insignificant number of unions in the public hospital field but for each category of employee there tends to be only a few that are significantly active. For example, with respect to service employees the Canadian Union of Public Employees (CUPE) and the Service Employees International Union (SEIU) are very significant. Similarly for engineers the International Union of Operating Engineers and the Canadian Union of Operating Engineers dominate. The nurses in each province have in the past been organised by one professional association which usually has evolved out of a professional licensing or educational body. The same has been true for some paramedical groups.

Collective bargaining in the health sectors of all of the pro-vinces demonstrates a very strong tendency towards the esta-blishment of centralised collective bargaining structure. For example, in British Columbia approximately 105 hospitals belong to an accredited employers' association and province-wide col-lective agreements are negotiated with registered nurses, para-professionals, and nonprofessionals. Local issues tend to be treated by way of appendices to these master agreements. Pro-vince-wide agreements are found in nearly all of the jurisdictions for all or many of the groups of employees discussed above. However, a few provinces, such as Manitoba and Ontario, are very much in an evolutionary state, moving toward province-wide bargaining structures in a halting but consistent fashion.

Indeed, it might be useful briefly to describe Ontario's experience in order to convey the application of the general principles and determinants noted above. Until ten or fifteen years ago the only hospital employees organised into unions in any significant degree were service groups comprised of dietary, housekeeping, laundry, maintenance and stationary engineering employees. Many hospitals had no unions whatsoever. However, the passage of the Hospital Labour Disputes Arbitration Act almost fifteen years ago had the effect of changing the climate for union organisation of hospital workers and the financial ability of unions to launch organising campaigns for new members. It would appear that the funds that unions received from the compulsory-dues-conditions awarded by arbitrators (that the hospitals had previously refused to concede), coupled with the elimination of any risk to employees who might have been called out on a strike, led to considerable union success in organising new hospital units. As well, the support of collective bargaining by the Registered Nurses' Association of Ontario rapidly led to the certification of many nursing bargaining units across the province. Technicians and technologist groups commenced to be organised for collective bargaining and greatly increased the number of separate bargaining groups in the hospital field.

The rapid escalation in the number of employees becoming organised and the proliferation of separate bargaining units created severe 'whipsawing' or 'leapfrogging' pressures, both within hospitals and between hospitals. To some degree, this situation existed in other fields, such as municipal and school board collective bargaining, but there was only one bargaining agent dominant in the field. In hospitals, there were many different unions creating a rivalry that simply magnified the whipsawing pressures. Moreover, it should be noted that these whipsawing pressures were present despite the absence of the right-to-strike. As each agreement was settled, either directly or by arbitration, it appeared to create a new plateau or floor for other negotiations related either geographically or by job similarity. In addition to the direct monetary costs, the multiplicity of negotiations caused the negotiation expenses of hospital and resource personnel, consultants, conciliators and arbitrators to rise sharply over this period. Where arbitrators tended to lag behind collective bargaining developments in the private sector, threatened unlawful activity caused severe political pressure and traumatic catch-up settlements. The chaos generated by these pressures led to the Ontario 'Report of the Hospital Inquiry Commission' (Johnston Report) dealing with ways in which negotiation procedures could be improved.[1] It was the Commission's view that the parties should work towards a system of province-wide bargaining on a voluntary basis rather than having the system imposed through legislation. At least it recommended voluntary efforts to be tried before compulsion considered.

On the employer's side, the Ontario Hospital Association (OHA) is a voluntary organisation which has as its members all of the public hospitals and a number of private psychiatric hospitals and nursing homes in Ontario. The OHA offers its members a variety of services relevant to collective bargaining including representation to the Ministry of Health on budget issues and the distribution of information on wages and fringe benefits. However, the specialised industrial relations function rests not with the OHA but with the Hospital Employees Relations Services which was established as an independent body to provide hospital managements with industrial relations data and consultation and direct negotiation services. It currently provides consultation and negotiation services to the 180 public hospitals in its membership while the department's long-term goal is to provide a broadly based employee relation service to all of the OHA member hospitals and to develop a more rational collective bargaining system. Collective agreements continue to be the responsibility of individual hospitals.

Even before the report of the Johnston Commission there had been strong tendencies toward multi-hospital bargaining, and broader-based bargaining has been increasing since the publication of that report in 1974. Group bargaining is important with respect to paramedical employees where 37 out of a possible 45 hospitals currently are participating in province-wide bargaining. There is also strong group-bargaining tendencies in the operating engineer area. Province-wide agreements for service employees have been negotiated through the auspices of the Hospital Employees Relations Services Department with both the SEIU and CUPE for a number of years. However, the rivalry between the SEIU and CUPE, exacerbated by employer attempts to impress the pattern of one union on the remaining unsettled union, may be causing serious setbacks to this particular structure. Moreover, each union, particularly the SEIU, has experienced discontent by member locals and in some instances these locals have broken away to form separate sets of negotiations with individual or groups of hospitals.

Setbacks in the attainment of centralised bargaining are further illustrated by the experience between hospitals in Ontario and the Ontario Nurses' Association. One province-wide agreement was successfully negotiated in 1975 involving 110 participating hospitals and over 20 000 nurses. However, in 1976 the Ontario Nurses' Association reverted to individual hospital level negotiations because it was not prepared to accept the earlier method utilised for resolving local issues and the parties could not agree on an alternative. In their first attempt at province-wide bargaining, issues with major monetary significance were referred to as central issues and bargained at the central table while all other issues were referred to as local and bargained by hospitals individually with the corresponding union local. However, the method of settling unresolved local issues was to refer them to the central table if they continued to be outstanding. Indeed, this has been the general approach to local issues in almost all efforts at province-wide negotiations. The nurses have taken the position that this approach results in local issues being put aside in an effort to achieve an overall agreement. They have therefore taken the position that unresolved local issues ought to go to local binding arbitration. To date the employers have disagreed and the parties have therefore reverted to hospital-by-hospital arbitration although relatively few arbitration awards have been needed to establish a pattern for the province.

The one area where there has not been any substantial group bargaining is in respect to negotiations for office employees, although four Toronto hospitals have at least begun to bargain on a joint basis with respect to these employees. However, the effort is restricted to that city and to only a few hospitals located there.[2]

The United States

The situation in the US is similar to the Canadian experience although it tends to be more fragmented reflecting the absence of a single main funding source. As originally enacted, the National Labor Relations Act was applicable to both private and non-private hospitals. However, in 1947 legislation was passed to exclude non-private hospitals from coverage. The National Labor Relations Board, nevertheless, continued to assert jurisdiction over private proprietary hospitals and related health-care facilities which met the Board's legal and discretionary jurisdictional standards. However, because the exemption from coverage under the Act resulted in numerous strikes and work stoppages, Congress enacted the Health Care Amendments in 1974 which brought nonprofit hospitals again within the purview of the Act. Although the new amendment made no distinction between profit and nonprofit health-care institutions, prior exemption for 'the United States or any wholly owned government corporation or any federal reserve bank or any state or political subdivision thereof' remained unaffected by the new legislation. Accordingly, health-care facilities operated by municipalities, states or the federal government are still not defined as employer within the meaning of section 2(2) of the Act, although such facilities may be subject to executive orders which provide for a modicum of collective bargaining without the right-to-strike. Since the passage of this Act, the Board has indicated that it will continue to apply the same discretionary standards for asserting jurisdiction over health-care facilities.

In its numerous cases in the health-care field the Board has included the following groups of employees as appropriate for collective bargaining: nurses; technical employees (licensed practical nurses, radiological technicians, respiratory therapy technicians, etc.); service and maintenance employees; clerical employees; and maintenance employees. The Board has granted single-location-units in the health field and reiterated its well-established principle that a single facility unit is presumptively appropriate where there is no bargaining history on a more comprehensive basis and the degree of functional integration with other facilities is insufficient to negate the separate identity of the facility the union seeks to represent.[3]

As noted by Abelow and Metzger,[4] in their study of New York City, Minneapolis-St Paul and San Francisco-Oakland, most of the unionised voluntary hospitals have joined together to bargain with one or more of their unions on a formal, multi-employer association basis. Generalising from these three areas, Abelow

and Metzger have suggested that this kind of hospital bargaining arrangement is more likely to emerge (1) in large metropolitan areas, (2) among hospitals of a similar type, (3) where
bargaining histories are similar, (4) where there is a strong
union adversary, (5) where the union has organised a substantial portion of its jurisdiction, and (6) where the union represents either nonprofessional employees or the 'bread and butter'
concerns of professional employees rather than professional
issues.

Similarly, Feuille, Maxey, Juris and Levi[5] concluded that
union strength, union coverage, employer geographical concentration, and employer homogeneity were important influences
in the development and stability of multi-employer bargaining
structures in the six cities that they studied. They concluded
that in a large metropolitan area with a substantial degree of
union penetration, organised hospitals with similar characteristics will implement some form of inter-employer bargaining co-
operation. Moreover, even if a hospital declines to come within
the negotiating unit, it may fall within the unit of direct impact
because of pattern bargaining. They further concluded that
multi-employer bargaining would be appropriate for most hospital
occupational groups and, based on developments in San Francisco
and Seattle, saw a role for master agreements in the area of
professional issues. However, unlike in Canada where funds for
the operation of hospitals primarily come from the state, a fact
which brings employers together on this basis alone, rate regulation in the United States is just beginning and external financial regulation has not yet had a decisive or dramatic influence
on bargaining structures in the cities that have been studied.
However, there is the concern that such regulation may exacer-
bate the difference among hospitals over bargaining strategies
because of disparate financial conditions.

United Kingdom
In the health sector, as in the civil service in general in Britain,
collective bargaining formally is conducted by labour and
management representatives in Whitley Councils, which are
outgrowths of the Whitley Committee established in 1916. Following the report of the Whitley Committee, the government
persuaded itself that if voluntary collective bargaining was the
ideal system for private industry it was also appropriate to
the civil service. Accordingly, a series of joint Whitley Councils
were established to negotiate pay and conditions of employment
for the civil service. However in order to lessen the possibility
of strikes, differences were to be settled in the last resort by
arbitration. Pay standards have been elaborated by a succession
of Royal Commissions on the Civil Service and until recently
there was a Civil Service Pay Research Unit which conducted
periodic investigations into the work and remuneration of outside analogues for each class for non-industrial civil servant.[6]
These studies formed the basis of negotiations on the Civil

Service Whitley Councils and, if needed, of submissions to
arbitration.

With the nationalisation of health care in 1948 the government
became the paymaster for the NHS and a number of Whitley
Councils were set up to determine, through national collective
agreements, the pay and conditions of all health service employees. At present there is a General Whitley Council which negotiates on issues common to all NHS staff and eight other Councils, who cover specific issues to administrative and clerical
staff, ambulance personnel, ancillary staffs (manual), nurses
and midwives, optical staff, pharmaceutical staff and two professional and technical groups. In addition maintenance craftsmen have their own separate negotiating committee and doctors'
and dentists' pay is assessed by an independent review body.
In effect therefore the Whitley Councils, which encompass almost
one million employees represented by 43 unions and staff organisations, are one of the most complex bargaining systems in the
UK. However the extreme centralisation and bureaucracy of
decision-making has increasingly come under pressure, due to
the growth of union organisation and the effects of labour
legislation. These two factors have pushed hospital managements
to bargain over a wide range of issues on which the highly
centralised system was unable to make a rapid response.

The growth of union organisation has led to a more militant
posture by staff organisations in national pay bargaining in
the Whitley Councils. From 1973 onwards there has been considerable unrest and widespread industrial action by various
groups within the NHS. In 1974 a number of special reviews were
carried out by the Halsbury Committee into the pay of nurses
and paramedical grades. Against the background of these difficulties it was felt the time had come for a thorough review of
the NHS negotiating machinery and Lord McCarthy was appointed
as a special adviser by the Secretary of State for Social Services
in April 1975. His published report noted that the Whitley system
was one of the most centralised bargaining arrangements in the
UK and that variations from established conditions can only be
made with the approval of the DHSS. This situation has meant
that local management cannot respond to special conditions and
circumstances and disputes over local problems may escalate
to national level.

Lord McCarthy therefore recommended a move towards multi-
level bargaining in order to deal with these problems. The
report[7] recommended that in each region a regional Whitley Council should be established. In addition to bargaining over the
flexible elements (which henceforth could be provided for within
national agreements), the regional councils could negotiate on
matters outside the purview of the national level: these could
include aspects of work arrangements such as shift work, overtime and changes in manning levels. A third function for the
regional councils would be to act as an appeal body under grievance procedures, disciplinary procedures and similar matters.

A major flaw within the McCarthy Report was its failure to recognise the amount of decentralisation that had already taken place within industrial relations in the NHS. The growth of unionisation at hospital level had pushed their managements into establishing local consultative and negotiating committees to discuss and agree on local matters which affected the operation of health services. In consequence the report's proposals for multi-level bargaining seemed likely to overturn existing local arrangements. Additionally the problem of the institutional inertia of the centralised system remained, particularly in regard to the staff sides of the Whitley Councils. While there is a trend towards decentralisation it has taken place because of the pressure of events within hospitals which has required the Whitley Councils to react accordingly.

GENERAL OVERVIEW OF EVOLUTION OF DEGREE OF CENTRALISATION

The previous discussion of the *specific* experiences in each jurisdiction allows for a number of observations on the general determinants of bargaining structure as outlined in Weber.[8] However, in making these observations the fundamental differences in the legal regime between North America and Britain must be kept in mind. In North America any approach to collective bargaining begins at the atomistic level of the single hospital and an appropriate unit therein, whereas in the United Kingdom collective bargaining in the health sector, based on the Whitley Councils, is highly centralised with a haphazard pulling-down of authority for negotiations at lower levels. In a general sense, North America suffers from the evils of too much fragmentation and local bargaining, and in the United Kingdom the health sector has been burdened by the problems of extreme centralisation in collective bargaining.

In North America it is important to note that the appropriate bargaining unit is not intended to define the ultimate shape of the negotiating structure. In effect, labour relations boards have refused to take affirmative stands on structural grounds beyond the point of enabling the establishment of collective bargaining relationships. Given this room to move, the parties have evolved arrangements that public policy has seen fit neither to approve nor disapprove.

We have observed the general trend in North America towards co-ordinated and centralised collective bargaining in the health sector. This voluntary rationalisation of bargaining structures has manifested itself in a wide variety of shapes with the ultimate structure chosen in each bargaining relationship being dependent upon the particular effect of market, institutional and interpersonal factors. However, the experience in the health sector also demonstrates that the evolution towards more centralised and co-ordinated bargaining structures is a very gradual

process in which the level of formality increases and the extent
of geographic coverage expands haltingly as collective bargaining relationships mature. Before a wider-area centralised multi-
employer bargaining structure comes into existence, it is likely
to have been proceeded by a variety of less formal efforts at
co-ordination and co-operation including information sharing,
parallel bargaining and pattern bargaining.

While the precise form finally settled upon is always a product
of specific economic, institutional and tactical variables, the
health industry does demonstrate a marked appetite for centralised collective bargaining structures. A number of the general
explanations for centralised bargaining outlined above help
explain this evolution.

The large number of small-scale employers in the North
American health sector encourage a galvanised response to collective bargaining in order to fight off whipsawing pressures by
a handful of prominent trade unions. Combining together by
hospitals employers also permits the development of certain
economies in the hiring of specialists and the provision of other
labour relations services, and it encourages a uniformity in
wages which permits a uniform approach to government funding
sources. The grouping together of employers also permits a
more sophisticated response to the growing complexity of collective bargaining with its pension and insurance plans, supplementary unemployment insurance, job evaluation, technological
change, and other legal issues. A group employer response
may also result in a better collective bargaining relationship
with a more centralised trade union. In this respect, some observers believe that the healthy respect generated by two large
forces at the bargaining table carries over into the administration of the collective agreements on a hospital by hospital basis.
Indeed, many employer associations continue to play a very
active role in contract administration.

On the other hand, the disadvantages associated with greater
centralisation explain why wider-area bargaining in North
America has not been fully embraced and why extreme centralisation in the United Kingdom has been eroding in the private
sector of the economy for some time and in the National Health
Services as of late. The remoteness of central negotitiations may
give the impression that local issues are being sacrificed for the
overall benefit of the entire group. This remoteness may be compounded during the administration of any contract negotiated
at a level far above the local workplace. With local officials play-
ing little if any role in the negotiation of a collective agreement,
their involvement in contract administration may be rancorous
because they need never face each other at the bargaining table.
While individual employees and local trade unions may fear their
loss of autonomy, individual employers or groups of employers may
experience an equal anxiety where, for example, uniformity of
wages takes the form of the highest paid wage in a particular
area. All of these factors, then, fight against any growing trend

towards centralisation in North American or against its maintenance in Britain.

Some health-care occupations, like that of nursing, are particularly receptive to centralising forces. Such professional
occupations tend to construct bargaining structures which are
co-extensive with their homogeneous labour market rather than
structures centred on one employer or an entire product market.
These broad-based bargaining structures reflect the common
skills and professional qualifications of such employees and the
fact that they can shift readily from job to job within and
between regions. By way of contrast, in the case of office
workers in the health-care sectors of Canada and the United
States, bargaining structures are much more local in focus and
even broader-based service bargaining does not have the geographical scope of professional and paraprofessional occupations.
Office workers' skills are not unique to the health-care sector
and tend to be somewhat enterprise or labour market specific.
Hence, the local labour market is the most central variable in
determining their bargaining structure.

Professional and paraprofessional staff in the health-care
sector commonly identify more with their profession than with a
particular employer. This attachment has its roots in the professional concern for maintaining high standards of competence
and responsibility, and a concern for the preservation of professional jurisdiction against the encroachments of other allied
workers. Also of concern would be a fair and uniform rate of
pay for all members of the profession regardless of where they
are employed. Highly centralised collective bargaining structures
can more effectively tend to these broad and uniform themes.
Such issues then reinforce the tendency of these medical groups
to construct bargaining structures that would broadly coincide
with the contours of their labour market. The absence of special
or divergent interests within the professional or paraprofessional ranks also makes for a more secure and central framework
for collective bargaining. By way of contrast, the quite different
circumstances of service and office employees where there are
competing trade unions and heterogeneous skills, illustrate
labour market phenomena that impede centralising forces. Indeed,
the enormous variety of classifications which are difficult to
compare have inhibited these groups in their efforts towards
more centralised collective bargaining. Service employees, however, have been organised by trade unions for a considerable
period of time and through the passage of time have overcome
many of these problems.

Multi-hospital bargaining structures also reflect the tactical
factors which have an impact on collective bargaining structure.
This is particularly the case in Canada and the United States
where labour relations boards have certified bargaining units
on an individual hospital basis. The resulting large groups of
individual employers in the North American health-care industry therefore represent a classic example of an industry of

employers who are particularly susceptible to whipsaw and
pattern-bargaining tactics by trade unions who have a much
broader and centralised presence in the particular collective
bargaining arena. We see this even in those jurisdictions where
compulsory arbitration is the terminal event for resolving collective bargaining disputes.

Indeed, with labour costs representing such a high percentage
of overall health-care service costs, employers cannot afford to
confront funding sources without a common front on the issue
of the compensation which is necessary to pay employees in the
circumstances. This high concentration of employers being
dependent on a common source of governmental funding would
appear to be the most dominant variable in explaining the centralised bargaining structures that exist in most provinces in
Canada. The extreme case is Britain where the national government is paymaster and national centralised settlements exist.
Yet, in neither country can the needs of the local hospital be
ignored.

Centralised collective bargaining must constantly strive to
accommodate the needs of individual participating hospitals.
Any failure to do so generates stresses that threaten wider-
based bargaining, a situation which recent experience in
Britain illustrates. However, centralised bargaining structures
may even enhance the participation of individual hospital units
in the negotiation process. A formalised multi-employer structure
can provide a vehicle by which small and particularly vulnerable institutions can better express their views, rather than
being obligated to simply 'pick up' the pattern that has been
negotiated or arbitrated elsewhere. Moreover, to the extent that
the multi-employer bargaining structure delegates responsibility
for negotiating local issues and contract administration to individual hospitals, the local parties to collective agreements will
be able to focus their attention on matters over which they have
the greatest expertise. But the difficulty of making meaningful
distinctions between local issues and central issues cannot be
over-emphasised and the failure of parties to develop consensus
on such important distinctions has caused a number of setbacks
to wider-based bargaining in North America. The best example
in this respect is the efforts of province-wide bargaining by
hospitals with nurses in Ontario.

It is interesting to note that trade unions in the hospital service sectors have not strenuously opposed the drift towards
the centralisation of collective bargaining structures, in spite
of the fact that centralised bargaining reduces their power to
whipsaw and utilise pattern-setting tactics. The reason for the
lack of resistance probably reflects the interest of the trade
unions in greater administrative efficiency, an interest which is
often entirely coincident with the wishes of employers. The
expense and time in negotiating a myriad of separate collective
agreements across its jurisdiction together with a concern for
the quality of the representation it can provide its members,

all tend to push trade unions towards more centralised bargaining structures. In addition, trade unions tend to favour uniform wages and working conditions throughout an industry, a possibility that is enhanced when negotiations are highly centralised. Centralisation forces the group of employers to develop a uniform and logical presentation on most issues and guards against the fears that one employer is being treated differently than another.

Two other institutional concerns of trade unions that are somewhat unique to the health sector also contribute to centralising tendencies. The first arises out of the fact that where the government has become the primary source of health-care funds for individual hospitals, there will be a strong desire on the part of employees to address their concerns directly to a responsible representative of the funding source. This usually results in demands that representatives of the government sit at the negotiation table together with representatives of the various employers. The prospect of this request being honoured is considerably enhanced where there is one formal set of all-inclusive negotiations. Moreover, because the government will quickly come to appreciate the monetary significance of centralised negotiations, it will be encouraged to monitor and if possible, impact on, such negotiations.

The second institutional factor stems from the closed nature of the health-care sector in the sense that many of the jobs are unique of that particular industry. This uniqueness causes employers to look at compensation and benefits in other hospitals as standards of comparison for their own set of negotiations. Trade unions often view this type of comparison as amounting to a vicious circle, and it is a viewpoint from which arbitrators have not been immune. All-embracing multi-employer collective bargaining obliges both the parties and arbitration tribunals to look for external and usually non-health-care comparisons as standards against which health-care wages and working conditions can be agreed upon or determined. Trade unions usually have an interest in encouraging these broader comparisons and centralised negotiations are therefore attractive to the extent that they encourage the adoption of a world view.

To this point we have emphasised those factors that have pushed the parties towards more centralised multi-employer bargaining structures. However, the health-care sectors of all three countries continue to be subjected to a number of countervailing and fragmenting forces which also need emphasis.

We have already noted that the labour market orientation for service and office employees tends to be local in nature and therefore wider-based bargaining based on these occupations, particularly office workers, has been difficult to achieve. But one of the most fundamental barriers to extended bargaining structures in North America centres on the autonomy ascribed to a local hospital by either the government or the labour relations agency that issues a single-unit certification. Compounding this situation is the opportunity it presents for the encourage-

ment of trade union rivalries and the recognition of competing
and conflicting power centres in both employer and trade union
circles.

Indeed, trade union rivalries are exacerbated by government
policies that encourage and facilitate the development of trade
unions which are specific to a particular group of employees.
Nursing unions, craft unions for operating engineers and
various industrial unions for service and office staff, all illustrate the fragmented forces with which collective bargaining in
the health sector must cope. Moreover, it is important to understand that this kind of fragmentation results in a specific distribution of bargaining power and the development of rigid and
competitive inter-occupational comparisons for the purposes of
compensation. For example, in some jurisdictions registered
nurses have been able to achieve a very positive and large differential between their own remuneration and that received by
other paraprofessional groups. Where this is the case, it is
understandable that nurses will resist any form of broader-based
multi-union bargaining structure that might cause an internal
employee review of the differential and its justification. Indeed,
competitive rivalries between various professional and paraprofessional occupations have impeded the very formation of
trade unions that are capable of organising a majority of the
employees in a bargaining unit that a labour board in North
America would find appropriate. These kinds of divisive factors
explain why co-ordinated multi-*union* bargaining structures of
a horizontal nature almost never have been erected in the health-
care industries of North American and Britain.

Indeed, even within a group of employees who might otherwise share a wide community of interest, and for whom a centralised bargaining structure would be of advantage, government
policies in some Canadian provinces and in the USA certifying
trade unions on a single hospital basis set off a train of political
and jurisdictional rivalries, personal loyalties and disparate
histories which interfere with co-ordination even between groups
of very similarly situated employees. There is a good deal of
evidence, particularly in the United Kingdom, that where these
rivalries do not exist because government policies *began* with
more centralised structures, the opportunity to create or maintain multi-employer bargaining structures has been greatly
enhanced. This belief appears to have been the basis of the
recommendation by the Johnston Commission appointed in Ontario
wherein it was recommended that existing craft units for operating engineers should be eliminated retrospectively and that in
the future all such employees should be combined with a province-wide bargaining unit of service employees, so as to
rationalise hospital bargaining.

The centrifugal forces unleashed by sanctioning such rivalries
are exacerbated when a multiplicity of negotiations results in a
confusing patchwork of classification schemes for employees who
might otherwise be regarded as performing very comparable

work. The difficulties of making meaningful comparisons in the
face of such heterogeneous classification schemes become an
impediment to the centralisation of collective bargaining negotiations. In fact, the Johnston Commission saw the need for a comprehensive province-wide job evaluation scheme as a prerequisite
to facilitate the centralisation of bargaining for all groups on a
province-wide basis. There are, of course, parallel forces
operating against wider-based bargaining on the employer's side
as well. We have noted that atomistic bargaining structures are
emphasised by government policies defining the appropriate
bargaining unit on the basis of a single hospital in North America,
and this approach reinforces strong local community attachment
to neighbourhood and regional hospitals. Indeed, the concern
for local autonomy in the abstract has been a very significant
impediment to the development of employer associations in hospitals, although as the Johnston Commission in Ontario concluded,
it may be that real local autonomy in the financial aspects of
collective bargaining does not presently exist, given the fact
that financial sovereignty for hospital care ultimately rests with
provincial or national governments. In fact, as pointed out earlier, centralisation of bargaining on the financial issues can
allow individual hospitals to concentrate their resources on areas
where there is genuine local autonomy, for example, resolving
grievances and improving work techniques. However, to the
extent that the parties to the collective bargaining process are
unable to develop a clear demarcation between central and local
issues, concern for local autonomy will continue to plague efforts
at devising more centralised collective bargaining structures.

SUMMARY OBSERVATIONS ON PROS AND CONS OF CENTRALISATION

Although collective bargaining in the health sectors started off
by being decentralised in North America and centralised in Britain, both are moving towards a similar state of fairly centralised
bargaining with accommodation to local needs. Their starting
points, determined by legislature decisions reflecting their
own peculiar circumstances, have affected their current progress
in this evolution towards a similar structure; nevertheless, the
initially imposed structures had to adapt to the realities of their
particular circumstances. The realities of health sector bargaining appear to demand a fairly centralised structure, but one
that can accommodate local needs.

From a policy viewpoint, a number of advantages and disadvantages can be associated with a fair degree of centralisation.
It permits much more sophisticated representation for small and
middle size employers and there is an obvious convenience for
both labour and management in limiting the number of separate
negotiations that must take place. Greater centralisation may
contribute to a lower strike frequency in the sense that the

parties more clearly appreciate the costs of economic conflict and thus are more determined to settle issues at the bargaining table without the need to incur such costs or government intervention. Wider-based bargaining can result in more uniform compensation, a feature that is attractive to trade unions. A key advantage to employers is the ability to resist whipsawing and leapfrogging tactics of trade unions. Wider-based bargaining may also permit the negotiation of more generous fringe benefits if there is group-wide funding.

Disadvantages of centralised collective bargaining also exist, including the possible loss of trade union autonomy and employer independence that comes with centralisation. With these concerns comes the tendency for local issues to be sacrificed for the overall benefit of the entire group, a fact that erodes good labour-management relationships at the hospital level. With wider-based bargaining also comes the concern that wages may drift up to the highest level in the group, resulting in inflationary wage costs and insufficient wage variation to ensure the efficient allocation of labour. Of additional concern is the fact that with centralised bargaining comes more serious strikes if they occur or, in a compulsory arbitration setting, the magnifying of arbitral errors.

Public Policy Issues
The existence of such conflicting factors would appear to explain the absence of any conscious thread of integrating public policy in the area. To a large extent, the legal framework for both North America and Britain is permissive in terms of policy with respect to wider-based bargaining and, given room to move, the parties have evolved arrangements that public policy has seen fit neither to approve nor disapprove. This is not to deny that the concept of exclusive-bargaining-agent in North America is a feature of great significance. Bargaining units determined to be appropriate by labour relations agencies become basic building blocks in the context of centralised bargaining structures. While more elaborate structures can be built, the blocks themselves give shape to the structure; the lack of 'legal cement' provided by public policy means that a central bargaining structure is always subject to the risk of collapse. However, at the same time, these building blocks provide a degree of flexibility that allows parties to design a structure most accomodative to their needs. Laws of general application would be difficult to design so that they would have the same effect; moreover, bargaining-structure laws of general application run the risk of deterring the parties from combining together where the required structure may not meet particular needs over time.

While it can be argued that the original emphasis on the 'local unit' in North America may have contributed to the fragmentation of bargaining structures, experience in Britain suggests that too strong a bias in favour of centralised bargaining is also

unwise. Recent experience suggests that local needs and autonomy cannot be ignored. Thus, any enshrinement of centralised
bargaining in the law would need to provide a real accommodation for local labour relations considerations. It would be an
understatement to characterise this balance as delicate and
difficult to achieve by legislative dictate. Indeed, we have seen
that the appropriate level of bargaining may differ from issue to
issue and the appetite of the parties for wider bargaining may
vary over time and with regard to changes in economic and
technical contexts. Against this reality, there would appear to
be no easy way for public policy either to provide meaningful
blanket solutions or to help with the needs of individual groups.
It may therefore be a mistake to move public policy more deeply
into the structures of collective bargaining than has been the
case. This policy response takes the view that labour and
management have the primary responsibility for maintaining the
vitality of their organisations and devising solutions that cope
with their mutual problems. The growing sophistication of bargaining structures in North America and Britain is consistent
with this belief.

The principal problem in this area for public policy is to
design laws that facilitate the advantages of wider-based-
bargaining and at the same time protect against potential costs
and abuses. In all three jurisdictions it can be asked whether
there is sufficient positive public policy to 'facilitate' more
centralised collective bargaining if that is what is desired by
the parties. For example, should group bargaining always depend
upon unanimous employer and trade union consent? In the health-
care industries of North America this has usually been the case
and the progress towards effective centralised structures has
been halting to say the least. In Britain centralised nationwide
bargaining in its health-care industry is in place but with an
apparent insufficient accommodation of local interests. Obviously,
the optimum for public policy lies somewhere in between these
two extremes. Rather than pursuing a policy of certifying unions
for broader and more encompassing groups of employees, which
would undermine representational and organisational policies in
North America, in this middle area we have in mind such initiatives as accreditation schemes or the imposition of a council of
trade unions at the request of the majority of employees affected.
These devices can be constructed in a way which will ensure
the effective participation of local and minority interests. For
example, employer accreditation schemes in North America
require a double majority and the resulting bargaining agent
may be subject to a duty of fair representation. The more centralised schemes in Britain in the National Health Service operate
within a different legal tradition however and more responsive
bargaining may only be achieved through a process of evolution.

The paucity of public policies in the structural area of collective bargaining in Canada, the United States and Britain
reflects the positive and negative consequences that can arise

out of the concentration of economic power. Unfortunately, however, this absence of public policy means a lack of support where wider-based bargaining would be in the public interest and an absence of regulation where concentrated collective bargaining is currently taking place and is being abused. While we do not see a role for the mandatory regulation of bargaining structure in any general sense, we do think that public policy should take more account of the structural considerations of collective bargaining. Whereas the third quarter of the twentieth century focused upon the mere establishment of collective bargaining between employees and their employers, the last quarter ought to focus greater attention on the quality of the resulting relationships.

REFERENCES AND NOTES

1 Ontario (1974), 'Report of the Hospital Inquiry Commission' (Johnston Report), November.
2 Moga, M. (1972), The Impact of Joint or Multi-Employer Bargaining in Hospital Labour Relations in Ontario, unpublished thesis, University of Toronto.
3 Farkas, Emel (1978), The National Labor Relations Act: The Health Care Amendments, 'Labor Law Journal', vol.29, no.5, May, pp.259-74.
4 Abelow, W.J., and Metzger, Norman (1976), Multi-Employer Bargaining for Health Care Institutions, 'Employee Relations Law Journal', vol.1, pp.390-7.
5 Feuille, P., Maxey, C., Juris, H., and Levi, M. (1978), Determinants of Multi-Employer Bargaining in Metropolitan Hospitals, 'Employee Relations Law Journal', vol.4, no.1, Summer, pp.98-115.
6 In 1981 the UK government discontinued the Civil Service Pay Research Unit as one aspect of its policy towards incomes in the public sector.
7 McCarthy, Lord (1976), 'Making Whitley Work', Department of Health and Social Security.
8 Weber, A. (1967), Stability and Change in the Structure of Collective Bargaining, in L. Ulman (ed.), 'Challenges to Collective Bargaining', Prentice-Hall, pp.13-36.

10. COLLECTIVE BARGAINING AMONG NURSES: CANADA, USA AND UK

A.S. Sethi, G. Rowsell, N. Solomon and
M. Carpenter*

INTRODUCTION

This chapter will outline the evolution of unionisation and some
of the principal collective bargaining issues in nursing in
Canada, the USA and the UK, together with comparisons highlighting key aspects in nurse bargaining. Because of the traditional earnings comparisons between nursing and allied professional groups in the UK the bargaining behaviours of the latter
group are discussed in this chapter.

CANADA

The evolution of unionisation of nurses in Canada covers the
entire range of peculiarities inherent in labour relations and
legislation. In 1928 the first union, Catholic Nurses Union,
was formed in the Quebec City area. In 1944 the Canadian Nurses
Association publicly approved the principle of collective bargaining for nurses. It believed that the bargaining authority
for its members should be vested in the professional nurses'
association in each province. As a result, it was the professional
associations in the majority of provinces which established the
structure and constitution, and proceeded to organise nurses.
Nurses' acts and by-laws were also changed to permit them to
bargain collectively and to become the bargaining agent.
    In 1946 the Registered Nurses Association of British Columbia
(RNABC) was the first to apply for certification for all registered
nurses under the Labor Relations Act of British Columbia. Certification was granted and the RNABC became the first provincial
association to become a bargaining agent. The remaining nine
provincial nurses' associations assumed responsibility for the
social and economic welfare of their members. They published
recommended personnel policies yearly and distributed them to
employers of nurses and to their members. The main objective
was to provide nurses with employment standards and recommended salaries that could be used to support negotiations for
better working conditions and salaries.
    These policies brought about little change in the employment
situation: too frequently they were regarded merely as sugges-

* The sections on Canada and USA are written by Sethi, Rowsell
and Solomon, and the UK section by Carpenter.

tions by employers, and ignored. The realisation that other
methods had to be used if change was to be effected, brought
about a revolution in the approach to employment relations.
   In the 1960s as a result of pressure from their members,
professional associations began to develop collective bargaining
structures and prepare for negotiations with employers. In this
structure, nurses organised in groups known as 'local staff
associations' which are the same as industry's local union or
bargaining units.

Current Status
The overall unionisation rates for nurses in Canada are given
in Table 10.1. Out of 192 747 registered nurses in Canada, (of
which 148 827 are working), a total of about 91 000 are unionised (Table 10.1).

Provincial Bargaining Strategies
A province-wide picture is depicted, outlining the internal and
external pressures on collective bargaining affecting the nursing profession, bargaining strategies employed by them, and
the outcomes and trends. Provincial Nurses' Associations
assumed responsibility for collective bargaining through the
sixties. Between 1970-7 individual nursing unions were formed,
thus separating the collective bargaining function.

British Columbia. In 1940 the RNABC was concerned because
if they did not accept collective bargaining as a viable route to
negotiate for salaries and fringe benefits, unions would begin
to infiltrate their membership. In 1945 the Hospital Employees
Union (HEU) won certification for 'lay' members at the Vancouver
General Hospital, which resulted in the HEU urging staff nurses
to join. This resulted in the RNABC becoming certified in 1946
for all registered nurses under BC labour legislation.
   A Supreme Court decision in 1973 affected most professional
associations in Canada. It ruled that the Saskatchewan Registered Nurses Association could not become a certified bargaining
agent because it was not a union but a 'company dominated'
organisation. In 1977, the labour relations programme of the
RNABC was transferred to a separate and autonomous Labour
Relations Division (LRD).
   The outcome has been a modern labour organisation with many
new locals being certified in the nursing home industry. In
1980 the RNABC-LRD took a strike vote in an attempt to settle
their contract. The result of the threat of a strike resulted in a
settlement, and the highest nurses salaries in Canada. It is
expected that by summer 1981 the nurses in BC will dissolve
the LRD and a British Columbia Nurses Union will take its
place, severing all legal ties with RNABC.

Alberta. In the early 1960s nurses in Alberta hospitals and
public health units were suddenly aware that great activity was

Table 10.1: Approximate Membership and Membership Dues for Nursing Unions, Canada, 1980/81

Union[a]			Union[b]		
Name	Number of Members	Monthly Dues $	Name	Number of Members	Monthly Dues $
Registered Nurses Association of British Columbia – Labour Relations Division[b]	16 440	1% of regular pay	Fédération des Syndicats Professionels d'infirmières et d'infirmiers du Québec (Federation of 6 Unions)	14 000	16.00
United Nurses of Alberta	7 600	1% of regular pay (min. $7.50)	New Brunswick Nurses Union	2 900	10.00
Saskatchewan Union of Nurses	3 800	8.00[c]	Nova Scotia Nurses Union	2 100	12.75
Manitoba Organization of Nurses' Associations	6 000	7.00[c]	Prince Edward Island Nurses Provincial Collective Bargaining Committee	400	15.00
Ontario Nurses Association	27 900	18.00	Newfoundland Nurses Union	2 500	16.50
Les Infirmières et Infirmiers Unis Incorporé	6 000	12.00	Professional Institute of The Public Service of Canada – Nursing Group	1 900[d]	13.11

a. There are more nurses unionised than the table indicates. For example, many public health nurses and nursing school instructors belong to the civil service union in their province.
b. The RNABC-IRD and the PEI-CBC are under the umbrella of their respective professional associations but they function completely independently with a separate board, financing, etc.
c. This figure represents provincial dues. In addition, local dues vary from $1.00 to $3.00.
d. PIPSC is the union that represents the federal government nurses. There are a total of approximately 1900 nurses in PIPSC, working in various federal government agencies across Canada.

going on around them by unions who were organising health workers for the purpose of collective bargaining. As a result of these pressures, nurses turned to their professional association, the Alberta Association of Registered Nurses (AARN), for leadership and guidance in organising for collective bargaining.

During the early years of collective bargaining Alberta nurses negotiated individual contracts with hospitals and public health units. In 1969 they were involved in group bargaining for hospitals. The outcome of the Supreme Court decision in Saskatchewan forced the nurses to develop a separate independent union known as the United Nurses of Alberta (UNA). Since its inception in 1977 UNA has had many difficult problems to overcome. In July 1977, seven hospitals went out on a legal strike. The membership has grown from 3000 in 1977 to 7000 in 1980. In the spring of 1980 UNA was faced with a province-wide strike which ended with substantial salary increases.

Saskatchewan. Nurses employed in areas except the civil service had no involvement in collective bargaining prior to 1968. Hospital employees other than nurses received substantial improvements in their salaries and working conditions in the mid-sixties due to the organisational efforts of Service Employees International Union (SEIU) and Canadian Union of Public Employees (CUPE). Nurses began to realise that they were losing ground rapidly with respect to salaries and working conditions.

In 1972, an amendment was passed to the Saskatchewan Trade Union Act. Nurses who once belonged to a Saskatchewan Registered Nurses Association (SRNA) bargaining unit could no longer use their association to bargain for them. This resulted in the local nurses units applying for certification under the Saskatchewan Labor Relations Board as independent bargaining units. Late in 1972 the SEIU challenged the involvement of SRNA in organising nurses for the purpose of collective bargaining. The case was finally taken to the Supreme Court of Canada and the court ruled that SRNA was an 'employer dominated' organisation.

The outcome was the formation of the Saskatchewan Union of Nurses (SUN) in January 1974. SUN has developed and expanded as a trade union and negotiates provincially on behalf of 3800 plus members.

Manitoba. The first nurses to become involved in collective bargaining were nurses employed by the City of Winnipeg who became aware in 1953 that they were included in the Federation of Civil Employees when compulsory check off of dues was applied. In 1965 they were successful in obtaining certification as an independent bargaining unit. Later licensed practical nurses joined the Winnipeg Civic Registered Nurses Association.

In 1975 the Saskatchewan experience prompted the complete independence of nurses from the provincial nurses association. The Manitoba Organisation of Nurses' Associations (MONA)

was formed. Today MONA is a strong organisation of nurses
and licensed practical nurses in the same union. MONA negotiates a master agreement for all its units except for hospitals
in Winnipeg who have chosen to revert back to local bargaining.

Ontario. At an annual meeting of the Registered Nurses Association of Ontario (RNAO) in May 1964 the members passed a
resolution instructing the Board of Directors of the RNAO to
make the necessary representation to the Ontario Government
to secure the enactment of legislation which would provide collective bargaining rights for registered nurses. 'The Nurses
Collective Bargaining Act 1965' was prepared and sent to the
Minister of Health in February 1965. When the Ontario Government took no action on the proposed Act the RNAO members
voted to proceed with collective bargaining under existing
labour laws.
  Today there are over 250 certified bargaining units in hospitals, public health units and occupational health schools of
nursing in Ontario. All are independent units with their own
collective agreements. Because of the 'Hospital Disputes Act'
nurses working in hospitals do not have the right to strike.
Public health nurses have this right and have exercised it in a
few units. The Ontario Nurses Association is the nurses union
and broke away from the RNAO in the mid seventies.

Prince Edward Island. Late in 1960, the government of Prince
Edward Island initiated a study of labour legislation. The nurses were asked to wait for the results of this study before proceeding with plans for collective bargaining. In 1972, the
subsequent report by Professor Revell, 'Collective Bargaining
in the Public Service of Prince Edward Island' was released to
the public. It recommended new labour legislation which would
give all public and civil servants, including nurses working
in hospitals and public health, the right to collective bargaining.
  The government did not adopt the recommendations of the
report, but instead suggested that the nurses, teachers and
civil servants amend their own legislation to provide collective
bargaining rights. Section 12 of the Prince Edward Island
Nurses' Act, assented to on 14 April 1972, gave the PEI Nurses
Association the right to bargain collectively.
  Regulations dealing with Section 12 of the Nurses' Act were
developed. The Provincial Collective Bargaining Council negotiates for hospital nurses in Prince Edward Island.

Newfoundland. In the late 1960s the Association of Registered
Nurses of Newfoundland (ARNN) presented to the Newfoundland
Government a Salary Brief; they were successful in gaining
increases in salaries only. Conditions of work were established
for the civil service nurses in the Civil Service Act and Regulations. Individual hospital personnel policies covered all other
nurses. In June 1970 the Newfoundland legislature passed the

Public Service Collective Bargaining Act (PSCBA) in respect to
collective bargaining between the government of the province
and its employees and certain other employees. This enabling
legislation gave the government the right to proceed towards a
Collective Bargaining Act and Regulations. In 1971 the ARNN
signed a collective agreement under voluntary recognition
covering all nurses including public health nurses. It excluded
only one hospital owned and operated by a private industry.
The Newfoundland Nurses Union was formed following the passing of PSCBA as a separate nurses union because the ARNN was
precluded from acting as bargaining agent.

Quebec. In 1970 the United Nurses' of Montreal (Les Infirmières
Unies de Montréal) became the United Nurses' Inc. (Les Infirmières et Infirmiers Unis Inc.). Management nurses incorporated
as the United Management Nurses' Inc. The trend in negotiations
for Quebec's public sector employees has been a three-year
contract. The United Nurses' Inc. joined the Corporation des
Organismes Professionels de la Santé (COPS) for the purpose of
negotiations in 1975.

The membership of COPS which represent over 80 per cent
of the unionised nurses in the Province of Quebec and the
majority of health professionals includes: La Fédération des
Syndicats Professionnels d'infirmières et d'infirmiers du Québec
(FSPIIQ); la Fédération des Infirmières et Infirmiers Unis
(FIIQ); L'Association Professionnelle des Technologistes Médi-
caux du Québec (APTMQ); L'Association Professionnelle des
Inhalothérapeutes du Québec (APIQ); le Syndicat Professionnel
des Diététistes du Québec (SPDQ); Association of Medical Social
Service Workers of the Province of Quebec (AMSSWPQ); Association of Ville-Marie Social Service Workers (AVMSSW); L'Association Professionnelle des Techniciens en Radiologie Médicale
du Québec (SPTRMQ); Les Syndicats des Infirmières et Infirmiers auxiliaires de Québec; L'Association des Techniciens en
Diététique de Québec.

New Brunswick. The Public Service Labour Relations Act
(PSLRA) was proclaimed in December 1969 giving nurses legal
bargaining rights in the public sector. The Industrial Relations
Act (1971) gave nurses in the private sector the right to
organise. The proclamation of the PSLRA resulted in the development of two collective bargaining councils, one for hospital
nurses and a second for public health and psychiatric nurses.
The latter voted to move out from under the New Brunswick
Public Employees Association. In 1978 the two councils and the
nurses private sector unions (nursing homes) merged into the
New Brunswick Nurses Union.

The PSLRA includes a section on the designation of essential
employees and nurses working in hospitals have subsequently
received a high designation. This has militated against nurses'
strikes. Added to this, the nurses cannot select the arbitration

route unless the employer agrees. The employer has agreed to arbitration only once in ten years: for a group of non-nursing employees.

UNITED STATES

Prior to World War II, the American Nursing Association did not endorse collective bargaining nor did it sanction nurses to strike. The pioneer in breaking with this policy was the California State Nursing Association (CSNA). The CSNA was able to implement an economic security programme in 1942 in part as a result of an award by the War Labour Board. The decision helped set a pattern that the nurses in San Francisco sought to emulate. The American Nursing Association (ANA) gave its approval in 1946 towards the establishment of state nursing associations as collective bargaining agents; in part out of the fear that the Nurses Guild (C10) would seek to organise ANA members. Also, in the late 1940s employers in certain areas, such as San Francisco, preferred to establish a bargaining relationship with the relatively quiescent ANA rather than with a traditional trade union. Therefore, employers tacitly encouraged the ANA to organise for collective bargaining. The ANA only formally endorsed the right to strike *after* the California Nurses Association struck for better wages and working conditions in the mid-1960s.

Until the 1970s, the unionisation of nurses in the USA had been comparatively slow.[1] As pointed out by Miller, some of the reasons for this include the lack of financial resources allocated for collective bargaining by the national and state associations, the high hospital turnover rates of younger RNs, lack of co-ordinated collective bargaining policies, and the low participation rate of general duty nurses in the national and state associations.[2] Miller writes:

In many respects all of the above factors continued to operate throughout the 1970s. Thus, in April 1978 only 70000 registered nurses were under contracts administered by state affiliates of the ANA, with an additional 25000–30000 covered by contracts of independent nurses associations or trade unions including 1199, Retail Clerks, Service Employees, and Teamsters. Interestingly enough, the ANA has fared significantly better than other labour organisations with the NLRB's representation machinery, winning nearly 80 per cent of the 176 elections it has contested over the period 1973 to 1977.[3]

Critical Issues
One of the thorny problems has been the representation issue both in Canada and USA. The National Labor Relations Board, in the years immediately following the 1974 amendments,

encountered this problem with respect to registered nurses.
Miller summarises this issue as follows:

> In the first place, the existence of hospital nursing super-
> vision personnel among the officials of national and state
> nurses associations was a signal to hospital management that
> the ANA and its state affiliates did not meet the definition of
> labor organisations for purposes of certification. Although
> the NLRB accepted a policy by which bargaining functions
> might be delegated to local hospital chapters or related organ-
> isations, this did not find acceptance with appellate courts.
> The Board also encountered difficulty in distinguishing
> between supervisory and nonsupervisory personnel. Their
> responsibilities for patient care often involve registered
> nurses in overseeing the activities of aides, orderlies, and
> LPNs. In addition the RN may be in charge of wards or
> floors on evening or graveyard shifts. Thus, the standard
> criteria historically used by the NLRB for judging super-
> visory status at times have not been easily applied. More-
> over, the parties themselves have confused the issue through
> changes in assigned duties or titles in an attempt to have
> nurses excluded from bargaining units. While the Board has
> attempted to clarify its policies, the apparent inconsistency
> of its position on unit determination, points up the limitations
> for service and professional workers of labor law procedures
> based in industrial or manual blue-collar experience.[4]

The problem of deciding at what level a nurse becomes
management (within the meaning of the labour act) has plagued
employers and provincial labour boards. This has resulted in
a variety of decisions across Canada: British Columbia, New
Brunswick and Prince Edward Island include all positions except
director and assistant director of nursing. In contrast Alberta,
Saskatchewan, Manitoba, Nova Scotia and Newfoundland include
large numbers of head nurses in their bargaining units. Quebec
has two separate units; one including general staff nurses and
assistant head nurses; and a second including head nurses and
supervisors. In Ontario panels of the labour board have handed
down awards that include supervisors in a few units, head nurses in others, with the majority including assistant head nurses
and general staff nurses only.

Certification
In the USA, the American Nursing Association followed the
practice of receiving certification in its own name while the
actual election district or bargaining unit is the hospital chapter. Miller explains the policy as follows:

> The National Labor Relations Board has accepted the prac-
> tice, conditioning its certification on the delegation of the
> actual bargaining activities to the hospital chapter. The

delegation was required on the assumption that since the
state association officers are so frequently employed as nursing supervisors or administrators, they could not avoid al-
legations of management domination or interference. In 1977,
the Fourth Circuit Court of Appeals ruled in the Anne Arundel Hospital case, however, that it was illogical and illegal
'to certify a bargaining agent on the condition that it not
bargain.' If the Anne Arundel decision were to prevail,
several hundred bargaining certifications held by state nurses' associations among private-sector hospitals will become
invalid. In addition, even if the Fourth Circuit's position
were ultimately overturned, years would likely pass during
which the ANA's right to bargain was in limbo. Hospital
employers would feel no compulsion to bargain, and many
bargaining units would cease to exist.[5]

The certification issue will not be soon settled. Thus, in 1979
in Sierra Vista Hospital Inc. and California Nurses Association
(241 NLRB No.107) the NLRB ruled out the argument that state
nurses' associations cannot fairly represent staff nurses in
collective bargaining because their memberships include supervisory nurses. The Board will not require a nurses' association
to delegate bargaining authority to any other entity as a condition of certification and it will deny certification to a nurses'
association only when a hospital or other party can prove that
the membership of supervisory nurses causes such a conflict of
interest that the association no longer represents the undivided
interests of the nurses for whom it must bargain.[6] The Board
decision in this case, as in others, can be subject of appeal.
It therefore seems that the certification issue represents a long-
term legal problem. Canada's nursing organisations, many of
whom acted on a voluntary recognition basis, faced a similar
problem until the early 1970s. However professional associations
can no longer act as bargaining agents.

Nursing Code
Another area of conflict has occurred when nurses attempted to
incorporate the American Nursing Association's (ANA) nursing
code which reads in part:

Provision 3 - The nurse maintains individual competence in
nursing practice, recognising and accepting responsibility
for individual actions and judgements.
Provision 5 - The nurse uses individual competence as a
criteria in accepting delegated responsibilities and assigning
nursing activities to others.[7]

This issue has resulted in a number of strikes, in Youngstown,
Ohio, Chicago, Seattle, San Francisco and St Louis. Further,
it has caused strains for collective bargaining between hospitals
and their committees of interns and residents 'when housestaff

organisations have sought to limit such assignments as drawing blood, clerical tasks, and setting up I.V. Systems. At times demands have also been made that nurses and paramedics be trained to handle work formerly assigned to interns and residents.[8]

In Canada, professional responsibility clauses were included in contracts for handling nursing care activities. A few of the unions are in the process of negotiating such clauses in their contracts. A CNA ad hoc committee is in the process of redrafting a CNA Code of Ethics that will presumably include guidelines for nursing practices.

Competition

Another issue is the competition faced by ANA from other independent units. The United Nurses Association of California in the Los Angeles area has about 2000 members, the bulk of whom are in Kaiser-Permanente Facilities. By comparison the Connecticut Health Care Association which represents 3300 nurses, technical workers and other professionals broke from the Connecticut Nurses Association in 1976. Similar developments have occurred in Wisconsin, Massachusetts, Pennsylvania and Michigan.[9]

Another example of competition comes from outside unions, such as the American Federation of Teachers (AFT). In 1977, the AFT decided to open its membership to non-teachers. The reason for adopting this policy was in response to initiatives taken by professional nurses and nursing assistants, librarians and labourers who have sought to gain an AFL-CIO affiliation.[10] Rival unionism has flourished because the ANA has not squarely faced the issue of its proper role in collective bargaining. Miller states that, 'If it (the ANA) is to continue with its collective bargaining activities, it must reorganise. The internal politics of the association, however, seems to suggest it won't.[11]

In Canada, there have been relatively few raiding activities from outside unions. In 1977 in all provinces separate union organisations for nurses were set up.

THE UK: NURSES AND ALLIED PROFESSIONALS

The National Health Service is Britain's single largest employer. Nursing and midwifery staff in 1977 formed 430 500 of the approximately 1 million strong labour force, the largest single occupational group. In a service where wage and salary costs upwards of 70 per cent of total revenue expenditure, control of nurses' salaries has been a prime means of combatting the rising costs of the service. Other professional and technical staff (excluding works) formed a much smaller proportion of the total, just under 65 000. These covered 20 separate groups in 1977, ranging from the whole time equivalent of 11 medical artists to 16 000 medical laboratory scientific officers.

The State Assumes Responsibility
While not quite a monopoly employer of nurses and professional
and technical staffs, the vast majority of most of these staff
groups work for the National Health Service. This means that
the state plays a decisive role in setting not just pay and conditions, but also in establishing professional standards and recognition of qualifications.

For nurses (as with doctors) professional recognition occurred
prior to the creation of the NHS. The Nurses Registration Act
1919 established a register of trained nurses and the creation
of an elected General Nursing Council (GNC).[12] Other professional staffs did not enjoy state recognition at this time. The
earliest group to begin to professionalise were physiotherapists
whose Chartered Society dates back to the 1890s. Radiographers
followed a similar path in the 1920s. Both groups co-operated
in the 1930s with the British Medical Association (BMA) which
established a Register of Medical Auxiliaries.[13]

Before the NHS, there were no nationally recognised rates of
pay for such 'medical auxiliaries'. Mental nurses' pay and conditions were in theory nationally determined by a Joint Conciliation
Committee between employing authorities and the Mental Hospital
and Institutional Workers Union (MHIWU). However, by no
means all employers were party to these collective agreements
or followed them. There were no similar arrangements in either
local authority or voluntary (i.e. charity) hospitals before the
war. Trade unions were weak among nurses and professional
staffs in these hospitals. The main nurses' organisation, The
College of Nursing, established in 1916 - later to become the
Royal College of Nursing (Rcn) in 1939 - regarded itself as a
professional association and was reluctant to take on trade union
functions. However it did publish recommended scales before the
establishment of the Whitley Council structure and from 1926
the 'Nursing Times', when it became the College's official organ,
refused to accept advertisements which fell below them (the
official organ is now the 'Nursing Standard').

The Second World War served as a main catalyst for change
and the state took over the running of the hospital service in
1939. When the service proved it could cope with the worst strains
imposed by the war, attention shifted towards bettering the service as a whole. The most immediate problem was the shortage of
nurses, particularly of students. A Nurses Salaries Committee
was established under Lord Rushcliffe which recommended scales
for all grades and reductions in hours. In addition the Nurses
Act of 1943 established a roll of practically trained nurses alongside the Register, also under the supervision of the General
Nursing Council.[14] Both unions and professional associations had
nominated members on to the Rushcliffe Committee, with the majority of seats held by the Rcn and other professional associations
of whom the Royal College of Midwives (RCM) was most significant.
Almost inevitably, this pattern was reproduced in the setting up
of the Nurses and Midwives Whitley Council after the NHS came

into being in 1948. The management side tended to overrepresent local authorities against the hospitals, but the real weight was with the Ministry of Health officials who, in any case, were the paymasters.[15]

With professional and technical staff, the position was very different. A highly fragmented bargaining structure was created, with considerable variations in pay and other conditions between different categories of staff. The government had hoped to create a unified functional council covering all professional and technical workers. However, when the Professional and Technical Council was established it was divided into an A Council covering mainly patient contact occupations and a B Council for the remainder. Groups like almoners, chiropodists, occupational therapists, physiotherapists and radiographers were included in A Council and groups like medical laboratory technicians and hospital engineers in the B Council. Those regarded as 'scientists' rather than 'technicians' - like hospital physicists - found themselves upon the higher status A Council.

As with the Nurses and Midwives Council, a multiplicity of organisations claimed to represent the interests of staff, approximately half of all recognised Whitley organisations, covering a relatively small proportion of total staff. Professional associations predominated on the A Council, many of which had originated as qualifying associations. Unions predominated on the B Council. One of these, the Association of Scientific Workers - from 1968 part of the Association of Scientific, Technical and Managerial Staffs (ASTMS) - subsequently became the main union representing laboratory workers.

Developments to the 1970s
Nurses are sometimes regarded as a quiescent group of workers. Despite this reputation, there were periodic signs of discontent from 1948, before the eruption of militancy in 1974. The first protest occurred in 1948 over the deduction of national insurance from student nurses salaries. In subsequent years mental hospital nurses conducted an overtime ban in the mid 1950s and in 1962 widespread demonstrations against the government's 'Pay Pause' helped to win a backdated pay award. In the late 1960s the Rcns 'Raise the Roof Campaign' once again brought nurses on to the streets.

The situation was somewhat different with scientific and professional staff. In the first place there were no common scales between different grades, even within the same occupation. During the 1950s, psychiatric social workers were the best and chiropodists the least well remunerated 'medical auxiliaries' - probably a fair reflection of the status hierarchy at that time.[16] However the same pattern of delay and resort to arbitration similar to that in the Nurses and Midwives Whitley Council continued through the 1950s only to be halted by successive incomes policies from the 1960s. Although shortages emerged, and wage levels of most types of staff failed to keep up with the general

level, many of the professional and technical occupations were
better placed than nursing.

An important consequence of NHS control was moves to
strengthen recognition of these occupations. The Cope Committee Reports in 1951 recommended the establishment of state
registers similar to those of doctors and nurses. Eventually in
1960, the Professions Supplementary to Medicine Act 1960 was
passed, establishing state registers for many of these groups.
However one condition imposed was the acceptance subordination within a male and medically dominated division of labour,
a factor which may have influenced speech therapists' decision
to stay off the register.[17]

It is some significance that a review of the professional status
of nurses had to wait much longer since the cost implications
were much greater. The Wood Report in 1947 had recommended
something akin to full student status, by the separation of
training from service provision. However it was not until a
further report in 1972 of a Committee under Lord Briggs that
recommendations to reorganise nurse training appeared. In the
meantime, increased status had been accorded to nurse managers
following the Salmon Report in 1966 and the reorganisation of
the service in 1974. At the same time, while student nurses
remained 'pairs of hands', increasing numbers of untrained nursing assistants and auxiliaries were recruited to perform basic
care.[18] Since this change had already taken place, the implementation of Briggs through the Nurses, Midwives and Health
Visitors Act 1978, was hardly revolutionary. How the new
generic system of training will work out in practice, remains
to be seen.

The Breakdown of Whitleyism
Whether Whitleyism is judged a success or failure depends very
much on the objectives set for it. Its cumbersome, arms-length
machinery has served the government well as a means of containing costs by depressing health workers' salaries. However,
as a system intended originally to promote harmony and consensus through joint co-operation to improve both staff conditions
of employment and the service in general, it has proved an
abysmal failure. Although staff-side organisations had a recognised place at national level, in only a few places did local
management show any inclination to involve staff in decisions
affecting the service or staff conditions.[19] At national level
staff's commitment was not built upon but taken for granted.
This, more than anything, brought Whitley Councils into dis-
repute, combined with a failure of staff-side organisations,
particularly professional associations, to respond effectively to
the government's neglect of staff pay and conditions.

The first indications of failure occurred during the 1950s,
with staff sides being forced to go outside the Whitley system
to obtain settlements from arbitration. In the incomes policies of
the 1960s and 1970s the government intervened directly in the

collective bargaining process. Perhaps in some respects it is to be preferred, for it is at least more apparent than the Treasury's hidden influence on the size of management-side offers. Looked at this way, the NHS has never enjoyed 'free' collective bargaining.

While incomes policies have generally snared nurses and other professional health workers, they have sometimes promoted change, precisely because they are framed outside the Whitley system. For example, in 1968 the National Board for Prices and Incomes 'Report No.60' on nurses' pay as well as recommending 'catching up' increases in pay criticised the conditions of discipline under which student nurses lived and worked. Another example of externally imposed change through incomes policies was the £6 flat rate pay policy agreed between the Labour Government and the TUC for the phase of the Social Contract during 1975-6. This cut right across the arguments about differentials that have tended to dominate discussions on those Whitley Councils which span long staff hierarchies.

Quite apart from these externally imposed constraints upon Whitleyism, health workers' protest activity has during the 1970s placed strains on the system, which the government only resolved by going outside its structure. In the turbulent year of 1974, wage militancy erupted on an unprecedented scale. Health workers vented their frustration at three successive phases of Conservative incomes policy on the incoming Labour Government. Militant demonstrations and industrial action by nurses and radiographers forced the government to cool the situation by appointing a Committee of Enquiry to examine the pay and conditions of nurses and midwives. Its terms of reference were subsequently extended to cover the group of occupations represented on Professional and Technical Council A, whose pay had been broadly linked to nurses and midwives since 1959. The model was the Review Body system in operation for doctors. The system involves no bargaining. However pressure can still be mounted if the quasi-judicial atmosphere is disturbed by industrial action. All nurses' organisations suspended industrial action on the setting up of the Halsbury enquiry, with the exception of the Confederation of Health Service Employees (COHSE).

Among radiographers the Society of Radiographers had been reluctantly pursuing a campaign of industrial action under pressure of intense competition for membership from ASTMS. Medical laboratory workers had done relatively well in recent years, and this invited comparisons of the relative effectiveness between the professional associations on Council A and the unions on Council B.[20] In the event the Society of Radiographers decided to suspend its industrial action and put its trust in the Committee of Enquiry.

The Halsbury Reports on Nurses Pay and Professions Supplementary to Medicine appeared in 1974 and 1975 respectively. Overall, as John Berridge has suggested, the recommendations

of the two Halsbury Reports were unadventurous, even though
the Committee's terms of reference covered the structure of
occupation as well as pay and conditions.[21] In particular, no
recommendations appeared which might have disturbed traditional patterns of subordination to the medical profession.

Medical laboratory workers on B Council had been relatively
quiet. Yet in February 1975, the unions while accepting a 19
per cent pay deal, instituted a ban on emergency on-call duties
in response to management's attempt to alter the system of
payments. These would have been in line with the Halsbury
recommendations to which they were not, in any case, a party.
By April 1975, management had revised its original offer in line
with the claim of ASTMS and other unions.

The Road to Comparability
The relative lack of success of the Halsbury Reports in permanently correcting the failures of Whitleyism can be judged by
the fact that a similar exercise proved necessary within a space
of only a few years. This time the spur was the actions of, in
particular, public sector manual workers (including NHS ancillary workers), who revolted in 1978-9 against a further stage
of incomes policy. In response the Labour Government established a 'Standing Commission on Pay Comparability' for public
sector pay. The scheme retained elements of British 'voluntarism' by only accepting references made to it jointly by unions
and the government. However, its approach, of linking public
sector pay to that of 'comparable' occupations in the private
sector, left little room for argument, based as it was on such
supposedly scientific techniques as 'factor analysis' of jobs.

Thus the overall effects of the Comparability Commission have
been to widen differentials. This is because its recommendations
have fairly accurately mirrored the wider hierarchies in private
industry. The Commissioners have also been accused of sexism
in choosing equivalent female rather than male jobs in the private
sector as their basis for comparison. As before the justification
is that a comparability exercise merely seeks to reproduce an
existing state of affairs rather than alter it. If the comparability
exercise was not primarily concerned with issues of wider social
justice, neither was it concerned to remedy specific shortages
if they could not be justified by criteria of comparability. For
example, though there is a national shortage of midwives, the
Commission did not favour an additional payment for midwifery
qualifications because most midwives 'are already registered
nurses' and the 'findings do not give any greater weight to a
job of a midwife than to the job of a nurse'.[22]

Both Reports 3 and 4 established that the value of the Halsbury
awards had been whittled away in the years since 1974, regret-
ted the fact, and hoped that it would not happen again. However
this seems rather pious. The Comparability Commission has now
gone and there is no reason to believe that it, any more than its
successor, has dealt effectively with Whitleyism's periodic

tendency to collapse. All it has done is give the system enough medicine to keep it going to the next crisis, when another variant might be tried. At the present moment, there seems little prospect of an end to the present pattern of longer periods of erosion of salaries, characterised by industrial peace, followed by shorter catching up periods characterised by militancy resulting from staffs' accumulated anger and frustration.

CONCLUSION

Collective bargaining is a complex process for determining the relationships between nurses and their employers. In Canada, as well as in UK and USA, both structural and negotiation environments play important parts in determining particular strategies employed by the nurses. Nurses in Canada have used strategies to emphasise the following three main categories: (1) the levels of compensation and insured fringe benefits; (2) conditions of work; and (3) the desire to be part of the decision-making process. First, collective bargaining is seen by nurses as a legitimate means for improving their economic status. Emphasis is on increased compensation, improved fringe benefits, and protection against inflation. Secondly, working conditions in the contracts in Canada, are increasingly spelled out in more specific terms. Thirdly, nurses are determined to have a greater say in policy formulation and determination affecting health care. These demands manifest themselves in some cases in specific contractual clauses clearly stating the nurses' or their union's role in administrative and policy matters. In other cases, broadly defined internal and arbitral procedures for ensuring nurse input into policy matters have been negotiated.

On the other hand hospitals in Canada, as employers, have certain limitations and objectives within which they conduct negotiations, because they represent the public, and as trustees of a public institution, they are ultimately responsible to the public for the welfare of patients and the health-care system. Their desire for quality health care within the constraints of financial stringencies pose difficult strains at the bargaining table.

In the case of the USA two difficult issues are noteworthy. First, the American Nurses Association and its state affiliates face the challenge of the organisation's status as a bargaining representative because of supervisor domination. This may likely develop into either internal changes within the American Nurses Association, or 'strong takeover challenged by other labour organisations'.[23] Second, the third-party payer issue - more pronounced in New York and on the west coast - is affecting the size of settlements and bargaining procedures. 'In many situations, it is the reimbursement or state agency to which both parties must plead their cases, and to whom strike action is directed. Because of third-party payers, bargaining is frequently extended three to six months beyond the expiration date, settlement sizes are reduced and bargaining is perfunctory. As a cost containment policy at the national level becomes more pronounced, the traditional bilateral bargaining may be exchanged for the multilateral bargaining emerging in some areas.[24] It seems that the US nursing bargaining strategies may develop rather rapidly into the direction of the Canadian bargaining models, although the precise nature of such developments will incorporate the unique American constraints and objectives of their industrial relations system.

In the UK a collective bargaining role tended to be thrust on nurses' professional associations and they have been accorded the majority representation in the centralised negotiating machinery. However both the professional associations and the trade unions have found it difficult to escape government's control within the collective bargaining process. Paradoxically, the major instances of betterment of nurses' pay and conditions (together with those of the professions supplementary to medicine), occurred when government intervened directly in NHS pay bargaining in the 1960s and 1970s. The external pay inquiries, linked to government incomes policy, highlighted the unsatisfactory employment circumstances of these two groups and promoted better results than had been obtained by collective bargaining within the Whitley system.

REFERENCES AND NOTES

1 The number of registered nurses under collective contracts grew very slowly after 1946, reaching about 9000 in 1964 and 30 000 in 1969. Two-thirds of the RNs under contract in the latter years were in four states: California (6805), New York (5597), Minnesota (4103), and Washington (3713), quoted in Miller, R.U. (1980), Hospitals, in G.G. Sommers (ed.), 'Collective Bargaining: Contemporary American Experience', Industrial Relations Research Association Series, p.405.

2 Miller, Hospitals, p.405.

3 Ibid.

4 Ibid., p.385.

5 Ibid., p.407.

6 Metzger, Norman (1980), Hospital Labor Scene Marked by Union Issues, 'Hospitals', 1 April, p.105.

7 Quoted in Miller, Hospitals, p.421.

8 Ibid., p.421.

9 US Department of Labor (1979), 'Impact of the 1974 Health Care Amendments to the NLRA on Collective Bargaining in the Health Care Industry', Federal Mediation and Conciliation Service, p.95.

10 Health Labour Relations Reports 1 (September 19, 1977): 6, Quoted in ibid., pp.95-6.

11 Miller, Hospitals, p.408.
12 For a full discussion see Abel-Smith, B. (1960), 'A History of the Nursing Profession', Heinemann.
13 Aleszewski, A., Meltzer, H., and Hainsworth, M. (1979), 'Management, Deployment and Morale of NHS Remedial Therapists: An Extended Final Report', Institute for Health Studies, Hull, pp.33-4.
14 For a fuller account see Ferguson, S., and Fitzgerald, H. (1954), 'Studies in the Social Services', HMSO, chapter on The Nursing Services.
15 Baly, M.E. (1980), 'Nursing and Social Change', Heinemann, 2nd edition, p.215.
16 Kahn, H. (1962), 'Salaries in the Public Service in England and Wales', Allen and Unwin, p.129.
17 Aleszewski et al., 'NHS Remedial Therapists', pp.194-6.
18 These developments are discussed at length by Carpenter, M. (1977), The New Managerialism and Professionalism in Nursing in M. Stacey et al., 'Health and the Division of Labour', Croom Helm, pp.165-93.
19 Miles, A.W., and Smith, D. (1969), 'Joint Consultation: Defeat or Opportunity?', King Edward's Hospital Fund for London. In this chapter I say relatively little concerning local relations between workers and employers. See instead Chapter 5, The Labour Movement in the NHS.
20 For a critical look at the operation of the A Council see Time to End this Whitley Charade, 'Health Team', August 1975, pp.46-7.
21 Berridge, John (1976), 'A Suitable Case for Treatment: A Case Study of Industrial Relations in the NHS', Open University Press, pp.46-7.
22 Standing Commission on Pay Comparability (1980), 'Report No. 3 Nurses and Midwives', HMSO, paragraph 84.
23 US Dept. of Labor, Impact of the 1974 Health Care Amendments..., p.440.
24 Ibid., pp.440-1.

11. COLLECTIVE BARGAINING AMONG NON-PROFESSIONAL AND ALLIED PROFESSIONAL EMPLOYEES IN THE HEALTH SECTOR

A.S. Sethi, R.H. Stansel, N. Solomon and S.J. Dimmock*

INTRODUCTION

The purpose of this chapter is to outline a broad overview of collective bargaining experience in the Canadian, American and British hospital sector pertaining to the nonprofessional hospital workers and allied health-care professionals. The following pages will summarise the bargaining structure, bargaining strategies employed, internal and external pressures, and outcomes and trends.

CANADA

Public hospitals in Canada constitute the second largest segment of the public sector. Hospitals employed approximately 420 000 workers in 1979, or over 17 per cent of the total public sector employment in Canada - representing 4 per cent of the total Canadian employment, and 2 per cent of the Canadian population.[1] Historically, the hospital sector expanded on account of the introduction of universal hospital care and medical care programmes between 1950s and mid-1960s.[2] During 1960-79, the annual employment growth of Canadian public hospitals averaged 3.7 per cent compared with 3.5 per cent for the total public sector and 2.8 per cent for private sector employment in Canada.[3]

Collective Bargaining Roles
Collective bargaining is perceived by hospital workers as a means of achieving their economic and other goals. In the last decade, unionisation of hospital employees has increased in all provinces in Canada. The proportion of unionisation, however, varies among hospitals and among occupational classes.

Role of Unions in Hospitals. There are a total of about 70 national, international and provincial unions involved in hospitals. The majority of them are affiliates of central labour bodies, and a few are independent unions. The Canadian Union of Public Employees (CUPE) is the only union that has bargaining units in

* The section on Canada is written by Sethi and Stansel, the one on the US is authored by Solomon; and the UK section is authored by Dimmock.

public hospitals in nine of the ten provinces - in British
Columbia the Hospital Employees Union is a breakway from
CUPE.[4] In general, there is a proliferation of unions involved
in the Canadian hospital collective bargaining.

Role of Management Sides. In all provinces there is a two-tier
committee structure to provide input into the bargaining process by hospital managements. In most of the provinces, there
is a Labor Relations or Employee Relations Committee of the
Hospital Association (or equivalent). In Prince Edward Island,
the law provides a Health Negotiating Agency which includes
representatives of the Hospital Association. In British Columbia,
the Health Labor Relations Association, separate from the
Hospital Association but with essentially the same voluntary
membership, is the largest constituted employers' bargaining
agent.

In all the provinces there are one or more Negotiating Committees or Teams which include representatives of hospitals. In
most cases, the chief spokesman of the Negotiating Committee
or Team is a labour relations specialist on the staff of the
Hospital Association (in British Columbia, the Health Labor
Relations Association). In those provinces where government
is directly represented on the Committee, the role of chief
spokesman at the bargaining table may be carried by one of the
government officials (e.g., New Brunswick).

Government's Role. The government's role varies from total
involvement into the bargaining process to no formal involvement in various provinces. The highest level of government
involvement is in Quebec, where the bargaining mandate is set
by the Treasury Board and representatives of the Social Affairs
Department are members of the negotiating committees. In
Newfoundland, the Treasury Board and the Department of
Health are represented on the Hospital Association's Labor
Relations Committee and on negotiating committees.

In Prince Edward Island the Health Negotiating Agency acts
for the employers, consisting of representatives of the Hospital
Services Commission, Treasury Board, and representatives of
the Hospital Association. In New Brunswick the employer is
the Treasury Board which delegates to hospitals the authority
to negotiate providing: (1) there is province-wide bargaining;
and (2) each negotiating team includes representatives of the
Department of Health and Treasury Board.

In Ontario, a representative of the Ministry of Health is a
member of the Steering Committee (policy) in a liaison capacity.
In Manitoba, the government is usually invited to have an observer at major bargaining sessions. In Saskatchewan, government
has an observer on each negotiating committee. The observer's
role is sometimes expanded to that of a mediator. In other
provinces (Nova Scotia, Alberta and British Columbia) there is
no formal involvement of government.

Participation in Central Bargaining. There exists in all ten
provinces some mechanism to allow hospitals to participate in
province-wide bargaining or at least to encourage a trend in
that direction. Participation in this process is voluntary except
in Quebec.

The level of participation by hospitals in central bargaining
is high - 100 per cent in Newfoundland, Prince Edward Island,
New Brunswick and Saskatchewan; almost 100 per cent in
Alberta and British Columbia and 87 per cent in Ontario. In
Nova Scotia, about one half of all contracts are bargained
regionally (four to eight hospitals per bargaining table) and
the other half are negotiated individually.

On the union side, province-wide bargaining has been practised by the unions on an individual basis. However, in one
province the CUPE and the SEIU bargained as council of trade
unions. The general pattern is that the union's negotiating
committee consists of: (a) representatives of the union's local;
and (b) staff of the union's provincial body.

The Issues Involved - Central Versus Local
In most provinces, the process is highly centralised, in the
sense that province-wide bargaining includes nearly all issues.
Some provinces have master contracts; other have central
settlements which are the basis for individual agreements.
Ontario's system provides for province-wide bargaining on
issues of common application and local bargaining of issues unique to each hospital. The system of 'central versus local' split
is being constantly refined, with greater numbers of issues
coming to be negotiated on a province-wide basis. The Canadian
collective bargaining experience faces the constant challenge
of determining which issues are central and which are local.

Bargaining Strategies. As there is no national uniform system of
bargaining, a review of bargaining strategies employed by
hospital workers is given for some of the provinces to provide
an insight into the nature of the negotiation process used by
the parties to achieve their goals.

British Columbia. Bargaining in British Columbia hospitals is
conducted on a province-wide basis. The structure has evolved
over time from individual hospital bargaining in the early 1950s
to regional bargaining in the 1960s culminating in province-wide
bargaining as it is presently structured.

As in Ontario, the individual hospital is legally responsible
for negotiating and abiding by the terms of a collective agreement. However, in practice, each public hospital delegates
bargaining authority to the British Columbia Hospital Association (BCHA). British Columbia law would permit the BCHA to
bargain as the accredited bargaining agent of all public hospitals
but, hitherto, the membership has not given the Association the
necessary mandate to apply for accreditation. Consequently,

an agreement negotiated by the BCHA must be approved by a two-thirds majority of its membership to be binding on those who so approve. If this majority is obtained, the agreement is not legally binding on dissident member hospitals but, in practice, dissidence is rare. If a two-thirds majority is not obtained, there is no agreement binding on any hospital.

Province-wide bargaining in British Columbia appears to have been facilitated by the relatively small number of unions on the scene. Service employees are almost exclusively organised by the Hospital Employees Union (HEU). Paramedical employees are represented by the Health Sciences Association (HSA). Province-wide bargaining does not transcend existing union jurisdictions - that is, there is no joint union bargaining. However, for each union, a master contract is negotiated for major items of pay and working conditions. Certain local items exist and are settled at the level of the individual hospital.

The administration of the master agreement is undertaken at the local hospital level and some problems arise. There is not always a consistent interpretation of any disputed clause from one hospital to another and the BCHA finds it difficult to impose a uniform interpretation across the board. The master contract with the HEU has a provision that job evaluation be undertaken province-wide for employees in the bargaining unit. This provision was imposed by the government in order to resolve equal-pay-for-work disputes. To date, a steering committee has been established with the power to establish a working committee which will have equal management/union representation.

In summary, the British Columbia system of province-wide bargaining has evolved with the co-operation of all parties. The evolution has been facilitated by the relatively small number of unions in the hospital field and by the fairly clear policy of the Labor Relations Board with respect to appropriate bargaining units. There is fairly general agreement that the main improvement in the system would be the accreditation of the BCHA to avoid the delays and uncertainties inherent in the present bargaining relationship.

Ontario. The principle underlying collective bargaining in the public hospital sector is that each hospital is an autonomous unit responsible for signing and complying with the terms of a collective agreement.[6] Therefore, any bargaining entered into by a hospital on a group or province-wide basis is done so on an entirely voluntary basis.

In 1965, the Hospital Labor Disputes Arbitration Act was enacted to protect the community from disruptions in the delivery of health care. However, it also had the effect of changing the climate for union organisation of hospital workers and the financial ability of unions to launch organising campaigns for new members. The newly found funds unions received from compulsory dues (conditions awarded by arbitrators that the hospitals had previously refused to concede), coupled with the elimination of any risk to employees of being called out on legal strike, led to considerable union success in organising new hospital units. Technician and technologist groups commenced to be organised for collective bargaining and greatly increased the number of separate bargaining groups in the hospital field. To illustrate the trend, in a period of three years, 1971-3, the number of bargaining units of medical and radiological technologists increased from two to over 60.

The rapid escalation in the number of employees becoming organised and the proliferation of separate bargaining units created severe 'whipsawing' or 'leapfrogging' pressures, both within hospitals and between hospitals. The prevalence of a multitude of different unions has created a rivalry that multiplies whipsawing pressures. As each agreement was settled, either directly or by arbitration, it created a new plateau or floor for other negotiations related either geographically or by job similarity. (One need only mention the Toronto CUPE settlement of 1974 or the Ottawa Civic Award of 1974 with their repercussions throughout, and indeed beyond, the hospital industry.) In addition to the direct monetary costs, the multiplicity of negotiations caused the negotiation expenses of hospital and resource personnel, consultants, conciliators and arbitrators to rise sharply over this period.

In 1974 the Johnston Commission was established to make recommendations for improvement in negotiation procedures by reducing the bargaining groups to three - service, nursing and paramedical. The Johnston Commission also supported province-wide negotiations on central matters with local issues being left for settlement within each hospital. The Commission's view was that the parties should work towards a system of province-wide bargaining on a voluntary basis rather than having the system imposed through legislation, and it recommended that the bargaining agents work towards the goal of bargaining in councils of trade unions. The Commission stated that if the unions could not reach this goal voluntarily, then it should be legislated.

Since the publication of the Johnston Commission Report 17 settlements have been reached on a province-wide or near province-wide basis.[7] In no case have the unions established a council for bargaining purposes. The participation of hospitals and unions has been on an entirely voluntary basis, and hospital participation in some cases has ranged as high as 99 per cent of those eligible to participate. In one case, a split within the union involved -- SEIU -- resulted in 14 hospitals being forced to negotiate with one of the union's locals while 44 hospitals negotiated as a group with the other locals of that union..

In summary, the historical development of collective bargaining in the industry points clearly towards more group or province-wide bargaining as influenced by the following factors:

the legislative imposition of compulsory arbitration and the

elimination of legal strikes leading to rapid increases in trade
union membership.
proliferation of separate bargaining units and increased trade
union competition and rivalry.
consequent 'leapfrogging' and 'whipsawing' with rapid escalation
of wage and salary levels through the multiplicity of negotiations and attempts of each union to satisfy its members.

Quebec. In the province of Quebec, province-wide bargaining
in public hospitals has existed since 1966. In that year, all
public hospitals delegated bargaining authority to the Association of the Hospitals of the Province of Quebec (AHPQ) which
bargained separately with the Quebec Federation of Labor
(QFL), the Confederation of National Trade Unions (CNTU) and
the United Federation of Nurses. The AHPQ has developed a
system of canvassing the views of individual hospitals on the
priorities of bargaining. Voluntary delegation persisted up to
1971 but, in that year, Bill 46 made such delegation a requirement of law.

Labour Board certification policy in Quebec permits an almost
unlimited number of unions in any hospital. In practice, as many
as twelve separate unions exist in one hospital and the AHPQ
is required to negotiate with all groups. So, while province-
wide bargaining is a legal requirement, it need not transcend
union jurisdictions. In practice, the CNTU and the QFL, with
a combined representation of some 80 000 hospital employees,
have agreed to bargain jointly with the AHPQ. It should be
noted that, while a number of different unions may negotiate
for the same occupation across the Province, the wages and
working conditions of such an occupation are uniform. To a
large extent, this reflects the bargaining policy of the AHPQ
that aims at standardisation across the Province.

The Ministry of Social Affairs plays a direct role in public
hospital negotiations. A representative of the Ministry is present
at each bargaining table and acts in partnership with the AHPQ.
Development of bargaining policy and strategy is undertaken
jointly by the Ministry and the AHPQ so that a common front is
presented at the various bargaining tables.

There are signs of a trend toward consolidation of bargaining
activity by unions in Quebec. The common front of the QFL and
the CNTU in 1972 bargaining is one indication.

In summary, the Quebec system is province-wide in character
but only on a union basis. The number of unions representing
all categories of employees makes for a multiplicity of bargaining tables. To some extent, potential problems due to fragmentation are obviated by the predominance of the CNTU and the QFL.
Generally, settlements by these unions set the pattern for
other groups. The trend appears to be towards voluntary joint
negotiation by unions though this is not provided for by legislation.

New Brunswick. In 1968 Public Service Labor Relations Act
was passed, and the Public Service Labor Relations Board
(PSLRB) was created to administer the Act which specified the
Treasury Board as the employer of hospital employees. The
public hospitals are represented on the 'employer' bargaining
committee but, in negotiations on monetary matters, the Treasury Board plays the predominant role. The hospital representatives play a more active role in bargaining on nonmonetary
issues.

The transition from individual-hospital to province-wide
bargaining in New Brunswick was facilitated by the absence of
competing unions in any of the employee categories. Only three
unions are now involved in representation of employees in the
six separate bargaining units.

In the event of deadlock during hospital negotiations in New
Brunswick, a conciliation officer is appointed at the request
of either party. Should the conciliator fail to bring about accord,
the Treasury Board is required to furnish the union with a list
of 'designated' employees whose duties affect the health, safety
and security of the public. Should the union object to specific
designations, the PSLRB rules on the matter. Employees so
designated are prohibited by law from strike action should this
course be taken by the union. As is the case in the federal
government, the process of designation can cause delays. Further, the designation process does not place an equal burden
on all hospitals. One hospital might have a relatively large
number of designated employees and might therefore cope reasonably well with a strike. In contrast, a hospital with few
designated employees might suffer considerably from a strike.
The employer representatives are concerned about the fairness
of informing designated employees of their status prior to any
strike vote. Evidently, such employees might be more disposed
to vote for a strike in the knowledge that they would not be
required to withhold their services.

Outcomes and Trends
From the above discussion a number of outcomes and trends are
worth noting.

The Structure of Negotiations. In so far as the structure of
negotiation is concerned, there is a trend towards regional,
co-ordinated negotiations or a province-wide bargaining system,
i.e. a broader based bargaining. In most provinces, the process
is highly centralised, in the sense that province-wide bargaining includes nearly all issues. Some provinces have master contracts; other have central settlements which are the basis for
individual agreements. The system of 'central versus local' split
is being constantly refined, with greater numbers of issues
coming to be negotiated on a province-wide basis. The Canadian
collective bargaining experience faces the constant challenge of
determining which issues are central and which are local.

Standardisation. In seven provinces, standardisation has been
virtually achieved at least in relation to pay rates. In Newfoundland and Manitoba, there has been substantial progress towards
standardisation. Ontario is moving toward standardisation of
several matters, including rates of pay.

Right to Strike and Compulsory Arbitration. Except in Ontario
and Prince Edward Island, hospital workers have the right to
strike. In Ontario, the non-medical hospital workers went on a
week's strike in 1981 and demanded the restoration of the right
to strike.

The implication of opposition to compulsory arbitration is that
hospital workers perceive that collective bargaining is distorted
by compulsory arbitration resulting in delays in settling contracts. Hospital workers would concur with Professor Woods'
view that compulsory arbitration has a 'potentially corrosive
effect on the decision-making process, both within and between
unions and managements'.[8] It is argued that the compulsory
arbitration system serves as a 'crutch for leadership' to the
extent that it enables union and hospital officials to take all
politically embarrassing disputes to the arbitrator and 'let him
make the unpopular decisions'. 'In the long run', says Woods,
'the effect would be to undermine both the leadership in question
and the collective bargaining process itself'.[9]

Future Direction. Based on the collective bargaining experience
of hospital workers in Canada, a few comments are offered
which may point out the direction of collective bargaining in
the health sector: health-care negotiations will tend to be
increasingly difficult in 1981-2 because of continued economic
containment policies on hospitals and the overall sluggish rate
of growth of the economy. Some of the hospital workers will
generally continue to hold a weak position in earnings, while
their real average weekly earnings will actually decline. Increases in earnings for health-care workers in May 1981 average to
about 10 per cent and the rate of inflation, as estimated by
the Conference Board in Canada will be about 11.7 per cent.[10]

The health-care unions will be increasingly militant in their
demands as exemplified by 1979, 1980 and 1981 strikes by
health-care workers in some provinces.[11] Bairstow predicts that
'...the aggressive union activity will come from hospitals and
other less well-paid service sectors, where they are lagging
even further behind than are most of the groups that will be
bargaining in 1981'.[12] This demand may compel the governments
to deviate from their stated policy of restraint in public sector
wage settlements.

The government's role as a regulator is likely to increase in
light of the fact that health services industry is an essential
industry where the patient's welfare must be protected. The
government's role as a legislator is well known in Canada
through the setting up of Anti Inflation Board in 1975. A return

to wage and price controls is not predicted by most industrial relations experts in the country.[13] However, controls may become a reality, if the United States resorts to such a measure, and if the rate of inflation exceeds 12 per cent.

Collective bargaining strategies in the health-care sector are not confined to a choice between work stoppage on the one hand and government control of wages and working conditions on the other. There is a middle road, and as one labour leader puts it, 'The middle road is labour-management cooperation; or, better still, labour-management-government cooperation.'[14] The trend towards positive collective bargaining in the health sector will ultimately depend upon the maturity of the parties, rationalisation of the union institutions, the skills of negotiators, the attitudes of management, the nature of the consultative assistance provided by the government, and the overall economic and political climates.

Summary
During the decade 1970-80, bargaining demands have been built around issues such as wages, paid holidays, vacations, union security, notice of layoffs, reduced hours of work, shift premiums and sick leave. There is an increasing trend in the eighties to stress issues in the collective bargaining such as pensions, human rights, participation in the decision-making process, equal pay for work of equal value, health and safety committees, and flexible retirement policies. Parties in the past have relied on the criteria of cost of living and comparable employments. Such criteria will continue to be applied in the new economic and political reality in the eighties. Bargaining strategies will be subject not only to new expectations of the hospital worker but also upon the internal and external economic and political impacts on the health care delivery system.

US: INTERNAL AND EXTERNAL PRESSURES AFFECTING COLLECTIVE BARGAINING STRATEGIES: NONPROFESSIONAL HOSPITAL WORKERS AND ALLIED HEALTH-CARE PROFESSIONALS

There are at least three sets of external pressures affecting the collective bargaining strategies of unions representing nonprofessional and allied professional health-care workers in the USA; legislation, third-party payers and employer structure for bargaining. Internal pressures affecting bargaining strategies include the structure and composition of the unions at the local, regional and national levels.

Prior to 1974, the lack of federal labour legislation covering nonprofit hospitals was accompanied by a patchwork quilt of state legislation in the area. In 37 states, nonprofit hospitals were not required to recognise or bargain collectively with their employees; the remainder of states had legislation varying in

their favourableness towards collective bargaining.[15] The kind
of state legislation had a direct impact on the early development
of trade union bargaining strategies.

Labour organisations in states without legislation favourable
to hospital collective bargaining were often forced to resort to
the strike or the threat of a strike to achieve recognition. Thereafter, the strike strategy either became a regular part of the
bargaining process, or the parties developed private mechanisms,
such as pre-election consent agreements, to avoid strikes. Pre-
election consent agreements required recognition elections to be
held and also required submission of interest disputes to binding arbitration. The 1974 Amendments eliminated the need for
pre-election consent stipulations and the unions involved in such
stipulations now pursue traditional strike-related bargaining
strategies.

States which guaranteed hospital workers the right to bargain
collectively prior to 1974 also limited the workers right to strike.
These limitations have, in some cases, had a permanent impact
on the bargaining strategies of the trade unions involved. The
most notable situation is that which occurred in Minnesota. In
that state, the Charitable Hospitals Act of 1947 required arbitration of contract disputes. Several bargaining relationships,
especially those in Minneapolis-St Paul, relied heavily on
interest arbitration. As a result, when the 1974 Amendments
superseded the state legislation, interest arbitration language
was written into several Twin City area collective agreements.
The bargaining strategies followed by the parties in these
relationships often reflect the fear that an arbitrator will 'split
the difference'. That is, the parties take positions at opposite
ends of the bargaining continuum and freeze their positions.

The bargaining units established as a result of pre-1974
legislation have also had an impact on the contemporary bargaining strategies of trade unions. Certain state labour boards,
such as those in Minnesota and in New York, pursued a policy
of certifying narrowly defined bargaining units in an effort to
promote employee free choice in collective bargaining. In Minnesota, this policy encouraged the establishment of separate
labour organisations to represent small technical groups such
as pharmacists and radiologic technicians. In New York, the
policy encouraged Local 1199 to organise itself into occupationally
based divisions (see Chapter 4).

The bargaining policies the independent technical organisations develop are specific to their members occupationally based
needs. Lack of co-ordination among several labour organisations
representing different bargaining units in the same hospital
makes it difficult for labour to exercise bargaining power based
on an ability to shut down the institution. A union such as Local
1199 has the problem of internally resolving bargaining policy
clashes based on occupational differences.

The 1974 Amendments, as well as subsequent NLRB decisions,
have encouraged broad-based bargaining units. To the extent

such units develop labour may be in a better position to exercise effective bargaining power. On the other hand, trade union leaders and attorneys have argued that management efforts to destroy bargaining units established under state legislation -- on the grounds that they fail to meet the NLRB's criteria for eliminating fragmentation -- are eroding labour's hold in the hospital sector.[16]

The role of third-party payers in the collective bargaining process is ubiquitous yet not clearly understood. That it is ubiquitous is a result of the growing concern of policy-makers with health-care costs (see Santos and Helburn, Chapter 18); that it is not clearly understood is a result of the complexities involved when a third-party payer looks closely at labour costs when determining its reimbursement policies.

Richard U. Miller states that in the Northeast and especially in New York, reimbursement policies have affected the structure of bargaining and the behaviour of the parties, resulting in a hardening of positions and an increase in conflict.[17] He states that, in a variation of multilateral bargaining typical of the public sector, labour and management in seeking bargaining leverage, draw the third-party payer into negotiations. He points out, however, that the difference is that in health care the bargaining is not multilateral. Instead, it is a series of bilateral negotiations: employer and union, employer and public authority, union and public authority, and perhaps union acting together with employer against public authority.[18] The final result of the public authority's intervention has been to 'chill' bargaining. Thus, states Miller, the settlement must be fashioned either by an outside arbitrator or by the rate decisions of the public authorities themselves.[19] The latter decisions, at least in the case of New York City hospitals, have often been made as a response to strikes or threatened strikes by militant unions.

Employer structures for bargaining have been a function of union bargaining strength and, simultaneously, have affected union bargaining strategies. Thus, in highly organised areas -- such as New York City, Minneapolis-St Paul and San Francisco-Oakland -- when employers began to co-ordinate bargaining activities to counter union whipsaw tactics, the unions pushed for and obtained multiple employer agreements.[20] Alternatively, in areas where unions have not been as successful in organising, at least part of the reason has been due to the very effective 'preventive' labour relations programme co-ordinated by local and regional hospital councils. Local unions which have organised in the latter areas sometimes find it difficult to extend their jurisdiction. This is because the hospital councils encourage their member institutions to implement policies, procedures and benefits which would eliminate the incentive for workers to join unions. Also, unions in these regions are very susceptible to decertification drives by disgruntled members who see workers at non-unionised institutions receiving the same or better benefits without the responsibility of having to pay union dues.

In Chapter 4 of this volume, Schoen explored the unique structural configurations of the largest labour organisations in the health-care sector. She concluded that: the National Union of Hospital and Health Care Employees (NUHHCE) centralises its bargaining authority in the national headquarters; while the American Federation of State, County and Municipal Employees (AFSCME) delegates authority to regional bodies; and both the Service Employees International Union (SEIU) and the United Food and Commercial Workers International Union (UFCWIU) give their locals much discretion in bargaining matters. Schoen also stated that while each organisation represented a large number of health-care workers only the NUHCCE had the health-care sector as its sole focus of activity. These structural and member-ship configurations have had a direct impact on the bargaining strategies employed by the NUHHCE, SEIU and UFCWIU. Other factors specific to the public sector have shaped AFSCME's bargaining strategies.

The Constitution of the NUHHCE gives effective power over collective bargaining activities to the union president.[21] Since the union president also acts as chief negotiator in the major New York City bargaining relationship, he attempts to use the union's organisational base there to establish bargaining pat-terns. The importance of the New York City agreements to Local 1199 has led it to engage in a number of bitter strikes since the late 1950s.[22] Its importance has also led the union to reject or threaten to reject arbitrated decisions.[23] Furthermore, the union has, in certain cases, appealed directly to third-party payers in New York State in an effort to achieve better wages increases.[24]

SEIU locals are dispersed, with a single local often covering many workers employed across a large number of companies and organisations, in a variety of industries and occupations.[25] Miller states that local unions may improve the services they offer by belonging to a Joint Council. A Joint Council is com-posed of a minimum of 15 local unions and provides back-up for negotiations, assists with arbitration cases and provides research and other expert services for affiliated locals.[26]

Miller discusses several implications of this structural con-figuration which, in turn, have relevance for bargaining strate-gies:[27]

1. The presence of the Joint Council permits the individual locals to pool their resources to ensure that expert bargain-ing help is locally available as the need arises.
2. The business representatives appointed to the locals, with the aid of the research specialists from the Joint Councils, are able to use in individual negotiations, their knowledge of wage levels, working conditions, and contract settlements in competing health-care institutions as well as in similar occupations in nonhealth industries.

3. The vertical integration of hospital bargaining units attached
   to a dispersed local union which in turn is a unit within a
   Joint Council may create problems of emphasis in bargaining
   and 'reactive' organising. For example, in large locals where
   only a minority of the members are hospital workers, priorities may be placed elsewhere, or the expertise required to
   deal with the hospital sector may not be available. Also,
   union resources may be thinly spread across a number of
   demands. The results may be that hospital members do not
   receive the attention they need and bargaining progress will
   reflect this. Similarly, organising may not be systematic,
   and may be limited to responding or reacting to outside
   requests.

The UFCWIU co-ordinates the activities of health-care members
by means of a Professional Health Care Division.[28] The purpose
of the division is to encourage affiliations of independent organisations and to provide a superstructure for the UFCWIU in the
health sector.[29]

The independent organisations, representing such diverse
groups as medical technologists and operating room technicians,
were formed when the professional organisations to which the
workers belonged refused to represent them in collective bargaining. The UFCWIU permitted the independents to affiliate
by forming their own local unions, assuring that their members
would have control over collective bargaining policies affecting
them. Several of the locals, backed by the International, engaged
in long strikes, especially in the Seattle and Portland areas.
The locals lost these strikes because the hospitals were able to
continue operation without the specialised workers. None the
less, viewing this as an area of potential membership growth,
UFCWIU continues to provide strong financial support to its
health-care locals.

The major factors affecting AFSCME's bargaining strategies
are more deeply rooted in the problems of public sector bargaining than in internal union structure. Miller states that:

AFSCME not only shares with other public sector organisations the burden of governmental fiscal dislocation, but also
the weight of a state or local public policy in opposition to
trade unions and collective bargaining .... Until state legal
barriers are lowered, public hospital unionism will be an
exception rather than the rule.[30]

Thus, AFSCME must pursue a legislative strategy designed to
achieve positive public policy for public sector unionism and
it must also deal with public sector budget cutbacks. In New
York City in the late 1970s, AFSCME sought to deal with budget
induced layoffs by means of a massive strike. Although the
strike prevented some of the layoffs, it is unclear whether
this strategy has long-range viability in jurisdictions facing

real and long-run fiscal constraints.

THE UNITED KINGDOM

The category of 'nonprofessional employees' covers three groups in the National Health Service (NHS): the ancillary staff of approximately 220 000, who constitute about one-fifth of all NHS staff, and who are employed primarily in the 'hotel services' side of the hospital sector: the 31 000 works and maintenance staff who also work almost exclusively in the hospital sector; and the ambulance staff of about 21 000 who since the 1974 reorganisation have become the direct employees of the NHS.[31] Both the ancillary workers and the ambulance staffs have separate functional Councils within the Whitley centralised bargaining structure. In addition they are represented by the same four trade unions: the Confederation of Health Service Employees (COHSE); the General and Municipal Workers' Union (GMWU); the National Union of Public Employees (NUPE); and the Transport and General Workers' Union (TGWU).[32] These four unions are affiliated to the British Trades Union Congress (TUC), as are the unions representing craftsmen and hospital maintenance workers. This latter group negotiates separately with government's Health Departments to determine rates of pay consistent with those for craftsmens' national scales in industry.

Prior to the 1970s the bargaining activities of the principal nonprofessional group, the ancillary staffs, were especially low key. In the past decade the increasing militancy of this group has been primarily responsible for creating a new climate in health service industrial relations. Since entering the NHS the ambulance staffs too have adopted an aggressive posture in pay bargaining. However because of their wider influence on NHS industrial relations this section will concentrate upon ancillary workers.

Internal and External Pressures

The development of ancillary staffs from a weakly organised occupational group in the 1960s to their present state of organisational strength is perhaps one of the most critical elements in the recent history of the NHS. It has been argued that the growth of trade unionism and the changes in their bargaining behaviour was stimulated by the events surrounding the introduction of large district hospitals in the late 1960s and early 1970s.[33] In essence the argument holds that the introduction of managerialism as a necessary corollary to the increasing size and complexity of the hospital sector was a significant internal pressure on the unionisation and bargaining activities of the ancillary staffs. Hence, health service managerialism, based on the principles of industrial management, acted to undermine the traditional attitudes and behavioural patterns of the ancillary staffs. In particular their previous attitude of deference was replaced by the notion of the cash nexus and a rationale more akin to manual workers within a capitalist system of production. These internal innovations and the changed attitudes they produced were the stimulus to trade union growth. More significantly they encouraged a sense of collective consciousness among ancillary workers within hospitals and the subsequent emergence of a workplace-based system of trade union organisation. The leaders of this system were union stewards elected by individual work groups within the ancillary labour force.

In this context the ancillary staffs national pay dispute in 1973 was especially significant: although defeated over their national pay claim, one of its significant by-products was the consolidation of the emergent system of workplace trade unionism. Moreover the ancillary staffs' unions' decision to apply direct sanctions in support of national pay bargaining directly challenged the taboo against taking action which could be seen as hazarding patients. (Although the medical profession had offered threats, it had, until that time, retreated from taking direct sanctions.) In the years immediately following 1973 virtually every NHS occupational group took up the ancillary staffs' example.

The absolute increase in union membership and the growth of workplace trade unionism is all the more remarkable given the severe organisational difficulties which confront the four trade unions. A large proportion of the ancillary staff are female part-time employees.[34] In addition ancillary staffs have traditionally fallen into the category of the low paid, both relatively in the NHS and absolutely in the UK's labour market. These two factors together with the traditional attitude of deference tended to depress union membership and thereby acted as a brake on the collective bargaining behaviour of the ancillary staffs' trade unions. After the 1973 dispute the four unions encouraged the development of workplace organisation. For example, with the support of the TUC these unions commenced training programmes for health sector stewards; while NUPE adapted its internal structure to enable greater involvement for ordinary members in the government of the union.[35]

However the growth in membership and workplace organisation has taken place within a multi-union context. In consequence there has been a number of difficulties arising from inter-union competition.[36] The entry of the ambulance services into the NHS in 1974 introduced a new element of competition. Their assimilation into the NHS necessitated a series of mergers between previously separate services to create new organisational forms. The result of these various mergers was to highlight the existence of differentials in pay and conditions that had grown up under local government. Attempts by health authorities to equalise pay and conditions within the newly formed ambulance services met with strong opposition from those staff who wished to preserve their distinctive sets of arrangements.

The overriding external pressure has been the low pay levels

for nonprofessional staff, in particular for ancillary and ambulance workers. On government's part a central and underlying
feature of centralised Whitley bargaining structure is the opportunity it gives for the control of earnings which constitute
approximately 70 per cent of NHS expenditure. In the area of
ancillary employment the traditional weakness of the trade
unions led them to rely on third-party arbitration as a means
of improving on the pay offers of the management side. The
incidence of low pay among ancillary staffs first received public
attention in 1967 in a Report of the National Board for Prices
and Incomes (NBPI): 25 per cent of male workers in this group
fell within the low paid category.[37]

After the 1966 disclosure of the extent of low pay among
ancillary staff it could be argued that the best means of amelior-
ating their position would have been an 'across the board'
increase. However the ability of government to undertake this
course is severely restricted. In the first instance the percept-
ible decline of the British economy from the 1960s has led
government to limit spending on the public sector services. An
increase sufficient to remove ancillary workers from the low
paid category would have considerable consequences for NHS
expenditure. Secondly, such an increase would have significant
effects on the established differentials between ancillary staffs
and other NHS occupations: nursing and other allied medical
professions also see themselves as low paid by reference to
their skills. Thirdly, of the four unions representing ancillary
staffs three are also the principal representatives of manual
workers in local government. The past bargaining weakness of
ancillary staffs encouraged these unions to establish a link over
pay between them and local government's manual workers. Thus
pay settlements for the latter group generally provide the bargaining parameters for the subsequent national pay agreement
for NHS ancillary staffs: local government employees would
undoubtedly have attempted to retain the same pay levels. Moreover because local government receives considerable financial
support from the national Exchequer, state expenditure would
be further squeezed. The NBPI recommended the work measured
payment systems.

The high rate of inflation and the consistent use of national
incomes policies by successive governments in the 1960s and
1970s has been a further external pressure on the pay bargaining of the NHS's nonprofessional employees. From another direction the labour legislation of both the Conservative and Labour
Governments in the 1970s has reinforced the development of
hospital-based trade unionism. The ancillary staffs' Whitley
Council acknowledged the legislation and the increase in steward
numbers when it negotiated an agreement in 1971 that set out
their rights and functions. However the effects of the 1971
legislation were felt more keenly within hospitals, as it exposed
the NHS's lack of appropriate 'local' procedures. The subsequent
introduction of grievance and disciplinary procedures by

hospital managements confirmed the representative role of the
union stewards. Following the Labour Government's legislation
of 1975 their role was given additional support by means of
statutory rights for appropriate time off to pursue trade union
duties and activities. These functions of the steward are critical
to the success of the unions. Acting as a go-between, both with
the membership and management and with the membership and
the union hierarchy, the steward may come to be seen as the
personification of the union in the eyes of the ordinary member.[38]

Nonprofessional Employees and Collective Bargaining
The development of hospital-level trade union organisation has
been an important factor in fashioning a new form and structure
of bargaining among these three occupational groups. Here again
the ancillary staffs provide the most pertinent example, although
ambulance and maintenance workers have followed a similar pattern. Prior to the last decade collective bargaining was almost
wholly encompassed within the ancillary staffs' functional Council. Increasingly in the 1970s hospital trade unionism has seen
the introduction of new structures within health authorities with
the aim of providing a forum for the joint determination of local
issues between management and their staff.

The precise form of these structures varies according to local
circumstances and in consequence it is not possible to give a
definitive description of either their form or purpose.[39] However
a number of general points can be made. First, these structures
have usually been established jointly by local managements and
trade union representatives in the absence of guidance from
either the Whitley Councils or the government Health Departments. Secondly, the need for hospital managements to create
and maintain a dialogue with locally militant ancillary staffs has
been a major reason for their introduction. Thirdly, although
local managements generally maintain that these committees are
only used for the purpose of 'consulting' staff it can be suggested that some aspects of their business are conducted by
straightforward collective bargaining.[40] Fourthly, while there
is no clear picture of items normally under consideration it can
be suggested that management inspired innovations to established working practices tend to be accompanied by concessions
on matters deemed important by the staffs' representatives.

Straightforward pay bargaining is still formally retained as a
prerogative of the national bargaining structure. However the
introduction of work-measured payment schemes provides some
opportunities for local pay bargaining. Local management concessions for example, the rearrangement of work shifts, rotas
and overtime, can also yield higher earnings to the ancillary
staff. Another area of concessions centres on staffs' request for
better working conditions and facilities. In this manner the
incidence and scope of locally determined pay increases can be
legitimately disguised by stewards and managers from the
scrutiny of the centralised bargaining structure. In addition

to these locally established consultative/bargaining structures, ancillary staffs' stewards have maintained the practice of approaching management on matters of specific concern to either the membership of an individual union or to a particular group of workers. Again the bargainable options can be as described above. By these means the growth of local bargaining has been built up on two fronts.

A variety of structural forms has also evolved locally on the trade union side. The basic organisational unit of British trade unions is the 'branch', with certain key officers elected by the branch membership. The location of the branch differs between unions. While there are a number of variables two broad distinctions can be applied. The branch can be based on a section of the membership residing in a defined geographical area, but employed in different industries or companies. Alternatively the branch may be sited at the place of work. In the NHS the latter organisational form is more common, and this may mean that within a health authority or a large hospital the branch is the cornerstone of local trade union organisation. Hence the branch officers may assume a wide responsibility for representing the membership to management on local issues. However another feature of workplace trade unionism in well-organised sectors of British industry is the stewards' own committee structure. In the NHS ancillary workers' stewards' organisations have tended towards two forms: a committee made up of stewards from within the same union, or more rarely, an inter-union committee. As the four unions recognised for ancillary workers also organise other NHS occupations these committee types may include stewards representing other occupational groups, e.g. nurses. The different union structures are not mutually exclusive and in practice trade union organisation within health authorities tends to be a combination of these structures. However, irrespective of its organisational form the significance of the structure is that it provides the means to determine and articulate collective opposition to local policies and practices that make up the prerogative of hospital managements.

The smaller concentrations of hospital maintenance workers generally precludes the establishment of workplace trade union branches. Moreover in their case the traditions of craft unionism tend to favour a geographically sited branch. For this group therefore the workplace trade union structure is more normally based upon stewards' committees.

Hospital level trade union organisation is perhaps the most significant determinant of the nonprofessional staffs' bargaining power. By comparison with the 1950s and 1960s the unions representing these occupational groups now enjoy not only an increased level of membership but also, and more importantly, a membership with a sense of collective identity and strength at the hospital level. Coincidentially the expression of that strength in national disputes has generally stimulated a further growth in union membership: NUPE in particular experienced its major expansion following the 1973 national pay dispute.

It is important to delineate between local and national bargaining. At the local level, usually in large hospitals, the existence of trade union organisation has required that managements adopt a negotiating stance with nonprofessional employees which would have been unthinkable before the 1970s. On some issues, e.g. the continuation of private medical practice within NHS hospitals, the initiatives taken by the local trade union organisation have overtaken the national policies of their trade unions. The ability of local union organisations to undertake direct sanctions may often exact concessions from hospital managements. However it has not as yet been sufficient to overcome government's resolve to retain a tight control over national pay scales.

Bargaining Strategies
Hospital-based trade unionism has generally been concerned with the improvement of local circumstances in terms of earnings increases (where possible) and more favourable working conditions. The extent to which this can be viewed as a deliberate strategy on the part of the ancillary staffs' trade unions is a moot point. The national leadership of these unions comment on the importance of the stewards' role in safeguarding and advancing the interests of the members locally.[41] It may however be more realistic to see this as an acknowledgement of the existing situation rather than as a coherent policy agreed between national and local representatives.

Within the last few years, and particularly following the election of the Conservative Government in 1979, the ancillary staffs' trade unions have become concerned over the reductions in state spending both for the NHS and other social services. In this regard they have had relatively few successes in resisting either hospital closures and service reductions locally, or nationally increased charges for services.[42] This may in part be an illustration of the lack of cohesiveness between national and local levels within the four unions. However it also emphasises the basic dilemma of the TUC unions: whilst ideologically committed to the continuation and expansion of the NHS, in advancing their members' interests they are inevitably cast in the role of 'attacking' it. This dilemma is acute as their principal strategy remains that of gaining significant increases in national pay bargaining to ameliorate the relatively low level of their members' earnings. In this context they have found it necessary, despite their recent increase in bargaining strength, to fall back on third-party intervention as a means of improving management side's pay offers (or more accurately, the financial limits set by government).

In 1973 and again in 1979 the ancillary staffs' trade unions applied direct sanctions in support of national pay bargaining. In the 1979 dispute they were joined by ambulance workers. Although strikes were a feature of these disputes in some health authorities (particularly in the case of ambulance workers), the more usual sanctions were works-to-rule, overtime bans, and restrictions of output. In general therefore some form of staff cover was provided in order to maintain hospitals' emergency services.

The direct cause of the 1973 dispute was the break in the comparability link between ancillary staffs' and local government manual workers, due to the onset of an incomes policy. The dispute can be judged a success in terms of the stimulus it gave to both the level of union membership and the consolidation of hospital-based trade union organisation. However the dispute failed to persuade the Conservative Government, acting through the management side of the ancillary staffs' functional Council, to breach its newly introduced incomes policy.

The 1979 disputes gave the Labour Government greater cause for concern. The original trigger was again the application of an incomes policy and its perceived unfairness to low-paid workers in an inflationary period. However the 1979 dispute contained a number of additional features. In 1973 both management and union representatives locally found themselves in a novel situation. By comparison, in 1979 many hospital managements had in some sense come to terms with either the possibility, or the effects of union sanctions. The trade unions had gained lessons from the 1973 dispute. In 1979 they tended to take more selective industrial action, aimed at either major hospitals or critical areas within the production side of hotel services, e.g. laundries. In some instances managements' responses to sanctions were more determined, e.g. a reduction of the bonus element in wages and the use of volunteer labour. Government too became directly involved with its decision to introduce the ambulance services of the armed forces.

Faced with a more resolute resistance than in 1973 the unions found that despite their new internal strength and solidarity they were unable to achieve major concessions within the NHS's collective bargaining machinery. It was because of this perhaps that divisions between and within the national organs of the unions began to emerge. The eventual means of resolution was provided by the Clegg Commission, charged with the task of comparing ancillary and ambulance staffs' pay with that of similar groups of workers in the public and private sectors. Although this represented a concession by the Labour Government it was probably motivated by the prospect of an imminent General Election rather than by the sanctions of the NHS unions. The subsequent recommendations of the Commission were generally unsatisfactory from the unions' viewpoint.[43] Ambulance staff received a relatively large increase, as the emergency element in their work allowed for comparisons with the better paid police and fire services. Ancillary workers however failed to secure increases on the scale originally sought by their trade unions, as the comparability studies demonstrated that their pay was not unfavourable with that of similar occupations in other sectors of the labour market.

Outcomes and Trends
The results of the 1979 dispute suggest that ancillary workers
in particular will tend to remain in the category of the low paid,
albeit with marginal improvements. Unlike the medical profession
they do not control a body of knowledge and skills which could
make them indispensable to the NHS. (Among nonprofessional
employees only the hospital maintenance staff could claim this.)
Moreover events in the 1979 dispute have tended to encourage
hospital managements to believe that a more retaliatory approach
reduces the likelihood or at least the duration of unions' sanctions. Official advice from the Health Departments supports this
view.[44] If management should pursue a harder line one probable
consequence is an escalation of hostilities within both national
and local disputes. While national level bargaining remains as
the principal focus of nonprofessional employees' trade unions
nationally, it seems likely that third party arbitration will
continue as a means for resolving national disputes over pay.
At the hospital level however trade union organisation may be
further strengthened by the present proposals to restructure
the management arrangements.[45] The proposed devolution of
increased authority and responsibility to hospital management may
serve, in practice, to widen the scope of local joint determination.

REFERENCES AND NOTES

1 Conference Board in Canada (1980), Employment Growth in
  the Public Sector, 'Executive Bulletin', no.12, May, p.4.
2 Ibid., p.4. The Hospital Insurance and Diagnostic Services
  Act was passed in 1957 covering all Canadians, under which
  the federal government agreed to share with the provinces
  the cost of providing hospital care. In 1966 the Medical Care
  Act was passed. By 1972 all provinces and territories had
  joined this programme which provided federal contributions
  to provincial medical care insurance programmes.
3 Ibid., pp.8-9.
4 In addition to CUPE, other unions found in more than one
  province are: Health Science Association (HSA), HSA and
  Association of Allied Health Professionals (AAHP), HSA is
  active in Saskatchewan, Alberta and British Columbia.
  AAHP is in Newfoundland and Ontario (no central bargaining in Ontario with this group). Other unions include:
  International Union of Operating Engineers (IUOE) (no
  central bargaining in Ontario), and Service Employees
  International Union (SEIU). The remaining unions are each
  in one or more hospitals but in only one province or are in
  more than one province but with such a small number of
  bargaining units that central bargaining is not appropriate.
5 The paramedical group embraces laboratory technologists,
  X-ray technologists, dietitians, pharmacists, occupational
  therapists, physiotherapists, remedial gymnasts, medical

social workers, medical records librarians and a number of
smaller groups of this nature. Labor Relations Board policy
now recognises only these groups as appropriate for certification. Some 29 separate operating engineers groups
organised by the International Union of Operating Engineers
exist on a 'grandfather' basis but no new certifications of
separate operating engineers units are now possible in
British Columbia hospitals.
6 Johnston, D.L. (1974), 'The Report of the Hospital Inquiry
  Commission', Toronto, November. For the purpose of certification for collective bargaining the Ontario Labor Relations
  Board has recognised five groups of employees: service
  employees, office employees, operating engineers, professional nurses and paramedical employees. Service employees
  are mainly kitchen staff, maintenance staff, cleaners,
  laundry workers and registered nursing assistants. Some
  150 hospitals have service units, most being represented
  either by the Canadian Union of Public Employees or the
  Service Employees International Union (around 30 000
  employees in total). Office employees are represented mainly
  by these same two unions; about 25 per cent of the office
  employees are represented.
7 Hospital Employees Relations Services Division Unpublished
  Research Paper, Ontario Hospital Association, Toronto,
  September 1979. Ontario's system of group bargaining is
  currently supported by three levels of committees:

  1. Employee Relations Policy Committee, a standing com-
     mittee of the Ontario Hospital Association Board of
     Directors.
  2. Steering Committee (Chief Executive Officers, Trustees
     and Personnel Directors). The participating hospital
     delegates authority to bargain to the Steering Committee
     which establishes the mandate for each set of negotiations.
     This Committee includes an officer of the Ministry of
     Health who provides liaison with government.
  3. Ad Hoc Negotiating Teams (generalist administrators,
     Personnel Directors). There has been one team for each
     set of provincial negotiations. (ONA)

  There are about 80 bargaining units exclusively for operating engineers accounting for around 1000 employees. These
  generally small units are held by the International Union
  of Operating Engineers (50 units) and the Canadian Union
  of Operating Engineers (30 units). Paramedical units consisted mainly of medical laboratory and X-ray technicians,
  but latterly have included pharmacists, physiotherapists,
  dietitians, medical records librarians, technologists,
  psychometrists and other similar occupations. However,
  the expanded units are few in number. This coincided with
  an upsurge of unionisation among these employees, and a

determination by the Labour Relations Board to define
'paramedical' in broad, rather than in narrow, terms. Some
70 hospitals have paramedical units. Of the 240 public
general hospitals, 175 have one or more bargaining units.
In 25 of these, all employees eligible to be represented are
organised. There are 13 unions in the industry, of which
7 have 10 or more units.

8 Woods, H.D. (1969), 'Canadian Labour Relations'.
9 Ibid.
10 Chartier, A.R. (1981), 'Industrial Relations 1981 Outlook
   and Issues', Conference Board in Canada, February,
   pp.5-18.
11 The rate of strikes and lockouts in Canada is as follows:

Strikes and Lockouts in the Health and Welfare Sector and
all Industries in Canada 1975-80

	Health & Welfare		All Industries	
	No. of Strikes	Person-days Lost	No. of Strikes	Person-days Lost
1975	46	91 650	1171	10 908 810
1976	56	769 490	1039	11 609 890
1977	37	123 260	803	3 307 880
1978	59	131 020	1058	7 392 820
1979	50	461 350	1050	7 834 230
1980	79	224 500	1033	8 482 000

Source: Labour Data Branch, Labour Canada (February 1981),
'Strikes and Lockouts in Canada', Labour Canada (1979 and
earlier issues).

12 Chartier, Industrial Relations Outlook & Issues, p.6.
13 Ibid.
14 Finn, Ed (1980), Let's take tripartism out of the closet,
   'MacLean's', vol.93, no.39, 29 September, p.6.
15 Pointer, Dennis D., and Metzger, Norman (1975), 'The
   National Labor Relations Act: A Guidebook for Health Care
   Facility Administrators', pp.55-60.
16 D'Alba, Joel A. (1980), Health Care Bargaining Units and
   the Law: Recent Trends and Problems, in Ronald J. Peters,
   Helen Elkiss and Helen T. Higgins (eds.), 'Unionisation
   and the Health Care Industry: Hospital and Nursing Home
   Employee Union Leaders' Conference Report', pp.35-7.
17 Miller, Richard U. (1980), Hospitals, in Gerald G. Somers
   (ed.), 'Collective Bargaining: Contemporary American
   Experience', Industrial Relations Research Association,
   p.146.
18 Ibid.
19 Ibid., p.417.

20 Solomon, Norman A. (1980), The Emergence of Multiple Employer Bargaining in the Nonprofit Hospital Sector: An Exploratory Analysis, unpublished PhD thesis, University of Wisconsin, pp.251-9.
21 Block, Richard N. (1978), Unionism in the Health Care Industry: An Overview, 'The Journal of Health and Human Resources Administration', October, pp.5-7.
22 Solomon, The Emergence of Multiple Employer Bargaining, pp.137, 191, 204-10.
23 Ibid., pp.205, 208-9.
24 Nash, Abraham (1972), Labor Management Conflict in a Voluntary Hospital, unpublished PhD thesis, New York University, p.79.
25 Miller, Hospitals, p.396.
26 Ibid.
27 Ibid., pp.396-7.
28 Communication from Richard J. Perry, International Vice-President and Director, Professional Health Care Division, UFCWIU, 30 January 1981.
29 'Retail Clerks International Union, Official Proceedings, Reports, and Resolutions', 27th International Convention, Honolulu, July 25-27, 1976, p.6.
30 Miller, p.400.
31 'Royal Commission on the National Health Service, Report', Cmnd. 7615, HMSO, London, 1979, p.178, Table 12.2.
32 COHSE is overwhelmingly an NHS union although it has a small membership in the local government sector. The GMWU, NUPE and TGWU are also recognised for other NHS occupational groups and have seats on a number of Whitley Councils. These three unions are also recognised for collective bargaining purposes in other areas of the public sector and the GMWU and the TGWU organise in private industry. The TGWU is the largest union in the UK with over two million members. Figures supplied by the Department of Health and Social Security in 1979 identified NHS membership of these four unions as follows: COHSE - 244 000: GMWU - 22 000: NUPE - 244 000: TGWU - 12 000. The fact that the DHSS gave equal membership figures for COHSE and NUPE of itself is probably an indication of its awareness of the general sensitivity which surrounds the competition for membership between these two unions.
33 Dimmock, Stuart, and Farnham, David (1975), Working with Whitley in today's NHS, 'Personnel Management', vol.7, no.1. Manson, Tom (1977), Management, the Professions and the Unions: A Social Analysis of Change in the National Health Service, in M. Stacey et al., (eds.), 'Health and the Division of Labour', Croom Helm.
34 For an analysis of the role of NUPE's female stewards see, Fryer, R.H., Fairclough, A.J., and Manson, T.B. (1978), Facilities for Female Shop Stewards: The Employment Protection Act and Collective Agreements, 'British Journal of

Industrial Relations', vol.XVI, no.2.

35 Fryer, R.H., Fairclough, A.J., and Manson, T.B. (1974),
   'Organisation and Change in the National Union of Public
   Employees', NUPE.

36 'Royal Commission on the National Health Service: ACAS
   Evidence', Advisory Conciliation and Arbitration Service,
   1978.

37 'The Pay and Conditions of Manual Workers in Local
   Authorities, the National Health Service, Gas and Water
   Supply', National Board for Prices and Incomes Report
   No.29, HMSO, 1967.

38 'Your Job as a Union Steward: a Handbook for Union
   Stewards Representing Health Service Ancillary Staffs',
   NUPE, BD/PL/10.71.

39 For a discussion of the various forms of local joint structures see, Dyson, Roger, Consultation and Negotiation;
   Bosanquet, Nick, op.cit., 1979.

40 Roger Dyson, ibid.

41 See for example the discussion of stewards' representative
   roles in NUPE, op.cit., BD/PL/10.71 and in, 'Union
   Stewards Handbook', COHSE, 1976.

42 Recent action against hospital closures has tended to take
   the form of 'occupations' or 'work-ins'. In general however
   incidents of this type are relatively uncommon as local
   managements have normally closed individual wards rather
   than hospitals. This piecemeal and diffuse approach has
   reduced the opportunity for concerted action by local trade
   union organisations. Resistence to the Conservative
   Government's national policies has taken the form of TUC
   organised 'Days of Action' which have centred upon formal
   protest marches. The unwillingness of the TUC or its
   affiliated unions to exercise their industrial strength
   against the present government's policies is probably a
   function of the declining economic position of industry and
   their current poor public image.

43 'Local Authority and University Manual Workers: NHS
   Ancillary Staffs; and Ambulancemen', Standing Commission
   on Pay Comparability Report no.1, Cmnd.7641, HMSO, 1979.

44 'If Industrial Relations Break Down', (HC(79)20), Department of Health and Social Security, 1979.

45 Department of Health and Social Security, 'Patients First',
   HMSO, 1979.

12. BARGAINING STRATEGIES AMONG PHYSICIANS : CANADA, USA AND UK

E.J. Moran, T.A. Barocci and S.J. Dimmock *

CANADA

The medical profession in Canada has been involved with various provincial governments in the determination of payment for medical services for about ten years. This roughly coincides with the period during which governments, for practical purposes, have served as the sole source of such payments. Negotiating arrangements in the various provinces vary in marginal ways, and have evolved over time.

Table 12.1 illustrates the decline in physicians' real income since 1971. It will be noted that general pricing in Canada as measured by the Consumer Price Index has increased 91 per cent since 1971 whereas physicians' net incomes have increased only 34 per cent.

Table 12.1: Index of Physicians' Net Incomes vs. Price Inflation - 1971 = 100

	Physicians' Net Income[a]	Consumer Price Index[b]
1971	100.0	100.0
1972	100.8	104.8
1973	101.3	112.7
1974	101.5	125.0
1975	108.7	138.5
1976	111.3	148.9
1977	117.0	160.8
1978	123.1[c]	175.2
1979	133.6[c]	191.2

a. Department of National Health and Welfare Canada
   (for physicians who netted $15,000 or more per year)
b. Statistics Canada
c. Estimate Based on Benefit Schedule Increase.

Most physicians believe that the current negotiations are a sham. They believe that the Cabinet, the Executive Committee

* The section on Canada is written by Moran. The US portion is authored by Barocci and Dimmock has contributed the UK section.

of Government, identifies a maximum percentage increase which
is acceptable to it in relation to overall political and fiscal
pressures; and then the physician negotiators play a funny
little game called 'guess the number'. The profession's negotiators do in fact use income levels, economic indices and the
usual trappings that accompany the bargaining ritual, but the
consensus is that such presentations just help to carry off
the charade and do not influence the end point very much, if
at all.

The ultimate bargaining weapon of the profession is the ability
to impose sanctions, a euphemism for withdrawal of service in
some form or other. Up to this point, such a strategy has been
repugnant to physicians, largely because of their professional
instincts and because of the very vital nature of the service
they provide. However, professional associations are subject
to ever increasing pressure from members to establish some
sort of meaningful negotiating leverage. Given the current
direction of the negotiating process, professional associations
will be under increasing pressure to evolve effective bargaining
tools.

External Pressures
In the early 1960s when government formulated its plan for
publicly funded health care, it was anticipated that the system
would be financed through increases in the growth of the
Canadian economy. Such luxury no longer exists. With our
flagging economy, revenues have diminished but expenditures
have continued to rise. Economic forecasters suggest that this
will not change in the foreseeable future. It is generally agreed
that financial pressures on government are creating a general
and increasing state of underfunding throughout the whole of
the health-care system, and within that framework physician fee
bargaining has been even more selectively constrained.

Another pressure which bears on physician negotiations
derives from the crass politicisation of health care in Canada
by political parties in opposition and by a variety of other
politically oriented groups. As a political issue, health care has
great populist appeal and it lends itself to a wide variety of
melodramatic presentations. Under the guise of 'consumerism'
physicians are often identified as villains and the amount as
well as the method of determination of their incomes become the
subject of raucous political debate.

Internal Pressures
After the global dollar for physicians' services is negotiated with
government, it must be distributed among the various interest
groups within the professional association - surgeons, paedia-
tricians and so on. This responsibility falls on the provincial
medical associations and not infrequently it generates intense
political cross currents.

In pursuing the exercise, the associations use the average

incomes of the various groups as one of the determining factors.
An attempt is made to create income equity (although not equality) among the groups and the identification of equity is rather
hazy in the light of widely variant workloads and degrees of
responsibility. The 'Robin Hood' approach has been used in the
past, but in the light of an increasingly inadequate global dollar,
the exercise is getting very sticky. The objective of most
associations is to create an equal amount of unhappiness among
all groups, but there are continuing threats that some will break
off and go it alone. Associations therefore have to be concerned
about their own survival.

Another source of pressure is the level of aggression and the
degree of success demonstrated by other groups which negotiate
within the health-care system; nurses as well as interns and
residents come to mind. Both of these groups have moved into
rather advanced forms of collective bargaining, both have used
the strike weapon and both have achieved results which far
surpass those of physician groups. Awareness of the success
of others and knowledge of their strategies is creating considerable unrest within professional associations as they search
for a winning approach.

Collective Bargaining by Interns and Residents
Housestaff began organising into provincial associations as early
as 1968. The purposes were multiple, including promoting excel-
lence in clinical training as well as improving salaries, benefits
and working conditions. Two facts became clear to housestaff
over those twelve years. First, to bargain at all, one must have
an identifiable employer. Second, to bargain effectively, one
must have some form of power.

To have an identifiable employer with whom one negotiates
seems simple and reasonable, but it took most provincial housestaff organisations seven years to establish this, and one
province, Saskatchewan, is frustrated to this day.

It has taken interns and residents at least five additional
years to understand the meaning of power in the negotiations
process. There are only two avenues by which power can be
achieved in the collective process, in the absence of an amicable
agreement - withdrawal of services or third-party adjudication.
There are no other avenues in an employer/employee relationship.
For obvious reasons, interns and residents across the country
have opted for third-party adjudication or 'binding arbitration'
as their form of 'power'.

Not surprisingly, this has been opposed by government which
traditionally has had all the power. In British Columbia, interns
and residents were able to achieve binding arbitration indirectly
by first succeeding in having the BC Labor Relations Board
declare them a union. Manitoba interns and residents were able
to agree with the hospitals on a voluntary form of binding arbitration without threat of work action. Alberta, Ontario, Nova
Scotia and Newfoundland housestaff have all obtained binding

arbitration, but only after having to threaten or actually carry out a withdrawal of services. Saskatchewan obviously has no chance of achieving arbitration until they have accomplished step one, which is that of identifying an employer.

Except for Saskatchewan, the housestaff situation is largely settled. The employer is identified and the ultimate method for dispute resolution should negotiations fail, is established.

Collective Bargaining - Alternate Strategies
Most observers of the democratic process have at least a loose awareness of the various strategies used by employee groups in negotiating their objectives. The medical profession has been exploring alternatives to the classic adversarial approach. According to the rational approach, there is some merit in presenting one's case in a clear, concise, accurate fashion to government. In short, to appeal to their sense of fair play. To this point, such as approach seems to have staved off total disaster but as a long-term strategy it will not suffice by itself.

The fundamental flaw in the financial aspect of medical practice is an inadequate price structure. Compelling arguments have been presented and government negotiators usually can see the point. However, the profession's price arguments are quickly buried in concerns about incomes, utilisation and overall fiscal pressures on the public purse.

Another major determinant in government decision-making is public opinion. Medical associations are attempting to identify physicians as competent, concerned observers who will watch-dog the system on behalf of the public. By increasing communications activities, associations hope to reinforce the public's awareness that physicians are a very valuable social resource and that society must not allow governments to conscript the profession so that it becomes just one more resource in the system.

Currently, there is some experimentation involving the presence of a competent, third-party neutral at the bargaining table, an arbitrating presence. There has been no hint of binding arbitration by either side but one must presume that the profession hopes that government may be embarrassed into a more realistic position because of the arbitrating presence. Once again, the jury is out.

A recently released report on health care,[1] commissioned by the federal government, recommends compulsory binding arbitration as a means of resolving impasses on fee negotiations between provincial governments and medical associations. Nine out of ten provinces have rejected this recommendation out of hand. One can only presume that the provinces deem it inappropriate to relinquish self-determination in a major fiscal matter. Medical associations too are rather lukewarm to the recommendation presumably because such a measure would in a symbolic way be supporting of employee status for physicians.

Outcomes and Trends
The process through which fee bargaining between physicians
and government occurs is at a crossroads in Canada. The combination of declining incomes along with the frustrations of
working in a progressively underfunded system has created a
massive corrosion of physicians' attitudes. Doctors are becoming
progressively disillusioned and alienated from the system.

If the government purse is to continue to be the only source
of income for physicians, a cap-in-hand approach to the bargaining table can no longer be tolerated. The profession must and
will acquire the tools to pursue collective bargaining effectively
- in short, either strike action or binding arbitration becomes
the bottom line.

Many of the leaders of the profession believe that the pursuit
of formal collective bargaining as outlined will consolidate and
entrench an adversarial relationship between the medical profession and society through its government. The fear that like
so many other groups the profession will become an inward
looking, self-serving group, entrenched in a sort of 'rampart
mentality' - the ultimate in deprofessionalisation. To so sequester
a profession that deals with such vital and sensitive services
seems contrary to the public interest.

The only alternative is to provide the means whereby funds
from sources other than the public purse are incorporated into
payment for physicians' services. The profession believes that
private money is needed to buffer the predictable inadequacies
of government benefit levels and that a proper role for government is to devise ways and means to encourage and not suppress
its introduction. Doctors accept that charges for health care
can be harmful. That is why they supported, indeed pioneered
health insurance in Canada - to protect the sick. They equally
believe that a state monopoly with its implicit need for rationing
has immeasurable potential for harming the health-care system,
and submit that supplementary funding by users of the system
can in large measure defend against such harm and still maintain
acceptable access to care. Ways and means can be found to protect those with limited means from the impact of direct charges.

The profession believes that the most important transaction
in health care occurs when the individual patient presents with
a need, and all must strive to ensure that individuals are able
to have their own personal needs or wants served on acceptable
terms. They state with absolute conviction that the greatest
hazard to the individual reaching that goal rests with government and not with the medical profession. A free and independent
physician advocate is the patient's best protection.

Summary
There is at least one clear consensus which arises out of the
confusion and the conflict about the role of the state in health
care. Surely all parties - consumers, providers and government
- agree that all must continue with their efforts to provide the

best possible health care. The dispute arises over the decisions
which are more likely to achieve the agreed upon goal. Such
decisions are both complex and hazardous and must receive
serious and tempered consideration.

The medical profession believes the answers are not to be
found in the extremes of ideology or in political polarisation
over the merits of various economic systems. Market place
medicine with price as the sole allocative determinant is unacceptable on humane grounds. The alternative of state medicine
with its progressive rationing and institutionalised mediocrity
is not good enough either. The challenge is to provide the
proper mix of both state and market, so that the strength of
each can defend against the hazards of the other.

The profession does not pretend to know the precise formula
required. It does believe that both elements must be built in
and protected as integral, structured components in the organisation of health care. The strength of such a melding comes
from the inevitable ebb and flow that will occur with this design.
The rationing of health services in Canada has already begun,
and almost certainly will become more stringent unless alternative measures are employed to maintain and expand existing
resources. Charges to patients will never be popular, but
patients in the future would better be faced with user charges
than with the spectre of needed services and facilities not being
available at any price.

THE USA

This section explores the current status of physicians unions
in the USA and explains why they sprang up after 1970, the
legal and practical considerations responsible for their present
uncertain position, and prospects for their future. Fee-for-
service physicians, salaried physicians, and housestaffs will
be discussed separately, because their legal, professional and
social positions in the health-care industry are, as we will show,
quite different.

The rise of collective bargaining among physicians was a
phenomenon of the 1970s. At present (1981), the prospects for
survival of those unions that remain in existence can best be
described as uncertain. Factors such as physicians' own sense
of their professional identity, the legal implications of their
supervisory status, anti-trust and labour laws, and income
levels that are already among the highest in the country threaten
the survival of existing bargaining units. Countering these
pressures are trends toward cost containment in hospitals, the
possibility of national health insurance, an increasing number
of salaried physicians, and collective movements among hospital
housestaffs (interns, residents and clinical fellows).

Physicians are the highest paid professionals in the United
States.[2] Their incomes and perquisites are admired by some,

resented by others, and deemed appropriate by most of the general public. In 1976 physicians in the United States averaged $59 544 in net income.[3] Until recently, the vast majority of MDs were paid on a fee-for-service basis. Over the last 15 years, however, many publicly owned and run health facilities have hired physicians on salary. In addition, private institutions, both profit and nonprofit, and including such facilities as nursing homes, health maintenance organisations, and for-profit hospitals, often pay fixed incomes to doctors. This trend has arisen as part of the institutions' cost containment strategies. Not surprisingly, it has served as a motivation for collective organisation among physicians.

Among housestaff, interns in particular, traditional incentives to organise are clearly present. Internship involves both patient care and educational activities; an internship is necessary for qualification for the examination to practice medicine. (Residents and clinical fellows, the other constituents of the housestaff, choose these optional continuations in order to acquire a specialty skill.) Interns are low paid, relative to their skills and importance to the operations of the hospital; they work long hours, often unscheduled and unpredictable; they are subject to both job and educational discipline, since they have not yet attained physician status; and they have little voice in the policies and processes of the hospital. Though they perform many of the same services to patients as regular staff physicians, they are compensated by yearly stipends that are always far less than a staff physician would receive for the same services.

None the less, as with physicians unions in general, there have been only isolated organising drives by groups of interns (usually with residents and clinical fellows); there is nothing among housestaffs or physicians that could be called an industry-wide drive for unionisation. Legislative inconsistencies are no doubt responsible for many of the difficulties facing organising efforts among physicians and housestaffs. Before looking in some detail at the history of these efforts, it is worthwhile to set out the causes of physicians' incentives to unionise.

The initial growth of physicians unions had its roots in the erosion of the fee-for-service role traditionally held by US physicians. Since the mid-1960s, government intervention, third-party health insurance company pressures, and hospital managerial policies have significantly limited the professional and economic independence of the profession.[4] The American Medical Association (AMA), surprisingly and no doubt unwittingly, also played a key role. Professional associations of physicians, such as the AMA, state medical societies, and specialty organisations, have existed for over 100 years in the US. Historically, their function was primarily to set and police standards of education and training, encourage professional development, and act as censuring bodies for physicians who did not act in the best interest of patients.

But these associations became more political in nature as a

response to the federal government's involvement in the business of health care. This involvement began in the late 1940s, when the government passed legislation to finance capital expansion in hospitals (the Hill-Burton Act); it continued in the 1960s with increasing funding for the education and training of physicians, nurses and other health professionals. But the government's major threat, as perceived by the medical profession, was its enactment of Medicare and Medicaid legislation, which provides federally sponsored care for the poor and aged.

The AMA, perhaps understandably, was opposed to the enactment of this legislation. Conservatives in the Association were concerned to preserve their heretofore unchallenged economic independence. The AMA finally came around to supporting Medicare/Medicaid on the condition that the fee-for-service principle remain in effect for these federal reimbursements. In this, the Association was successful. However, its adamant opposition to federally sponsored care apparently alienated a great number of younger physicians who were educated and entering practice in the 1960s and 1970s. This cohort, opposed to the conservative stance of the AMA, responded by not joining its ranks. According to the AMA's files, in the 1950s over 55 per cent of medical school graduates joined the Association; by the 1960s this percentage had dropped to between 35 and 40 per cent; in 1975 only 16 per cent of these graduates joined. Though part of this drop is no doubt attributable to the tendency of younger physicians to join specialty societies instead of the AMA, the fact remains that the more liberal young physicians were alienated by the Association's lack of social concern, as evidenced by its bitter, strenuous lobbying against the passage of Medicare and Medicaid.[5]

Meanwhile, the more conservative among the physician population also turned against the AMA, feeling that their independence had been weakened by the Association's capitulation to this legislation. Ironically, the AMA lost the memberships of both its liberal and its conservative supporters. Both groups turned their organisational loyalty to local medical associations; a few began at the same time to entertain thoughts of collective organisation. Physicians' organisations, called unions, federations or guilds began to form. Bognanno's 1975 survey indicated that at least 16 000 physicians were members in some 26 labour organisations, some of which had National Labor Relations Board (NLRB) certification.[6] These organisations faced substantial difficulties, primarily in the form of legislative inconsistencies posed by the National Labor Relations Act (NLRA) and its regulatory board (the NLRB), as well as from anti-trust laws.[7] Physicians work either as independent fee-for-service professionals or as staff physicians, on salary with a hospital or other medical facility. In order to be protected under the NLRA's provision for union recognition and bargaining rights, organised workers have to fall under the definition of 'employee' that exists in the Act and in subsequent judicial decisions. Even the most liberal interpretation of employee, however, could not apply to fee-for-service physicians, and it is very difficult for staff physicians to be defined as employees. The profit motive of some of these bargaining units, and physicians' already high incomes, have also inhibited success in gaining NLRB certification.

For instance, the Union of American Physicians (UAP), which does not have certification, had as one of its goals a $100 000 per year salary for seasoned practitioners.[8] Though it has claimed to represent 8000 of California's 40 000 MDs, legal problems have prevented the UAP from representing any fee-for-service physicians. It has been able to offer its members mainly a 'grievance procedure', which is simply an organised force, mainly lawyers, who collect unpaid insurance and Medicare/Medicaid bills. It has also negotiated two contracts for physicians on salary in two small facilities in the state.

Most early organising drives owed their success to the energy and dedication of strong leaders. Most notable among these are Harold Yount of the American Physicians Guild, Kenneth Burton of the American Physicians Union, Sanford Marcus of the Union of American Physicians, and Stanley Peterson of the American Federation of Physicians and Dentists. However, their efforts often failed to sustain the union in the face of NLRA limitations. A typical experience is the one of a group of physicians on staff at a Nevada hospital. They formed a union in 1972, which, though it did not get NLRB certification, did affiliate with a national union. The efforts of their leader, Dr Holmes, brought them some successes; most notably they won a $50/hour reimbursement fee for all time spent in committee work. But once Dr Holmes stepped down, because of illness, the organisation dissolved.

A survey by Reynolds in 1976,[9] which was supplemented by a telephone survey we conducted in 1979, revealed that at least a substantial portion of the organisations mentioned in the Bognanno survey of 1975 has disappeared. Those groups that have survived will face difficulty maintaining their legal bargaining status.

Of course, it is not necessary for physicians to be protected by the NLRA in order to organise to act collectively. But recognition under the Act is their only protection from federal antitrust laws. A collective action by a group of independent contractors or by any intra-state group against an organisation with inter-state connections (insurance companies, for example) would be subject to prosecution under the Sherman Act as a 'conspiracy in restraint of trade'. Only official ratification under the NLRA can protect a labour organisation from anti-trust prosecution. Any statewide efforts, even though they were contained within a single state, might still be subject to federal prosecution.[10] Even collective activities that do not cross state lines or involve more than a single employer, and which thus could possibly escape federal anti-trust provisions, might come up against various state anti-trust laws.

Aside from these legal problems, the general tenor in the
United States, of imposing constraints on rising hospital costs
(which, according to the Consumer Price Index, have been
surpassed in cost increases only by oil), also contributes to
the public forces opposing collective organisation by physicians.
Public opinion seems firmly attached to the belief that unionisation necessarily increases earnings.

Some fee-for-service physicians have begun to form corporations, combining a number of physicians into an organisation
that then contracts with one or more hospitals for services of
its members.[11] Clearly, these are not unions in the sense of
labour laws. Thus they remain a target for anti-trust prosecution, should their pricing policies be deemed in restraint of
trade.

Any chance to unionise in the traditional sense of the word
falls to the cohorts of physicians who work on salary for a
hospital (or part-time with several hospitals) and other health
facilities. However, these groups too have recently met with
legal setbacks. A recent US Supreme Court decision (NLRB v.
Yeshiva University, 78-857) cast a shadow over prospects for
NLRB certification of 'professional' bargaining units. Though
this decision was made with regard to university professors,
the implications for health-care professionals are undeniable.
Like professors, physicians supervise and manage workers in
their institutions and influence policy and promotion decisions;
thus they can be excluded from coverage by the NLRB's
jurisdiction.

As we said above, housestaffs, especially interns, have many
of the traditional incentives to unionise, low pay, long hours
and little voice in policy-making. But several factors work
against organisation. Interns are only temporarily in this
uncertain position (usually one year); their prospects for more
autonomy and higher earnings are great, and they have a
professional identity that has not traditionally been associated
with that of organised workers.

Not surprisingly, drives to organise groups of interns have
been isolated. They have also come under a great deal of scrutiny by the NLRB and state-level labour sanctioning bodies.
In 1974 Public Law 93-360 amended the Taft-Hartley Act of 1974
to remove the exemption of voluntary hospitals from the National
Labor Relations Act (1935), thus extending labour relations
protection to all employees of health-care institutions not under
government or public ownership. The question of whether or
not the housestaff (interns in particular) are students (since
they take courses), employees (since they are paid), or managers
(since they supervise nurses, among others) has been controversial until quite recently. Unions of housestaffs have been
formed, certified by state labour boards, and then decertified
by the NLRB (based on the fact that these members were students, not employees). In late 1979 a Congressional committee

tried to make clear that it had intended the 1974 amendments
to Taft-Hartley to cover hospital housestaffs, only to have its
amendment defeated by the House of Representatives.

Prior to the passage of the 1974 amendments, the Physicians
National Housestaff Association (PNHA) was formed 'to organise
the house staffs in hospitals throughout the US'. They met
with little success. In New York City the Committee of Interns
and Residents (CIR) was formed and represented (as an association, not a union) approximately 5000 housestaff in New York
hospitals. CIR's primary demands were restriction on hours
and 'out of title' work. Hospital management, united in the
League of Voluntary Hospitals (a loose association of New York
hospitals) was opposed to any contractual arrangement. No
attempt was made to gain official sanction of CIR as a bargaining agent, though a four-day strike in 1975 led to a compromise
settlement. Similarly, in 1975 in Chicago, the 450 member Cook
County Hospital Housestaff Association struck and subsequently
signed an agreement limiting work hours to 80 per week and
establishing a committee to discuss patient care issues.

These organising efforts of the 1970s began meeting setbacks
as early as 1976, when the NLRB dismissed (by a 4-1 vote) a
petition by the Ceders-Sinai Housestaff Association in Los
Angeles to have their organisation recognised by the NLRA.
The Board ruled that housestaff were not employees, but students.[12] The dissenting vote argued that the relationship between
student and employee is not mutually exclusive, since students
are not among the exclusions listed from the definition of
employee under section 2 (3) of the Act. Though this gave hope
to some housestaff organisations, and kept isolated movements
toward official recognition alive, the NLRB subsequently ruled
against union representation elections in two additional hospitals.
In the state of Massachusetts, however, the Labor Commission
ruled the other way, allowing an election under Massachusetts
law in April 1976.[13]

Because of the different interpretations by state bodies and
the NLRB, the US Circuit Court considered a case in which the
issue was whether housestaff working in nonprofit hospitals in
New York could be covered by New York State labour relations
law, instead of national law. The Court's ruling was that federal
law did not supersede state in this case; housestaff labour relations were not within the jurisdiction of the NLRB. In a further
turn of events, the US Court of Appeals reversed the Circuit
Court's decision. The battle continued with a bill sponsored in
the US Congress that would mandate inclusion of housestaff
under the bargaining laws. Though this bill was expected to
pass, it was soundly defeated in late 1979. For now, the issue
is settled: housestaff will not be considered employees within
the meaning of the national labour laws and are therefore
excluded from NLRA coverage.

Summary
The three separate cohorts of physicians (fee-for-service, salaried and housestaff) have each met legal opposition to any attempts to organise and bargain collectively. Fee-for-service physicians are most clearly outside the criteria for organisation, since they are independent entrepreneurs who could not be represented as a collective unit, according to the NLRA, even if they deemed this route the appropriate method for maintaining their rather privileged positions. Salaried physicians, though possessing a commonality of interest under the definition of an appropriate bargaining unit, have been severely limited by the recent NLRB v. Yeshiva decision of the US Supreme Court, which maintained that professional employees are essentially managers and cannot organise collectively. For housestaffs, the recent defeat of a bill to include them under the provisions of the NLRA precludes further attempts to organise in this area.

Though movements for unionisation in the medical profession have not been long-lived, they have been significant for pointing out inequities in the treatment of hospital housestaff. They have, however, failed to arouse public sympathy for the problems of the salaried or fee-for-service physician; the attempts of these latter groups to organise have met with only fleeting success. The passage of national health insurance in this country is probably the only factor that could breathe life into physician unionisation. Unless such insurance becomes a reality, collective organising will remain dormant, if not moribund, among physicians in the United States.

THE UK

The introduction of the NHS established a highly interdependent relationship between the state and the medical profession: two near monopolies in the field of health care. At the core of the relationship lay an employer-employee nexus. From the outset of the NHS therefore the profession was concerned with a number of 'market' issues; for example, the limitation of the number of doctors, regulation of professional standards and prescribing practices. The resolution of these matters was generally through the medium of government instituted committees whose working methods are not normally open to observation. On the determination of medical incomes however both parties had few alternatives to the more visible process of collective bargaining; a fact illustrated by the NHS's original bargaining structure which included national committees for negotiating doctors' pay. While there were a series of disputes over pay in the period up to the mid 1970s, successive governments sought to avoid confrontations with the profession on the scale of 1948. In the 1970s pressures from within the profession asserted themselves with some force, prompted in part by changed circumstances both in the NHS and the British economy. The intention of this section is to examine the behaviour of the profession and the British Medical Association (BMA) in pay bargaining. In so doing it will concentrate on the determinants of the profession's power; its approach to collective bargaining and other alternative strategies; and the changes to the pattern of collective representation which have been promoted by internal and external pressures.

The Determinants of Bargaining Power

The profession's bargaining power rests upon the awareness of its monopoly of medical knowledge and skills. This enabled the BMA to ensure, from the outset of the NHS, the pre-eminence of the doctors in both clinical and organisational terms. The post-war Labour Government's acceptance of the profession's definition of clinical freedom, with its emphasis on the primacy of the doctor-patient relationship, removed the threat of state interference from medical practice. In addition it required that other health occupations were to be either explicitly or implicitly subordinate to doctors. The hospital consultant's concern over the loss of private medical practice was met by a contractual formula which enabled its continuation within the NHS. Further, in recognition of the different standards of medical expertise approximately one-third of consultants would receive additional money on the basis of merit, and the definition of individual distinction was an intra-professional matter. The status of general practitioners (GPs) was that of an 'independent contractor' who provided medical care on behalf of the state. Financial assistance for their practices was available but interference in the running of them was minimal.

In organisational terms the profession insured itself against 'bureaucratic creep'. Consultants in the hospital sector were the most likely victims of this common organisational phenomenon: while not involved in the daily administration of hospitals they were represented at strategic points within the administrative structure. This enabled them to oversee and protect their especial interests.[14] Only junior hospital doctors (i.e. below the hospital consultant level) were exposed to the harsher realities of the employer-employee relationship. Consequently, taken as a whole the introduction of the NHS occasioned little diminution of the profession's bargaining power; indeed it has been argued that it promoted an increase in its independence.[15]

A further important determinant of their bargaining power was the monopoly of collective representation enjoyed by the BMA. There were other collective organisations representing doctors: for example, the Regional Hospital Consultants' and Specialists' Association (RHCSA) in the hospital sector; and the Medical Practitioners' Union (MPU) which mainly recruited GPs.[16] However the refusal of the government's Health Departments to recognise them for collective bargaining ensured that, for many years, they remained as small, ineffectual pressure groups. It would nevertheless be incorrect to portray the

medical profession as a homogeneous and well collectivised
group. There were a number of divisions of interests based on
differences in medical expertise and work expectations between
GPs and hospital doctors, and between hospital consultants and
their juniors. These distinct interests resulted in conflicting
pressures for the BMA in its approach to income determination.
In the absence of viable competitors the BMA managed to recon-
cile these pressures with relative success until the mid 1970s.
By comparison other health-care occupations were weakly
organised among both trade unions and professional associations.
This too was a critical factor in medical income determination
in that it allowed governments a certain flexibility. Thus precedents in medical pay bargaining could be made without serious
regard to their repercussions on other groups of health service
workers.

Collective Bargaining and Alternative Strategies

It had been made clear by Aneurin Bevan (the post-war Minister
of Health) that future terms and conditions of service would be
the subject of consultation and negotiation with the profession.[17]
The NHS's centralised bargaining machinery, set up in 1948,
included a Whitley Council for doctors, subdivided into three
separate committees: Committee A was concerned with the income
of GPs; Committee B with that of hospital doctors; and Committee C with medical staff in public health authorities (who
operated outside the boundaries of the NHS). The BMA's internal structure reflected the different interests within the profession and contained a number of semi-autonomous bargaining
committees, in particular the General and Medical Services
Committee (GMSC) and the Joint Consultants' Committee (JCC)
who represented the GPs and hospital consultants respectively.
The divisions within the profession and their implications for
the BMA were evident even in the early years of the NHS. The
initial issue was concerned with the income differential between
GPs and consultants. The reports of the Spens Committee
(1946-8)[18] had set out scales and methods of remuneration based
on earnings in 1939, and suggested that consultants might
expect to earn almost twice that of GPs. A subsequent failure
to agree between the GMSC and the Health Departments over
the capitation system which determined GPs' income led to an
ad hoc arbitration award in 1951 by a judge, Mr Justice Danckwerts. This early resort to arbitration (which gave GPs a
substantial increase) was a precursor of the dual system of
pay determination; a mixture of collective bargaining and third-
party arbitration. The consultants' response to the Danckwert's
award was to claim a similar increase to retain the 'Spens differential'.
A critical factor in NHS pay determination is the role of the
Treasury, which establishes the upper limits for management
sides' offers on the various Whitley Councils. Without recourse
to additional revenue the Health Departments were reluctant

to see 'whipsaw tactics' become an established feature of medical pay bargaining. Thus while an increase was conceded to consultants it did not fully reinstate the differential. Throughout this period the escalation of NHS finances had been a subject of government concern[19] and the consultants' award underlined their increasing unease over the 'political' implications surrounding their pay.

In 1956 matters came to a head. Anxious to offset the erosion of their incomes by inflation the GMSC and the JCC merged forces and presented a claim for a 24 per cent increase directly to the Conservative Government's Health Minister. Similar action was taken by the British Dental Association. The government's reaction was to offer a 5 per cent increase and the establishment of a Royal Commission to consider the whole question of medical remuneration.

The BMA's successful rejection of the collective bargaining structure as the arena for the determination of medical incomes was a major demonstration of the profession's power. In practical terms it marked the end of pay negotiations within the Whitley structure. Henceforth discussions in the doctors' functional Council were limited to the detailed application of agreements. Committee A had in fact never met as the GMSC preferred the pre-1948 arrangements that had dealt with the older system of National Insurance. Subsequent events led to the discontinuation of work in the other two Committees: neither the full Council nor its Committees have met since 1966.

In place of collective bargaining the Royal Commission[20] recommended the institution of a small standing body, comprised of public figures, who would be appointed by, but independent of government – the Doctors' and Dentists' Review Body (DDRB). Its purpose was to provide an 'independent assessment' of doctors' incomes from evidence submitted by the profession and the Health Departments. Disputes between the profession and government would thereby be avoided and the taxpayer would be protected from unjust demands. The DDRB's recommendations would be sent to the Prime Minister and, following Cabinet discussion, presented to Parliament.

The Royal Commission episode highlighted the internal divisions within the profession and the contradictions they presented to the BMA. Moreover the inability of the BMA to develop an effective means of handling its intra-organisational tensions, which had been a critical feature in its negotiations with Aneurin Bevan, came once more to the fore. Initially the BMA had denounced the Commission as a delaying tactic by government and threatened mass resignation from the NHS by its GP membership, if an immediate and substantial increase in incomes was not forthcoming. However the GPs and consultants were not united. As in the 1946-8 confrontation, the latter group, through the intervention of the Royal Colleges, rejected the BMA's policy of non-co-operation.[21] Wrongfooted by this development the BMA agreed to provide evidence to the Commission and

postponed indefinitely its resignation threat. A second feature
of its traditional intra-organisational difficulties - maintaining
close contact with the attitudes of rank and file doctors - also
became evident. Unlike 1948 the NHS was a working reality in
which a new generation of doctors had matured. The Royal
Commission's findings demonstrated that despite the BMA's
contrary claims doctors were in general well paid by comparison
with other professions. Contrary to the BMA's posturings the
notion of a return to a mythological golden age of private practice was an unwelcome financial prospect for many of its members.

Although the BMA argued against third-party intervention
it nevertheless accepted the introduction of the DDRB.[22] There
were advantages in this system of income determination for
both government and the profession. From the Health Departments' viewpoint an independent assessment loosened the grip
of the Treasury, as the Danckwerts award had shown.[23] The
BMA and the profession were probably attracted to the DDRB
on three grounds. First, its 'scientific' method of pay determination may have appealed to the intellectual instincts of
doctors. Secondly, its means of operation, which emphasised
a quasi-judicial approach rather than straightforward arbitration, had the advantage of distancing the determination of
doctors' incomes from collective bargaining, with its overtones
of trade unionism and the market place.[24] Thirdly, it had the
practical consequence, in theory, of removing the political and
economic pressures which had so clearly affected the determination of medical incomes since 1948. However collective bargaining
was not wholly replaced by the DDRB and in subsequent years
the BMA pursued it with vigour if the DDRB's awards were
adjudged unfavourable.

While the review system provided the instruments for peace
its findings on medical income established a new battle ground:
the Spens differential had increased by a ratio of three to two
in favour of the consultants. Thus by 1966 the method of
remunerating GPs was the subject of conflict. The events that
followed took on a familiar shape: the BMA threatened mass
resignations; the relationship between the GMSC and the JCC
became visibly strained; and the College of General Practitioners
appeared, for a short time, to be taking the lead in negotiations
from the BMA. The DDRB's report was generally favourable.[25]
The GPs received a new deal (the Doctors' Charter) and junior
hospital doctors too received a large percentage increase. However the award for consultants was less generous. During this
episode two additional factors emerged. For the first time alternative collective organisations presented a more credible threat
to the monopoly position of the BMA[26] and the dispute took place
in the context of a national incomes policy. In future these two
factors would provide an additional dimension to medical pay
determination.

In the years immediately preceding the mid-1970s the review
system appeared increasingly fragile. Since the NHS's inception,

post facto cost of living increases had taken an inordinately long
time to achieve from the profession's standpoint. The upturn in
inflation in the late 1960s exacerbated the 'catching-up cycle'.
Prior to the 1970s the absence of powerful collectivities among
other staff groups and the overwhelming power of the doctors,
in both clinical and organisational terms, within the NHS,
allowed government sufficient flexibility over medical incomes.
A declining British economy and the advent of national incomes
policies from the middle 1960s reduced government's options.
Expenditure on the NHS became a broader political issue: pay
concessions to doctors had politico-economic implications for
other organised groups of workers in both public and private
sectors of industry. Thus in 1970 a Labour Government refused
to accept the DDRB's recommendations in full and referred them
for further consideration to the National Board for Prices and
Incomes. With its 'independence' threatened the members of
the DDRB resigned. The BMA canvassed its membership on
resignation although it took no direct action. The matter was
eventually resolved by a change of government which largely
conceded the BMA's claims and established a new DDRB.

These events again highlighted both the vulnerability of an
'independent' review of incomes and the BMA's contradictory
attitudes to pay bargaining.[27] The final outcome was determined
by the profession's monopoly position which ensured that the
state met its income aspirations, albeit with an inbuilt delay.
By contrast the BMA's bargaining behaviour had appeared to
produce few additional benefits. Indeed in trade union terms
the BMA exhibited the symptoms of an ill-organised and unstable
collectivity, that because of the professional monopoly succeeded
in spite of itself. Shortly these criticisms of the BMA were seen
to have substance.

External and Internal Pressures
The first set of external factors that exerted significant influence
on medical pay determination in the 1970s had been shaped by
changed circumstances in the hospital sector.[28] Occupational
growth, the increased size of hospitals and the complexities of
the services supporting the delivery of health care had been
organisational phenomena of the 1960s. These prompted a number
of developments which, although unconnected in character,
produced a different organisational climate. Its principal features were the growth of trade unionism among other health
occupations; the desire of nursing and allied medical professions
for greater professional autonomy; and the rise of managerialism,
culminating in the 1974 health service reorganisation. All of
these acted to undermine the clinical, organisational and collective predominance of the senior hospital medical staff, and in
some instances impinged directly on medical pay bargaining.
The second set of external factors arose from developments in
the political economy of Britain: national incomes policies operated by successive governments sought to establish guidelines

or maxima for pay increases; and the regulation of industrial
relations by legislation introduced new categories of definitions
for trade unions which exposed the medical profession's dilemma
over its attitudes towards trade unionism.

The intrusion of incomes policy into medical pay in 1970
presaged the end of 'independent' reviews of income. Thus
attempts by the BMA to argue in its evidence to the newly established DDRB, in 1971, for a redress of income levels to offset
inflation, were thwarted by the new Conservative Government's
guidelines on pay. The DDRB's reports of 1973 and 1974 left
the profession frustrated and angry. The DDRB's lack of independence was again underlined in 1974, when its chairman
resigned following his refusal to exceed government pay norms.
Although the 1975 report gave a 30 per cent increase (outside
a statutory income policy) the profession remained aggrieved.
In retrospect the events of 1975 can be seen as a watershed in
medical pay determination. While the DDRB had been providing
reports almost annually in the early 1970s the BMA had been
pursuing, through collective bargaining with the Health Departments, a separate issue of new contracts for both hospital consultants and junior hospital doctors. In 1974 the consultant's
contract became embroiled with the continuation of private
practice in the NHS.

The 1973 national dispute of hospital ancillary staff (manual
workers) had impinged directly on the contractual freedoms of
consultants when action was taken by local groups against
private wards in NHS hospitals. In 1974 the issue assumed
national proportions following the local 'blacking' by manual
workers of the private wing in the new Charing Cross Hospital,
London. In early 1975 against the background of grievances
over pay levels, the seemingly endless negotiations over the
new contract and a threat against the continuation of private
practice, the consultants began a work-to-rule. The organisation of direct sanctions presented the BMA with a novel problem: it had uttered threats in the past but had always with-
drawn from the brink. While the first consultants' dispute was
shortlived it again demonstrated the lack of cohesion within the
BMA and its contradictory attitude towards the use of direct
sanctions.[29] The BMA's organisational ability was tested again
in the junior hospital doctors' dispute. The flashpoint of this
strike occurred over the interpretation of the terms of their
new contract.

The traditional 'exploitation' of the juniors was carried over
into the NHS. By the early 1970s, however, an additional com-
plication had emerged. The Royal Commission on Medical Education had recommended an increase in the numbers of British
medical students to lessen the NHS's dependence on non-UK
doctors.[30] The effect was to reduce the juniors' chances of
progression to consultant posts.[31] One response from the juniors'
representative bodies was to argue for a closed contract of 40
hours per week with set payments for additional overtime - a

point grudgingly conceded by the DDRB in 1975. The actual dispute centred on the pricing of the additional units of medical overtime, following the onset of a statutory incomes policy introduced by a Labour Government, which constrained the pricing recommendations of the DDRB. Although the BMA's junior representatives accepted the DDRB's pricings, grass-roots opinion was opposed: in the autumn of 1975 junior doctors began to take spontaneous forms of industrial action.

At this point the issue of private practice again flared up with the decision of the Labour Government, following a resolution at its annual party conference, to withdraw facilities for private medicine from NHS hospitals. The BMA again threatened to canvas its membership for undated resignations and advised consultants to follow an emergency only service. The juniors' dispute was resolved nationally before Christmas 1975. However the eventual settlement, on the type of overtime payment, was left for piecemeal negotiations between the junior doctors and Area Health Authorities (AHAs). The consultants' action was eventually settled by third-party intervention. As in previous disputes the monopoly position of the profession was the decisive factor and the final agreements were clearly in their favour. The Health Services Act 1976 assuaged many of the consultants' fears over government's intentions for private practice. While the juniors subsequently breached the statutory incomes policy in the bargaining with AHAs.[32] However the long-term effects were seen more directly in the changes in the profession's pattern of representation: specifically in the BMA's loss of its near monopoly of collective representation.

In the hospital doctors' disputes the tempo was increased by the competition for membership between the BMA and its small rivals. As previously mentioned the BMA had faced competition even before 1948 from alternative doctors' associations. However the first major challenge to the BMA's hegemony came from within its own ranks. Traditionally the BMA had paid little regard to the circumstances of hospital juniors. In response to this leading members of the BMA's representative committee for juniors, the Hospital Junior Staffs Council (HJSC), formed the Junior Hospital Doctors' Association (JHDA). It was orginally intended to act as an internal pressure group, to focus attention on the juniors' pay and conditions. The continuing exclusion of juniors by the BMA from its negotiations with Health Departments[33] plus its seeming indifference to their special problems led to the JHDA's succession in 1969. Thereafter the JHDA competed with the BMA and by 1975 it claimed 5000 members. The BMA reacted by setting up in 1975 (immediately before the junior doctors' dispute) the Hospital Junior Staffs Committee, to bargain on behalf of its own junior members. The JHDA and the juniors who remained in the BMA had maintained links prior to 1975. These, however, were severed by the strike. The hostility between these two bodies led the JHDA to form an alliance with the RHCSA.

The RHCSA had originally been founded in 1948 as a counter to the London dominated BMA. Until the 1970s its membership was small with approximately 250 members.[34] After that date its membership grew rapidly as a result of its more militant stance over consultants' pay, and in 1974 it changed its name to the Hospital Consultants and Specialists' Association. The HCSA's support for direct industrial action following the breakdown of discussions on the consultant's new contract forced the BMA to follow suit. By 1975 the HCSA claimed some 5000 members; over 40 per cent of all NHS consultants.[35] The merger of the HCSA and the JHDA in 1977, to form the British Hospital Doctors' Federation (BHDF), now represents a considerable counter-weight to the BMA in the hospital sector. (Although in the light of the traditional division of interests between consultants and their juniors it may be a fragile alliance in periods of industrial conflict.)

The rapid growth of these two organisations and their subsequent merger was the culmination of the BMA's consistent failure to come to terms with its intra-organisational problems. Moreover the BMA's bargaining behaviour in the course of the consultants' dispute was a further illustration of its inability to gauge accurately the feeling of its membership. Thus despite its threat of resignations, the subsequent ballot on government's plans for phasing out private practice from the NHS showed its members to be generally unwilling to support its proposed course of action. Finally the hospital doctors' disputes laid bare a central issue which the BMA has still not resolved: whether or not it should publicly accept a trade union role. On this point the attitude of its competitors are more sure.

Outcomes and Trends
The rejection of a distinctive 'professional' approach in favour of trade unionism became a major topic for the BMA in the 1970s. Initially the issue was crystallised by the Conservative Government's 1971 Industrial Relations Act, which prompted the BMA to register as an organisation involved in collective bargaining. The subsequent legislation of the Labour Government - the 1974 Trade Union and Labour Relations Act - also contained a legal definition of a 'trade union', although in an altered form. The BMA therefore chose to retain its legal trade union status. A decision which had also been taken by its two principal rivals, the JHDA and the HCSA. Thereafter the BMA debated and rejected the proposition of affiliation to the British Trades Union Congress (TUC). As with the BMA's preference for the DDRB in place of collective bargaining, TUC affiliation appears to symbolise the rejection of the ethos of professionalism. In contrast the HCSA saw its role more clearly as a trade union representing hospital consultants and in 1979 it joined the TUC. Its decision seems to have ended any hopes of a rapprochement with the BMA. Moreover the formation of the BHDF gives greater organisational viability to both of its constituents. It seems reasonable

to predict that juniors who join the JHDA (now the Hospital
Doctors Association) will progress naturally to the HCSA on
achieving consultant status. The HDA may also apply for TUC
affiliation. The overwhelming majority of the BMA's 53 000
members are GPs.[36] This may in any event cause a flow of membership by hospital doctors towards the BHDF which more clearly
represents their special interests. If this should happen the
BMA may no longer be able to claim sufficient membership of
hospital doctors to warrant its continued sole recognition by the
Health Departments. From the Health Departments' viewpoint
the dangers of a continued refusal to recognise the BHDF could
be more real than sanctions threatened by the BMA, in its claim
to retain sole recognition for hospital doctors. In this context,
employer recognition of the BHDF with its suggested consequences for trade union growth[37] could see a more rational structure of medical representation: the BMA would represent GPs
and the BHDF the hospital doctors.

The BMA's recent decision to establish an internal system of
workplace representatives in the hospital sector may, in part,
be a recognition of both its previous failures in accurately
representing its members' views and the need to pursue a more
active recruitment policy at hospital level. The introduction of
'Place of Work Accredited Representatives' is in the latter sense
a reflection of recent policies made by nursing and allied professional organisations in their attempts to combat membership
competition from TUC trade unions. Ironically the BMA's reluctance to adopt the more common trade union title of 'steward'
for its workplace representatives is another indication of its
ambiguous attitude towards the acceptance of a trade union role.
In the short term the continued non-recognition of the HCSA
and the HDA may not necessarily reduce their representational
effectiveness. The DDRB's method of working, i.e. through
the consideration of evidence submitted by any interested party
within the profession, enables both organisations to represent
their members within the formal channel of pay determination.
Likewise their exclusion from the collective bargaining meetings
between the BMA and the Health Departments may not be a
real handicap as both the HCSA and the HDA may force events
from the edge of the formal arena. Thus their reactions to
trends in pay determination may persistently shape the behaviour of the BMA in its endeavour to retain the membership of
hospital doctors. In short inter-organisational competition could
be a continuing feature in medical pay determination with a
resultant spiralling of militancy. Given the likelihood that doctors will retain their professional monopoly in the foreseeable
future, a greater consolidation of the now fragmented representation between GPs and hospital doctors seems the most probable
outcome.

REFERENCES AND NOTES

1 Hall, Emmett M. (1980), 'Canada's National–Provincial Health Program for the 1980's: A Commitment for Renewal', 29 August.
2 'Medical Economics', 18 September 1978.
3 Eisenberg, Barry (1979), Trends in Physicians' Income, Expenses and Fees, in 'Profile of Medical Practice', American Medical Association, p.71.
4 Marcus, Sanford (1975), The Purposes of Unionization in the Medical Profession: The Unionized Profession's Perspective in the United States, 'International Journal of Health Services', vol.4, no.1.
5 'Medical Economics', 23 May 1970.
6 Bognanno, M. et al. (1975), Physicians' and Dentists' Organizations: A Preliminary Look, 'Monthly Labor Review', June, pp.33-5.
7 Private Physicians Unions: Federal Antitrust and Labor Law Implications, 20 'UCLA Law Review', 983.
8 The Time has Come to Bargain for Higher Income, 'Medical Economics', 17 March 1975.
9 Is the Doctor Union Movement Dead?, 'Medical Economics', 23 August 1976.
10 See Goldfarb v. Virginia State Bar, 43 USLW 4723 (US June 16, 1975), where the court found that state professional societies can indeed be subject to federal prosecution for 'conspiring to benefit the economic interests of their members'.
11 The physicians dealing with the Kaiser Permanente Health Plan in California operate under this type of organisation.
12 Ceders-Sinai Medical Center (Los Angeles, California), v. Ceders-Sinai Housestaff Association, 31-RC-2983, June 10, 1976, 224 NLRB, No.90, 92 LRRM 1303.
13 See MCR-2153, 29 April 1976, 'Massachusetts Labor Relations Reporter', vol.2, 1143.
14 Stevens, Rosemary (1966), 'Medical Practice in Modern England: the Impact of Specialization and State Medicine', Yale University Press, p.266.
15 Parry, N., and Parry, J. (1975), 'The Rise of the Medical Profession', Croom Helm.
16 The Medical Practitioners' Union was formed in 1913 and although separately affiliated to the TUC it merged with the Association of Scientific, Technical and Managerial Staffs in 1970. Its membership is largely made up of GPs.
17 'Report of the Ministry of Health for the Year Ended 31st March 1949', Cmnd. 7910, HMSO, 1949, pp.302-3.
18 Ministry of Health (1946), 'Report of the Inter-departmental Committee on the Remuneration of General Practitioners', Cmnd. 6810, HMSO, (Spens Report on General Practitioners); Ministry of Health (1948), 'Report of the Inter-departmental Committee on the Remuneration of Consultants and

Specialists', Cmnd. 7420, HMSO, (Spens Report on Consultants and Specialists).

19 Central Health Services Council (1956), 'Committee of Enquiry into the Cost of the National Health Service', Cmnd. 9663, HMSO.
20 'Royal Commission on Doctors' and Dentists' Remuneration 1957-1960, Report', Cmnd. 939, HMSO.
21 Stevens, Rosemary (1966), 'Medical Practice in Modern England, p.135.
22 Rosemary Stevens, ibid., pp.136-7.
23 Rosemary Stevens, ibid., p.134.
24 'Medical World Newsletter', Medical Practitioners' Union, 1966.
25 Rosemary Stevens, Medical Practice in Modern England, p.318.
26 Gordon, H., and Iliffe, S. (1977), 'Pickets in White: the Junior Doctors' Dispute of 1975 - a Study of the Medical Profession in Transition', MPU Publications, p.21.
27 Gordon and Iliffe, ibid., p.21.
28 For a discussion of these factors and their effects on medical representation see, Stuart Dimmock (1979), Dilemmas of Medical Representation - a View, in N. Bosanquet (ed.), Industrial Relations in the NHS - the Search for a System, King Edward's Hospital Fund for London.
29 Gordon and Iliffe, Pickets in White, p.39.
30 'Royal Commission on Medical Education, 1965-1968, Report', Cmnd. 3569, HMSO, 1968.
31 Elston, Mary Ann (1977), Medical Autonomy: Challenge and Response, in K. Barnard and K. Lee, 'Conflicts in the National Health Service', Croom Helm, p.39.
32 Gordon and Iliffe, Pickets in White, p.67.
33 Generally these negotiations were concerned with the implementation of the DDRB's recommendations.
34 Mary Ann Elston, Medical Autonomy, p.50 fn.
35 Mary Ann Elston, ibid., p.50 fn.
36 Dyson, Roger, and Spary, Katherine (1979), Professional Associations, in N. Bosanquet, 'Industrial Relations in the NHS', p.148 Table. The figures quoted include retired members but exclude overseas members.
37 Bain, G.S. (1970), 'The Growth of White Collar Unionism', Oxford University Press.

PART V

CONFLICT RESOLUTION

Introduction

In Part V, the various authors explore the different methods of
conflict resolution. Kelly describes the combined method of
mediation-arbitration as it has been used in Canada, and suggests that mediation is an effective force for conflict resolution
in health care and other sectors of the industrial relations
system. Kelly also makes the suggestion that 'strikes and lockouts, and the threat of these types of industrial action, are
an integral part of the dynamics of a democratic collective
bargaining system'.

Subbarao compares the procedures for the resolution of
hospital labour disputes in Canada and the USA, and examines
the operation of each system. The acceptability of the system
to the parties involved is clearly a critical factor in establishing
a basis for industrial peace and Subbarao highlights this aspect
of dispute procedures. In the UK the role of arbitration and
conciliation is less apparent than in Canada and the USA, as
the traditional emphasis on 'voluntarism' has resulted in a much
lesser involvement in conflict resolution by legal means. Against
this different cultural background Harnden describes the role
of interest arbitration in Canada, the USA and the UK. The
chapter examines the criteria employed by arbitrators in determining cases and discusses the issues of their perceived abilities.
Harnden then explores a number of key questions of public
policy which arise in the use of arbitration as a mode of impasse
resolution in the health sectors in the three countries.

13. CONFLICT RESOLUTION[1]: THE CANADIAN EXPERIENCE

W.P. Kelly

INTRODUCTION

The purpose of this chapter is to present the method of dispute settlement as it is dealt with at the federal level in Canada. It seeks to portray the general philosophy which guides the formulation of labour relations legislation at the Canadian federal level and the selection of approaches and procedures for dealing with any particular dispute or disputes. An attempt will be made to draw on the federal experience in a way which can have particular interest to and application for the labour-management community in the health services industry, not only in Canada but possibly also in the USA and the UK.

Jurisdiction over labour relations in Canada is divided between the federal and provincial levels, with the great majority of collective bargaining coming under provincial jurisdiction. This chapter will be largely confined to a discussion of the process of mediation and conciliation of labour-management disputes at the federal jurisdiction level.[2]

PRESSURES AND RESPONSES

In Canada, as in most Western economies, the contraction of economic fortunes during the 1970s, which was coupled with changing social forces has given rise to an urgent need for a careful re-evaluation of government's role and responsibilities for economic management, not least in importance being the assurance of relative stability and harmony in the labour-management relationship in key sectors. Directly related is the question of the public interest which looms large in any discussion on conflict resolution, with the health services sector being one of those activities which draws much attention from the public, the media and in the political arena. Government austerity has led to major cost-cutting efforts in areas such as the health-care services. These budgetary constraints have been occurring at the same time that inflationary pressures have led workers, including those in the health services sector, to place a high priority on wage and other compensation items. There is evidence to suggest, for example, that the bulk of labour disputes in the health services field since 1970 have occurred over the issue of wages and related fringe benefits.

As a consequence of these opposing forces, with workers in

the health field on the one hand seeking substantial wage and
fringe benefit improvements and the government, on the other
hand, exerting a strong fiscal restraint and pursuing a number
of cost-cutting measures, it should not be surprising to find a
noticeable increase in the incidence of labour disputes in the
health services field. To the informed industrial relations observer, it will be apparent that these stoppages are explained
partly as a result of the forces referred to above, and also, as
a result of the fact that unionisation has come rather recently
to this important sector of the economy.

Whenever a labour dispute threatens or erupts in important
sectors, such as the health services field, one detects a wide
spectrum of public and political feelings about the matter and
the alarmists, in particular, would have government undertake
whatever steps necessary to confine the negative impact of
such disputes, including a permanent withdrawal of the right
to strike or lockout.

Much is being written today about taking the conflict out of
labour-management relations and, through various techniques
of employee participation, moving away from the adversarial
approach in collective bargaining. This indeed sounds like a
noble objective and should be fully explored, not only on a
theoretical basis, but hopefully, with a certain amount of
experimentation. In our reactions to industrial relations disputes, whether ongoing or threatened, it is of fundamental
importance that these situations be judged and seen in their full
perspective and that haste be avoided in prescribing solutions
which are inappropriate. It must be remembered that industrial
relations is, above all, a field of practice involving the interaction of people with very real concerns, objectives and needs.
Sometimes, even with the best intentions and a spirit of compromise which are reflected in the give and take at the bargaining table, serious disagreements cannot be avoided. It is within
such a context that dispute resolution procedures are looked to
for a durable settlement. Perhaps least helpful to both the
parties and the conciliator/mediator is an outpouring of hysteria
and rhetoric based on misconceptions and ill-founded notions
about the industrial relations process and its end result.

For one, the fact that we have labour-management disputes
should not necessarily be viewed as evidence that our collective
bargaining system and institutions have completely broken down
and are unable to cope with the challenges of today. It is suggested that strikes and lockouts, and the threat of these types
of industrial action, are an integral part of the dynamics of a
democratic collective bargaining system. For the foreseeable
future, employers and employees will have both common and
divergent objectives, and conflicts of interest will inevitably
arise from time to time, and especially during negotiations over
a new collective agreement. When these conflicts occur, they
are typically resolved through consultation and the collective
bargaining process, which are the accepted procedures for

resolving differences. Inevitably, a strike or lockout can be the outcome of such a system in certain cases, but it should be remembered that they represent only a small proportion of all collective bargaining situations.

It is appreciated that the question of disputes in the health services field raises some imposing questions. The crucial question facing policy-makers is the guarantee that essential health-care services be maintained. There are some who see the hospital's basic responsibilities and the employee's rights to strike should not be permitted.

An acceptable formula for the settlement of disputes without resort to strike or lockout would clearly be ideal. However, experience has shown that strikes can and do occur, even where they are forbidden by law. Importantly too, one finds amongst the provinces considerable diversity of views on how to deal with the question of strikes in the health services field, no doubt explainable by the fact that each jurisdiction adopts the most appropriate approach based on their particular experience over time with the question of how to handle such work stoppages.

For the federal private sector, there has been a deliberate decision by policy-makers to resist pressures to adopt legislation which prohibits strikes, even those in essential services,[3] and instead, to place emphasis on procedures and mechanisms to further improve the functioning of industrial relations and to assist the parties to negotiate meaningful agreements and improve their day-to-day relationships. Undoubtedly, the best and most successful method of settling labour-management disputes is by direct negotiations between the parties. This philosophy notwithstanding, there have been occasions in the past where strikes and lockouts have taken place at the federal level which have become detrimental to the public well-being. In these cases, where an individual right becomes a public wrong, Parliament has rightly been called upon to terminate the dispute and bring about a resumption of operations.

Making strikes illegal does not put an end to our industrial relations problems. Illegal strikes do occur and even if workers do not go to this extreme in expressing their concerns, such actions as work-to-rule, organised use of sick leave and industrial sabotage are possible outcomes when the safety valve of strike action is not available.

Industrial relations, no matter how well functioning, is not static nor are the issues with which it must deal constantly. What then, if anything, can and should be done to ease some of the strains inherent in our system of collective bargaining and to foster a continuing dynamism that enables the industrial relations system to respond to changing pressure and circumstances?

In Canada, we bargain for wages and working conditions for a set term which generally varies in length from one to three years. This means, in theory, that the parties can remain isolated from each other during the term of the agreement, and only renew the marriage in the short 'open period', which is usually defined as the date provided for in the collective agreement when notice can be served, until a new agreement is reached or the collective agreement is renewed. If there is no meaningful consultation over the course of the life of the agreement, severe strains can be put on the system during the short, open period and problems surface then that really are more susceptible to resolution outside the pressure of bargaining over a new contract.

Under the Canadian collective bargaining model, it is during this limited open period that all the ills and shortcomings of the labour-management relationship, real and imagined, are to be resolved to the satisfaction of both parties and their principles, and a collective agreement concluded which will keep everybody happy for the next two or three years. This, in itself, is quite a feat, and it is a tribute to the practitioners of collective bargaining that it does work with a fair degree of success.

Dispute Resolution in the Closed Period

Many items that are of fundamental importance to the parties require exhaustive study and are too complex to deal with during the short, critical period when the collective agreement is open. If the system is overloaded with these complex items that often have little direct relevance to the renewal of a collective agreement, breakdowns occur and strikes take place.

Much can be done to avoid such situations through a process of meaningful consultation which, in the end, calls for accommodation, adaptation and innovation. Collective bargaining today involves many issues other than the compensation and so-called standard fringe benefit items. It is suggested that if the union has a problem, it is also management's problem and many of these issues need to be tackled as an exercise in problem-solving rather as a process wherein one party is dedicated to win at the expense of the other.

The Federal Mediation and Concilation Service (FMCS) has had extensive experience with and continues to be involved in dispute resolution during the life of a collective agreement, a process widely known as preventive mediation. The basic thrust of this policy is to assist labour and management, not only during negotiations, but as well to help them identify and deal with complex issues during the closed period of the collective agreement. While collective agreements traditionally provide for remedial measures, such as a grievance procedure and ultimate arbitration for the resolution of disputes that arise during the closed period, the approach of FMCS is to eliminate some of the issues which tend to clog the bottleneck of the open period and thereby facilitate the bargaining process. As a consequence, some work stoppages have been avoided where there was great potential for strike action. These preventive mediation activities

have contributed largely to a greater degree of industrial relations stability in some key industries under federal jurisdiction,
and particularly, the longshoring industry on both the East
and West coasts.

The consultations involved can take many forms and can be
either highly structured or completely informal. The important
thing, however, is that if a consultation procedure is established,
it must be meaningful and must be entirely voluntary. From the
viewpoint of the FMCS, contact with the parties is on a regular
basis to give advice, guidance and, in some cases, direction
to the parties in the handling and resolution of difficult union-
management affairs that do not lend themselves to long-term
solution through short-run ad hoc arbitration proceedings
established under the collective agreements, and short of confrontation.

Dispute Resolution in the Open Period
Under the Canada Labor Code, the parties to a dispute do not
acquire the right to proceed with legal strike or lockout action
until they have fully exhausted the compulsory conciliation
procedures established by that legislation. Under these procedures, the Minister of Labor may appoint a conciliation officer,
board or a commissioner, or a combination of them, to a dispute
where the parties are unable to resolve their differences. In
the event that he is satisfied that no such appointment will be
successful in bringing about a resolution, he may decide not
to make such an appointment. In any case, however, the parties
are not free to proceed with legal strike or lockout action until
after the provisions of the Code dealing with compulsory conciliation procedures have been adhered to. These conciliation
procedures, which have been periodically updated and made
more responsive, have proven to be highly successful in bringing about a peaceful conclusion to disputes between labour and
management, on a consistent basis over the past 30 years. This
high rate of success has been achieved in the face of increasingly diverse and complex situations with which conciliators and
mediators have had to deal.

In more recent years, within the FMCS, there has been an
increasing emphasis placed on mediation, in its various forms,
as a process for bringing about a resolution of disputes. It is
to the topic of mediation that much of the rest of this chapter
will be devoted since it is felt to be a procedure which offers
the most flexibility for dealing with the increasingly complex
issues in the labour-management arena, and an increasing
sophistication into the art of dispute resolution.

Role of Mediator in Dispute Resolution
A mediator, through some control over the dynamics, can narrow
the area of disagreement in a dispute, issue by issue, and can
head off an impasse on any given issue, sometimes an emotional
one, before it occurs. By exercising control over offer and

counter-offer, a mediator can also avoid that which often turns into an impasse situation, even as to whose turn it is to make an offer. A skilled mediator can anticipate and head off situations in which one side is particularly adept at manoeuvring the other into an awkward position, which can be satisfying to the ego, but does little to achieve a collective agreement.

He can probe and develop and modify a position on a given issue, while protecting the parties' official postures. When he detects that a gap in the positions can be bridged, he can push an item forward aggressively, and through negotiations, and sometimes a proposal, resolve the particular issue.

A skilled mediator at a negotiating table can help the parties save face and avoid embarrassment during a heated discussion when neither side can afford to retreat gracefully.

Frequently, a breakoff in negotiations is threatened over contract language, when actually the parties are not too far apart on substance. Pride of authorship can come into play, and a mediator should be able to come up with alternative language capturing the intent of the parties. He must also be creative and innovative, and produce the proper contract language when the parties are grasping for words to reflect their intent.

Primarily, it is the role of a mediator to resolve conflict. This conflict is not always just between the parties. There is often conflict within a union negotiating committee and a company negotiating committee. A mediator can also be very helpful to the parties in their ongoing relationship, and especially, in the final stages of a protracted dispute where possibly tempers have flared and animosity exists. Much can be done during the final stage of mediation to create goodwill between the parties, or at least, restore some form of normalcy.

Role of Arbitration in Dispute Resolution
In the Canadian federal jurisdiction, permanent compulsory arbitration of interest disputes has not been considered a viable alternative to voluntary collective bargaining. However, it is recognised that arbitration on a voluntary basis is a legitimate and viable technique for resolving a collective bargaining impasse under certain circumstances and on particular issues in a given dispute. It is unfortunate that in North America, the word 'arbitration' has been stigmatised by many trade union leaders. This would seem to be especially true in Canada where much of the trade union movement can hardly use the word arbitration without the automatic insertion of the prefix 'compulsory'.
When two parties agree to the use of arbitration in the resolution of a particularly difficult question or issue, it is most likely a voluntary procedure and one which deserves to be utilised more frequently.

The Med-Arb Concept
In recognition of the virtues of mediation and the existence of voluntary arbitration as a legitimate, but underutilised 'tool'

in the resolution of collective bargaining impasse, considerable experimentation has taken place with combining the two procedures, into what is now commonly referred to as the 'med-arb'.[4] It is a process that possesses great potential as one of the more creative and promising alternatives that exist for resolution of collective bargaining disputes without recourse to strikes or lockouts, and health services' disputes do seem to lend themselves to successful application of such procedure.

The process is a combination of mediation and arbitration where the parties arm a skilled mediator with the powers of an arbitrator who has the muscle to cope with deadlock situations on any given issue. The most important factor contained within this concept is that the union and management negotiating committees, while party to an arbitration proceeding, still are afforded the opportunity to carry out the negotiating process.

Where med-arb has been agreed to, in addition to the employer and employee representative at the bargaining table, there is a third person participating directly in the bargaining process. This third party combines the skills and functions of a mediator with an ultimate mandate to make a final and binding decision, if necessary on issues which cannot otherwise be resolved. He serves primarily as a mediator, but his influence on the outcome of negotiations is more than that of the conventional mediator because the parties know that if they fail to reach an agreement, this same person will be switching hats from the role of the mediator to that of arbitrator.

Med-arb places heavy emphasis in reliance on negotiations during which the med-arbitrator is present. Throughout this process, there is, in fact, definite incentive for the parties to negotiate frankly and conscientiously, and the presence of the med-arbitrator has the tendency to keep them honest in the negotiation process. In practice, it has been found that as the process goes on, very few matters remain to be resolved through arbitration, and if there are outstanding issues, the range of differences usually have been narrowed considerably through the mediation process.

The med-arbitrator can take a more active role than the conventional mediator, armed as he is at the end of the process with the power to impose a final and binding settlement. Meeting with the parties, both separately and jointly, he gains a full appreciation of the issues and the real distance which separates the parties. As the process evolves, he makes suggestions and proposals, the timing of which he can assess on the basis of his experience. It should be stressed that med-arb is a voluntary negotiations as a means to bring about an acceptable agreement. The emphasis is on the parties to shape their own agreement through direct negotiation.

In the federal jurisdiction, existing legislation gives flexibility in the use of the med-arb concept where there is mutual agreement by the parties. The first time this concept was used was in the Port of Montreal in a dispute involving longshoremen in 1968.

The med-arb concept was also agreed to in three successive negotiations for renewal of collective agreements by grain handlers employed in the West Coast terminal grain elevators, and thereby, ensured a continuation of grain export activities that are so important to the economy.

Despite its attractions, trade union leaders have difficulty coping with the necessary approval of their membership to apply med-arb. It must be understood that if med-arb is to be used, there should be a formal agreement between the parties stating specifically that the med-arbitrator's award is final and binding. This, of course, comes into conflict with the ratification procedure practised by the unions.

If a union decides in any given negotiation to submit their dispute to med-arb, they must first seek approval from their membership, as the agreement reached is not subject to ratification. Hence, the reluctance of union leaders to ask their membership to relinquish the right to strike, in a particular negotiation.

CONCLUSION

In the Canadian industrial relations model, conflict is normal. Conflict has a number of positive functions, the most important being its role in clarifying for the parties, the items that need to be dealt with so that the system can continue to function properly. Equally important to an understanding of the Canadian industrial relations model is the fact that our system, and its day-to-day functioning, is dynamic not static, and that attempts to resolve its inherent conflicts and tensions cannot bring about peace and stability unless these pressures are addressed in an imaginative and constructive way.

Attempts to suppress conflict through such measures as strike prohibition, for example, are likely to lead to counter-reactions which serve to release tensions that build up and exist in the system. Such responses are often expressed through work sabotage, poor motivation and resistance to change. Clearly, effective solutions to labour-management disputes in health care cannot be found by simply dealing with symptoms of conflict. They must instead confront the underlying causal elements if the industrial relations system in health care is to continue to be able to respond positively to the pressures exerted upon it, both from within the system and from outside social and economic forces. Given the dynamic nature of the problems and pressures to which the health-care industrial relations system and its parties must respond, it is clear that creative experimentation in conflict resolution techniques deserves priority attention by all those with a vital stake in the functioning of the system.

REFERENCES AND NOTES

1 This chapter had its genesis in a speech given by the author
   to a seminar on labour disputes settlement in health services, sponsored by the School of Health Administration,
   University of Ottawa in February of 1977. It is not intended
   to reflect the position of the federal government on a number of the important issues which will be discussed, but
   rather, are reflective of the personal beliefs and opinions
   of the author which have evolved over the past 30 years
   during which he has been very deeply involved in the
   Canadian collective bargaining system, first, during negotiating and executive roles with the Brotherhood of Railroad
   Trainmen and since 1966 in senior positions with the Federal
   Mediation and Conciliation Service, of which he has been
   head since 1972.

2 Involved here specifically is the panorama of procedures
   and approaches that find their basis in the Canada Labor
   Code (Part V - Industrial Relations), which is the legislation which establishes rules and procedures governing the
   certification of unions, arbitration of rights disputes, and
   dispute prevention and resolution activities for the federal
   private sector. The Canada Labor Code (Part V - Industrial
   Relations) which came into effect on 1 March 1973, applies
   to inter-provincial and international railways, airlines and
   highway transport; telephone, telegraph and cable systems;
   pipelines, canals and ferries; banking, primary fishing;
   most Crown corporations; and certain undertakings that
   have been declared by Parliament to be for the general
   advantage of Canada, including grain elevators, uranium
   mining and processing, and feed and flour mills. The Code
   also governs labour-management relations in the private
   sector in the Yukon and Northwest Territories. At the
   federal level, the public service comes under the Public
   Service Staff Relations Act for labour relations purposes.
   While the Canada Department of Labor has little to do with
   employees in such important areas of economic activity as
   the health services industry, it is widely accepted that the
   practice of mediation and conciliation, in whatever jurisdiction, can yield a variety of important innovations and
   experiences which are both informative and, to some extent
   at least, are transferable from one jurisdiction to another.

3 It is recognised that the concept of essential services is both
   complex and one on which there is little agreement.

4 Med-arb is not a new concept. In its earlier application by
   Senator Wayne Morse of Oregon, it was a process termed
   'mediation to finality'. The term 'med-arb' gained currency in
   the early 1970s after its successful application by California
   lawyer Sam Kagel in a number of disputes in the health
   services field.

14. DISPUTE RESOLUTION METHODS

A.V. Subbarao

This chapter presents a brief comparison of the procedures for resolution of hospital labour disputes between the Canadian and the United States legislations, and covers the methods of dispute resolution namely negotiations, mediation and conciliation, boards of conciliation and fact-finding and final offer arbitration. Different arbitration systems as they obtain in UK and North America are discussed by Lynn Harnden in Chapter 15 of this volume.

Procedures for resolution of hospital labour disputes[1] as well as the laws regulating collective bargaining in Canadian hospitals differ from province to province as hospitals in Canada fall within the provincial jurisdiction. While hospital employees in some provinces are covered under general labour relations legislation, they are covered by the public sector labour relations legislation in other provinces. The differences among provinces are even more significant with respect to procedures for resolving hospital labour disputes.

For the purpose of collective bargaining, hospital employees in Ontario are covered under the Ontario Labor Relations Act[2] which regulates collective bargaining in the private sector. But hospital employees in Ontario, unlike their counterparts in the private sector, do not have the right to strike. Instead, Ontario enacted a separate legislation, the Hospital Labor Disputes Arbitration Act,[3] and provided compulsory arbitration for resolving disputes between hospital employees and their employers. Employees of public hospitals in British Columbia are also covered under the Labor Code[4] which regulates collective bargaining in the private sector. But, hospital labour disputes in British Columbia are subjected to different procedures for resolution under the Essential Services Disputes Act of 1978.[5] Under the Act, the Lieutenant-Governor-in-Council may refer hospital labour disputes for investigation by the Essential Services Advisory Agency and if the agency recommends the minister may appoint a fact-finder. Hospital employees in British Columbia acquire the right to strike only after the procedures specified under the Essential Services Disputes Act are complied with.

Under the Essential Services Disputes Act, binding arbitration option is available and a trade union representing hospital employees in British Columbia can elect to resolve a dispute by arbitration, if the parties, after bargaining in good faith, have failed to conclude a collective argument. Hospital employees in

New Brunswick who are covered under the Public Service Labor Relations Act,[6] too, have an option to choose between the strike and arbitration routes. Hospital employees in Quebec, have the right to strike. But, the Government of Quebec can delay the strike by imposing a 'cooling-off' period for 80 days, under section 99 of the Quebec Labor Code.[7] Neither restrictions on the right to strike nor any requirement of compulsory arbitration exist in Saskatchewan. In fact, all employees in both public and private sectors including those in Saskatchewan hospitals are covered by the same legislation, the Trade Unions Act of 1944.[8]

On 26 July 1974, the National Labor Relations (Taft-Hartley) Act[9] was amended extending the provisions of the legislation to employees of private, nonprofit hospitals in the USA. The Act now applies to over 1.5 million hospital employees who constitute more than 55 per cent of all hospital workers in the United States. The 1974 Amendments[10] to the Taft-Hartley Act contain specific procedures for resolving hospital labour disputes. The procedures consist of notice requirements with specific time limitations and different methods of dispute resolution that the parties are required to go through before they resort to work stoppage.

NEGOTIATIONS

Negotiations are the most important part of the collective bargaining process. The purpose of negotiations is to reach a collective agreement between employer(s) and its employees represented by a trade union. This purpose is clearly spelled out in every labour legislation enacted to regulate collective bargaining between employers and trade unions. All other methods of dispute resolution prescribed in different labour relations legislation are supplementary to negotiations. However, the availability of the right to strike or compulsory arbitration, more than being supplementary, may have a significant differential impact on negotiations.

Negotiation is a process of exchange of information between the parties. The information consists of facts and tactics including threats and bluffs. During negotiations, the exchange of information starts with the exchange of proposals and counter-proposals. This exchange, of course, takes place after the parties have issued notice to bargain and have agreed to meet at a specified place on a specified date and time. During the first meeting, the trade union, traditionally, presents its proposals to the employer. The proposals consist of demands that the union would like to incorporate into a collective agreement, in case of a first agreement, or to amend the clauses in case of an existing contract. In the following meeting, the employer presents its counterproposals which are considered the employer demands. Invariably, the demands in proposals and counterproposals are developed in such a way that neither party would agree to the others' demands without negotiations. Such an agreement would involve a party giving away everything to the other. In other words, parties negotiating under adverse circumstances initiate negotiations with demands which, if agreed upon, will accrue maximum advantage to its own constituents at the cost of the other's. Hence, it is appropriate to call these demands the initial offers of the parties, implying that a party develops its initial position on issues not necessarily expecting an immediate settlement, but with the hope of negotiating towards an agreement.

The union's initial offer (U_I) will be so high that the employer would not be able to accept because of the cost that it would impose on the establishment. Similarly, the employer's initial offer (E_I) would be so low that the union would not accept because of the fear of its very survival. Invariably, the parties making initial offers do not expect and may not wish the others to accept. If the employer accepts the union's initial offer and if the costs increase beyond control, employees' job security may be threatened. On the other hand, if the union accepts the employers' initial offer, employees may leave for jobs elsewhere and the employer may not be able to compete and recruit in the labour market. Hence, the parties negotiate and make concessions for the purpose of reaching an agreement which would be mutually beneficial.

Besides initial offers, each party attempts to identify its own target point and resistance point either before commencement of negotiations or during negotiation process.[11] Both parties' target and resistance points are shown in Figure 14.1. The union target point (U_T) is a position at which the union would prefer an agreement and would continue to negotiate for the purpose of making the employer move to that position. Similarly, an employer would prefer an agreement at its target point (E_T) and would continue to negotiate, with the hope of making the union move to its own position (E_T). On the other hand, the resistance points are the party's sticky positions. The union would either accept a settlement at its resistance point (U_R) or be prepared for a strike or lockout rather than moving below U_R. The employer, too, would not move beyond E_R and would rather lockout or accept a strike. If the employer's resistance point (E_R) is above that of the union (U_R), then the parties have a positive contract zone. They have a negative contract zone if the employer's resistance point (E_R) is below that of the union (U_R).[12]

The parties may have identified their own target and resistance points. But, they would not know the other's target and resistance points. A party would not believe even if the other openly declares its target and resistance points. In fact the purpose of negotiations is to make the other believe party's target point and to assess the other's resistance point. During negotiations, each party uses tactics[13] for the purpose of making the other concede and move towards party's position as well as

to convince the other that the other's position is unreasonable
and warrants concessions. Of the tactics, the parties frequently
refer to 'comparable' conditions and cite those facts that would
support their own positions. Parties also resort to threats of
work stoppage indicating that unless the other makes a concession, the threat will be actually effected. The purpose of the
threat is to suggest an expected cost of disagreement.[14] A party
concedes if the expected cost of disagreement is higher than its
expected cost of agreement. Union's expected cost of disagreement is the expected loss of wages to its members, if the threat
of work stoppage becomes effective. Expected loss of production
and profits will be the expected cost of disagreement to the
employer. A party's expected cost of agreement is the difference
between its target position and the position at which the agreement is offered. A party would stand firm and would expect the
other to make another offer of agreement if the party's expected
cost of agreement is greater than its expected cost of disagreement.

Figure 14.1: Contract Zone

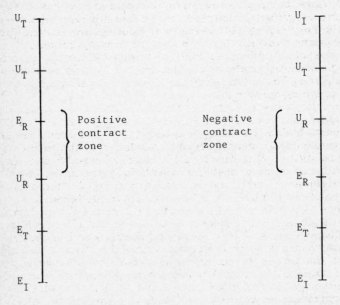

A party will continue to negotiate and make concessions until
the time at which the offered position of agreement is close to
its resistance point. If both the parties reached that situation
and if they are able to communicate with each other, then they
may be able to settle. In other words, the possibilities of a
settlement are greater in a positive contract zone situation than

in a negative zone situation. In a negative contract zone, negotiations are likely to reach a stalemate and a work stoppage may take place. During work stoppage, parties may, in realisation of costs of disagreement, revise their own resistance points and may be able to reach an agreement. In the absence of the right to strike, the trade unions representing employees in Ontario public hospitals may not be able to threaten and make the employer to concede. Moreover, the employers of Ontario public hospitals may not know their own resistance and target points. Both the Ontario hospitals negotiating committee and the unions representing hospital employees are aware of the announced budget increases for Ontario public hospitals. Both may use those increases as employer's initial offers on economic issues.

Even in other jurisdictions where hospital employees have the right to strike, negotiations may be subject to a number of factors. One, in most of the jurisdictions, hospital negotiations take place within the context of multilateral collective bargaining.[15] The inter-organisational and intra-organisational conflicts among hospital managements are likely to influence and delay collective bargaining negotiations between hospitals and trade unions. Two, being political institutions and inexperienced in collective bargaining, the trade unions representing employees of public hospitals may often resort to political process and give up negotiations process for achieving contract agreements.[16] These special circumstances surrounding hospital collective bargaining will have to be kept in mind for the purpose of understanding the effect of dispute resolution processes discussed in the following pages.

Conciliation and Mediation
Conciliation and mediation are the most frequently used but the least researched methods of dispute resolution in the field of labour relations.[17] Traditionally, mediation is considered as an art and hence is not amenable to scientific investigation.

Mediation and conciliation are used synonymously, although they are used differently in labour relations legislation with reference to different kinds of appointments. For illustration, under the Ontario Labor Relations Act, a career officer appointed by the Minister is referred to as a conciliation officer[18] whereas a person chosen by both the parties and willing to mediate between the parties is referred to as a mediator.[19] But, the purpose of both mediation and conciliation as well as their roles in labour-management disputes are one and the same. Mediation and conciliation are processes in which a neutral party helps union and management negotiators to reach a voluntary agreement. In other words, a mediator or a conciliator, unlike an arbitrator, has no binding force on the parties. It is precisely because of this voluntary nature of the process of conciliation or mediation, its effectiveness is attributed to the mediator's or conciliator's intelligence, understanding, empathy, assertiveness, aggressiveness and tactfulness.[20]

Mediator Strategies. Besides the personal characteristics of a
mediator, the effectiveness of mediator in health-care disputes
also depends upon the strategies the mediator uses. Kochan
categories these into noncontingent and contingent strategies.[21]
The former are those that a mediator uses normally in every
dispute he is involved and the latter he chooses depending upon
the dispute situation. One of the most universalistic noncontingent strategies of health-care mediation is that a mediator first
has to gain the trust and confidence of the parties. Unless the
parties perceive the mediator as trustworthy, they are not likely
to respond to his efforts later in mediation. How a mediator
establishes trust with the parties depends upon his interpersonal skills to deal with people and, at times, also upon the
dispute situation. Once an initial level of trust is established
between the parties and the mediator, the mediator begins the
search for information regarding the causes of the dispute, the
nature of the relationship between the parties, the internal
distribution of power within the parties and the relationships
between negotiators and their constituents. In short, a diagnostic or search process takes place so that the mediator can
begin to understand both the visible issues which are in the
dispute and the underlying impediments of 'hidden agendas'
to a settlement. This diagnostic process is the second most
important noncontingent strategy and the data collected in this
process will affect the choice of strategies for reaching a settlement. A third noncontingent strategy is assessing the underlying attitudes of the parties toward their adversaries. Allowing
the parties to express these attitudes is often felt to have a
cathartic effect on the parties. It allows them to vent their
emotions on the mediator rather than directly on the opposite
party.

In order to understand the attitude of the parties and to give
them an opportunity to vent their emotions, mediators normally
meet with the parties separately, in separate rooms and if necessary, in separate sessions over a period of time. These sessions
are essentially nondirective and the mediator takes the role of
a patient listener and absorber of the party's tension while
interpreting the level of hospitality that exists in the dispute.
During separate sessions, a mediator also tries to find out the
resistance and target points of the parties. It may not always
be possible to find out these positions of the parties. The
parties themselves may not know if they are confused and
inexperienced or if the parties did not negotiate sufficiently
before seeking the assistance of mediation. In those jurisdictions
where conciliation is compulsory under the law and the parties
are required to go through before seeking arbitration or acquir-
ing the right to strike, parties tend to request conciliation
before reaching impasse and even before seriously negotiating
between themselves. A mediator would know if such a situation
exists between the parties and would arrange a joint session. A
joint session is also useful between those parties who are con-

fused and inexperienced and it will give them an opportunity clearly to identify the issues in dispute. During joint sessions, depending upon their attitudes toward each other, a mediator helps the parties to identify and exchange their target positions.

Once the issues and parties' target positions are identified and enough information is uncovered to make a preliminary diagnosis of the impediments to the dispute, a mediator chooses a contingent strategy that is appropriate to the dispute situation. Some mediators prefer a nondirective contingent strategy. They meet with the parties in separate rooms for the purpose of finding out the party resistance points. After finding out the resistance points of both the parties, if the mediator believes that there exists a positive contract zone, he brings the parties together in a joint session, allowing them to exchange their final positions. In other words, a mediator who believes in non-directive strategy, allows the parties to reach their own agreement while acting as a catalyst between the parties. Those mediators who believe in direct strategy use different tactics.[22] The tactics include a mediator strategy of making substantive suggestions for a compromise, pressing one or both of the parties hard to change their bargaining positions or their expectations for settlement, strongly criticising one or both of the parties for intransigent behaviour. A mediator, of course, has to be extremely cautious in using these 'strong arm' tactics. If pressure and suggestion for an agreement come from a mediator and are turned down by one of the parties, a mediator becomes ineffective and he may be perceived as trying to sell his recommendation for an agreement. Hence, the 'strong arm' tactics should never be used unless a tacit agreement already exists between the parties, i.e. where a positive contract zone exists and the parties are ready to make it explicit and reach an agreement.[23]

Those favouring a more active or aggressive direct strategy argue that a mediator must engage in pressuring the parties to change their positions, suggesting alternatives for settlement and bringing expectations in line with reality if the process is to be effective in producing settlements.[24] In hospital collective bargaining situations, as in Ontario, even directive mediation may not produce settlements. The mediator's pressure on the parties to settle may be misplaced, if the hospital employers' negotiating committee is not delegated with sufficient authority to negotiate and to settle. Instead, the mediator has to reach the source of authority over funding, and put pressure on that party to settle rather than allow the dispute to go on to the next stage of the impasse procedure. Even in those jurisdictions where hospital employees have the right to strike, mediation may not be effective unless the parties have sufficient experience and authority to negotiate on behalf of their constituents.

Mediation Effectiveness.   The ultimate criterion of the effectiveness or success of mediation is whether or not a mediator

helped the parties to reach a settlement. A mediator's intervention may not always result in a settlement. But that does not
mean that mediation was altogether ineffective. Kochan[25] suggests three other measures of effectiveness of mediation. Mediation is a continuous narrowing process in which the parties
start with a large number of unresolved issues and narrow them
down until none are left unresolved and the total agreement is
reached. Consequently, according to Kochan, an additional
measure of mediation effectiveness is the proportion of issues
that are resolved during the mediation process. It is possible
to make progress in bringing a dispute closer to an ultimate
settlement even though no issues are actually resolved. The
parties may have made movements and narrowed differences
over issues. The degree of movement towards an agreement by
the parties during mediation intervention is another partial
measure of effectiveness of mediation. Kochan's final measure
of mediation effectiveness is the extent to which the parties held
back concessions in anticipation of going on to the next stage –
the more they held back, the less effective the process.

The stages following mediation and conciliation, particularly
the final stages in the procedures, namely the right to strike
and arbitration, are expected to have a significant effect on
mediation effectiveness. If the parties are required to go through
fact-finding and compulsory arbitration after mediation, they
may hold back in mediation believing that any movement by a
party would be construed by the other as the party's initial
position in the procedure following mediation. In other words,
the parties tend to hold back until arbitration stage is reached
and even during arbitration (see the discussion below). Even
if the employees have the right to strike, the parties tend to
hold back until the 'eleventh hour' bargaining. Perhaps because
of this, under the Essential Industries Disputes Act of British
Columbia, special mediators are appointed after the parties have
gone through all the prior procedures and the employees have
acquired the right to strike. At this stage, according to
Stevens,[26] mediation can be most successful because the negotiation process has progressed to the point where the parties
may be under great pressure to settle.

Boards of Inquiry and Boards of Conciliation.   Inquiry and
conciliation by boards into disputes between management and
trade unions are the procedures following mediation. Boards of
Inquiry are also known as fact-finding boards which are appointed in a number of public sector jurisdictions in the US.
The Canadian equivalent to the fact-finding board is the Board
of Conciliation. The mandate of a board of conciliation is to
investigate the facts on issues in dispute and to try to bring
a settlement acceptable to the parties. The fact-finding boards
are also required to search the factual basis of the parties'
positions and to identify an acceptable compromise settlement.[27]
If the parties settle as a result of the efforts of the board of

conciliation or fact-finding, the agreement is submitted to the appointing authority. On the other hand, if the parties fail to settle, the boards are required to submit to the appointing authority, detailed reports of their investigations outlining the issues involved in the dispute, steps taken to resolve the dispute, intensity of the dispute including the differences between parties on issues and steps, if any, that could be taken either by the parties themselves or the authorities for resolving the dispute. The boards may also be required by the appointing authority to outline the consequences, if the dispute is not settled and the effects on the community as well as the recommendations for a settlement.

Appointment of Boards. The procedures for constitution of boards of conciliation and fact-finding are also more or less similar. After the conciliation officer's report is received indicating the failure of the parties to reach agreement, the appointing authority determines to constitute a conciliation board if he believes that such a board might be able to produce a settlement. The parties to the dispute will be required to appoint their nominees on the conciliation board within a stipulated period and the nominees so appointed will be required to select a third neutral person who will be appointed as the board's chairman. If the parties fail to nominate their members and if the two members fail to select the third party, the appointing authority appoints the conciliation board. The chairman as well as members of the conciliation board should not have any pecuniary interest in the dispute they are appointed to investigate and report. Although provisions exist in industrial relations legislation in Canada, conciliation boards are not appointed frequently. The only exception is in the disputes between the Canadian Union of Postal Workers and the Treasury Board. Every time the parties reached impasse, the conciliation boards were appointed and the boards submitted voluminous reports each time after lengthy proceeedings. The most recent 1979 conciliation board's report was accepted by the Canadian Union of Postal Workers while the same was rejected by the employer, the Treasury Board.[28] Negotiations continued, based on the conciliation board's report and an agreement was finally reached, averting a strike by postal workers. Thus, the reports of the conciliation boards as well as those of fact-finding boards help the parties clearly to identify the issues, if they were not done so by then, and to negotiate for the purpose of reaching an agreement. The appointing authority has the right to make the board's report public. Following publication the parties negotiate under the pressure of public opinion. In fact, public opinion plays a very important role in the health sector labour-management disputes.

Government intervention in labour-management disputes also depends upon the course of action suggested in the reports and the expected consequences on the community if the dispute is not settled. Provisions for appointment of boards of inquiry in

hospital labour-management disputes exist in a number of
jurisdictions in North America. The procedures for investigating
and reporting by the boards of inquiry in hospital collective
bargaining are similar to those of the boards of conciliation and
fact-finding in the North American public sector jurisdictions.
In Canada, there is very little research on the functioning of
either the boards of conciliation in general or the boards of
inquiry in hospital labour-management disputes in particular.[29]
In the US, however, the functioning of the fact-finding panels
in the public sector disputes[30] and the boards of inquiry in
hospital collective bargaining are studied and they form the basis
for the discussion in the following paragraph.

Experience with Boards of Inquiry.   A board of inquiry is a
unique feature of the 1974 health care Amendments to the United
States National Labor Relations Act and is designed to provide
fact-finding in an attempt to avoid strikes. It is at the discretion
of the National Director of the US Federal Mediation and Conciliation Service that an impartial board may be appointed to investigate the issues involved in a dispute and to provide the parties
and the Service with a written report of the factual findings
and a set of recommendations for settling the dispute. The Act
stipulates that the appointment of a board of inquiry should
take place no later than 30 days prior to the expiration date of
the contract or within 30 days of the 60-day notice to the Federal
Mediation and Conciliation Service, whichever date is later. In
the case of initial contracts, the board of inquiry, if convened,
must be appointed with ten days of the receipt of the 30-day
notice to the Federal Mediation and Conciliation Service that a
dispute exists. The Act also specifies that a board of inquiry
may be appointed only if a threatened or actual work stoppage,
if permitted to occur or continue, substantially interrupts the
delivery of health care in the locality concerned.

During the four months after the effective date of the Amendments, 24 boards of inquiry were appointed. The Federal Mediation and Conciliation Service reviewed the initial experiences to
determine the effectiveness of the boards of inquiry in resolving disputes. The review indicated that in a number of situations,
particularly first contract situations, the boards were faced with
several unresolved issues. In other words, little bargaining had
occurred prior to the board's appointment and the negotiating
parties left major provisions of a contract for the board's determination. On the basis of the findings, the Federal Mediation
and Conciliation Service decided to use the following two factors
to determine the appointment of a board of inquiry: (1) the
potential impact of a strike or lockout on health services in the
community and - if the impact is found to be substantial -
(2) the possible impact of the introduction of the board of inquiry
on collective bargaining in the case.[31] This second factor is
viewed from the point of view of the status of negotiations,
relationship between the parties and the types of issues involved.

The Federal Mediation and Conciliation Service devised a
voluntary arrangement for appointment of special fact-finders
instead of the boards of inquiry, in cases where the Service
determined that the parties did not negotiate sufficiently and
the impact of a threatened strike or lockout was not substantial.
Under the arrangement, the parties would sign on a stipulation
form developed by the Service requesting the appointment of
a special fact-finder and setting a definite date for receipt of
the fact-finder's report. The date set by the parties could be
either the date of expiry of the contract or the final date for
appointment of a Board of Inquiry, as stipulated under the Act.
Between August 1974 and March 1977, a total of 129 boards and
special fact-finders were appointed.[32] The boards of inquiry as
well as special fact-finders are required to submit reports and
recommendations only to the parties with copies to the Federal
Mediation and Conciliation Service. The parties have the right
to release the report to the public at any time, but the Service
would not release as long as it believed that the parties were
negotiating following the receipt of the report and were likely
to reach an agreement. In other public sector collective bargaining situations, the parties tend to negotiate and settle after the
receipt of the fact-finding report. In fact, the fact-finders are
believed to develop their recommendations in such a way that
the parties would either accept or use them as a basis for
negotiating an agreement.

Final-Offer Arbitration. For the first time in 1971, the city of
Eugene, Oregon State, provided the final-offer selection system
of arbitration for resolving industrial disputes between the city
management and its employees.[33] Later on in Wisconsin[34] and in
Massachusetts,[35] the statutes were amended to allow final-offer
selection arbitration of disputes of police and firefighters. The
Major League Baseball Players Association and the Baseball Club
Owners also agreed in 1973, voluntarily to resolve their salary
disputes under the final-offer arbitration. The theoretical impact
of this system of arbitration on negotiations was, for the first
time, discussed in 1966 by Carl Stevens,[36] who then, called it
'either-or' type; later it became known as 'final-offer' arbitration. In final-offer arbitration, the parties failing to reach an
agreement submit their respective final positions and the board
of arbitration awards by selecting either the employer's or the
union's final positions. Under the Wisconsin and Massachusetts
systems, the arbitrators are required to select either the
employer's or the union's total package of offers on all issues
in dispute between the parties. Whereas under the Michigan and
Iowa systems, a board of arbitrators is allowed to develop an
award by selecting on each issue either from the employer's or
the union's final positions. These two are also differentiated by
referring to them as the final-offer-selection and the last-offer-
by-issue systems of arbitration.[37] Under both the systems,
arbitrators are required to consider the 'criteria' specified in

the legislation, in their decision-making process.

These two systems of final-offer arbitration are expected to have different effects on bilateral negotiations. Unlike in conventional arbitration, the threat of arbitration under these two systems is expected to induce the parties to concede during negotiations. The 'threat of arbitration' implies that either party may indicate its intention to refer the dispute to an arbitration panel whose award will be final and binding on the parties. A party's threat of arbitration may cause the opponent to concede and compromise, provided it has the effect of increasing the opponent's subjective estimate of the costs of disagreeing. In pre-arbitration negotiations, a party's subjective estimate of the cost of disagreeing with the opponent is a function of the party's expectations of the arbitration award. The cost of disagreement is the cost of the award. The greater the 'uncertainty' associated with an award, the greater will be the expected cost of disagreement. (The 'uncertainty' of an award is defined to mean the probability that the arbitration would result in an outcome to a party less desirable than the party could have obtained through a bilateral settlement.) The party's threat of arbitration will cause the opponent to concede if the 'threat' imposes a cost of disagreeing which exceeds the cost of agreeing on the party's offer. In other words, the 'uncertainty' of an award in a system of binding interest arbitration is expected to encourage free negotiations. The parties' threats of arbitration may generate concessions and compromises.

In the final-offer-selection system, the award is 'uncertain' to the extent that the arbitrator may order either of the parties' final package of offers. One party's 'threat' of arbitration will generate concessions from the other only if the other expects the cost of disagreeing to be greater than the expected cost of agreeing on such terms. The expected cost of agreeing with the opponent is the difference between the opponent's offer and the expected award. Since the third party's order is of the strictly 'either-or' variety, the cost of disagreement is minimised if one expects his offer to be ordered. If, however, one expects the arbitrators to rule in favour of the opponent, then the expected cost of disagreement is high. Negotiators reduce their respective expected costs of disagreement through concessions and compromises. They negotiate (i.e. concede and compromise) at least until their respective expected costs of disagreement are perceived as equal and their negotiations may result in settlements.

In the last-offer-by-issue system, the arbitrators will award by picking on each issue either the party's or the opponent's offers. In other words, the 'uncertainty' of the award in this system is reduced to the extent that the arbitrators are given discretion in issuing an award. The negotiators may expect that the arbitrators would award by selecting some issues from the party's offers and the rest from the opponent's package of offers. By so doing, they may expect the arbitrator to issue an

award which would compromise the interests of both the negotiators. The cost of such an award to either party is less than
the cost of agreeing with the opponent. Hence, the negotiators
may not settle in the last-offer-by-issue system. A party may,
however, concede on some issues so that the neutral may order
his last offers on those issues. If the bilateral negotiators concede on different issues, the difference between their last offers
at the termination of negotiations is expected to be large, and
the negotiations are not expected to result in bilateral settlement
of contract negotiations. In the conventional arbitration system,
arbitrators are expected to compromise the interests of the
parties who employed them for resolving their dispute and may
award by splitting the difference between the parties' final
offers.[38] A party's expected cost of disagreeing is the difference
between his offer and the expected award. Since the cost of the
expected award to a party in this system is less than the cost
of agreeing at the opponent's terms, the threat of arbitration
by the opponent may not induce the party to negotiate. In other
words, the system may have a 'chilling effect' on negotiations
and the parties may not settle bilaterally.

The expected effects of these different systems of arbitration
were tested under controlled experimental conditions and the
results confirmed that the parties were induced to concede more
under the final-offer-selection than under the last-offer-by-
issue or conventional systems of arbitration.[39] But the results
of other studies that compared these systems of arbitration in
different jurisdictions are not conclusive.[40] There may be other
uncontrolled factors in those jurisdictions which may have
influenced the results. Under the Michigan's final-offer-by-
issue system, the chairman of the arbitration boards mediate
between the parties and the parties are allowed to revise their
final positions during arbitration proceedings. Because of this,
the system is also known as med-arb, or mediation-arbitration.
Arbitrators who are vested with authority to render awards that
will be binding on the parties, mediate between the parties.
Mediation under the threat of binding award might make the
parties revise their positions, resulting in agreements. If the
objective of the system is to produce agreements, irrespective
of the stage at which they are reached, then med-arb might
serve the purpose. On the other hand, if the objective of the
system is to make the bilateral parties negotiate for the purpose
of reaching agreements and to reduce their dependence on third
parties, the policy-makers may have to examine more seriously
the final-offer-by-package system of arbitration in which the
arbitrators are only required to render awards based on the
final positions submitted by the parties at the commencement of
arbitration proceedings. Negotiators may not like such a system
of arbitration if they are not experienced and are unable to
develop final offers that are considered 'reasonable' and acceptable to arbitrators. In such situations, negotiators may face the
risk of loosing in arbitration and may find it difficult to explain

to their constituents. Perhaps because of these reasons, including the 'loss of face', some unions and public sector employers expressed their concerns about the final-offer selection system of arbitration.[41]

Some public sector unions seem to favour conventional arbitration while others want only the right to strike. The effect of the strike-based system of collective bargaining seemed to have been better than the systems of arbitration in terms of inducing the parties to concede and negotiate for the purpose of reaching bilateral agreements. The right to strike also yielded higher wage outcomes than those under arbitration.[42] On the basis of the comparison of the effects of the various systems of dispute resolution on negotiation process and outcomes,[43] they can be ranked from the most to the least effective in the following order: strike-based system, final-offer-by-selection system, last-offer-by-issue system and the conventional arbitration system. The systems, however, are still under experimentation in different jurisdictions and the results of their effects can be established conclusively only by continuous research. Until that time, policy-makers and practitioners of labour relations may speculate and prefer those methods of dispute resolution that serve their needs and interests.

CONCLUSION

A system of conflict resolution consists of different procedures available to the parties for resolving their disputes. The final procedure in any system may have a significant impact on the prior procedures and their effectiveness in making the parties resolve their own disputes. The right to strike or the right to final-offer-by-package arbitration may help the parties to negotiate, to avail mediation and to resolve their own disputes. But, the parties' preferences are the most important for a system to be acceptable, and to become effective in any jurisdiction. A system that is overimposed on the parties by policy-makers may not yield the expected results and may not help the cause of establishing industrial peace. On the other hand, those systems that were voluntarily adopted by the parties may have helped the parties to resolve their own disputes[44] and to establish industrial peace. In the public sector collective bargaining too, the emerging trends indicate that the systems provide for alternative procedures and let the parties choose those that serve their interests. Public servants in the Canadian federal public service and in the New Brunswick Province are provided with a choice of the right to strike and binding conventional arbitration.[45] The public sector employees in Iowa state have the choice between conventional arbitration and the final-offer-by-issue arbitration.[46] The New Jersey public sector collective bargaining statutes provide for the right to strike as well as the various systems of arbitration.

Collective bargaining in hospitals is similar to those in some respects with the private sector and in other respects with those in the public sector.[47] Hence, the results of experimentation with different procedures and methods of dispute resolution in different sectors and in different jurisdictions should be useful for developing a system of collective bargaining for hospitals. The following system of impasse resolution for hospitals is worthy of consideration:[48]

First, create a board of promote collective bargaining in hospitals and health services with the primary function of prompting joint decision-making by mutual agreement.

Second, designate this board as the agent to decide when direct negotiations are no longer possible or productive and to determine what procedure should be followed as an alternative. If the board does not believe the parties have exhausted the utility of negotiations, it would be able to insist on further meetings with mediation. If it decides that fact-finding or recommendations are called for, it would have power to direct this procedure. No fixed procedure would be mandated in advance. The board would have full flexibility to design procedures that met the particular situation.

Third, the board should have authority to restrain a strike for a limited period, perhaps 20 days, to give it time to consider the next step to be taken.

Fourth, as a last resort, the board would have power to submit a particular remaining issue or issues to arbitration. The board would also frame the issue for the arbitrator. By holding this possibility in reserve, the process would have sufficient uncertainty to spur effective negotiations.

This system was suggested for those jurisdictions where work stoppages by hospital employees were not acceptable. In view of the emerging trends of work stoppages in hospitals, prohibition of strikes may not ensure continuous hospital services. But, provision of the right to strike and lockout along with alternative choice procedures may reduce work stoppages and may improve industrial relations in hospitals. Final-offer arbitration may be offered as an alternative to work stoppage.

REFERENCES AND NOTES

1 Disputes in this chapter refer to only contract disputes and not to grievance or rights disputes.
2 Revised statutes of Ontario, 1970, Chapter 232.
3 Revised statutes of Ontario, 1970, Chapter 208, as amended by 1972 Chapter 152.
4 Revised statutes of British Columbia, 1960, Chapter 122.
5 As proclaimed in B.C. Reg. 465/77 Part II, Gazette; vol.20, p.853.
6 Statutes of New Brunswick, 1968, Chapter 88.
7 R.S. 1964, C.141 as amended in Feb. 1978.

8 Saskatchewan's Trade Union Act, 1944.
9 Act of 26 July 1974, Pub. L. No. 93-360, 88 Stat 395 amending National Labor Relations Act, 29 U.S.C. 1971.
10 For a detailed discussion see, Vernon, R.G. (1975), Labor Relations in the Health Care Field Under the 1974 Amendments to the National Labor Relations Act: An Overview and Analysis, 'North Western University Law Review', vol.70, no.1, pp. 202-19; Kennedy, E.M. (1975), Preface: Public Concern and Federal Intervention in the Health Care Industry, 'North Western University Law Review', vol.70, no.1, pp.1-5 and Pointer, D.D. (1975), The 1974 Health Care Amendments to the National Labor Relations Act, 'Labor Law Journal', vol.10, no.6, June, pp.350-9.
11 Walton, R.E., and McKersie, R.B. (1965), 'A Behavioural Theory of Labor Negotiations', McGraw-Hill, pp.41-6.
12 Kochan, T.A. (1980), 'Collective Bargaining and Industrial Relations', Irwin-Dorsey Ltd, pp.243-8.
13 Stevens, C.M. (1963), 'Strategy and Collective Bargaining Negotiations', McGraw-Hill, pp.41-6 and Chamberlain, N.W., and Kuhn, J.W. (1965), 'Collective Bargaining', 2nd edition, McGraw-Hill, pp.173-82.
14 Chamberlain and Kuhn, 'Collective Bargaining', pp.170-3.
15 Kochan, T.A. (1974), A Theory of Multilateral Collective Bargaining in City Governments, 'Industrial and Labor Relations Review', vol.27, no.1, July, pp.525-42.
16 Kochan, T.A., and Wheeler, H.N. (1975), Municipal Collective Bargaining: A Model and Analysis of Bargaining Outcomes, 'Industrial and Labor Relations Review', vol.29, no.1, October, pp.46-66.
17 For a discussion of mediation process based on empirical analysis, see Kochan, T.A., and Jick, J. (1978), The Public Sector Mediation Process: A Theory and Empirical Examination, 'Journal of Conflict Resolution', vol.22, no.2, June, pp.209-40.
18 Section 15 of RSO 1970 C. 232.
19 Section 16 of RSO 1970 C. 232.
20 Landsberger, H. (1955), Interaction Process Analysis of Professional Behavior: A Study of Labor Mediators in Twelve Labor-Management Disputes, 'American Sociological Review', vol.20, no.5, pp.566-75.
21 Kochan, The Public Sector Mediation Process, pp.216-19.
22 Kressel, K. (1972), 'Labor Mediation: An Exploratory Survey', Association of Labor Mediation Agencies.
23 Stevens, C. (1967), Mediation and the Role of Neutral in J.T. Dunlop and N. Chamberlain (eds.), 'Frontiers of Collective Bargaining', Harper and Row, pp.271-90.
24 For a review on mediation, see Rehmus, C. (1965), The Mediation of Industrial Conflict: A Note on the Literature, 'Journal of Conflict Resolution', vol.9, no.2, pp.118-25.
25 Kochan, The Public Sector Mediation Process, pp.211-12.
26 Stevens, Mediation and the Role of Neutral.

27 Kochan, T.A. (1979), Dynamics of Dispute Resolution in the Public Sector, in B. Aaron, J.R. Grodinnand J.L. Stern (eds.), 'Public Sector Bargaining', Industrial Relations Research Association, pp.150-90.
28 Report of the Board of Conciliation.
29 Goldenberg, S.B. (1979), Public Sector Labour Relations in Canada, in B. Aaron, J.R. Grodin, L. Stern (eds.), 'Public Sector Bargaining', Industrial Relations Research Association, pp.254-91.
30 McKelvey, J.T. (1969), Fact-finding: Promise or Illusion, 'Industrial and Labor Relations Review', vol.22, no.2, July, pp.528-43.
31 Scearce, J.F., and Tanner, L.D. (1976), Health Care Bargaining: The FMCS Bargaining, 'Labor Law Journal', vol.27, no.7, July, pp.387-98.
32 Barret, J.T. (1972), Collective Bargaining in Hospitals: A Discussion, 'Labor Law Journal', vol.7, no.8, August, pp.525-31.
33 Long, G., and Feuille, P. (1974), Final Offer Arbitration: Sudden Death in Eugene, 'Industrial and Labor Relations Review', vol.27, no.2, Jan., pp.196-203.
34 Section 111-77 (6) of Wisconsin Statutes of 1973.
35 General Laws of Massachusetts, Sec.4, Ch. 1078 Acts of 1973.
36 Stevens, C.M. (1966), Is Compulsory Arbitration Compatible with Bargaining, 'Industrial Relations', vol.15, no.2, Feb., pp.38-52.
37 Subbarao, A.V. (1978), Final Offer Selection vs. Last Offer by Issue Systems of Arbitration, 'Industrial Relations', (Laval), vol.33, no.1, pp.38-57.
38 Horton, R.D. (1975), Arbitration, Arbitrators and the Public Interest, 'Industrial and Labor Relations Review', vol.28, no.4, July, pp.497-507.
39 Subbarao, A.V. (1978), The Impact of Binding Interest Arbitration on Negotiation and Process Outcome: An Experimental Study, 'Journal of Conflict Resolutions', vol.22, no.1, March, pp.79-103.
40 Stern, J.L., Rehmus, C.M., Loewenberg, J.J., Kasper, H., and Dennis, B.D. (1975), 'Final Offer Arbitration', Lexington Books, pp.223.
41 Witney, F. (1978), Final Offer Arbitration: The Indianapolis Experience, 'Monthly Labor Review', vol.96, no.1, May, pp.20-5.
42 Subbarao, A.V. (1979), Impasse Choice and Wages in the Canadian Federal Service, 'Industrial Relations', vol.18, no.2, Spring, p.235.
43 Subbarao, A.V. (1979), The Systems of Industrial Conflict Resolution, 'Proceedings' of the 5th World Congress of the International Industrial Relations Association, International Labour Organisation.
44 Abel, I.W. (1973), Basic Steel's Experimental Negotiating

Agreement, 'Monthly Labor Review', vol.96, no.9, Sept., pp.39-42.

45 Goldenberg, S.B. (1979), Public Sector Labour Relations in Canada, in B. Aaron, J.R. Grodin and J.L. Stern, 'Public Sector Bargaining', IRRA Series, pp.254-91.

46 Gallagher, D.G., and Legnetter, R. (1979), Impasse Resolution Under the Iowa Multi Step Procedure, 'Industrial and Labor Relations Review', vol.32, no.3, April, p.331.

47 For discussion of collective bargaining in hospitals, see R.U. Miller, Brian E. Becker, Edward B. Krinsky (1979), 'The Impact of Collective Bargaining on Hospitals', Praeger; R.U. Miller, B.B. Becker and E.B. Krinsky (1977), Union Effects on Hospital Administration: Preliminary Results from a Three State Study, 'Labour Law Journal', August, pp.512-25; and Brian E. Becker, Glen G. Cain, Catherine G. McLaughlin, Richard U. Miller, Albert E. Schwenk (1981), 'The Union Impact on Hospitals: A National Study', University of Wisconsin, prepared for the National Center for Health Services Research, US Department of Health and Human Services.

15. ROLE OF ARBITRATION IN HEALTH SECTOR DISPUTE SETTLEMENT: CANADA, USA AND UK

L. Harnden

One of the basic tenets of collective bargaining systems in UK, Canada and the United States is the freedom of employees to withdraw their services at some point in a collective bargaining dispute. The resultant interruption of the employer's operation is the lever which is expected to enable employees to negotiate a satisfactory settlement of the dispute.

The right to strike was considered by many to be inappropriate for the health-care sector by reason of the damage to the public welfare which was considered to inevitably follow any work stoppage in health-care institutions. Thus, with the rapid unionisation of health-care employees in the 1960s there developed substantial public pressure for the removal of the right to strike from health-care employees. Legislators in several jurisdictions in Canada and the United States responded to this sentiment by enacting legislation prohibiting strikes in health-care facilities. As a means of counterbalancing the consequent loss of bargaining strength by employees, the legislators offered compulsory third-party arbitration of the matters which could not be voluntarily negotiated with employers.

The purpose of this chapter is to trace the use of arbitration in the settlement of collective bargaining disputes in the health-care sector of UK, Canada and the USA. It will be seen that, in most instances, public demands for compulsory arbitration were rejected in favour of other types of dispute settlement procedures although the right of parties voluntarily to refer their disputes to arbitration was commonly retained. It will also be noted that the focus of public concern is starting to turn from the impact of the strike weapon on the public interest to the propriety of referring collective bargaining disputes to a third party. The attraction of arbitration as a peaceful dispute settlement technique is becoming tempered by a recognition of the deficiencies of arbitrated settlements. Such factors as the detrimental impact of compulsory arbitration on the collective bargaining process and the lack of public accountability of arbitrators have caused a decline in the popularity of arbitration and a renewed interest in alternative schemes for dispute settlement.

THE NATURE OF ARBITRATION

Labour arbitration is a dispute-settling procedure whereby a trade union and employer refer disputes to a third party for determination. A distinction is generally recognised between rights or grievance arbitration and interest arbitration. Interest arbitration occurs where the parties are unsuccessful in negotiating the terms of a collective agreement and their disagreement is referred to a third party for resolution. In rights or grievance arbitration, a third party is called in to resolve a dispute about the application or interpretation of a collective agreement. In effect, interest arbitration involves a dispute over the formation of the contract between the employer and the trade union while rights arbitration involves disputes over the performance of that contract. This chapter will concern itself only with interest arbitration in health-care institutions in the three countries under review.

Interest arbitration is normally preceded by an attempt by the parties to the collective bargaining relationship to negotiate the terms of a collective agreement. In some jurisdiction, prior negotiations or resort to other dispute settlement mechanisms such as fact-finding, conciliation or mediation may also be required by statute before a dispute may be referred to arbitration.

The third party to whom the dispute is referred will normally be a sole arbitrator or a three-person board of arbitration. Where a three-person board is established, it is often composed of the nominee of each party and a chairman selected by the two nominees. There are several variations on this practice including the referral of disputes to a panel of judges, as occurs under a 1974 statute covering health-care employees of the State of Nebraska, or referral to an industrial labour court as occurred in Britain for many years.

Arbitration proceedings are said to be adjudicative in nature in that each party is allowed the opportunity to participate by way of presenting evidence and argument. Evidence is typically presented by way of statements by the parties' representatives and written briefs rather than through sworn testimony. The arbitrator is then expected to reach a decision based on a reasoned analysis of the positions of the parties.

There are a number of variations on the traditional arbitration format. In 'final offer' arbitration the arbitrator is obliged to choose the last offer of one of the parties and to include the terms of that offer in the award. In 'mediation arbitration' the arbitrator is authorised to attempt to mediate the dispute prior to issuing an arbitration award. 'Advisory arbitration' is identical to conventional arbitration except in so far as the award of the arbitrator is not binding on the parties.

Arbitration in Health-care Sector: UK, Canada and the USA

UK. Referral of collective bargaining disputes to arbitration in the UK only occurs with the mutual consent of the employer and trade union except in limited circumstances where unions

seek information for bargaining purposes. In most instances it
follows the completion of a series of procedures aimed at settlement of the dispute. This general approach was codified in
statute law in 1975 with the passage of the Employment Protection Act: referring to the Advisory Conciliation and Arbitration
Service, Section 3 of the Act provides:

3(1) Where a trade dispute exists or is apprehended the
Service may, at the request of both parties to the dispute,
refer all or any of the matters to which the dispute relates
for settlement to the arbitration of --
   (a) one or more persons appointed by the Service for that
       purpose (not being an officer or servant of the Service);
       or
   (b) the Central Arbitration Committee constituted under
       Section 10 below.
2 In exercising its functions under subsection (1) above, the
Service shall consider the likelihood of the dispute being settled by conciliation and where there exist appropriate agreed
procedures for negotiation or the settlement of disputes, shall
not refer a matter for settlement to arbitration under that
subsection unless those procedures have been used and have
failed to result in a settlement or unless, in the opinion of the
Service, there is a special reason which justifies arbitration
under that subsection as an alternative to those procedures.

The use of arbitration thus remains voluntary in that the consent
of all parties to a dispute is required before a referral to arbitration occurs. In addition, arbitration remains the dispute
settlement method of last resort in that the referral only occurs
where other procedures have failed unless there is a 'special
reason' justifying immediate referral.

The Advisory Conciliation and Arbitration Service (ACAS) was
created in 1974 without statutory mandate.[1] It was placed under
the control of an independent council rather than the government department responsible for labour matters. The assignment
of arbitration and conciliation services to an independent body
represented an attempt to allay suspicions held particularly by
trade unions that conciliators and arbitrators were influenced
by current government policy.[2] The independence of the ACAS
was confirmed in Schedule 1 of the Employment Protection Act
which provides that with the exception of discharging in financial accounts satisfactorily:

... the Service shall not be subject to directions of any kind
from any Minister of the Crown as to the manner in which it
is to exercise any of its functions under any enactment.

The Employment Protection Act also provided for the establishment of the Central Arbitration Committee. It plays the role of
a permanent arbitration body and is thus comparable to the

role played in earlier years by the Industrial Court.[3]

The basic structure for collective bargaining in the health-care sector in Britain was established in 1948 at the time of the creation of the National Health Service (NHS). It was decided that the system of Whitley Councils which was then operating successfully in the civil service would be adapted for use in the NHS.

The Main Constitution of the Whitley Council provides that where it is impossible to accommodate differences of opinion between the two sides of the Council, 'it shall be open to the management or the staff organisations concerned to seek arbitration in accordance with terms of an arbitration agreement to be determined by the General Council'. In earlier years, where the parties agreed to resort to arbitration, the services of the Industrial Court were employed. Although there is no formal arbitration agreement between management and staff organisations issues may be referred to ACAS. Referral to arbitration of collective bargaining disputes in the NHS was frequent from 1948 to the mid-1960s. However one result of the incidence of strikes in the NHS and in other sectors in the early 1970s was the British government referral of several wage disputes to specially created committees which were mandated to conduct inquiries into these disputes and to make recommendations. In the NHS, in the period 1974 to 1976, several disputes, including that over nurses' pay, were referred to pay inquiries under the chairmanship of Lord Halsbury.

In March 1979 the Standing Commission on Pay Comparability (SCPC) was established under the chairmanship of Professor Hugh Clegg,[4] in response to several NHS pay disputes. The Commission subsequently examined the pay claims of other public sector groups.

In its first series of inquiries the parties agreed to be bound by the Commission's findings with the result that its recommendations were treated in the same manner as an arbitration award. However, the procedures of the Commission did not fit the traditional pattern of an arbitration proceeding. While it held public hearings with all parties present it also conducted its own research and held private meetings with each of the interested parties.

Canada. Apart from persons in the health-care sector who are directly employed by the federal government, the labour relations of employees in Canadian health-care institutions are regulated by the ten provinces.

Two of the provinces currently impose compulsory arbitration on health-care employees. In Ontario, a strike by the support staff of Trenton Memorial Hospital in 1963 prompted the provincial government to appoint a Royal Commission to inquire into the 'feasibility and desirability' of applying compulsory arbitration in collective bargaining disputes in hospitals. The Commission recommended that compulsory arbitration be introduced

but only in situations where the Provincial Cabinet found that
patient care was adversely affected or seriously threatened or
where either party to a collective bargaining dispute had been
convicted of bargaining in bad faith. The provincial government
responded to the Commission's Report in 1965 by enacting 'The
Hospital Labour Disputes Arbitration Act'. The statute implemented a compulsory arbitration system but did not assign any
discretionary power to the Provincial Cabinet. Instead, all
unresolved disputes had to be referred to arbitration. Strikes
and lockouts were prohibited. The Act remains in effect in
1981 and applies to most health-care institutions in the province
including hospitals, nursing homes and homes for the aged.

The Province of Prince Edward Island also has enacted legislation providing for the compulsory arbitration of interest disputes involving persons required for the maintenance of hospital
services and employees of nursing homes.

The Province of British Columbia has enacted 'The Essential
Service Disputes Act' which provides for 'unilateral arbitration'
in essential service industries including health-care institutions.
The Act allows a union representing health-care employees to
elect to have an interest dispute referred to arbitration. The
request for arbitration can only be made after an effort has been
made to bargain in good faith with the employer. While the right
to compel arbitration of collective bargaining disputes is frequently relied upon by trade unions in British Columbia, there
have also been a number of instances where the right to strike
has been exercised in preference to the arbitration route.

The Province of Newfoundland at one time imposed compulsory
arbitration on hospital workers and prohibited strikes and lockouts. This legislation was repealed in 1973 following an illegal
strike of hospital employees. The statute which currently regulates the majority of health-care institutions in the province
provides for compulsory arbitration only in circumstances where
an emergency has been declared by the Newfoundland legislature.

A similar development occurred in Quebec where a 1975 statute
imposing compulsory arbitration on health-care employees was
repealed in 1978. Currently, health-care workers are subject
to no restrictions beyond those imposed on other private sector
employees. Strike action is allowed although there is legislation
granting authority to a commissioner for essential services to
determine which essential health services must be maintained
during a strike.

Employees of the Government of Canada working in federally
funded health-care facilities fall under the jurisdiction of the
Parliament of Canada. The Public Service Staff Relations Act
enacted by Parliament in 1967 allows a trade union to follow
either a conciliation and strike procedure or the route of compulsory arbitration. The choice must be made prior to the
commencement of negotiations. The vast majority of collective
agreements are settled through arbitration although the bargaining agent representing nurses has opted for and exercised its

right to strike in both the 1976 and 1978 rounds of bargaining.

The situation of physicians in Canada bears special comment. Physicians are excluded from participation in the collective bargaining schemes in most provinces although physicians employed by the Government of Canada are covered by the Public Service Staff Relations Act. Continuing disputes over fee levels chargeable by physicians under Canada's universal medicare programme resulted in the review of this and other matters by a Special Commissioner appointed by the Government of Canada in 1979. The Report tendered by the Commissioner in 1980 recommended that any impasse in negotiations between provincial authorities and physicians over fee levels should be resolved through binding arbitration. The recommendation has not been acted upon to date.

United States.   Prior to 1974, jurisdiction over most private health-care institutions in the USA fell within the legislative realm of individual states. Nine states passed labour relations statutes which covered these institutions. Two states, Minnesota and New York, prohibited strikes by health-care employees and imposed compulsory arbitration.

Jurisdiction over certain private nonprofit health-care institutions fell to the National Labor Relations Board. The criteria employed by the Board in deciding on its jurisdiction varied over the years. The confusion which resulted from this fragmentation of labour regulations was largely clarified in 1974 through amendments to the National Labor Relations Act. As a result of the amendments nonprofit health-care institutions were brought within the coverage of the Act and thereby within the jurisdiction of the National Labor Relations Board. In 1974, this represented more than 55 per cent of hospital employees.

The amendments also created a legal framework for collective bargaining in health-care institutions which differs in many respects from that imposed in other industries. The most distinctive feature is the rigorous time limitations on parties to collective bargaining particularly in first contract negotiations. While provision is made for the establishing of a fact-finder or a Board of Inquiry (BOI) to investigate and report on unresolved disputes, the idea of compulsory arbitration was considered and rejected by the United States Congress. It was felt by some legislators that the findings of fact and recommendations of the BOI would provide the basis for a voluntary referral of collective bargaining disputes to arbitration.[5] In practice, the use of arbitration subsequent to a BOI report has been infrequent. Moreover, the rate of BOI appointments has declined since 1974 as has the number of fact-finding boards appointed.[6]

Since employees of state and municipal health-care facilities are not covered by the National Labor Relations Act, individual states have the legislative authority to govern collective bargaining disputes in those institutions. Most states prohibit arbitration of bargaining disputes involving state and municipal health-care institutions. Some states have imposed compulsory arbitration while others allow voluntary referral of disputes to arbitration.

One can discern in recent years a trend towards increasingly sophisticated arbitration schemes at the state level. In 1969 Michigan enacted legislation covering certain essential services including emergency medical personnel. Mediation and fact-finding may be used by the parties. Thereafter, economic issues must be submitted to 'final-offer arbitration' while other disputed areas may be referred to conventional arbitration.

In 1974 Iowa passed a statute requiring arbitration for all public employees. The parties are obliged to follow mediation and fact-finding procedures before submitting the remaining issues in dispute to final-offer arbitration on an issue by issue basis. The arbitrator is entitled to choose either of the parties' final offers on each issue in dispute or, alternately, the recommendation made by the fact-finder.

The State of Nevada passed legislation in 1975 imposing compulsory arbitration on all local government employees. Mediation is mandatory and fact-finding may be requested by either party. Where fact-finding is requested, both parties can agree that it be binding or the governor may order it binding at the request of either party based on considerations of public interest, fiscal interest or public safety.

In Wisconsin, a 1977 statute provides for a mediation-arbitration scheme. A single arbitrator or a tripartite board conducts mediation and, if unsuccessful, final-offer arbitration. A limited right to strike is given when both parties withdraw their final offers.

At the federal government level, prior to 1978, there was no statute governing collective bargaining of federal health-care employees. However, two executive orders, one issued by President Kennedy in 1962 and the other by President Nixon in 1970, authorised collective bargaining with respect to certain issues. Significantly, monetary issues were excluded. Both orders prohibited federal workers from resorting to strikes. The 1970 order provided for the creation of the Federal Mediation and Conciliation Service. Disputes which were not settled were then referred to the Federal Services Impasses Panel (FSIP) which was empowered to recommend procedures for settlement including arbitration. The parties were not allowed to refer their disputes to arbitration without the consent of the FSIP.

In 1978 the Civil Service Reform Act put into statutory form many of the practices imposed by the Executive Orders. Prohibition of strikes has been continued as has the prohibition against collective bargaining monetary issues. The FSIP continues to be empowered with the exclusive right to refer disputes to arbitration.

AN OVERVIEW

The legal framework governing most health-care workers in the
three countries under review may be characterised as permissive
in relation to the right to refer collective bargaining disputes
to arbitration. Legislators have been willing to allow parties
voluntarily to use the arbitration mechanism although certain
preliminary steps in the negotiating process may be imposed as
prerequisites to arbitration.

The significant split at the policy level occurs over the issue
of whether to grant a right to strike to health-care employees.
In Britain, and in most jurisdictions of Canada and the United
States, the right to strike has been retained. In light of the
degree of public concern which normally attaches to work stoppages in health-care institutions, it is apparent that legislators
have significant reservations about the use of arbitration as a
means of resolving collective bargaining disputes.

One of the most commonly expressed criticisms is that referral
of interest disputes to an arbitrator is contrary to fundamental
democratic principles. The arbitrator is authorised to render
decisions in a forum which is essentially a closed legislative
process from which other competing political forces are excluded.
Interest arbitration is said to be 'inimical to a basic precept of
political democracy, namely, that authoritative political decisions
should be reached by government officials who are accountable
to the public'.[7]

These concerns are increasing in situations where arbitration
awards involve large expenditures of public or private funds.
A recent award in the Province of Ontario was said to involve
the expenditure of approximately one-half billion dollars of public
funds in so far as it established a pattern for other settlements
across the Province.[8]

A related criticism is that the skills of the individuals who are
appointed as arbitrators are not equal to the complexity of the
task. The following frank assessment of this difficulty is provided by one of Canada's leading arbitrators:

> The one thing that the arbitrator fraternity has in common
> is that we all know little or nothing about basic public finance,
> about the long-term impact on an employer's budget of ap-
> parently innocuous changes in working conditions, about the
> elasticity of demand for an employer's product, about the
> substitutability of capital for labour as proposed wage or
> benefit increases make labour more expensive, about the
> long-range costs of funding pension increases as the com-
> plexion of the work force changes, and about all the other
> material necessary for an intelligent response to the questions
> posed by the statutes or the parties.[9]

In fact, the array of skills which might be brought to bear in
many modern-day interest disputes is not possessed by any one

individual even when assisted by the parties' nominees.

One proposed solution to this difficulty is suggested in the report of the Hospital Inquiry Commission appointed in 1974 to investigate the system of bargaining and dispute settlement in public hospitals in the Province of Ontario. The Commission recommended that a pay research centre be established to accumulate data on prevailing wage rates and other information pertinent to collective bargaining in public hospitals. It was also recommended that arbitrators be specifically authorised to use whatever information they considered relevant including that supplied by the pay research centre. The Commission further recommended that a panel of arbitrators be established to ensure that the persons appointed in interest disputes would develop experience adequate to deal with the matters in dispute.

The pay inquiry procedure which has been relied upon in the UK in recent years may also reflect a desire to buttress the skills and credibility of the third party assigned to resolve a collective bargaining dispute. The pay inquiry commissions were provided with sufficient resources to support the generation of research data independent of that submitted by the parties to the dispute. This would presumably have increased the prospect of developing objective data as well as remedying any lack of expertise on the part of members of the pay inquiry commission with respect to particular issues which arise. However both the Halsbury Committees in 1974 and the 1979 Clegg Commission were accused by the staffs sides of committing major errors.

An alternative policy response adopted in several jurisdictions is the inclusion in the statute authorising arbitration of specified criteria which must be taken into account by the arbitrator. It is reasoned that this legislative direction ensures continued consideration by arbitrators of appropriate public policy considerations. In the United States, inclusion of criteria in the enabling statute was necessitated by court decisions which found that imposition of compulsory arbitration was unconstitutional unless the arbitrator was guided by criteria.[10] Legislation in the State of Nebraska directs that terms imposed by arbitrators must be 'comparable to the prevalent rate... and conditions of employment' enjoyed by similarly situated workers and that consideration must be given to the public employer's ability to pay within existing revenue sources. Several other states direct arbitrators to take account of the total compensation package (wages and benefits) and to consider specific ability to pay factors such as tax levy limitations, long and short term bonded indebtedness and comparative equalised tax rates.[11]

In the Province of British Columbia, section 7 of The Essential Service Disputes Act provides the following detailed statement of the criteria to be adhered to by arbitrators:

(a) the interest of the public,
(b) the terms and conditions of employment in similar occupations

outside the employer's employment, including such geographic, industrial, or other variations as the single arbitrator or arbitration board shall consider relevant,

(c) the need to maintain appropriate relationships in the terms and conditions of employment as between different classification levels within an occupation and as between occupations in the employer's employment,

(d) the need to establish terms and conditions of employment that are fair and reasonable in relation to the qualifications required, the work performed, the responsibility assumed and the nature of the services rendered, and

(e) any other factor that the single arbitrator or the arbitration board considers relevant to the matter in dispute.

Several studies have concluded, however, that such statutory directions to arbitrators have little actual impact on the arbitrator's approach.[12] While cursory reference may be made to the criteria set out in the statute, the general approach taken by arbitrators does not appear to differ from that where the development of criteria is left to the discretion of the arbitrator.

The defects in the arbitration process from a public policy standpoint are not the only reasons for the resistance of legislators to a compulsory arbitration system in the health-care field. In those jurisdictions where compulsory arbitration has been imposed a number of problems have been encountered.

The longest experience with compulsory arbitration in the three countries studied occurred in the State of Minnesota between 1947 and 1974. Over this period, over 1300 collective bargaining agreements were concluded under the legislation. Arbitration accounted for all but 251 of the agreements.[13]

In 1963 the State of New York enacted a compulsory arbitration system for nonprofit hospitals and residential care centres in the City of New York. An estimated 10 to 20 per cent of the collective bargaining disputes were referred to arbitration.[14]

Similar results have occurred in the Province of Ontario where compulsory arbitration in health-care institutions has been imposed by statute since 1965. While many settlements are reached voluntarily, they usually follow and are closely patterned on the arbitration awards brought down in major cities in the Province.

Experience in these jurisdictions indicates one of the central defects of a compulsory arbitration system - the undermining of the collective bargaining process. Compulsory arbitration is said to have a 'narcotic effect' on the parties who become incapable of reaching voluntary agreements without the intervention of a third party.[15] This is reflected not only in the number of disputes which are resolved through arbitration but also in the number of unresolved issues which are referred to arbitration. A recent study in the Province of British Columbia - where a system of unilateral arbitration is employed - revealed that an average of 45 issues were referred to arbitration by parties in the health-care industry in comparison to an average of six issues in industries where interest arbitration was not compulsory.[16]

In the United States, the use of alternative forms of arbitration has been experimented with as a means of reducing certain of the problems of excessive reliance on arbitration in a compulsory arbitration system. Both final offer arbitration and mediation-arbitration have been imposed by states in conjunction with other dispute-settling mechanisms such as mandatory fact-finding and conciliation.

Studies of final-offer arbitration indicate that it has achieved significant success in reducing the number of cases which proceed to arbitration and the number of issues which remain to be resolved by the arbitration.[17] The primary difficulty with the procedure arises from the fact that the arbitrator is not provided with the discretion to find the reasonable middle ground between the parties' bargaining positions. The implementation of one party's position may result in inclusion of contract terms that do significant damage to the bargaining relationship which must be corrected through subsequent rounds of bargaining.[18]

Apart from deleterious effects on voluntary negotiations, a compulsory arbitration system has also been found to fail in its primary purpose – the avoidance of work stoppages by health-care employees. Unions have effectively employed both the threat of illegal strikes and illegal strikes to win favourable contract settlements. In the Province of Ontario the threat of an illegal strike by nonmedical employees in twelve Toronto hospitals in 1974 brought about a wage settlement which increased wages of health-care employees by as much as 60 per cent. The settlement resulted in a major upward adjustment of wages for all health-care employees in the Province. The adjustments resulted from voluntary settlements as well as several arbitration awards which determined that the wage gains obtained in Toronto settlement should be passed on to employees of other health-care instititions. In 1981 nonmedical employees conducted a one-week strike in support of their bargaining position. The employees returned to work only after a cease and desist order was obtained from the Ontario Labour Relations Board and an injunction was issued by the Supreme Court of Ontario.

Trade unions representing New York City health-care employees employed similar tactics in a compulsory arbitration setting. The unions shifted between bargaining, illegal strikes and arbitration to suit immediate needs and to maximise settlements.[19]

One legislative response to the problems associated with compulsory arbitration is implementation of a system which allows the right to strike with provision for imposing arbitration where circumstances require. The Province of Newfoundland rejected compulsory arbitration in 1973 in favour of legislation which authorises the Newfoundland Assembly to order that a dispute involving health-care employees be referred to arbitration when it is deemed in the public interest to do so. The advantage of this procedure is that the parties enter negotiations without any assurance that arbitration will be available to resolve the dispute and the chilling effect of compulsory arbitration on the negotiations is thereby reduced.

Other jurisdictions have chosen to allow health-care employees the right to strike while reserving authority to intervene to ensure continuance of essential services. In the Province of British Columbia the Labour Relations Board has been assigned jurisdiction to designate services, facilities and employees as essential and to order the employees to perform services during a strike in order to avoid 'immediate and serious danger to life, health or safety'. The Board was called upon to exercise this authority in a 1976 strike of nonprofessional hospital employees at Vancouver General Hospital. Of the 2200 employees who were eligible to strike, the Board concluded that approximately 100 performed essential services and directed them to continue work during the strike. The work of the employees who engaged in strike action was carried out by professional staff and volunteers. It was considered by most persons involved that safe patient care had been provided during the strike.[20]

A similar system has been relied upon in the State of Hawaii where a civil court is empowered to enjoin partially or totally any strike which is considered to jeopardise public health and safety.

Aside from the fact that a legislative prohibition against strikes is often ineffectual, there is also an increased recognition that strikes in health-care institutions are not as hazardous as many had predicted at the time when collective bargaining rights were granted to health-care employees.[21] Moreover, the incidence of strikes is less than had been predicted.

In general, there is a marked trend in North America away from the use of compulsory arbitration systems which employ conventional arbitration. In the UK, there has traditionally been a reliance on an external system which bears some resemblance to arbitration but which rejects some of the procedures of conventional arbitration found in North America. While voluntary referrals to arbitration are encouraged in most jurisdictions, there is an increasing reluctance on the part of legislators to impose arbitration on the negotiating process. While arbitration will undoubtedly have a continuing role to play in health-care collective bargaining in the 1980s, it seems probable that the decade will also bring experimentation with new arbitration procedures as well as a continuing search for more effective methods of achieving peaceful resolution of bargaining disputes in the health-care sector.

REFERENCES AND NOTES

1 The ACAS was initially called Conciliation and Arbitration Service and in 1975 its name was changed to Advisory

Conciliation and Arbitration Service.
2 Kessler, Sid (1980), The Prevention and Settlement of
Collective Labour Disputes in the United Kingdom, 'Industrial Relations Journal', vol.11, no.1, p.17.
3 The Industrial Court had become the Industrial Arbitration
Board in 1971. A review of the functioning of the Central
Arbitration Committee is contained in Kessler, The Preven-
tion and Settlement of Collective Labour Disputes in the
United Kingdom, pp.25-7.
4 Discussion of the Standing Commission on Pay Comparability
is derived from the study by Swan, Kenneth P. (1980),
Apples and Oranges: Comparability as a Criterion in Interest
Arbitration, prepared for Continuing Legal Education
Interest Arbitration Seminar, Queen's University.
5 Vernon, Richard G. (1975), Labor Relations in the Health
Care Field under the 1974 Amendments to the National Labor
Relations Act: An Overview and Analysis, 'Northwestern
University Law Review', vol.70, no.1, p.213.
6 Tanner, L.D., Weinstein, H.G., Ahmuty, A.L. (1980),
Collective Bargaining in the Health Care Industry, 'Monthly
Labour Review', p.50.
7 Horton, R.D. (1975), Arbitration, Arbitrators, and the
Public Interest, 'Industrial and Labor Relations Review',
vol.28, p.499; Anderson, J. (1977), 'St John's Law Review',
vol.51, p.506.
8 Kingston General Hospital v. Ontario Nurses Association
(1979), unreported (Swan).
9 Weiler, Paul (1980), 'Reconcilable Differences - New
Directions in Canadian Labour Law', Carswell Company
Limited, p.226.
10 See for example, State (Van Piper) v. Traffic Telephone
Workers Federation, 66 A 2d 616 (1949).
11 Miller, Ronald (1980), Compulsory Impasse Procedures:
Recent American Experience, 'Industrial Relations Journal',
vol.10, no.4, p.47.
12 Mironi, M. (1980), Arbitration as a Strike Substitute in
Labour Negotiations -- Public Policy Reconsidered, 'Alberta
Law Review', vol.XVIII, p.178; Weiler, J. (1980), Interest
Arbitration in Essential Services: The British Columbia
Experience, University of British Columbia, p.23.
13 Howlett, Robert G. (1973), Contract Negotiations Arbitra-
tion in the Public Sector, 'University of Cincinnati Law
Review', vol.42, no.1, p.47.
14 Loewenberg, J.J. (1976), Compulsory Arbitration in the
United States, in J.J. Loewenberg, W.J. Gershenfield,
J.H. Glasbeck, B.A. Hepple and Kenneth F. Walker,
'Compulsory Arbitration', D.C. Heath and Company, p.150.
15 Miller, Compulsory Impasse Procedures: Recent American
Experience, p.47; Weiler, Interest Arbitration in Essential
Services, p.17-18; Anderson, John C. (1980), Arbitration
in the Federal Public Service, presented at a conference,

'Interest Arbitration -- A Matter of Public Policy', p.7.
16 Weiler, Interest Arbitration in Essential Services, p.17.
17 Gallagher, D.C., and Pegnatter, R. (1978-9), Impasse
   Resolution under the Iowa Multistep Procedure, 'Industrial
   and Labor Relations Review', vol.32, p.327; Weiler, J.M.
   Interest Arbitration in Essential Services, p.17.
18 P. Weiler, 'Reconcilable Differences', p.231-5.
19 Miller, 'Compulsory Impasse Procedures: Recent American
   Experience, p.47.
20 Weiler, 'Reconcilable Differences', p.212.
21 Jones, S.A. (1977), Note - Alternative Proposal for the
   Regulation of an Emergency Strike in the Health Care
   Industry, 'Vanderbilt Law Review', vol.30, p.1033.

PART VI

POLICY

Introduction

Many of the major aspects of health-care decision-making take place within a political context. While the UK, with its state financed NHS is an obvious example of this, neither Canada nor the USA are immune from developments within public policy and legislation. In industrial relations terms one important feature of public policy is the concern to contain or control income. In each of these three countries governments have turned to some form of incomes policy in an attempt to contain the collective bargaining behaviour of unions in order to influence wage costs. The continued growth of inflation in the 1970s increasingly pushed governments to adopt this approach as a necessary corollary to their commitment to full employment.

In Canada, the 1975 wage and profit controls were in part concerned to lessen pay increases in the public sector and in particular health. A concern to resist pay increases in the public sector has been a recurring theme in the successive incomes policies of UK governments since 1948. On a number of occasions health workers have been used as an example, by UK governments, of their determination to resist public sector pay increases. In the USA wage and price controls have caused hospitals to become more cost conscious and have acted to depress health workers' pay. However, in the sphere of public policy it is not uncommon for the decisions of policy-makers to produce different results to those intended. The experience of incomes policy in the health sector provides some examples of this difference in intention and outcome.

The authors of the following chapters examine and analyse the impact of incomes policy on industrial relations in the health sectors of the three countries. In Chapter 16 Reid explores the effect of this policy initiative which 'had more impact on industrial relations in Canada than any other government policy initiative in the post-war period'. In Chapter 17 Dimmock discusses the relationship between incomes policy and health service pay determination in the UK and identifies a number of unforeseen consequences that have emerged and their effect on industrial relations in the health sector. In the final chapter of Part VI, Santos and Helburn analyse the impact of incomes policy and other programmes on health industrial relations in the USA. The future of incomes policy is uncertain in each of these countries. Santos and Helburn draw some lessons that can be shared between Canada, the USA and the UK on the operation of incomes policy in industrial relations in the health sector.

16. EFFECT OF INCOMES POLICY ON HEALTH INDUSTRIAL RELATIONS IN CANADA

F. Reid

INTRODUCTION

On 13 October 1975 Prime Minister Pierre Trudeau shocked the Canadian nation by announcing a comprehensive three-year programme of wage and profit controls. The programme had an immediate and dramatic impact on the conduct of industrial relations in Canada. The fundamental right of management and labour to bargain wage rates and fringe benefits was drastically altered by the intrusion of a powerful third party in the negotiation process. It is no exaggeration to say that the imposition of the three-year controls programme had more impact on industrial relations in Canada than any other government policy initiative in the post-war period.

For those involved in industrial relations in the health sector the programme was especially important. It will be argued below that certain parts of the health sector suffered a particularly severe impact from the controls programme. In addition, large wage settlements in the health sector were one of the contributing factors leading to the government's decision to implement controls.

The approach taken in this chapter is to begin by analysing the economic situation prior to controls in the Canadian economy in general and in the health sector in particular. After discussing the events leading to the implementation of controls, the actual structure of the controls programme is described, followed by an analysis of the effects on industrial relations in the health sector. The chapter concludes with a brief discussion of the impact of the controls programme on the Canadian economy.

THE SITUATION LEADING TO CONTROLS

The main reason controls were introduced was the government's concern over the sharp rise in wage settlements and inflation in

* I am very grateful to Mr Robert Bass of the Ontario Hospitals Association, and Ms Evelyn Wong of the Ontario Nurses Association for very helpful discussions and access to data and to Mr Pat O'Keefe of the Canadian Union of Public Employees for comments on the paper. This does not, of course, imply agreement with either the analysis or the conclusions in this chapter.

1974 and 1975. Table 16.1, which plots the annual inflation rate since the mid 1960s, shows a substantial increase in the inflation rate in 1973, reaching 'double-digit' levels by 1974.

*Table 16.1:   Inflation and Unemployment, Canada,
1967:1 to 1980:2*

Year and Quarter	Inflation	Unemployment
1967: 1	2.1	3.7
2	4.9	3.7
3	5.5	3.7
4	2.7	4.2
1968: 1	4.8	4.4
2	2.8	4.5
3	3.7	4.5
4	5.3	4.5
1969: 1	3.4	4.3
2	6.5	4.4
3	3.9	4.4
4	4.0	4.6
1970: 1	4.1	4.9
2	2.6	5.8
3	0.9	6.2
4	1.0	6.1
1971: 1	2.4	6.2
2	4.7	6.3
3	4.8	6.1
4	4.3	6.1
1972: 1	5.1	5.9
2	2.8	6.1
3	6.8	6.4
4	5.5	6.5
1973: 1	7.9	5.9
2	8.5	5.4
3	10.1	5.4
4	8.5	5.5
1974: 1	10.2	5.2
2	12.8	5.2
3	10.7	5.3
4	12.0	5.7
1975: 1	9.5	6.7
2	8.2	6.9
3	12.6	7.0
4	8.7	7.1
1976: 1	6.2	6.8
2	5.6	7.0
3	4.8	7.3
4	6.8	7.4

Table 16.1: (*continued*)

Year and Quarter	Inflation	Unemployment
1977: 1	9.4	7.9
2	8.8	7.9
3	7.6	8.3
4	9.5	8.4
1978: 1	8.2	8.4
2	9.2	8.5
3	9.2	8.5
4	6.2	8.2
1979: 1	9.0	7.9
2	10.5	7.6
3	7.9	7.1
4	9.2	7.3
1980: 1	8.9	7.4
2	11.1	7.7

Sources:
The unemployment rate is seasonally adjusted and revised to the new Labor Force Survey definitions introduced in January 1976, Statistics Canada catalogue 71-201 (1979), p.24. The inflation rate is the quarter to quarter percentage change in the Consumer Price Index at an annual rate, Statistics Canada catalogue 11-003.

The government was, however, even more concerned with the rising level of wage settlements in the economy. Maslove and Swimmer[1] conclude from numerous confidential interviews with those involved in the decision to implement controls that key government decision-makers, including those in the Prime Minister's office, recognised that the key problem was public-sector wage increases (especially at the municipal level) and in the quasi-public sector (i.e. education, hospitals). These settlements were running significantly higher than those either in the private sector or the federal public sector. Thus the health sector was one of the prime targets of the controls programme.

Table 16.2 presents quarterly averages for major settlements published by Labour Canada and the Ontario Ministry of Labor.[2] The data for Ontario are of particular interest since they are more disaggregated and show a separate series for the health and welfare sector. The Ontario data are also more comprehensive, including all bargaining units of 200 or more employees whereas the federal data apply to all bargaining units of 500 or more employees. The data are for changes in base wage rates, a measure which will overstate the increase in average wage rates somewhat in contracts where increases are a flat cents-per-hour increase rather than a percentage increase.

Table 16.2: Average Settlements in Major Collective Agreements

Year and Quarter	Ontario, Health and Welfare Sectors		Ontario, All Industries		Ontario, Manufacturing		Canada, Manufacturing	
	All agreements	Agreements without COLAs	All agreements	Agreements without COLAs	All agreements	Agreements without COLAs	All agreements	Agreements without COLAs
1971: 1	--	--	--	--	--	--	7.2	--
2	--	--	--	--	--	--	8.1	--
3	11.0	--	9.7	--	8.0	--	8.6	--
4	11.8	--	8.2	--	7.5	--	6.8	--
1972: 1	8.2	--	7.3	--	6.9	--	7.5	--
2	7.8	--	8.2	--	7.8	--	7.9	--
3	11.0	--	8.3	--	7.7	--	9.4	--
4	9.7	--	7.5	--	7.7	--	9.3	--
1973: 1	8.1	--	7.7	--	7.7	--	9.1	--
2	10.3	--	7.8	--	8.8	--	10.0	--
3	9.0	--	8.6	--	8.1	--	9.5	--
4	10.6	--	7.6	--	6.4	--	7.2	--
1974: 1	13.2	--	9.9	--	11.4	--	12.9	14.0
2	26.1	26.1	13.8	15.4	10.0	13.8	11.7	14.9
3	30.0	30.0	14.3	16.9	11.5	15.8	13.4	15.0
4	28.9	28.9	15.5	17.7	10.9	18.0	14.0	24.0
1975: 1	39.0	39.0	14.9	15.1	13.6	15.5	15.0	17.9
2	28.3	28.3	14.6	16.3	14.9	17.5	15.7	16.6
3	14.2	14.2	12.9	14.9	11.2	14.6	12.6	18.4
4	none	none	13.5	13.5	11.9	13.7	14.0	14.6
1976: 1	none	none	14.3	14.4	11.4	11.7	11.7	12.3
2	10.2	9.9	12.2	12.8	9.8	10.3	9.7	10.1
3	11.2	11.2	12.4	12.9	10.4	10.6	9.3	9.3

Table 16.2: (continued)

Year and Quarter	Ontario, Health and Welfare Sectors		Ontario, All Industries		Ontario, Manufacturing		Canada, Manufacturing	
	All agreements	Agreements without COLAs	All agreements	Agreements without COLAs	All agreements	Agreements without COLAs	All agreements	Agreements without COLAs
1976: 4	10.1	10.1	8.6	10.0	5.0	9.4	5.9	9.2
1977: 1	7.4	7.4	8.5	9.1	7.0	7.8	7.1	7.4
2	6.7	6.7	7.3	7.7	6.3	8.1	6.4	7.6
3	7.3	7.3	6.8	7.4	6.3	7.7	7.2	7.6
4	7.3	7.3	6.5	7.7	5.6	6.8	7.3	7.8
1978: 1	7.0	7.0	6.2	6.5	5.8	6.5	6.6	7.8
2	6.9	6.9	6.3	6.4	6.6	7.1	6.5	7.2
3	6.5	6.5	6.8	7.4	5.5	8.0	6.4	7.-
4	4.2	4.2	6.8	7.1	6.7	7.8	7.5	8.4
1979: 1	4.6	4.6	6.8	7.9	7.1	8.6	7.5	8.1
2	7.1	7.1	7.7	8.1	7.9	9.7	7.2	9.1
3	9.7	9.7	8.5	8.8	8.7	8.8	10.4	10.5
4	7.6	7.6	5.4	7.8	8.9	9.3	5.3	10.4
1980: 1	10.2	10.2	8.7	9.4	8.1	11.4	8.3	10.7

Source: Ontario data from the Ontario Ministry of Labour's quarterly publication 'Wage Developments in Collective Bargaining Settlements in Ontario'. Canadian data are from Labour Canada's quarterly 'Wage Developments' publication.

Notes: The table shows the change in base wage rates negotiated in collective agreements. The Ontario data covers all bargaining units of 200 or workers. The Canadian data are for bargaining units of 500 or more. In both cases the settlements are average annual compounded increased over the life of the contract, weighted by the number of employees in each bargaining unit.

Since Cost of Living Allowance (COLA) provisions are virtually non-existent in the health sector, settlements in agreements without COLAs in other sectors would be the most relevant comparison. Settlements in agreements without COLAs also avoid the difficulty of costing COLAs. Prior to 1974, however, COLAs were not prevalent[3] and separate data were not published for agreements without COLAs. For this reason both series are shown in Table 16.2.

The first two columns of Table 16.2 show the dramatic rise in settlements in the health and welfare sector in Ontario. Settlements which were averaging approximately 10 per cent in the 1971 to 1973 period jumped to an average of approximately 30 per cent in the period 1974: 2 to 1975: 2. The data for all Ontario industries show that the sharp increase in settlements was not unique to the health sector, although the increase was not so dramatic in the rest of the Ontario economy. The data for Ontario manufacturing illustrates that it was not just a case of the public sector raising the average for the economy as a whole -- comparable increases were being negotiated in the Ontario private sector. The final two columns show that a similar phenomenon was occurring across the entire country.

In understanding why controls were imposed it is important to determine the reason for these large wage settlements. Both common sense and economic research suggest that wage settlements tend to rise when (actual or expected) inflation increases and they tend to rise when a booming economy puts workers in a strong labour market position.

On the one hand, the inflation rate had increased substantially but not enough to explain all of the increase in wage settlements in 1974-5. Labour market conditions on the other hand, appeared weak, as indicated by the unemployment rate which was high compared to the boom period of the late 1960s (see Table 16.1). The high wage settlements which were observed during what appeared to be a recession generated a rather desperate feeling in government that previous economic relationships had broken down, 'things were out of control', and dramatic action was required.[4]

Subsequent research, however, has indicated that a substantial change in the relationship between the unemployment rate and labour market conditions occurred in the early 1970s, with the result that the government may have seriously misread labour market conditions in 1974-5. Taking account of this change, the high wage settlements during this period become more readily understandable.

Figure 16.1 plots the Canadian annual unemployment rate against the annual job vacancy rate for the period 1953 to 1978 (the numbered points in the figure indicate years). During the period 1953-71 the points generally lie in a negatively sloping band. During booms the economy moves to the right-hand end of the band with a low unemployment rate and a high job vacancy rate. In recessions the opposite is true -- the economy moves to

Figure 16.1: Canadian Unemployment-Vacancy Relationship, 1953-78

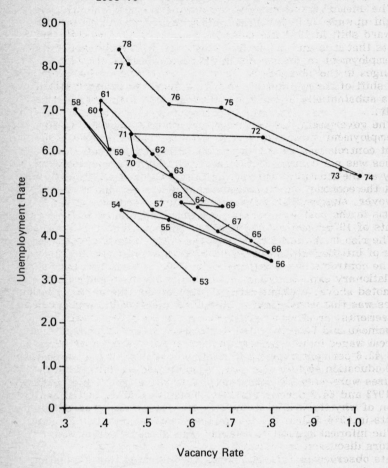

NOTES: The vacancy rate is calculated as the number of vacant jobs as a percentage of the number of jobs. Vacancy data are from Statistics Canada's job Vacancy Survey from the beginning of the survey in 1971 until its termination in 1978. Prior vacancy data are the Economic Council of Canada series constructed by Denton et al. (1975) to link the National Employment Service data, the Help Wanted Index and the Job Vacancy Survey data in a consistent series.
Source: Reid and Meltz, Causes of Shifts in the Unemployment-Vacancy Relationship, p.470.

the left-hand end where unemployment is high and the job
vacancy rate is low.

The unemployment-vacancy curve in Figure 16.1 shows a
slight upward drift during the 1950s and 1960s and a dramatic
upward shift in 1972. Research on the causes of this shift suggests that it is due mainly to the important liberalisation of the
Unemployment Insurance Act in 1971 and the demographic
changes in the labour force.[5] An important point is that after
the shift of the relationship in 1972 a 'boom' was characterised
by a substantially higher unemployment rate than prior to the
shift.

The government was generally not aware of this shift in the
unemployment-vacancy relationship when the decision to implement controls was made because the historical vacancy rate
series was not constructed until 1975 by Denton et al. Looking
only at the unemployment rate in 1974, one could easily conclude
that the economy was in recession. Looking at the vacancy rate,
however, suggests the economy was in one of the strongest
booms in the post-war period. In this light the high wage settlements of 1974-5 are much easier to comprehend.

The rise in the inflation rate in the early 1970s increased the
rate of inflation which people expected to occur over the life
of the contracts being negotiated in 1974-5 and this rise in
'inflationary expectations' contributed to the high settlements,
as noted above. Another related effect of the rise in the inflation
rates was that many groups fell behind inflation in their previous
agreements, creating a need for catch-up wage increases.
Cousineau and Lacroix[6] calculate that employees suffered losses
in real wages in 19.1 per cent of agreements expiring in 1973
and 43.6 per cent expiring in 1974. For agreements in the health
and education sectors (i.e. the 'quasi-public' sector) the loss
figures were even more dramatic: 50.0 per cent of the agreements
in 1973 and 64.3 per cent in 1974. This provides a partial explanation of why the health sector experienced even higher settlements in 1974-5 than the rest of the economy.

The informal arguments made above suggest that the various
factors discussed are capable of explaining the high wage settlements observed in 1974-5. This conclusion is supported by
economic research using multiple regression analysis which has
shown that the high wage settlements observed prior to controls
are just what one would predict given the strong labour market,
the high level of expected inflation and the catch-up factor.[7]
As an example, Figure 16.2[8] shows the actual wage settlements
in Canadian manufacturing and the predicted wage settlements
using a model in which labour market conditions are measured
by the vacancy rate (rather than the unemployment rate). The
model explains about 75 per cent of the quarter-to-quarter
variation in wage settlements and is able to explain the surge
in wage settlements in the 1974-5 period.[9]

The final point to be considered in explaining the government's
decision to impose controls is why the government did not

attempt to restrain wage settlements and inflation through the conventional means of a restrictive monetary and fiscal policy. Most economists agree that in the 'long run' inflation could be restrained if the government adopted sufficiently contractionary policies such as raising taxes, cutting expenditures and reducing the rate of growth of the money supply.

Figure 16.2: Actual and Predicted Wage Settlements, Canadian Manufacturing, 1967:1 to 1978:3

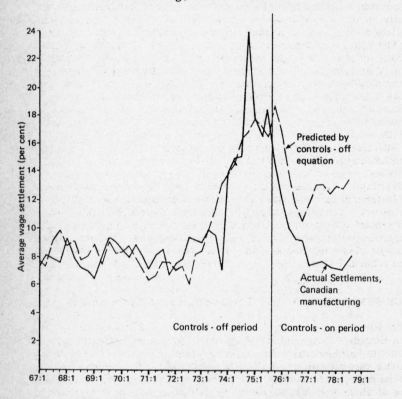

Source: Reid, Effect of Controls on the Rate of Wage Change in Canada, p.219.

The problem with contractionary policies however, is that they also cause a 'short run' reduction in production in the economy and an increase in unemployment. It is this induced recession which exerts restraint on wage settlements, lowers the rate of increase of unit labour costs and, so the theory goes, exerts a restraining influence on the rate of price inflation.

During the 1950s and 1960s the empirical evidence was generally consistent with this theory. During booms unemploy-

ment was reduced but inflation was increased and during recessions the opposite occurred. This created a policy dilemma for
government because if it stimulated the economy, unemployment
improved and inflation worsened and the converse occurred if
it restrained the economy.

Although most Canadian empirical research does indicate that
a rise in unemployment restrains wage settlements and inflation
(other things held constant), the magnitude of the restraining
effect is quite small, implying that a severe and prolonged
recession would need to be induced to reduce inflation substantially through contractionary policies alone.[10] Such a 'cure' for
inflation may well be worse than the disease!

The Liberal Government's awareness of this dilemma was no
doubt heightened by its previous experience with contractionary
policy in 1969-70. The result was a substantial rise in the
unemployment rate and a moderate reduction in inflation in
1970-1 (see Table 16.1). Many observers felt this rise in the
unemployment rate contributed significantly to the Liberals'
loss of their majority position in the House of Commons in the
1972 election.[11]

With monetary and fiscal restraint such an unattractive option,
the Liberal Government was driven to consider alternative
policies, even ones which it recognised had many other disadvantages. In this regard it should be remembered that in the
1974 federal election the Progressive Conservative Party
favoured a controls programme and the Liberals were elected
on a platform strongly opposed to controls. The imposition of a
controls programme the following year thus completely reversed
a major election promise and was an acute embarrassment for
the Liberal Party.

THE STRUCTURE OF THE ANTI-INFLATION PROGRAMME

The government's White Paper, 'Attack on Inflation[12] tabled in
the House of Commons on 14 October 1975 specified four components to the Anti-Inflation Programme: (1) gradual reduction
in the rate of growth of the money supply and a restrictive
fiscal policy; (2) restriction of the growth in government spending at all levels to the rate of growth of gross national product;
(3) structural policies to reduce the fragmentation of collective
bargaining and to make product markets more competitive; and
(4) formation of the Anti-Inflation Board (AIB) to directly control prices and incomes. The AIB was officially established in
the Anti-Inflation Act passed in December 1975[13] and made
retroactive to 14 October. Although the AIB was the most prominent part of the programme, the restrictive monetary and
fiscal policies also had important effects on the economy.

In the private sector the jurisdiction of the AIB included firms
with more than 500 employees, firms in the construction industry
with more than 20 employees, and self-employed professionals.

In the public sector coverage was more comprehensive -- all employees of the federal government and its various offshoots were covered.

Hospital employees were not directly covered since the Anti-Inflation Act was not binding on the provincial public sector. The Act provided, however, that provincial governments could 'opt in', making the province's public sector employees subject to the AIB. All provinces except Quebec and Saskatchewan opted into the federal programme, retroactive to 14 October 1975. Saskatchewan introduced a programme of voluntary restraint with provisions similar to the federal programme. Quebec administered its own compulsory controls programme with provisions identical to the federal programme. In November 1976, however, after about one year of controls, the Parti Quebecois government was elected in Quebec and within a few months the Quebec controls programme was terminated in March 1977.[14]

According to the Anti-Inflation Act (section 12) the duty of the AIB was to endeavour to obtain voluntary compliance with the programme's guidelines through 'consultation and negotiation with the parties involved'. If 'voluntary' compliance was not obtained the AIB could refer the case to an Administrator who had the power to enforce the AIB decision or a modification of it. A number of decisions in the first year of the programme demonstrated that the Administrator might well impose a more severe rollback than the AIB.[15] As a consequence the cases referred to the Administrator comprised only 358 of the 22 340 decisions by the AIB over the life of the programme on settlements which exceeded the guidelines. The Act also established an Appeal Tribunal to which decisions of the Administrator could be appealed.

The guidelines for maximum compensation increases established under the 'Anti-Inflation Act Regulations[16] had four components. First was a 'basic protection factor' of 8 per cent in the first year of the programme, 6 per cent in the second year and 4 per cent in the third year. These percentages equalled the government's target for the inflation rate during the controls programme. The 'Regulations' (section 46) also specified that if the actual inflation rate in the first (or second) year of the programme exceeded these target values then the basic protection factor would be increased by the amount of the excess in the second (or third) year of the programme. In the first year of the programme inflation was about 1.75 percentage points below the target level and in the second year about 2.75 percentage points above the target.[17] Instead of allowing the required increase in the basic protection factor for the third year, however, the government changed the regulations to maintain it at 4 per cent.[18]

The second component of the guidelines was a 'national productivity factor' of 2 per cent per year which approximated the long-run rate of productivity growth and the amount by which wage increases had exceeded price increases during the 20 years prior to the controls programme.

An 'experience adjustment factor' was the third component of the guidelines. If in either the two years prior to controls or the previous contract prior to controls (whichever was longer) a group's annual wage settlement exceeded the annual rate of increase of the CPI plus 2 per cent, then the group's guideline during controls would be decreased by this amount, to a maximum of 2 per cent per year. Conversely, the group's guideline would be increased if its settlement prior to controls was below the annual rate of change of the CPI plus 2 per cent. This resulted in considerable variability in the guideline -- in each year of controls it was possible for a group's guideline to vary 2 percentage points plus or minus from the basic pattern of 10 per cent, 8 per cent, 6 per cent. This provision was particularly important for health sector employees who had experienced large wage increases immediately prior to controls.

The final factor in determination of a group's guideline was that no group's average increase was permitted to exceed $2400 per year and no restriction was placed on increases of $600 per year or less. Thus in the first year of the programme, when the basic protection factor plus the national factor equalled 10 per cent, the general effect was to place no restriction on those earning less than $6000 per year and to place additional restrictions on those earning more than $2400 per year.

Increases in fringe benefits were to be included in the calculations and COLA clauses were to be costed on the assumption that inflation rates would equal the programme target rates.

There was some ambiguity concerning the treatment of 'increments' received for service or performance. Section 49 of the Regulations specified that increments were to be included as part of the compensation increase unless '...as a condition of the payment of the increment, that it shall be paid only if the employee to whom it is payable has improved or added to (his) skills or knowledge...' The interpretation of this provision proved troublesome but the conclusion which seemed to emerge was that increments would be exempted if there was a significant discretionary element related to job performance.

The programme allowed the AIB discretionary power to approve compensation increases above the guidelines for various reasons. Exceptions could be granted if an 'historical relationship' with another group was established. The Board generally ruled, however, that in the interest of restraining inflation increases would not be granted to restore fully the relationship immediately. The principle was that over the life of the programme the relationship would be restored by restraining one group more than the other. Increases to remove sex discrimination, to eliminate restrictive work practices, or to recruit employees for positions that had been vacant for three months or more were also exempt under section 54 of the Regulations.

Deferred wage increases received in contracts negotiated prior to 14 October 1975 were not subject to any restriction. Contracts which expired prior to 14 October but which were not settled until after that date were subject to approval by the AIB but the guidelines did not apply and the Board simply used its discretion.

For self-employed professionals the same basic principles applied as for other forms of compensation. Fees could not be raised by more than the amount which would allow the professional working the same amount as in the base year to increase his net income by the guideline or $2400, whichever was less. In professions in which fee schedules were negotiated provincially (e.g. physicians) the changes in the fee schedules were subject to AIB approval.

The Anti-Inflation Act imposed controls on prices indirectly by limiting price increases to the amount of unit cost increases. This implies that profits would be unchanged in absolute dollar amount and consequently profit margins expressed as a percentage of sales would decline somewhat. Firms which could not allocate costs to individual products were required to price in such a way that their profit margin would not exceed 0.95 of its base period profit margin. At the end of each fiscal year a check was made to ensure that the firm's pricing policy did result in actual profits which did not exceed the target specified by the Act. Any 'excess revenue' discovered was required to be returned to the market through an approved method. There were many complications concerning choice of base period, pricing of exports, etc. and the profit rules were modified in the third year of the programme. These points are not discussed in detail, however, since they are of less relevance to the health sector than the compensation provisions.

THE EFFECT OF CONTROLS ON HEALTH INDUSTRIAL RELATIONS

The major collective agreements data in Table 16.2 show that wage settlements in the Ontario health sector were sharply reduced during controls compared to the pre-controls period. Settlements in Canadian manufacturing also dropped substantially during the controls period but on average remained above the health sector settlements.

It would be incorrect to attribute all of this reduction to the effect of the AIB because the Anti-Inflation Program also included a restrictive monetary and fiscal policy which may account for part or all of the observed reduction in wage settlements. This point is of particular concern because approximately 70 per cent of the 91 000 compensation reports submitted to the AIB over its lifetime were at or below the arithmetic guidelines.[19] To assess the quantitative importance of controls it is necessary to specify how much settlements would have declined if the AIB had not been established. A number of studies have undertaken this task using an economic model to predict what wage settlements would have been without the AIB but given the economic conditions actually observed. Although there are naturally some differences of opinion about the exact specification which such a model should take, three studies using somewhat different methodologies have all concluded that the AIB did significantly reduce settlements beyond the reduction which would have occurred from the restrictive fiscal and monetary policy alone.[20] The broken line in Figure 16.2 shows that wage settlements in Canadian manufacturing were predicted to decline during the controls period and the solid line shows the path of actual wage settlements. The difference between them during the controls period is approximately 4½ percentage points and is highly significant by standard statistical tests. Although a separate estimating equation was not developed for the health sector, the similarity of pattern with manufacturing suggests an effect of equal or greater magnitude.

Table 16.3: *Effective Rate of Compensation Increases, By Programme Year, Health Sector*

	No. of Cases	No. of Employees	EFFECTIVE RATE OF INCREASE Proposed	Guideline	Effective
Prior to October 14, 1975					
Non-Union..............	152	2 944	8.3	9.2	7.6
Union	41	1 895	12.4	8.7	11.5
Total	193	4 839	9.9	9.0	9.2
October 14, 1975 to October 13, 1976					
Non-Union..............	3 250	86 667	8.0	8.5	7.8
Union	652	59 569	9.8	8.2	8.5
Total	3 902	146 246	8.7	8.4	8.1
October 14, 1976 to October 13, 1977					
Non-Union..............	3 105	71 440	6.3	6.5	6.1
Union	685	64 154	7.0	6.2	6.3
Total	3 790	135 594	6.6	6.4	6.2
October 14, 1977 to April 13, 1978					
Non-Union..............	1 806	40 813	4.4	4.8	4.3
Union	262	18 872	4.9	4.4	4.4
Total	2 068	59 685	4.6	4.7	4.4

Source: Anti-Inflation Board (1979), 'Final Report', Table A.2.

The employees in the health sector were hit particularly hard by the experience rating factor because of their large settlements in the two-year period prior to controls. Table 16.3 shows that the average guidelines for health sector employees for the three years of the controls programme were 8.4 per cent, 6.4 per cent and 4.7 per cent. These are substantially below the average guidelines for employees in all sectors which were 9.7, 7.4 and 5.6 per cent respectively for the three years of the programme.[21]

Table 16.3 also shows that in each year the average proposed settlement was below the guideline for non-union groups and, as one would expect, above the guideline for union groups. As a result of the below guideline settlements by non-union groups and the rollbacks of union settlements the average settlement for the health sector was below the average guideline in each programme year.

In addition to the restraining effect of a particularly low guideline, there is some evidence that the AIB was harsher than average towards health sector workers in its exercise of discretionary power under the Act. Empirically to test such a hypothesis a model of AIB behaviour is required. Early in its operation the AIB developed a rule of thumb whereby proposed compensation increases which exceeded the guideline by 2 per cent or less would be handled by senior staff members rather than the Board itself. Normal procedure in these cases was either to accept the full proposed settlement or reduce it all the way to the guideline.

Cases where the proposed settlement exceeded the guideline by more than 2 per cent were handled by a subcommittee of Board members. Several researchers have established, using multiple regression analysis, that in these cases the Board tended to roll back some fraction (about one-half to two-thirds) of the excess over the guideline, i.e. the Board tended to 'split the difference' between the guideline and the negotiated settlement.[22] Maslove and Swimmer explain the behaviour as a compromise between the Board's desire to exercise restraint and its desire to avoid serious confrontations with some groups which might have resulted if large negotiated settlements were rolled back right to the guidelines.

Maslove and Swimmer's regression results show that, for equal values of negotiated settlement, guideline and other control variables, approved increases for groups in the public sector were approximately one-half percentage point lower than groups in the private sector.[23] They also undertake a more detailed analysis of the public sector settlements in general and the Canadian Union of Public Employees (CUPE) in particular. They find that, for a given negotiated increase and guideline, CUPE groups in the quasi-public sector (mainly hospital service workers and school caretakers) received significantly lower awards (about one percentage point lower) than federal and provincial public employees (the comparison group). They also find that non-CUPE quasi-public sector groups (mainly nurses and teachers) were not subjected to such treatment by the Board. To explain this finding Maslove and Swimmer suggest that '...a strike by teachers or nurses (who compose a large part of this sample) would pose a greater political threat to the AIB than similar actions by school caretakers or hospital workers....'[24]

Another confrontation between the AIB and CUPE concerned

an agreement covering 1359 hospital workers at the Health
Sciences Centre in Winnipeg. A job evaluation plan was implemented by the employer and the union in 1974 prior to controls
in order to eliminate sex discrimination in wages. It was estimated that to raise female salaries to eliminate discrimination
would increase labour costs by 8 per cent. The AIB regulations
excluded such increases from consideration under the controls
programme. The guideline for the group was also 8 per cent and
in November 1976 a 16 per cent wage increase was negotiated.
In April 1977, however, the Board approved only a 10.9 per cent
increase in the first year of the contract and the arithmetic
guideline the second year. After much publicity and pressure
from the labour movement the Board reconsidered the case and
eventually permitted 4.3 per cent above the guideline in the first
year of the contract and the remaining 3.7 per cent the second
year, allowing for the cost of full implementation of the job
evaluation plan.[25]

The Anti-Inflation Board processed returns for about 34 000
self-employed professionals per year during the controls programme. For those professions the average increases in net
income were 9.0, -2.0 and 3.6 per cent over the three years of
the programme. This is an average of less than 4 per cent per
year and, if these figures are accurate, suggests that the $2400
limit had the intended effect of applying additional restraint on
high income groups. Most physicians were not included in these
statistics, however, since the AIB restrictions applied to the
provincially negotiated fees rather than individual net incomes.
For those Ontario physicians who were subject to the income
restraints because they had chosen not to participate in the
OHIP medicare programme, the average increase in net incomes
during the three years of the controls programme was 5.5, 0.4
and 5.8 per cent. Although the time pattern differed, the average for these physicians over the life of the programme was
similar to that for all professionals.

For the vast majority of physicians the AIB's influence was felt
only through the Board's influence on provincial fee negotiations.
Table 16.4 shows the percentage increase in physicians fees
approved in each province during each year of the controls
programme. While these figures do not seem greatly out of line
with the intent of the controls programme, they do suggest, on
average, that physicians fared better than other professional
groups since they were not subject to the $2400 per year limit
which applied to most professionals.

ASSESSING THE IMPACT OF CONTROLS ON THE ECONOMY

The discussion above indicated that the objective of the controls
programme was to reduce wage settlements with a smaller rise in
unemployment than would occur using fiscal and monetary policy
alone. The intention was that direct restraint of wage settlements

would reduce the rate of change of unit labour costs, and, other things equal, tend to reduce inflation. The evidence presented suggests that controls did significantly restrain wage settlements in the economy as a whole and by an even greater amount in the health sector. It is less clear, however, what effect controls had on inflation. This question requires a discussion of the link between new settlements, unit labour costs and inflation.

Table 16.4: Provincial Medical Payment Schedule Increases
Approved by the AIB (Over Preceding Year)

Province	1977 Per Cent Increase	1978 Per Cent Increase	1979 Per Cent Increase
Newfoundland	7.50	nil	6.40
P.E.I.	7.82	6.40	6.43
Nova Scotia	8.11	4.00	6.27 a
New Brunswick	7.78	6.30	
Ontario	8.10 b	6.50	6.25
Quebec (G.P.s	11.70 b	6.20	nil
Specialists)	17.50 b	nil	nil
Manitoba	9.15	7.00	6.88
Saskatchewan	7.44	6.90	6.49
Alberta	9.00	7.00	6.47
B.C.	8.16	5.50	7.20

a. Submission not received.
b. Quebec's fee schedule for 'specialists' remained frozen between 1970 and 1977. Also, the schedule for GPs was unchanged between 1972 and 1977.
Source: Anti-Inflation Board (1978), 'Third Year Report', p.18.

Although it was the AIB rollbacks of large settlements that attracted the newspaper headlines, much of the restraining effect of controls was on negotiated settlements before being submitted to the AIB.[26] This effect, in addition to the restraining effect of the restrictive monetary and fiscal policy during controls, caused 70 per cent of all compensation increases submitted to the AIB to be at or below the guidelines (particularly in the non-union sector) as indicated previously.

As a result of the experience rating factor the average guideline during each year of controls was somewhat below the initial specification of 10, 8 and 6 per cent. Furthermore, when the below guideline settlements are considered, the average settlement approved by the AIB was below the average guideline in each of the controls years. (See columns 2 and 3 of Table 16.5.) This establishes that controls were without a doubt, successful in achieving their intended restraint on new wage settlements.

Primarily because of the prevalence of multi-year collective agreements (which average about two years in length in Canada) there is a significant delay between a reduction in wage settlements and a reduction in average hourly earnings, and hence labour costs. This is illustrated in Table 16.5 by the rate of change of average hourly earnings which declines steadily throughout the programme but which is still above the average rate of change in new settlements in each year of the controls programme.

Table 16.5: Average Annual Rates of Change of Wages and Prices in Canada

Period	Guideline	Approved Settlements	Hourly Earnings	CPI	Real Hourly Earnings	CPI Exfood	CPI Food
Oct.55–Oct.75	--	--	6.63%	3.79%	2.74%	2.54%	3.14%
Oct.73–Oct.75	--	--	14.74	11.10	3.28	10.04	13.84
Oct.75–Oct.76	9.7	9.3	12.98	6.23	6.35	9.08	-0.90
Oct.76–Oct.77	7.4	7.1	10.64	8.77	1.72	7.30	12.73
Oct.77–Oct.78	5.6	5.3	7.02	8.67	-1.51	6.42	14.55
Oct.75–Oct.78	--	--	10.19	7.88	2.14	7.59	8.57
Oct.78–Oct.80	--	--	10.05	10.09	0.00	9.35	12.49

Sources: Guideline and average settlement are from Anti-Inflation Board (1979), 'Final Report', 1979.

Notes: Rates of change are shown for average hourly earnings in manufacturing (hourly earnings), The Consumer Price Index (CPI), average hourly earnings deflated by the CPI (real hourly earnings), and the food and non-food components of the CPI.

Average annual percentage rates of change are calculated allowing for compounding.

'Guideline' is the average guideline for all cases submitted to the AIB in each year. 'Approved settlement' is the average increase approved by the AIB in each year.

What about the effect on prices? The AIB applied profit controls to about 3400 companies and required them to return about 0.32 billion dollars in excess revenue to the marketplace.[27] This amount represented only about one-quarter of 1 per cent of the gross revenue of the companies concerned so one would not expect a noticeable effect on inflation from this return of excess revenue.

It is possible that, as with the wage settlements, controls may have exerted substantial effects on the behaviour of firms prior to submitting returns to the AIB. Such an effect would not show up in excess revenue -- its measurement requires an economic model to predict what price levels and profits would have been without controls. Results from such a test[28] indicate that, given the actual increase in unit labour costs, prices and profits were not significantly different from what would have been predicted in the absence of the AIB. Although the AIB does not appear to have had a direct effect on price increases, these results imply that controls did restrain inflation about 2 percentage points below what it otherwise would have been through its indirect effect on unit labour costs.

The data on the rate of change of the CPI (column 5 of Table 16.5) indicate that from a level of 11.10 per cent in the pre-controls period, inflation dropped sharply to 6.23 per cent in the first year of controls and then rose to 8.77 and 8.67 per cent in the second and third years. This rather erratic behaviour of the CPI is a reminder that inflation is affected by many factors other than unit labour costs -- two of the more prominent being food and energy prices. The last two columns of Table 16.5 show that the rate of change of all items in the CPI excluding food declined steadily during controls, roughly consistent with the decline of average hourly earnings. Food prices, on the other hand, actually decreased by nearly 1 per cent during the first year of controls then shot up 12.73 and 14.55 per cent during the final two years.

The conclusion from all of this is that the controls programme reduced the rate of change of unit labour costs and the rate of change of prices of many goods. Other things constant, this would have reduced the inflation rate by about 2 percentage points. Alas, other things (particularly food and energy prices, which were largely outside the scope of the controls programme) were not held constant. We are left to speculate that if the programme had not been implemented and these other factors had occurred the inflation rate would have been even higher than what was experienced. Regarding the impact of controls on prices, this is a probable but not a pleasing conclusion.

In retrospect, the labour movement's fear that the controls programme was simply an attack on workers seems unfounded. The data in Table 16.5 (column 6) show that on average over the three years of the controls programme wages increased 2.14 per cent per year faster than prices, a rate comparable to the long-run rate of increase without controls.

In considering the next advantages of the Canadian controls programme many factors must be taken into account and personal judgements about their importance will differ greatly.

The allocative effects from interference in the market system, about which economists are endlessly concerned, do not appear to me to have been of significant importance during the Canadian controls. More substantial, I think, are the administrative costs to the government and, more importantly, the time and effort involved by groups in complying with the controls.

Most important of all is the resentment by those involved in collective bargaining, the labour movement in particular. Organised labour was adamantly opposed to the controls programme from the beginning and took the unprecedented step of organising a one-day national strike in protest. Whether or not the effects of controls were actually harmful to workers, one must question the government's decision to expend in this way whatever goodwill it may have had with the labour movement.

REFERENCES AND NOTES

1 Maslove, Allan M., and Swimmer, Gene (1980), 'Wage Controls in Canada 1975-78', Institute for Research on Public Policy, p.8.
2 Canada Department of Labour, 'Wage Developments Resulting from Major Collective Bargaining Settlements', various issues, Ontario. Ministry of Labour, 'Wage Developments in Collective Bargaining Settlements in Ontario' (Toronto), various issues.
3 Cousineau, J.-M., and Lacroix, R. (1977), 'Wage Determination in Major Collective Agreements in the Private and Public Sectors', Economic Council of Canada, p.15.
4 This view was expressed to me in December 1977 in a conversation with Mr Thomas Axworthy, who was employed in the Prime Minister's Office during the period that controls were implemented. Maslove and Swimmer found a similar view in their research (Maslove and Swimmer, 'Wage Controls in Canada', p.11).
5 Reid, Frank, and Meltz, Noah M. (1979), Causes of Shifts in the Unemployment-Vacancy Relationship: An Empirical Analysis for Canada, 'Review of Economics and Statistics', 61, pp.470-5.
6 Cousineau and Lacroix, Wage Determination in Major Collective Agreements, p.76 and p.129.
7 Douglas Auld, et al. (1979), The Impact of the Anti-Inflation Board on Negotiated Wage Settlements, 'Canadian Journal of Economics', 12, pp.195-213; Reid, Frank (1979), The Effect of Controls on the Rate of Wage Change in Canada, 'Canadian Journal of Economics', 12, pp.214-27.
8 Reproduced from Reid, Frank The Effect of Controls on the Rate of Wage Change in Canada, p.219.
9 Wage settlements are predicted from the following equation estimated by Ordinary Least Squares regression:

$$W_t = 1.69 + 2.46\, v_t + 1.22\, PE_t.\ W_t, v_t \text{ and } PE_t$$

refer to wage settlements, a job vacancy rate variable and and expected inflation rate variable at time period t. The $R^2 = .75$, Durbin-Watson statistic is 1.83 and the slope coefficients are significant at the 5 per cent level on t-tests. See Reid (1979) for further details.
10 Reid, Frank (1979), Unemployment and Inflation: An Assessment of Canadian Macroeconomic Policy, 'Canadian Public

Policy', 6, pp.283-99.
11 Maslove and Swimmer, 'Wage Controls in Canada', p.7.
12 Canada, Minister of Finance (1975), 'Attack on Inflation:
   A Program of National Action', Supply & Services.
13 Canada (1975) Anti-Inflation Act, Bill C-73, Supply &
   Services.
14 Anti-Inflation Board (1979), 'Chronicles of the Anti-
   Inflation Board', Supply and Services, p.42.
15 Ibid., p.60.
16 Canada (1975) Anti-Inflation Act Regulations, Supply &
   Services.
17 Reid, Unemployment and Inflation..., Table 1.
18 AIB, 'Chronicles', p.64.
19 Anti-Inflation Board (1979), 'Final Report', Supply &
   Services, p.3; Anti-Inflation Board (1979), 'Inflation and
   Public Policy'.
20 Cousineau, J.-M., and Lacroix, R. (1978), L'impact de la
   politique canadienne de contrôle des prix et des revenus sur
   les ententes salariales, 'Canadian Public Policy', 4,
   pp.88-100; Auld, Douglas et al., The Impact of the Anti-
   Inflation Board on Negotiated Wage Settlements; Frank Reid,
   The Effect of Controls on the Rate of Wage Change in
   Canada; Denton, F. et al. (1975), Patterns of Unemployment
   Behaviour in Canada, Discussion paper 36, Economic Council
   of Canada.
21 Anti-Inflation Board, Table 4.
22 Reid, Frank (1977), AIB Wage Rollbacks: Tests and
   Implications of the Linear Rotation Hypothesis, Working
   Paper 7704, Centre for Industrial Relations, University of
   Toronto; Foot, D.K., and Poirier, D.J. (1980), 'The
   Compensation Decisions of the Anti-Inflation Board: An
   Empirical Analysis', Supply and Services; Osberg, L. (1977),
   A Note on the Wage Decisions of the Anti-Inflation Board,
   'Canadian Public Policy', 3, pp.377-80; Maslove and Swimmer,
   'Wage Controls in Canada 1975-78'.
23 Maslove and Swimmer, 'Wage Controls in Canada 1975-78',
   p.101.
24 Ibid., pp.142-4.
25 Ibid., p.146.
26 Douglas Auld et al., The Impact of the Anti-Inflation
   Board on Negotiated Wage Settlements.
27 AIB, 'Final Report', p.11.
28 Wilson, T.A., and Jump, G.V. (1979), 'The Influence of
   the Anti-Inflation Program on Aggregate Wages and Prices:
   A Simulation Analysis', Supply and Services.

17. INCOMES POLICY AND HEALTH SERVICES IN THE UK

S.J. Dimmock

The NHS is funded almost entirely by national taxation and the history of NHS pay determination since 1948 suggests that successive governments have sought to exercise a large measure of control within this process in an attempt to contain labour costs. The instruments of government control give the NHS a degree of uniqueness by comparison with other public sector industries in Britain. First, government is directly represented by officials of the health departments on the management sides of the various Whitley Councils.

Secondly, government has considerable power over those who administer the health services through its statutory powers under the National Health Service Act of 1946 and 1947 to issue directions and regulations to health authorities. Therefore, government has the means to influence NHS pay which are independent of either voluntary or statutory incomes policies. The aim of this chapter is to briefly describe the history of incomes policy in Britain since 1948 and to examine its impact on NHS pay determination.

INCOMES POLICY IN THE UK SINCE 1948

Incomes policy has been defined as an attempt by government to alter the level of wages and salaries, or to alter their pace of change. In this process government issues clear guidelines on the limits within which incomes should be permitted to move and takes overt steps to try to keep incomes within those limits.[1] Adopting this definition there have been a number of attempts at incomes policy in Britain since the end of the Second World War. The post-war Labour Government operated a voluntary policy, which largely rested on the support of the Trades Union Congress, between 1948 and 1950.[2] The policy crumbled under increasing trade union bargaining pressure following the outbreak of the Korean War. The Conservative Party was in government from 1951 to 1964 and during these thirteen years the Conservatives introduced two distinct policies between 1956 to 1957 and between 1961-2. Although the latter policy was more sophisticated, both had as their cornerstone a commitment by government to resist public sector pay increases. Between 1964 to 1969 the Labour Government operated an almost continuous statutory incomes policy which was subject to fairly frequent amendments in response to the changing national and inter-

national economic situation. In its early years the policy enjoyed
the support of the trade unions. However, as the decade passed
they became increasingly disenchanted, and the consequent
removal of controls in 1969 saw an escalation in the size of wage
settlements.

At the start of the 1970s the newly elected Conservative
Government initially abandoned the idea of incomes policy.
Instead it relied on the earlier Conservative approach of resisting public sector pay increases. An immediate effect of this was
to provoke a number of national strikes in the public sector.
Government subsequently introduced a statutory incomes policy.
This foundered on the second strike by the mineworkers' union
in 1974. The Labour Government, which was re-elected in 1974,
once more determined to operate a voluntary policy with TUC
support. The Social Contract was subsequently amended to a
statutory policy and adapted annually in the light of economic
circumstances. The attempt by the Labour Government to sustain
the policy between 1975 to 1979 encountered the same types of
problems that had characterised its policy of the 1960s: with
each successive year, the TUC, under pressure from its affiliated
unions, became increasingly disinclined to accept government
'pay norms'. In the winter of 1978-9 the resistance by trade
unions to incomes policy led to a series of national disputes.
Some of the most notable of these occurred among NHS staff.

The new Conservative Government of 1979 offered radically
different economic policies from any of its predecessors since
1948. It eschewed the Keynesian view of economics in favour of
monetarist policies. Within the government's economic theology
the regulation of collective bargaining in private industry was
better left to market forces. In the public sector government
introduced a system of 'cash limits' which left their managements
free to bargain within identified budgetary constraints. While
this approach echoed earlier attempts to resist public sector
wage pressures it served to distance government, albeit temporarily, from direct involvement in public sector pay determination.

The commitment to full employment by all post-war governments
until the late 1970s led the public to perceive an increase in the
power of the trade unions in collective bargaining. A low level
of inflation, which was held to be caused by wage increases,
was accepted by governments as an inescapable consequence of
full employment. However, this commitment limited the ability
of deflationary measures to reduce the volume of collective bargaining. Thus successive governments found it necessary to
intervene in the process of wage bargaining. On this aspect
of incomes policy a number of points can be concluded. First
that neither voluntary nor statutory policies can be continued
over a number of consecutive years without trade union support.
Second, that with each successive year within a period of
incomes policy the support of the trades unions is certain to
diminish (even when they are committed at the outset of the

policy) under the pressure from their membership.

THE IMPACT OF INCOMES POLICY ON THE NHS

Between 1948 and 1979 incomes policy tended to bear heavily on
collective bargaining in the NHS. The health service's experience
with incomes policy since 1948 can be broadly divided into three
distinct periods. Between 1948 and 1964 government ensured
that incomes policies were observed either through the exercise
of their influence within the national collective bargaining
machinery, or through direct intervention in pay settlements.
The years from 1965 to 1971 were notable for the investigations
into NHS pay by the National Board for Prices and Incomes
(NBPI), which had been created to monitor the operation of
incomes policy. The third period from 1972 to 1979 was characterised by a new phenomenon of outright opposition among health
service occupations generally, towards the incomes policies of
both Conservative and Labour Governments.

The First Period, 1948-64
The NHS came into existence shortly after the publication of
the Labour Government's White Paper in 1948.[4] A number of
public sector groups were then involved in pay negotiations and
subsequently received increases. The unions representing health
service ancillary staff claimed a similar increase to that given
to local government manual staff. The initial response of the
management side of their Whitley Council was that the policy of
national wage restraint should be respected, although it subsequently relented and agreed to a marginal weekly increase.
However, ancillary staffs' pay remained unchanged for the next
two years. The nurses' Whitley Council was initially concerned
with the question of living-in allowances. By the beginning of
1949 it was evident that a general increase needed to be considered. A common feature of NHS pay determination is the drawn
out nature of joint negotiations and although discussions on
nurses' pay had commenced in February 1949, the issue was still
unresolved by the following year. At this juncture the management side refused to consider an increase for local government
nursing staffs, whose pay also came within the purview of the
nurses' Whitley Council. Management, or more appropriately
government, feared possible repercussions among the vast majority of local government staff who had hitherto accepted pay
restraint.[5] The nurses' collective organisations, with the agreement of the management side, referred the issue to arbitration.
The award largely met with the staffs' claim and backdated the
increases to February 1949. Similar situations occurred in negotiations within the other Whitley Councils.
  In contrast, the remuneration of doctors received more generous treatment. The Reports of the Spens Committees were
accepted by the Health Minister as the basis for paying doctors

and dentists under the NHS.[6] The Reports took as their base
the value of money in 1939. This appeared to treat the doctor
as a special case, as incomes among professional groups had
suffered a relative decline during the war years. With the relax-
ation of the incomes policy after 1950, the BMA secured a size-
able increase for general practitioners through third-party
arbitration. The significant underlying determinant of doctors'
pay was their considerable power in collective bargaining. The
decision of the BMA in 1956 to present a significant pay claim
directly to the Health Minister led to a Royal Commission. Its
recommendation for an 'independent' body - the Doctors' and
Dentists' Review Body (DDRB) to consider the issue of medical
remuneration provides strong evidence of the profession's power.[7]
However the major clash between the BMA and government
incomes policy did not occur until the 1970s.

During the thirteen years of Conservative governments the
managements' stance in Whitley Councils' bargaining over pay
determinants shifted backwards and forwards. The management
side of one Council would accept an argument over labour shortages as the justification for an increase in pay; on another
occasion it would not. In parallel negotiations with other staff
groups the management sides challenged similar claims. This was
equally the case for other determinants such as the 'cost of living' and the need to retain 'relativities' with comparable groups
outside the health sector. The explanation which appears most
nearly to fit the circumstances of NHS pay determination during
this period was the external pressures acting upon government
which in turn affected the positions of the management sides.

As Clegg and Chester have commented,[8] governments are subject to external pressures when dealing with the pay of employees
in an industry that is funded from taxation. Governments therefore seek a political defence for public sector pay increases.
This was a significant factor in government acceptance of the
DDRB in 1960: it removed from government's direct jurisdiction
the vital, but politically hazardous, decisions, regarding the
remuneration of the most powerful occupation in the NHS.[9] It
is perhaps significant that generally in NHS pay determination
a large number of claims were settled by third-party arbitration.
Thus between 1948 to 1955, 26 of 53 'major' settlements were
the result of arbitration,[10] and by 1963 the total number of
referrals was 135.[11] In this way government could escape the
direct responsibility for agreeing pay increases.

Government cannot afford to be seen to be establishing a lead
over private industry. In the NHS this produced a depression
in earnings, over and above the effects of incomes policy, among
the majority of staff who continued to bargain within the Whitley
Council framework. By the end of 1954 for example, while the
pay of ancillary staffs (the second largest occupational group)
had kept roughly in line with inflation, they earned considerably
less than the average wage for manual workers in British industry, for longer hours.[12] Only the nurses (the largest occupa-

tional group) had received increases greater than the cost of living and the index of general wage rates;[13] other NHS salaried workers had fallen behind the national salary scales. The nurses' relatively better position may in part be explained by the considerable public good will they enjoyed, which of itself can be a political pressure on government. Prior to 1957 government had exercised wage restraint by the medium of national negotiations, primarily by the influence it was able to exercise through the health departments' representatives who 'advised' the management sides of the various Whitley Councils. However, on two separate occasions it found it necessary to intervene directly in NHS pay negotiations in order to enforce a principal aspect of incomes policy – wage restraint within the public sector.

Governments possess a number of powers in regard to health service pay, for example, decisions of Whitley Councils are in fact recommendations to the Health Minister. In 1957 the Health Minister vetoed part of a pay award to administrative and clerical staff. Salaries for this group had experienced both a relative and absolute decline. Since the last major review in 1951 the retail price index had risen by 34 per cent but on average health service administrative and clerical pay had increased by little more than 20 per cent.[14] In 1951 their pay was closely based, at various reference points, with that of Britain's civil servants. By 1957 a wide gap in the relative remuneration of the two groups had occurred. It was estimated that an increase of between 20 per cent to 30 per cent was necessary to restore the 1951 relativity.[15]

In the context of the NHS this method of enforcing public sector wage restraint marked a radical departure in pay determination. The power to veto wage awards had in the past been presented by government as a constitutional technicality, and it had given assurances that the essence of health service Whitleyism was 'free negotations'. Government's refusal to sanction the interim settlement called this into question. Indeed the refusal of government to allow third-party arbitration over its rights of veto provided further evidence of the underlying political and constitutional reality of NHS pay determination.[16]

A number of pay settlements for smaller groups of staff were made in the 1957-8 period without incurring the direct invention of government. However the atmosphere in which negotiations were conducted in some Whitley Councils suggested an imminent collapse of the centralised bargaining machinery.[17] The official acceptance in negotiations between 1958-9, of the need to improve most categories of health staffs' pay tended to reduce the disquiet among the staff organisations. However, in 1962 the question of government involvement in NHS pay resurfaced with its refusal to sanction an increase for nurses above the offer of the management side of the nurses' Whitley Council, which conformed with the second stage of government incomes policy.[18]

Government resistance to a larger increase provided further evidence of the relative uniqueness of NHS pay determination

both inside and outside the operation of incomes policy. By
comparison, the dockers (longshoremen) had only recently
received an increase in the region of 8 per cent. Commentators
pointed to the difference in bargaining power between the two
groups as the reason behind the Conservative Government's
attitude towards nurses' pay. In this regard the position of the
nurses' staff organisations was quite clear; the feasibility of
industrial action was never contemplated and they settled for
arbitration. A decade later many health groups would begin to
employ more traditional forms of industrial sanctions. Ironically,
the shift in circumstances that engendered a more militant attitude towards pay bargaining was partly caused by an initiative
undertaken during the next phase of the NHS's experience of
incomes policy.

The Second Period, 1965-71
Under incomes policy before 1965 governments chose to intervene
directly in NHS pay determination. The establishment of the
NBPI in 1965 enabled the Labour Government to employ a third
party to monitor NHS pay issues. The NBPI conducted three
separate investigations into NHS pay: one report concerned
nursing staff, the others looked at the position of ancillary
workers.

The examination of nurses' pay followed from the expiry of a
two year settlement in July 1967. The purpose of the NBPI's
reference was to examine the staff's claim for a major increase
together with other specialised issues which had arisen from
previous unsettled claims. In addition the NBPI was also to look
at the salary scales related to the introduction of a new managerial structure in nursing that had been recently recommended.[19]
The management side had resisted the claim on the ground that
the incomes policy criteria for exceptional increases were not met
by the salient points within the nurses' case.

The NBPI reported almost a year later.[20] It recommended a
pay increase of 14 per cent for the newly qualified nurse, taper-
ing to 9 per cent at the top of the nursing scale. These were to
be implemented in a series of stages, up to the spring of 1970.
The Report cleared up some of the existing smaller claims and
recommended that the new managerial grades should be introduced on a national basis. The NBPI also recommended an
increase in lodging charges for nurses accommodated in hospitals
in proportion to the new pay increases. Moreover it recommended
that these too should be backdated in line with the pay increase.
Not unnaturally this latter point raised a storm of protest from
both nurses and their collective organisations, although they
subsequently accepted it.

The NBPI's recommendations precluded any adjustments in line
with the trend of inflation over the period of the award. The
upward movement in inflation throughout the next two and a half
years meant that nurses' pay again required a considerable
increase to restore it to the 1967 position. As on previous

occasions the management side of the Whitley Council refused
a significant claim. In response the nurses' collective organisations launched a public appeal as a means to bring pressure on
government. The subsequent 'Raise the Roof' campaign of 1969-70
was a relative success. More importantly, it marked the beginning of a more outright militancy among nursing staff. However,
the major redress of their position had to wait until 1974.

The other area of interest for the NBPI was the pay and conditions of NHS ancillary workers. In 1966, during a period of a
severe incomes freeze, government called for an inquiry into low
pay among a number of industries, including the NHS. The
ancillary workers' three-year settlement made in 1963 was shortly
due to expire. The government proposed that given the difficulty
of assessing productivity in the non-trading area of the public
sector the NBPI should examine the principles determining ancillary workers' pay. By 1966 this group comprised some 266 000;
constituting the second largest occupational group in the NHS.
Nearly three quarters of them were female, of whom nearly one
quarter were part-time workers.

The findings of the NBPI were not auspicious for a government
determined to apply incomes policy:[21] it revealed that the NHS
contained large concentrations of male workers whose earnings
were among the lowest in Britain. Moreover the compression
within their wage structure meant that increases sufficient to
ameliorate the lowest paid would swamp existing differentials.
The NBPI concluded that the present wage structures and the
limited earnings opportunities precluded wage increases in favour
of the lowest paid: assistance to the low paid could only be
given through a general increase in wages. However, this would
result in an unreasonable burden for the taxpayer and precluded
a wage increase under the low pay exception of the incomes
policy.

The NBPI was in no doubt that the root cause of low pay was
poor levels of productivity: if payment schemes could be devised
that tied job performance to earnings the low pay condition would
be ameliorated. The Report identified a number of essential
conditions for securing a relationship between pay and more
effective use of labour. In general these boiled down to criticisms
of the existing poor standards of labour management. A significant obstacle was the absence of work study specialists. To
overcome this the Report suggested a form of interim scheme
based on a 10 per cent increase in productivity. There was a
recognition that the scheme could disturb the existing relationships between management and ancillary staff, but the NBPI felt
that the gains would justify the risks involved.

The NBPI's second examination of ancillary pay was published
in 1971[22] after the demise of the 1964-70 Labour Government.
The Report was concerned to re-examine the problem of low pay
and to review the progress made in implementing its earlier
proposals. While the revision of the pay structure had been completed, only slow progress had been made on introducing

incentive payment schemes. In the NBPI's view this served to
penalise the low paid male ancillary workers: while female
workers could also benefit from schemes they were not low paid
by the general standards of women's pay.[23] In the NBPI's view
the responsibility for the delay in implementing schemes was
largely due to the lack of management expertise within the hospital sector. The ancillary worker's trade unions also shared
a degree of blame: outside the arena of national negotiations the
NBPI adjudged them as inactive and ineffective. In an attempt
to speed up the introduction of productivity arrangements the
NBPI devised a model scheme which could be introduced more
rapidly. Although this new type of scheme was taken up, its
wider application within the hospital sector was prevented during
the 1975-76 period of incomes policy. By the 1980s the overall
coverage of incentive schemes remains relatively low.

An unforeseen consequence of the productivity schemes, at
least in terms of the scale of their effect, was the disturbance
of traditional relationships between ancillary workers and
hospital management. The NBPI had not been unaware of the widespread criticism of the effects on industrial relations of similar
payment systems in some sectors of British industry.[24] However
the wider introduction of incentive schemes between 1971 and
1973, coupled with other factors, acted to change the character
of health service trade unionism. Initially this transformation
occurred among ancillary workers. For the first time in the NHS,
important decisions about pay could be made locally. Some
managers recorded a new attitude among previously acquiescent
groups of ancillary workers, as they seized the opportunity to
bargain directly over their jobs, even to the extent of veiled
threats of industrial action.[25] By the end of 1972 with the onset
of a Conservative Government's temporary standstill policy the
ancillary staff in particular were in a stronger position to resist
government attempts to impose wage restraint than at any other
time in the NHS's history. Moreover other occupational groups
who remained within Whitleyism were also less disposed to accept
government pressure without a struggle.

The Third Period, 1972-1979
The operation of incomes policy in the NHS under both Conservative and Labour governments was characterised by a series of
national disputes: an entirely novel phenomenon in the NHS.
While the BMA on behalf of the medical profession had indicated
a readiness to apply sanctions over remuneration, its claims
had generally been accommodated. Even among doctors this was
to change. The first round of national disputes occurred between
late 1972 to 1976, and a second round followed during the winter
of 1979. The initial open challenge to incomes policy was undertaken by the ancillary workers.

The Conservative Government's Counter Inflation Act 1972
commenced with a temporary pay pause. This severed the traditional pay link between ancillary staff and local government

manual workers. The unions favoured selective strikes and in
March, at the end of the incomes standstill, up to 750 hospitals
were affected. Despite this the ancillary unions nationally were
unable to break the newly introduced Stage II of government's
policy. The major long-term effects were the change in attitudes
between ancillary workers and managers at hospital level, and
the consolidation of hospital-based trade union organisation. The
next examples of the changed attitudes towards the use of direct
industrial sanctions came from nurses who were also affected by
Stage I of Conservative Government's policy.

A claim concerned with a revaluation of nurses' pay structures
was interrupted by the November 1972 incomes standstill. The
claim was revised and resubmitted in January 1973 and again in
January 1974. In the intervening period the nurses received
general increases under the terms of Stages II and III of the
policy. The issue of revaluation was touched upon by an inquiry
of the Pay Board (established by the 1973 Counter Inflation
Act),[26] into pay relativities, which referred briefly to the position
of nurses. This seemed to be a tacit recognition of the nurses'
particular pay problems. Unfortunately, the 1974 miners' strike
intervened and with the election of the Labour Government the
chances of a thorough review appeared more remote. While nurses
received a further increase in line with Stage III of the incomes
policy, which was still being operated by the new government,
the revaluation issue remained unresolved. In late April 1974,
against a background of increasing inflation, nurses commenced
their first national dispute in the NHS.

The main professional organisation for nurses, the Royal College of Nursing (Rcn), had undertaken a collective bargaining
role in the NHS since 1948. During the early 1970s it had
increasingly adopted some of the characteristics of a trade union,
including the appointment of local stewards. The TUC trade
union with significant nursing membership - the Confederation
of Health Service Employees (COHSE) - had been ejected from
Congress during the period of TUC opposition against the 1971
Industrial Relations Act. The dispute provided an opportunity
for COHSE to re-establish itself and also for the Rcn to consolidate its more aggressive role. The Rcn threatened mass
resignations (a tactic used previously by doctors) and organised
marches and demonstrations. In some areas, especially in
psychiatric hospitals where COHSE traditionally was well organised, the nursing staff took direct industrial action. The pressure exerted was sufficient to provoke the Labour Government
to set up an independent pay inquiry 'to examine the pay structure and the levels of remuneration and related conditions'.[27]
The inquiry reached the general conclusion that over the preceding four years nurses' pay had fallen behind that of other
comparative occupations. It recommended the simplification of
job grades, a significant pay increase and the classification of
a number of items and anomalies that had evolved since the
previous major award.

The inquiry subsequently went on to examine the pay and conditions of the professions supplementary to medicine. This occupational group had also taken various minor forms of industrial action in support of its claim. Prior to the Stage III settlement for nurses, in April 1974, firm links existed between this group and key points of the nursing pay scale. The effect of the inquiry into nurses' pay had been to create a similar demand from these much smaller professional groups. However with the publication of the inquiry's report the comparative links became more tenuous.[28]

The next occupational group to take industrial action was the medical profession. Early incomes policy had relatively little effect on the doctors by comparison with other health service occupations and the DDRB was specifically excluded from the jurisdiction of the Conservative Government's National Incomes Commission in 1962. Likewise the Labour Government of 1964 implied that medical pay awards would not be referred to the NBPI. Hence as late as 1966 the DDRB was able to recommend a major award which escaped the attention of incomes policy. In 1969 the Labour Government challenged the notion of an 'independent' DDRB when it referred part of the recommended settlement to the NBPI. The action caused consternation within the profession and the members of the DDRB resigned en masse.

The Conservative Government which followed quickly re-emphasised the importance of the review system and a new DDRB was instituted in 1971. However, the DDRB's third report of 1973 confirmed the profession's suspicions as to its 'independence', when its recommendations confirmed with Stage II of government's incomes policy. The fourth report appeared during the period when the Labour Government was still operating their predecessor's Stage III policy. Once more the professions were faced with an unacceptable settlement. The control of medical pay by incomes policy was further strengthened in 1974, when the DDRB's chairman announced that the award would not be counter to the Labour Government's Social Contract with the TUC.

The principal impact of the Labour Government's 1975 statutory policy fell upon the junior hospital doctors, who had become increasingly reluctant to undertake the excessive hours of duty which had been a traditional feature of their work. In November 1975 the DDRB had recommended a basic 40-hour week, with additional overtime units to be paid at differential rates and the doctors received an increase within the incomes policy pay limit. In consequence, therefore, no additional funds would be available until the next review. In the circumstances, the DDRB suggested that money could only be found for the new contract by redistributing existing resources. The juniors took strike action and the eventual resolution of the dispute occurred after the publication of a further supplementary report by the DDRB in 1976.

The series of disputes between 1973 and 1976 however, were

to be a precursor to the next round of strikes which occurred
in 1979. Once more these arose from the Labour Government's
income policy. Government insistence in the autumn of 1978 on
a Phase Four of its policy comprising a 5 per cent pay limit, was
met with virtual outright opposition by the TUC. In the NHS
the trade unions representing ancillary staffs and joined by
ambulance personnel claimed increases significantly above the
level fixed by government. The substance of their claims was
for settlements of sufficient size to overcome the continued
incidence of low pay. After lengthy national disputes government
agreed to the establishment of a Standing Commission on Pay
Comparability to examine the whole issue of public sector pay
comparisons.

In their evidence the unions claimed that the twin effects of
inflation and the wage settlements that had taken place since
1974 in industries outside the NHS had effectively returned the
relative pay levels of ancillary staff to their 1970 position. The
claim of ambulance staff was different: the nature of the work,
particularly in regard to their emergency service, the historic
links with the other emergency services (i.e. police and fire),
and the general decline in their relative earnings constituted a
special case. The Commission's report partially vindicated the
ambulance staffs' claim. However, the ancillary staffs received
considerably less than they had anticipated.[29]

The Commission then turned to consider the respective claims
of the nurses and the professions supplementary to medicine.
These references too had been preceded by a national dispute.
The cycle of pay erosion followed by a 'catching-up' award has
in any event been a characteristic of NHS pay determination.
The operation of incomes policy by government throughout
almost the whole of the 1960s together with continuously high
levels of inflation merely exacerbated this cyclical process. In
an attempt to break out of this cycle the Standing Commission
was 'to report on the possibility of establishing acceptable bases
of comparison, including comparison with terms and conditions
for other comparable work, and of maintaining appropriate
relativities'. Its report recommended an overall increase of 19
per cent. However, its use of comparisons with occupations
outside the NHS revealed interesting results. On the bases
identified by the Commission, those nurses employed at or
immediately above ward level were entitled to increases, while
higher levels of nursing management received very small
increases, and in some cases no increase at all.[30]

The professions supplementary to medicine had experienced
similar problems of pay erosion. Accordingly, the Commission
undertook an examination of their pay on identical terms of
reference. The recommendations were similar to those for nurses:
within the overall increase in pay of 15 per cent larger sums
were reserved for those on lower job grades.[31] In considering
the feasibility of adopting pay comparisons between these groups
and other occupations within the NHS, the Commission commented

that 'such comparisons could lead to consistent results only if
the NHS as a whole had a coherent approach to pay'.[32] In its
view there were two sources of diversity. First, the apparent
lack of a common policy towards pay between the management
sides of the various Whitley Councils, second, the different
methods of settling pay between one occupational group and
another. In some cases, e.g. administrative and laboratory staff,
there were comparative links with equivalent groups in the
British civil service. In contrast medical remuneration was determined by an independent review.

CONCLUSION

The evidence suggests that pay determination in the NHS has
been subject to close government scrutiny. Inevitably therefore
the pay of health service workers has generally to be considered
by government in both economic and political terms. In this
context increases in pay seem always likely to be subject to
constraints. The influence that government can bring to bear
within the management sides of the Whitley Councils provides one
means of consistently setting the upper limits of pay offers and
government's statutory powers provide a means of monitoring
actual pay levels. With these two means at its disposal, together
with the absence of highly organised staff organisations until
recent years, government has generally operated a form of policy
for the control of incomes in the NHS. However, in terms of the
definition advanced previously this has not been a genuine
incomes policy; but rather a crude, unco-ordinated and incon-
sistent approach dictated by ephemeral political necessities. It
have nevertheless been effective in restraining income levels as
was demonstrated by Clegg and Chester and by the initial
government inquiries conducted during 1965–9 period of incomes
policy. In this regard however, the operation of incomes policy
has also played its part.
   In the NHS the interweaving of incomes policy with periods
of 'free collective bargaining' makes it difficult if not impossible
to delineate the impact of the former on health occupations'
earnings. The short experiments with incomes policy before
1965 clearly had an immediate impact on at least two occupational
groups: in 1957 for administrative and clerical staff, and in
1962 for nurses. Government's refusal to sanction pay increases
was explicitly undertaken as a political demonstration of its
determination to resist public sector wage increases, in line with
its declared national policy. Whether it would have adopted such
a positive approach with other, more powerful public sector
groups in 1957 and 1962 seems doubtful.
   The extent of wage restraint became particularly apparent in
the 1970s. The findings of the pay inquiries in 1974 and the
Standing Commission on Pay Comparability in 1979 show that for
a number of NHS occupational groups the effect of incomes policy

was to depress their earnings in relation to other occupations
both inside and outside the NHS. Nevertheless the immediate
result of these inquiries was to redress the erosion of their pay
which had taken place over the preceding years. In this context
it is perhaps important to reflect that one factor that produced
the decline in pay, both relatively with other occupations and
absolutely in terms of inflation, was the length of settlements.
Wage awards with a duration of two to three years were not
uncommon in the NHS. In periods of heightened inflation the
purchasing power of health workers' incomes was consequently
bound to decline. During the period of 1948-56 only in two years
was collective bargaining bound by national incomes policy. In
1957, the administrative and clerical staff had fallen well behind
their comparative groups in the British civil service. Moreover
this decline in their incomes had occurred over a seven-year
period of collective bargaining. These early results from bargaining identified by Clegg and Chester strongly suggest that
the staff organisations had insufficient bargaining strength to
exact concessions over pay from the management sides.[39] On a
few occasions the nurses galvanised public opinion in support
of specific pay increases. However independent assessment of
their pay by the NBPI in 1968 indicated that this had failed to
produce any long-term benefits. Alternatively the medical profession which possessed significant bargaining power and
indicated a readiness to use it, did appreciably better in securing pay increases via the DDRB than both other NHS occupations
and probably other comparable professions. In the light of this
it may be speculated that for those health occupations whose
pay continued to be determined within NHS Whitleyism, the
period of almost continuous incomes policy from 1965 to 1979 was
more beneficial than detrimental in its impact on their earnings.

In this context three important and inter-related effects of
incomes policy can be tentatively identified. First, incomes policy
was responsible, either directly or indirectly, for independent
examinations of pay levels among a number of NHS occupations.
The reports of the NBPI, the 1974 inquiries into nursing and
the professions supplementary to medicine, and the Standing
Commission on Pay Comparability were different in kind from
previous third-party involvement in NHS pay determination. The
latter had been concerned to examine the claims in relation to
specific cases. In consequence the general and more problematic
issues remained: the construction of coherent pay scales both
internally with other NHS occupations, and externally with non-
NHS groups. The issue of suitable external comparisons for
determining appropriate pay levels was and remains a problem
for many groups of NHS staff. And in instances where the NHS
is virtually a monopoly employer it is exceptionally difficult to
identify and agree comparative skills. The succession of third-
party assessments since the mid-1960s have served to mount
searches for suitable comparisons. Indeed the Standing Commission on Pay Comparability's terms of reference specifically

identified the need for comparative measures. While the Commission was unsuccessful in this, its terms of reference did indicate an acceptance of the problem by government. This in itself represents an important concession to some of these occupational groups and their staff organisations.

The second impact of incomes policy relates to the incidence of low pay in the NHS. The extent to which earnings declined under collective bargaining has already been discussed. However, while individual health workers may have experienced this directly it can be argued that except in specific instances a collective appreciation of the extent and degree of low pay was generally lacking. A further effect of the NBPI's inquiries was to identify this to health service workers, their staff organisations, and the public generally. The emergence of a collective will among NHS occupations enabled them to press more actively for the amelioration of low earnings. The slogans adopted during the disputes in the 1970s suggest that low pay, in the minds of NHS workers, was linked to government 'policy' which consisted of little more than the persistent exploitation of their vocational commitment to the health service.

The third effect of incomes policy lies in its impact on trade union growth and the emergence of hospital level trade union organisation. In 1967 the NBPI argued that on balance the inherent risks of incentive based payment schemes in regard to a deterioration in industrial relations were worth taking. Recognition of the embarrassment likely to be suffered by the Labour Government, following the disclosure of the incidence of low pay in the public sector and the tightly drawn exceptions to the current incomes policy, may have led the NBPI to present a politically feasible solution. Moreover the virtually strike free record of the NHS up to 1967 tended to support their gamble. However, the introduction of incentive payment schemes among ancillary staff was one of a number of significant elements in the increase in trade union organisation among ancillary staffs. Moreover this development among ancillary workers was one stimulus to increased unionisation among other hospital sector groups. The collective organisations representing NHS staff became generally more concerned with hospital level industrial relations whereas previously they had concentrated on national negotiations within the Whitley machinery. This found its most open expression in the recruitment struggles within hospitals, both between TUC affiliates, and between them and other professional associations. In consequence, professional associations such as the Rcn came to adopt the legal status of a trade union and to exhibit trade union forms of organisation. Increased unionisation subsequently enabled staff organisations to take a more militant posture in national level bargaining. These three interrelated effects of incomes policy provide some explanation of the change in attitudes and behaviour among NHS occupations towards the determination of pay in the 1970s.

In a democratic society government must generally make

judgements as to the acceptability of its policies. In terms of the introduction and operation of incomes policy in Britain the attitude of the TUC and its affiliated unions has generally been a decisive factor in its success. In the NHS the TUC trade unions and other staff organisations do not appear to have exercised the same degree of influence, both inside and outside periods of incomes policy, at least until the 1970s. Before then the circumstances of NHS pay determination strongly suggest that government could generally choose whether or not to give serious consideration to health staffs' claims in support of pay increases. In arriving at its decision government tended to take greater account of external political forces rather than those it met from within the NHS. Where it did meet claims from a powerful occupational group, as in the case of the medical profession, government sought a means to placate their demands for better pay. In the 1970s other NHS occupations required a degree of political power and received relatively similar benefits to those of the doctors: independent examinations of earnings. It is ironic that increased unionisation, which provided these groups with the means to challenge the established supremacy of government in pay determination, had in part been stimulated by incomes policy.

The present Conservative Government has partially returned to an earlier form of incomes policy, in that it has indicated a commitment to restrain public sector pay increases. The use of 'cash limits' within the NHS, however, has precluded direct government involvement. In essence pay settlements agreed within the Whitley system should conform to set budgetary constraints. The implication is that any additional pay increases for one occupational group have to be funded by appropriating resources away either from other health-care priorities or from the available money for other groups' pay awards. In theory therefore the decision to meet larger pay claims rests with the management sides of the Whitley Councils and their constituent employers. The extent to which government can distance itself from NHS pay determination over the long term remains to be seen. The present form of non-involvement, through the introduction of cash limits, may in any case be more of a cosmetic operation than a deliberate and permanent withdrawal from NHS collective bargaining. The decision on the size of the cash limit remains the responsibility of government and its influence in Whitley Councils' negotiations remains, due to the continuing presence of representatives from its health departments. It therefore seems unlikely that the central role of government in NHS pay determination will diminish in the foreseeable future.[34]

REFERENCES AND NOTES

1 Clegg, H.A. (1978), 'The System of Industrial Relations in
   Great Britain', 3rd edn., Basil Blackwell, pp.413-14.
2 Clegg, H.A., and Chester, T.E. (1957), 'Wage Policy and
   the Health Service', Basil Blackwell.
3 Clegg and Chester, ibid., p.v.
4 'Personal Incomes, Costs, and Prices', Cmnd. 7321, HMSO.
5 Clegg and Chester, Wage Policy, p.42.
6 Ministry of Health (1946), 'Report of the Inter-departmental
   Committee on the Remuneration of General Practitioners',
   Cmnd. 6810, HMSO; Ministry of Health (1948), 'Report of
   the Inter-departmental Committee on the Remuneration of
   Consultants and Specialists', Cmnd. 7420, HMSO.
7 'Royal Commission on Doctors' and Dentists' Remuneration
   1957-1960, Report', Cmnd. 939, HMSO, 1960.
8 Clegg and Chester, 'Wage Policy', p.96.
9 Stevens, Rosemary (1966), 'Medical Practice in Modern
   England: the Impact of Specialization and State Medicine',
   Yale University Press, p.137.
10 Clegg and Chester, 'Wage Policy', p.91.
11 Miles, A.W., and Smith, Duncan (1969), 'Joint Consultation:
   Defeat or Opportunity?', King's Fund, p.16.
12 Clegg and Chester, 'Wage Policy', p.76.
13 Ibid., p.76.
14 'The Hospital', December 1957, p.828.
15 'The Hospital', ibid., p.828.
16 'The Hospital', January 1958, p.2.
17 'The Hospital', June 1962, p.348.
18 'Incomes Policy: The Next Step', Cmnd. 1626, HMSO.
19 Ministry of Health (1966), 'Report of the Committee on
   Senior Nursing Staff Structure', HMSO.
20 National Board for Prices and Incomes (1968), 'Report
   No. 60: Pay of Nurses and Midwives in the National Health
   Service', HMSO.
21 National Board for Prices and Incomes (1967), 'Report
   No. 29: The Pay and Conditions of Manual Workers in Local
   Authorities, the National Health Service, Gas and Water
   Supply', HMSO.
22 National Board for Prices and Incomes (1971), 'Report
   No. 166: The Pay and Conditions of Ancillary Workers in
   the National Health Service', HMSO.
23 NHS pay scales do not discriminate between male and female
   staff. The NBPI's comment referred to comparisons with
   female rates of pay outside the public sector. Prior to the
   Equal Pay Act 1975 there was a large degree of discrimination between male and female workers.
24 'Royal Commission on Trade Unions and Employers' Associations 1965-68', Report, Cmnd. 3623, HMSO, 1968.
25 Gorham, M., Joint Consultation (1974), 'Health and Social
   Services Journal', vol.LXXXIV, no.4418-9, pp.2927-8.

26 Pay Board (1974), 'Advisory Report No. 2: Problems of
   Pay Relativities', Cmnd. 5335, HMSO.
27 Department of Health and Social Security (1974), 'Report of
   the Committee of Inquiry into the Pay and Related Conditions of Service of Nurses and Midwives', HMSO.
28 Department of Health and Social Security (1975), 'Report
   of the Committee of Inquiry into the Pay and Conditions of
   Service of the Professions Supplementary to Medicine and
   Speech Therapists', HMSO.
29 Standing Commission on Pay Comparability (1979), 'Report
   No. 1: Local Authority and University Manual Workers:
   NHS Ancillary Staffs: and Ambulancemen', HMSO.
30 Standing Commission on Pay Comparability (1979), 'Report
   No. 3: Nurses and Midwives', HMSO.
31 Standing Commission on Pay Comparability (1979), 'Report
   No. 4: Professions Supplementary to Medicine', HMSO.
32 Standing Commission on Pay Comparability, ibid., p.22.
33 Clegg and Chester, op. cit., p.119.
34 Lord McCarthy (1976), 'Making Whitley Work', Department
   of Health and Social Security.

18. EFFECT OF INCOMES POLICIES ON THE HEALTH CARE INDUSTRIAL RELATIONS SYSTEM IN THE USA

R. Santos and I.B. Helburn[*]

This chapter reviews the major studies which have examined the impact of incomes policies and other cost control programmes on the health-care industrial relations system in the USA. The focus will be on the impact of incomes policies and other cost containment programmes on the collective bargaining process in the health-care sector. Related issues such as the influence of cost containment on levels of health-care employment, delivery systems, and quality of care will be briefly covered. In order to examine the impact of incomes policies on the collective bargaining process, an overview of the health-care industrial relations system is first presented. Second, incomes policies are reviewed. The third section examines government cost control programmes such as rate reimbursements to hospitals. The fourth section discusses the implications of incomes policies and cost control programmes for the health-care industrial relations system. The experience of Canada and the UK with cost controls and collective bargaining is presented in the fifth section. Long-run trends and areas in which further research on cost control health care sector efforts is needed are discussed in the last section.

INTRODUCTION

Unabated inflation during the last decade in both the general economy and in the health care sector has made price stability one of the foremost economic goals of the eighties. In 1979 the US experienced an increase in the Consumer Price Index (CPI) of nearly 12 per cent. All sectors in the economy have contributed to the soaring price level, and the health care sector has been no exception. In 1979 the medical care components of the CPI showed an increase of over 9 per cent. In general, increases in medical care price levels have outstripped the inflation rate (see Table 18.1).

Efforts to curb inflationary trends and achieve price stability have fallen under the generic term of incomes policies or economic stabilisation programmes. Basically an income policy entails

* We are grateful to Dr Art Corazzini, US Council on Wage and Price Stability, for providing several studies on health-care costs. This does not, of course, imply agreement with the viewpoints or analysis expressed in this chapter.

Table 18.1: *Consumer Price Index for Urban Wage Earners and Clerical Workers, Annual Percent Changes by Components, 1967–79*

Year	All items	Food and beverages	Housing	Apparel and upkeep	Transportation	Medical care	Entertainment	Other goods and services
1967	–	–	–	–	–	–	–	–
1968	4.2	3.6	4.0	5.4	3.2	6.1	5.7	5.2
1969	5.4	5.0	6.2	5.8	3.9	6.9	5.0	4.9
1970	5.9	5.4	7.1	4.1	5.1	6.3	5.1	5.8
1971	4.3	3.1	4.4	3.2	5.2	6.5	5.3	4.8
1972	3.3	4.1	3.8	2.1	1.1	3.2	2.9	4.2
1973	6.2	13.2	4.4	3.7	3.3	3.9	2.8	3.9
1974	11.0	13.8	11.3	7.4	11.2	9.3	7.5	7.2
1975	9.1	8.4	10.6	4.5	9.4	12.0	8.9	8.4
1976	5.8	3.1	6.1	3.7	9.9	9.5	5.0	5.7
1977	6.5	6.0	6.8	4.5	7.1	9.6	4.9	5.8
1978	7.6	9.7	8.6	3.4	4.9	8.4	5.1	6.4
1979	11.5	10.9	12.3	4.3	14.5	9.4	6.5	7.2

Source: 'Monthly Labor Review', November 1980, Table 22.

three major concepts: (1) acceptable wage and price levels for
the economy are established, (2) individual sectors of the
economy such as construction, steel, or health can be given
specific wage and price levels to follow, and (3) a mechanism
is provided to ensure compliance with the desired wage and price
levels.[1] For example, in late 1978 President Carter signed
executive order 12092, which established a voluntary incomes
policy to curb inflation. The Carter incomes policy stressed
voluntary wage and price restraint, asking that pay increases
be held to no more than 7 per cent and that average price
increases be held to one-half a percentage point below a firm's
rate of annual price increases during 1976-7. Specific guidelines were also given to curb the health-care industry. Responsibility for monitoring of the programme rested with the Council
on Wage and Price Stability. While the programme was voluntary,
the President directed the federal government to engage in
contracts only with firms which were in compliance with the
established guidelines.[2]

Incomes policies are not the only approach for combatting
inflation in particular sectors of the economy. In the health-care
sector, for example, cost control efforts such as rate reimbursement reviews for hospitals can likewise serve as income policies.
Other procedures in the health care field also aid in curbing
inflationary processes. For example, the capital going into the
hospital industry can be partially reduced by requiring certificates of need before building or expanding medical facilities.
Better use and distribution of health care can also be accomplished by health system agencies that promote more effective
planning of resources. Other programmes to combat medical
care inflation include the requirement of second opinions before
federal reimbursement for surgery and the creation of Professional Standards Review Organizations (PSROs) to regulate
hospital costs by reviewing the care provided under Medicare
and Medicaid.[3]

Although incomes policies and other cost control programmes
attempt to reduce inflationary pressures, the impact of anti-
inflationary programmes, however, extends beyond the levels
of wages and prices. Excessive controls can cause product
shortages, labour shortages or deterioration of product quality.
In the health-care sector, for example, incomes policies and
other cost control programmes will impact on (1) health-care
workers and their union associations, (2) firms, i.e. hospitals
and other medical facilities, (3) physicians and the delivery of
medical services, (4) the quality and cost of care provided to
the patient, and (5) the regulatory role of government in the
health-care sector. Every component of the health sector is thus
likely to be influenced by incomes policies or cost containment
programmes.

The Health-care Industrial Relations Setting

Firms, labour unions and the government have generally been
viewed as the major actors in an industrial relations system.[4] A
variety of social, political, labour and economic factors define
the industrial relations system of a particular country or sector
of the economy. In the US, the development of a health-care
industrial relations system is of recent origin compared to other
sectors. As late as 1960, only about 9 per cent of hospital
employees were represented by labour unions, but by 1977, the
proportion of hospital workers represented by unions had
increased to slightly over one-fifth.[5]

The increase in union coverage of health workers reflects the
legislative extension of collective bargaining rights to the health-
care sector. For example, health care employees of the United
States Government, who for the most part work in Veterans
Administration facilities, as well as other nonpostal federal
employees, are now covered by the Civil Service Reform Act,
passed in 1978.[6] Title VII of the Act provided the first legislative framework for nonpostal federal employee bargaining,
replacing earlier executive orders. The law provides for bargaining unit determination, exclusive representation, bargaining,
grievance and arbitration procedures, unfair labour practice
constraints, and impasse resolution procedures, but bargaining
over salaries and fringe benefits is not permitted. In addition,
about half of the 50 states have laws which affirm bargaining
rights for some or all public employees in health care, although
these laws vary with regard to permitted scope of bargaining,
administrative arrangements, dispute resolution procedures and
the right to strike.[7]

Privately owned for-profit health-care facilities have been
covered by federal labour law since the passage of the National
Labor Relations Act in 1935. Private, nonprofit hospitals were
included after a 1942 US Court of Appeals ruling, but later
excluded under the National Labor Relations Act (NLRA) amendments to the earlier law. Public Law 93–360, enacted in 1974,
amended the NLRA to once again provide coverage for private
nonprofit hospitals.

A survey conducted by the Federal Mediation and Conciliation
Service (FMCS) from 25 August 1974 through 31 December 1976
provides a good picture of how the extension of collective bargaining affected the industry.[8] During this period 2585 collective
bargaining (contract) situations encompassing 414 000 employees,
or 25 per cent of the 1.7 million employed, were discovered.
The FMCS estimated that about 70 per cent of the bargaining
situations involved hospitals, with nursing homes accounting for
an additional 25 per cent. The greatest activity occurred in the
East (New York, Massachusetts, Pennsylvania, New Jersey),
Midwest (Michigan, Ohio, Minnesota, Illinois) and West Coast
(California, Washington).

Besides being of recent origin, the industrial relations system
in the health-care sector also has some other unique character-

istics. For example, over half of all medical care costs are incurred in hospitals, but the vast majority of hospitals are not-for-profit organisations. The goals of hospitals in industrial relations may be different from those of profit maximising firms.[9] In addition to the nonprofit nature of hospitals and the public emphasis on availability of medical care, the nature of medical care financing also influences the industrial relations setting. Over 90 per cent of medical expenditures in the United States are now paid either by insurance companies or by the government rather than by the patient. The health-care system thus has the potential to pass through costs.[10] Conversely, the public concern with spiralling medical costs and tax expenditures on health means that labour agreements between hospitals and trade unions are carefully scrutinised. More pointedly, there has been a concern, if not a suspicion, that collective bargaining will lead to higher wages and thus higher production costs. In the health-care industry, this concern centres on the cost of providing health-care services and the quality of those services.

The industrial relations system in the health-care sector thus has unique characteristics. Implementing incomes policies and cost control efforts to curb inflationary pressures in the health-care sector will affect its industrial relations system. Nearly three out of every four workers in the health-care sector are employed by hospitals.[11] Incomes policies and cost control efforts to combat hospital-based inflation will necessarily affect employer-employee relationships.

Incomes Policies in the USA: 1940-80
The post World War II experience with incomes policies in the USA has been relatively limited.[12] Inflation has generally been seen as an economic problem to be solved through the market system with minimum government interference. Restraint in government spending and control of the money supply have been preferred methods of combatting inflation. When needed, the government has established acceptable levels of wage and price increases to serve as voluntary guidelines for corporations and labour unions. The wage and price guidelines established in the sixties by the Kennedy and Johnson Administrations were voluntary and applied to specific sectors of the economy. The attempt by the government to 'jaw bone' wages and prices or appeal to the 'moral' instincts of labour unions and corporations was not applied to the health-care field. Until recently the health-care sector has generally enjoyed immunity from voluntary income policies. On the other hand, wage and price controls have also at times been imposed by the government on the economy. The legal power of the state to control wages and prices has been, with one exception, only used to solve emergency economic crises during war time. For example, during War World II and the Korean War, the government managed the economy directly through a variety of measures including direct wage and price controls.[13] Other than wartime emergency situations, the only

other enactment of wage and price controls in the United States occurred in the early seventies under the Nixon Administration. Wage and price controls were imposed in direct response to mounting political pressures to combat increasing inflation, and these controls included the health-care sector.

The Economic Stabilization Program was announced by President Nixon in August 1971 and entailed a comprehensive 90-day wage and price freeze. This freeze, which included the health sector, was the initial phase of a four phase programme to contain inflation. Lasting from August 1971 to April 1974, the Nixon stabilisation programme encompassed a series of wage and prices freezes, limits on wage and price increases, and a decontrol phase to limit inflation.[14]

The impact of the Nixon stabilisation programme permeated the economy as well as the health-care sector. The controls restricted the growth of both the CPI and its medical care cost component to under 4 per cent. Moreover, the average cost per patient day, relative to the CPI, increased by only 3 per cent during 1972-3 and less than 1 per cent during 1973-4. Except for the period under the Nixon controls, the average cost per patient day, relative to the CPI, increased more than 8 per cent in every year since 1966.[15] In short, increases in health-care costs have been effectively restrained only during the years of price and wage controls.

Table 18.2: The Carter Administration Guideline Efforts in the Health-care Field

Health Care Activity	Standard	Monitoring Agency	1st-Year Limit (%)	Actual 1st-Year Increase (%) [a]
Medical Care Commodities	Price	CWPS	5.8	7.3
Medical Care Services				
Professional Fees				
Physician Fees	Professional Fee	HEW	6.5	9.5
Dental Services	Professional Fee	CWPS	6.5	7.7
Other Professional Services	Professional Fee	CWPS	6.5	5.9
Other Medical Care Services				
Hospital & Other Medical Services	Expenditure Target	HEW	9.7-11.2	13.4
Health Insurance	Insurance	CWPS	N/A	N/A

a. October 1978 to October 1979

Source: Table extracted from unpublished paper, Medical Care Inflation, Council on Wage and Price Stability.

In contrast to the mandatory controls of the Nixon programme, the Carter Administration relied on voluntary wage and price guidelines to stem overall inflation as well as rising health-care costs. Under the Carter Anti-Inflation Program, the Council on Wage and Price Stability and the US Department of Health, Education and Welfare were given the responsibility for monitoring the level of health-care costs. Table 18.2 presents the agency that was responsible for monitoring the first year guidelines by health-care expenditure and the actual price increases in that year. In 1979, the government guidelines for physician fee was 6.5 per cent but actual fees rose by 9.5 per cent. Hospital costs increased by three to four percentage points above the guidelines. By and large, actual health care fee increases exceeded the voluntary guidelines.[16] According to the Council on Wage and Price Stability, the increases over the established guidelines cannot all be attributed to noncompliance but must also be attributed to the various required exemptions and exceptions in the health-care field.[17] Nevertheless, the President's Price Advisory Committee has concluded that monitoring of the health-care field, in particular, of hospitals and physician fees, has been delayed because of a lack of data. In addition, HEW has not taken effective measures to develop a monitoring programme.[18]

The effectiveness of incomes policies in controlling overall inflation in the United States has been difficult to assess.[19] By and large, incomes policies have been voluntary and the guidelines have not been applied to the health-care industry. Other than direct wage and price controls under the Economic Stabilization Program, incomes policies have not had much success in restraining inflationary pressures either in the total economy or in the health-care sector. Yet is is also impossible to gauge accurately what inflationary pressures would have been in the absence of a voluntary programme.

With the exception of the Nixon controls and the Carter programme, incomes policies have not specifically applied to health care. While the Nixon control temporarily froze health-care costs, inflationary pressures in that sector have generally not been restrained by incomes policies. However, other forms of cost containment efforts have been considered to halt the double digit price increases in health care. Federal legislation has been proposed to limit reimbursements to hospitals to where cost increases fall within established guidelines. Attempts to pass hospital cost control legislation have, however, not been successful. Nevertheless, some states through regulatory agencies have attempted to curb the rising costs of hospital care. These cost containment programmes are reviewed in the next section.

Cost Control Programmes

Besides through incomes policies, the federal government has made known its desire to curb inflationary pressures through a variety of cost control programmes. Foremost of the govern-

ment's cost control efforts has been the proposed Hospital Cost
Containment Act of 1977.[20] The Carter Administration proposed
that hospitals be limited in inpatient revenue increases and
capital expenditures. The limits on inpatient revenue would be
based on a formula that reflected both the general level of price
increases as well as increases in patient services. Capital expenditures would be limited to a lump annual sum. In limiting the
increases in patient revenues as well as capital expenditures,
the Carter proposal hoped both to contain inflationary pressures
and to set the stage for reforming the health-care system.

Passage of hospital cost containment legislation seems unlikely
given the election of a new president and the strong opposition
the Carter proposal encountered. The curbing of inflationary
pressures in the health care field will therefore have to rely on
the piecemeal cost containment approach developed by the
government since the introduction of Medicare and Medicaid
legislation in the sixties. The federal government has issued
guidelines for rate reimbursements, required medical review
committees, encouraged alternative health-care delivery systems
such as health maintenance organisations, and established health
system planning agencies as ways to control health-care costs.[21]
While not all of these approaches were specifically designed as
cost containment efforts, these programmes either increase the
supply of medical care personnel, alter the delivery system, or
stem demand for health care; thus, theoretically, they influence
the cost of health care.

The federal government has not been the only force to put cost
control pressures on health care. At least fifteen states have
experimented with either volunteer or mandatory cost control
programmes.[22] Some states have actually granted authority to
commissions to set rates for all nongovernment hospitals. At
minimum, states with cost control can monitor the budgets of
hospitals and review their rates. Other states play a more active
role and actually intervene in such hospital matters as wage
setting.[23] Cost containment efforts have also not been limited to
the government. A Voluntary Effort (VE) Program sponsored
by private groups such as the American Medical Association,
hospital associations, and Blue Cross and Blue Shield associations has formulated guidelines to control costs.[24]

As with the case of incomes policies, experiences with cost
control programmes have been limited. Cost control programmes
are largely fragmentary efforts and they have not been successful at stemming rising health-care costs.[25] Beyond the impact
of cost control efforts on inflationary pressures in the health-
care field, cost containment programmes should also be examined
by their impact on the health-care industrial relations system.
Although not much research has examined the impact of incomes
policies and cost control efforts on industrial relations in the
health-care industry, the next section reviews the major studies
in this area.

Impact on the Health-care Industrial Relations System
Incomes policies and cost control efforts influence the health-
care industry in a number of ways. By focusing on the rate of
price and wage increases, incomes policies cause hospitals to
become cost conscious. Unfortunately, the most likely candidates
for cost reduction are labour costs. Wages, fringe benefits and
extensive hospital staff are erroneously viewed as major contributors to inflation. According to most cost studies on health
care, wage increases are not the major cause of spiralling
hospital costs. Rather, the major contributors to health-care
costs have been the increase in third-party payments, advanced
technology, and greater quantities of labour and other inputs
required to provide greater levels of health care.[26] Yet a study
by Taylor indicates that employees in hospitals have borne the
major burden of incomes policies.[27] During the Economic Stabilization Program period, 1971-3 wage and price controls effectively
reduced hospital wage increases and, to a lesser degree, total
hospital employment. More important, hospital wage increases
were not only restrained during the control period, but the
increases actually lagged other industries with similar controls.
Hospital workers thus bore a large proportion of the burden
caused by incomes policies during the Economic Stabilization
Program.
    Evidence is also provided by Ginsberg that wage increases in
hospitals were curtailed by the Economic Stabilization Program.[28]
However, the impact on hospital costs was not very great. One
of the problems in assessing the effectiveness of the programme,
according to Ginsberg, is measurement. The controls were largely viewed as temporary, and the response by hospital and labour
unions might have been different if the controls had been viewed
as permanent.
    The voluntary incomes policy efforts of the Carter Administra-
tion also do not appear as yet to have had a major impact on
total employment or wages in the health-care field. According to
a survey report on community hospitals, full-time employment
in hospitals increased by 4 per cent in 1980 as compared to 2 per
cent in 1979.[29] Wage rates increased only slightly from the previous year, 10 per cent in 1980 compared to 9 per cent in 1979.
Overall hospital expenses increased by 17 per cent in 1980 as
opposed to 13 per cent in 1979. According to the survey report,
the increase in total expenses was due to overall inflationary
pressure on inputs, increased demand for hospital care, and
increases in total hospital employment.[30]
    Income policies in the health sector are more likely to influence
wages and total employment than other aspects of industrial
relations such as collective bargaining, union activity, or bargaining structures. On the other hand, cost control efforts,
particularly concerning rate reimbursement by third parties at
the state level, are more likely to affect collective bargaining
issues. For example, an in-depth survey by FMLS of 15 bargaining situations in New York State, 12 of these in New York City,

found the third-party payor issue the most important topic of negotiations.[31] Where the issue arose at the bargaining table, it was in the form of a management 'inability to pay' argument, where there was a refusal or concern that hospitals would not be reimbursed for increased labour costs. While third-party payors were not directly involved in labour-management negotiations, their bargaining impact was substantial, particularly prior to 1976, because they had to approve pass-through of negotiated increases in labour costs. In many instances, bargaining was perfunctory, involving union and management manoeuvres so that the state would have to respond with additional reimbursement. However, it did appear that there was a moderating impact on wages, as the wages settlements averaged under 5 per cent in the New York contracts studied, compared to an 8 per cent average for 21 agreements negotiated throughout the United States.[32]

In a study of three state cost control commissions -- New York, Maryland, Connecticut -- Schramm has gauged both the potential and actual impact of cost control programmes on the health-care system.[33] For example, the commissioner of health has on occasion intervened in the arbitration process to curb hospital wage increases and prevent the linking of wage hikes to Medicaid payment increases. In 1976, the Health Services Cost Review Commission in Maryland limited hospital costs to 5.3 per cent and also linked the increase to the CPI. According to Schramm, wage increases in previous years in Baltimore hospitals had ballooned to as much as 10 to 14 per cent. Nevertheless, the final bargaining agreement was in line with the established rate.

A review of published arbitration awards during the 1977-9 period indicated no undue constraints upon health-care management by third parties. Of the 14 awards published in Bureau of National Affairs, Inc. and Commerce Clearing House, Inc. publications, most dealt with issues similar to those arising in non-health-care cases. Two of the cases were related to the requirements of agencies external to the health-care facility, one dealt with the impact of state imposed qualifications for promotion in a public facility,[34] and the other concerned a District of Columbia requirement that employees in health-care facilities be required to take an annual physical if they had patient contact.[35]

Nevertheless, any issues that could impact on hospital costs could theoretically be 'fair game' for intervention into the collective bargaining process by cost control commissions. While it is difficult to predict this impact, the intervention of cost control commissions into collective bargaining could affect issues such as the growth of hospital unionisation, the number of bargaining structures, subcontract work, affirmative action and seniority rights. For example, active intervention by cost control commissions could either induce health workers to join unions for protection or render unions impotent. In addition, the intervention of the state could place a 'third chair' at the collective

bargaining table or require bargaining to be done with individual
hospitals or on a group basis. Cost control commissions could
thus potentially impact on the entire health-care industrial relations system.

Comparisons with Canada and UK
The United States does not have a national health insurance
programme.[36] In addition, medical care fees in the USA are
generally not paid on a predetermined fixed fee schedule; therefore the institutional mechanisms for establishing fees available
in other countries are not present in the US. For example, the
provincial governments in Canada have negotiated budgets with
individual hospitals.[37] In contrast, government involvement in
both the actual delivery of medical care services and the collective bargaining process in general has historically been
opposed in the USA.

Nevertheless, some lessons from other countries in the use of
incomes policies and cost control efforts are worth noting. Most
countries have suffered from inflationary pressures in both the
general economy and the health-care sector. Double digit inflation has in recent times characterised not only the United States
but also the UK and Canada. Counterinflationary pressures in
other countries have at times included wage and price controls
as well as selective cost control measures in the health-care
sector. Incomes policies in other countries have at best had only
limited success in controlling inflationary pressures.[38]

The cost control efforts of Canada and the UK have, however,
been much more extensive than those of the USA. In 1977,
Canada invoked the Federal-Provincial Fiscal Arrangments and
the Established Programs Financing Act to stem rising health-
care costs.[39] This legislation gave modified block funds to the
provincial governments rather than conditions grants that reimbursed provinces for a portion of their health-care costs. Under
the previous conditions grant system, wage increases in hospitals
were almost likely to be granted.[40] From 1966 to 1975, hospital
employees' wage increases averaged nearly 13 per cent, in excess
of the national average.[41] Although at times, major increases were
not approved, as was the case in British Columbia. Quebec has
at times participated in the wage negotiations of hospitals.[42]

The cost control provisions of the recent Canadian legislation
signal more participation by provincial governments in the activities of hospitals, including their industrial relations. By providing a fixed block grant to the province, the federal government monitors only the maintenance of national standards of
health care. The federal government assigns cost containment
responsibility to the provinces and provides financial incentives
to curb costs. The impact of this type of institutional arrangement is that the industrial relations system will more than likely
function in a public utility model in its collective bargaining
activities.[43]

In contrast to the regionalised cost control efforts of the

Canadian government, the UK has relied on a centralised governmental system, the National Health Service, to administer its health care services, including cost containment.[44] Responsibility for negotiating wage levels and other working conditions of health-care workers is given to the National Health Service. Under the British health-care system, labour relation negotiations in reality are carried out between the government and its employees. This public sector model partially parallels the US limited collective bargaining experience with governmental employees such as firemen, policemen and teachers.

For British doctors and dentists, their remuneration under the National Health Service is monitored by an 'Independent Review Body' which recommends the final award to the Prime Minister. At times, the Review Body has successfully gone against specific incomes policies of the government by granting larger pay increases than the established levels. The Review Body justified its position that these increases were needed for the proper operation of the National Health Service.[45]

The experience of the US, Canada and the UK briefly covered in this section suggests several lessons to be drawn from cost control effects and incomes policies. At one extreme, the US has experimented with only limited cost control efforts and consequently not ventured into the collective bargaining process in the health-care sector. Industrial relations are conducted in a quasi-private sector model with only occasional intervention by state rate control commissions. In contrast, the UK has centralised its cost control efforts in the National Health Service. Industrial relations issues are largely handled within the centralised bargaining machinery together with various forms of arbitration. In between these two approaches, Canada seems to be adopting a public utility model whereby provincial governments negotiate budgets within hospitals. Canadian health-care workers will thus have to consider these established budgets in their collective bargaining activities. Even though the United States has some unique elements in both its health-care delivery system and industrial relations system, worthwhile industrial relations lessons may be taken from other countries as the US considers ways to curb inflationary pressures in the health-care field.

Future Outlook

Predicting the impact that incomes policies and other cost control activities will have on the health-care industrial relations system in the USA remains largely a speculative task. No consensus emerges as to which types of incomes policies should be adopted, or for that matter what the best approach to contain health-care costs is. In addition, experience with incomes policies and cost containment activities has been piecemeal and limited. Moreover, the industrial relations system in the health-care sector is of recent origin and the system is in its early development stage.

Yet some tentative observations about health-care industrial relations can be made. From the consumer's viewpoint, the impact of bargaining generally seems minimal. Strikes, while infrequent, have caused concern but few major problems. In the UK the principal effect has been on those awaiting hospital treatment. On a day-to-day basis, unionisation does not seem to have decreased the quality of health care provided by constraining management in the use of personnel. And while the costs of health care have risen dramatically in recent years, available data suggest that the results of the bargaining process account for very little of the increase in Canada and the USA. Nevertheless, the public's concern in these two countries with rising health-care costs will more than likely increase the number of cost control programmes. The scant evidence available in the US and the UK as well as other countries suggests that cost control efforts can influence employer-employee relationships. By the same token, the industrial relations system can curb the increase in health-care costs. Through collective bargaining activities, effective industrial relations policy can reduce turnover, utilise workers more efficiently, and increase productivity.[47]

Furthermore, the current structure of the health-care delivery system has been influenced by the nature of collective bargaining in the USA. Since there is no system of universal health insurance, the accepted concept of employer/employee group health insurance is largely a product of collective bargaining. As trade unions and corporations wrestle with the increasing costs of health-care coverage, the approaches used to provide adequate coverage at a reasonable cost will undoubtedly affect industrial relations in the health-care field.[48]

The opportunity to contain health-care cost and influence the nature of industrial relations systems thus appears to be available to all parties engaged in bargaining, including health-care unions. As it considers the wide range of incomes policy options available to stem inflationary pressures in both the economy and the health-care sector, the federal government will also impact on the industrial relations system. As these issues are addressed, the influence of the industrial relations system on the health-care system and the potential impact of cost control activities on the industrial relations system will have to be carefully studied.

REFERENCES AND NOTES

1 Mansfield, Edwin (1980), 'Economics', 3rd edition, W.W. Norton and Company, pp.391-2.
2 US Congress (1979), 'Adequacy of the Administration Anti-Inflation Program', US Government Printing Office. Hearings before a subcommittee on Government Operations, 5-7 Feb., pp.454-5, 504-5.
3 Cost control programmes are discussed in American Enterprise Institute (1978), 'Proposals for the Regulation of

Hospital Costs', pp.11-15.

4 For a discussion of industrial relations system refer to Clark Kerr et al. (1960), 'Industrialism and Industrial Man', Harvard University Press.

5 An excellent overview of the unique characteristics of the health-care industrial relations system is presented in Miller, Richard U. (1980), Hospitals, in Gerald G. Somers (ed.), 'Collective Bargaining: Contemporary American Experience', Industrial Relations Research Association, p.373.

6 Chapter 71 of Title 5 of the United States Code.

7 These observations are based on a review of the following: US Department of Labor, Labor-Management Services Administration (1979), 'Summary of Public Sector Labor Relations Policies', GPO.

8 US Department of Labor, Labor-Management Services Administration and Federal Mediation and Conciliation Service, Office of Research (1979), 'Impact of the 1974 Health Care Amendments to the NLRA on Collective Bargaining in the Health Care Industry', GPO, Ch.4.

9 Newhouse, Joseph P. (1978), 'The Economics of Medical Care', Addison-Wesley, p.68.

10 Miller in 'Hospitals', p.415.

11 Ibid., p.375.

12 For a review of incomes policies refer to US Congress (1977), 'Incomes Policies in the US: Historical Review', Congressional Budget Office.

13 For review of incomes policies during war crisis refer to Derber, Milton (1972), Wage Stabilization: Then and Now, in Gerald G. Sommers (ed.), 'Proceedings of the 1972 Spring Meeting', Industrial Relations Research Association.

14 US Congress, 'Incomes Policies', pp.xii, xiii.

15 Feldstein, Martin, and Taylor, Amy (1977), 'The Rapid Rise of Hospital Costs', US Council on Wage and Price Stability, pp.9-10.

16 Price Advisory Committee (1980), 'Findings and Recommendations on Health Care Costs', Council on Wage and Price Stability, summary sheet.

17 Council on Wage and Price Stability, Medical Care Inflation, unpublished paper, pp.9-11.

18 Price Advisory Committee, Health Care Costs, summary sheet.

19 For analysis of incomes policies, refer to Popkin, Joel (ed.) (1977), 'Analysis of Inflation: 1965-1974', National Bureau of Economic Affairs.

20 Hughes, Edward F.X. et al. (1978), 'Hospital Cost Containment Programs', Northwestern University, Ch.4.

21 A review of control efforts is noted in Newman, John F. et al. (1979), Attempts to Control Health Care Costs: The US Experience, 'Social Science and Medicine', vol.13A, no.5A, pp.529-40.

22 Stodghill, William (1979), Discussion to Health Care Issues and Welfare Plans, 'Labor Law Journal', vol.30, no.8, p.513.

23 Most of the research on third-party reimbursements and collective bargaining has been done by Schramm, Carl J. (1978), Regulating Hospital Labor Costs: A Case Study in Politics of State Rate Commission, 'Journal of Health Politics, Policy and Law', vol.3, no.3; (1977), Role of Hospital Cost Regulating Agencies in Collective Bargaining, 'Labor Law Journal', vol.28, no.8; and (1978), Containing Hospital Labor Costs - A Separate Industries Approach, 'Employee Relations Law Journal', vol.4, no.1.

24 Newman, et al., Attempts to Control Costs, p.536.

25 Ibid., p.529.

26 Feldstein and Taylor, Rapid Rise of Hospital Costs, pp.2-3.

27 Taylor, Amy K. (1979), Government Health Policy and Hospital Labor Costs, 'Public Policy', vol.27, no.2, Spring, pp.203-24.

28 Ginsberg, Paul B. (1978), Impact of the Economic Stabilization Program on Hospitals, in Michael E. Zubkoff et al. (eds.), 'Hospital Cost Containment', Milbank Memorial Fund, pp.319-21.

29 American Hospital Association (1980), 'Trends: Community Hospital Indicators', Office of Policy Studies.

30 Ibid.

31 US Department of Labor, Impact of the 1974 Health Care Amendments, Chapter 9.

32 Ibid.

33 Schramm, Regulating Hospital Labor Costs, pp.367-9.

34 Washington Hospital Center, 79-2 ARB 8539 (1979).

35 Washington Hospital Center, 73 LA 535 (1979).

36 Comparative health-care system differences are well noted in Glaser, William A. (1978), 'Health Insurance Bargaining', Gardner Press, Inc., pp.181-91.

37 Hughes et al., 'Hospital Cost Containment Programs', p.8.

38 For review of comparative incomes policies, refer to Phlman, Jerry E. (1976), 'Inflation Under Control', Reston Publishing Company, Ch. 10 and Frank Reid, Effect of Incomes Policy on Health Industrial Relations in Canada, in A.S. Sethi and Charles Steinberg (eds.), 'Industrial Relations and Health Services', Croom Helm.

39 Analysis of the Canadian legislation is based on Van Loon, R.J. (1978), From Shared Cost to Block Funding and Beyond, 'Journal of Health Politics, Policy and Law', vol.2, no.4.

40 Hughes, et al., 'Hospital Cost Containment Programs', pp.74-5.

41 Van Loon, From Shared Costs to Block Funding and Beyond, p.459.

42 Hughes, et al., 'Hospital Cost Containment Programs', p.74-5.

43 Public utility model is discussed in Van Loon, From Shared
   Costs to Blocked Funding, p.472 and Schramm, Regulating
   Hospital Labor Costs, p.373.
44 Glaser, 'Health Insurance Bargaining', Ch. IX.
45 Ibid., pp.172-3.
46 Van Loon, From Shared Costs to Block Funding, p.472.
47 For union impact on hospitals refer to Miller, Richard U.
   et al. (1977), Union Effects on Hospital Administration -
   Preliminary Results, Industrial Relations Research
   Association, 'Proceedings of the 1977 Annual Spring Meeting', James L. Stern and Barbara D. Dennis (eds.),
   IRRA, pp.512-19 and Becker, Brian (1978), Hospital
   Unionism and Employment Stability, 'Industrial Relations',
   vol.17, no.1, pp.96-101.
48 Costs of health-care benefits for United Auto Workers are
   noted in Marshall, Eliot (1977), What's Bad for General
   Motors, 'New Republic', vol.176, no.1, pp.22-3.

19. HEALTH INDUSTRIAL RELATIONS: A CONCLUDING OBSERVATION

A.S. Sethi and S.J. Dimmock

The authors in this volume have examined some of the major industrial relations issues in health care in Canada, the USA and the UK. In their examinations the authors have employed John Dunlop's concept of an 'industrial relations system', as an heuristic device to identify and analyse the key elements within the 'system' and the principal interactions between them. Moreover the use of Dunlop's concept has enabled a range of comparisons and contrasts to be drawn between the three countries. The following areas have been discussed:

the health sector labour market in the three countries;
the structure of the labour movements;
the general legal frameworks and their specific application
   to the health sectors;
the experience of collective bargaining;
the different modes of conflict resolution;
the effects of income policy on industrial relations in the
   health sectors.

As such, therefore, this represents a working approach to the exploration of the nature of industrial relations in the respective health sectors in the three countries. In this concluding chapter the focus will be upon collective bargaining - the principal rule-making process in each of the three countries - and some of the suggested avenues of reforms and the direction of future research for industrial relations in the three health sectors.

In the UK collective bargaining has been the primary mechanism for regulating pay and conditions of employment in the health sector since the inception of the NHS in 1948. During the past several decades, in North America, collective bargaining has become an extensive feature for many groups of health sector workers, including doctors and nurses. The present collective bargaining structures and the range of contextual features acting on the rule-making process reflects the different industrial relations cultures and traditions of the three countries. Thus for example the present structures vary from an almost atomistic state in the USA, through to province-wide bargaining in Canada and national level determination in the UK. However despite these differences the experience of collective bargaining in the respective health sectors suggest a number of shared issues.

1. The unions involved in health institutions have only begun to initiate some form of rationalisation in their internal structures. Moreover they have yet to develop a coherent philosophy suited to the organisation of both professional and nonprofessional health workers. The question of jurisdictional overlap among unions and professional associations is also a contributory factor and in all three countries this is frequently exacerbated by the sheer proliferation of professional associations.
2. Arising from this is the present strength and role of union representation at local levels in each of the three countries. While the shop stewards movement in hospitals in the UK is further advanced than similar representative systems in North America, its present role within the rule-making process is still relatively obscure and ill defined.
3. An associated factor which is relevant here is the degree of competition over membership among many health sector unions and professional associations. Moreover the role of professional associations creates distinctive problems in health sector negotiations. The most obvious example of this is the medical profession. In the UK, for example, they have applied their considerable collective power to conduct pay determination outside the Whitley Council system.
4. The emergence of militant bargaining behaviour has sharply highlighted the issue of the most appropriate form of structure on the centralised-decentralised axis. Additionally representation of staff and management sides in the respective structures remains uneven.
5. The resort to arbitration is a persistent feature within health sector bargaining in all three countries. Given the relationship between the political and industrial relations systems, and the perceived need for the political and legal frameworks to react to the changed ideology of health workers, this is perhaps understandable. However one effect of persistent arbitration may be to undermine the regulative function of collective bargaining as a dominant mode of rule-making. Obversely, the often inordinate delay in arbitration procedures and the collective bargaining process itself may also serve to heighten militancy.
6. The emergence of militant bargaining, which appears as a dominant feature in the three health sectors, is both a proactive and a reactive element of the change in ideology within and between the groups of actors. Hence, hastened by contextual influences, the emergence of militancy has largely buried the notion of an unqualified commitment to the vocational nature of health care among many health sector professional and nonprofessional workers. It has been replaced by a more calculating attitude towards work and the nature of its financial rewards.

Together these issues have been interpreted as a challenge to the existing industrial relations systems in the respective health sectors. This has led to attempts at reform.

HEALTH SECTOR INDUSTRIAL RELATIONS AND REFORMISM

The overall concern in each country is to make the industrial relations system more flexible in order to provide a balance of centralisation and local interest. The actors within each system, and particularly those government agencies immediately involved, have tended to react to these issues as 'problems'. Accordingly there has been a tendency to perceive the 'unsatisfactory state of ... industrial relations as the outcome of what might be termed "institutional lag"':[1] that is, the developments have out-stripped the regulative capacities of established industrial relations institutions. The means adopted to reform the institutional and structural arrangements have differed between the three countries. This is a consequence of their respective industrial relations systems with their different traditions, such as the orientations of the actors, the legal framework and its relationship to the character of rule-making and of the rules. However the goals of reform have been similar: the provision of more finely tuned structural arrangements to meet the new demands placed upon them.

In the USA, the 1974 Health Care Amendments to the National Labor Relations Act have had an impact on structural and operational features. Among these can be included an increased emphasis on educational and training activities for union members to focus on health sector industrial relations; contracts which specify special patient care standards and institutional policies and procedures; the requirement that parties serve earlier notices on the Federal Mediation and Conciliation Service (and a new notice provision in initial negotiation situations) to encourage early bargaining; a requirement (under Section 213 of the Act) for a fact-finding process for all disputes which may substantially interrupt the delivery of health care, together with a ten-day notice period as a means to ensure continuity of patient care in a strike situation.

In the UK a similar concern has been shown, to effect structural and operational change. Although the role of the law in collective bargaining is less interventionist in the UK there is a shared concern to create more responsive bargaining structures. Thus the 1976 McCarthy Report[2] was primarily directed towards this end. Likewise the Advisory Conciliation and Arbitration Service (ACAS), the agency concerned with British industrial relations more generally, expressed its fears for health sector industrial relations to the Royal Commission.[3] ACAS too wished to see a more responsive system of local management-union relationships and stressed the importance of educational and training programmes as one means of achieving a change in behaviour.

The developments in industrial relations in Canada's health sector have produced both similar concerns and suggested avenues of reform. The movement towards province-wide bargaining rather than individual hospital negotiations is one example of this. However within this structure there has been an equal concern to retain local flexibility. The similarities between legal interventionism in industrial relations between Canada and the USA has raised the more general issue of the role of the law in contract settlement and grievance handling.

The state has become increasingly involved in the process of industrial relations in both Canada and the USA. In the UK state involvement in the health sector has been a predominant feature since the creation of government-funded health care. However the events of the last decade have seen a more overt involvement by UK governments. In North America the state has found it necessary to provide a framework of law for the regulation of the activities of professional and nonprofessional health manpower; to advance and protect their interests and those of the patients. Moreover the governments in each country have taken initiatives in defending the 'wider interests of the community',[4] and have actually intervened in the day-to-day processes of collective bargaining. The underlying philosophy of this intervention has been to ensure that the provision of health care is not frustrated by the pursuit of free collective bargaining. An integral feature of free collective bargaining is the principle of 'freedom to strike', which is ranked high in each country. While administrators and government are particularly concerned that patient care remain accessible, even during a strike, both would appear to accept the impracticality of denying strike action. The position of the unions is more problematic: although constrained by the fact that they are primarily concerned for the welfare of their members, strikes which clearly jeopardise patient care in the eyes of the public cause them considerable embarrassment. The emphasis on the retention of the strike principle with limited usage connects certain propositions in the ideology of industrial relations with major societal values in each of the countries. In this manner the actors attempt to legitimise strikes and other forms of industrial disputes in the eyes of the public.

THE PREDOMINANCE OF COLLECTIVE BARGAINING

Collective bargaining is seen by the authors as being the principal viable method for the regulation of labour relations in health-care institutions. Collective bargaining in North America has been traditionally seen as an adversarial system. In the UK it has assumed this dimension after the initial years of relative co-operation. It can be suggested that in the health sector both management and staff sides could take the initiative in formulating proposals for change if the best mutual results are to be achieved. In effect collective bargaining can be seen as a form of 'collective planning'. In the health sector collective bargaining may go beyond the orthodox 'conflict-type' pattern found in other areas of the economy. This point has been emphasised in Britain by Lord McCarthy.[5]

Collective bargaining 'is both a cooperative game and a conflict game'.[6] The labour problem in health services centres around the tension over how much the health-care worker should be paid, and how much participation he ought to make in the decision-making process. In the words of Barbash:

> ...it isn't the union that creates the labour problem; it is the labour problem -- that is, the inherent tension between order givers and order takers -- that creates the union. In point of fact, the division between workers and employers over how to distribute income and power existed prior to unionism. Unionism and collective bargaining simply channeled and, as it turned out, probably civilised the process of dispute resolution.[7]

The other side is that it is also a co-operative game. In a social survey conducted by Sethi in Canada and UK, in which he interviewed about 600 hospital administrators and union negotiators during 1972-4, a major finding was that the industrial relations actors regarded co-operation as a necessary part of the collective bargaining process. Despite differences in structural variables such as size, type of work, location, negotiation structure, financing mechanisms, etc. in Canada and the UK, the respondents whole heartedly supported co-operation as a significant value in the Canadian and British health industrial relations.[8] In the US, since 1974, 'the degree of linear co-operation between institutions has appreciably changed as measured by the formation of association coordinated demands, and increased discussion', although changes in the number of grievances or arbitrations have been unaffected by the post-amendment period in that country.[9]

Whether collective bargaining can assume a more co-operative dimension is an issue for the future. The past experience of joint consultation in the UK suggests a degree of reluctance among local management towards a greater involvement of staff in decision-making at hospital level.[10] Management side reluctance towards more co-operative forms of local bargaining may also be characteristic of management attitudes at higher levels. The unions' commitment to collective bargaining may also shape attitudes towards bargaining outside the context of an adversarial system. Indeed their experience has demonstrated that in general a share in decision-making is accorded to those who exercise power. It therefore seems unlikely that they would be prepared to settle for less than a major involvement in pertinent aspects of decision-making.

THE DIRECTION OF FUTURE RESEARCH

The suggested avenues of reform in each of the three countries constitute a search for an 'ideal' collective bargaining structure in the health sector. Given the essential pragmatism which inhabits the industrial relations system and the pragmatic nature of the relationship between its own contextual features and with those of the economic and political subsystems, some of them, in extremis, may represent little more than pious hopes. The criteria which can be derived from for reform can be summarised as follows:

1. There should be a joint determination to minimise sources of conflict and to maximise opportunities to promote and expand areas of mutual interest and profit. Greater attention should be given to adopting appropriate bargaining strategies.
2. Effective attempts must be made by unions (through shop stewards) and health managements (through personnel officers) to familiarise medical and nonmedical employees in health-care institutions with the various elements of collective bargaining process and with the basic economic principles which applied to the field of hospital and health care administration.
3. The right to strike is an integral part of a collective bargaining system and should be enjoyed by health workers. This right, however, should be used 'only as a last resort'.
4. Pre-bargaining study groups -- composed of equal numbers of management and staff representatives -- would be useful for delineating areas of potential conflict, and creating an atmosphere of co-operation. The present level of negotiation preparation can be improved by using a more effective information system. A critical area in joint participation is the need to appraise effectiveness of labour-management occupational health and safety committees.
5. Collective agreements should specify that during a strike of health workers, 'essential' services will be maintained which are crucial to patient welfare. This factor needs to be redefined in detail, and as clearly as possible.
6. Administrators of health-care institutions are the 'agents of change' in the system and exercise a significant role in the utilisation of human resources in achieving health-care goals. They must, therefore, increase their sensitivity to employee demands and must acquire knowledge of the collective bargaining process.

These suggested criteria for an 'ideal system' tend to beg the question: will they be operationalised in a changing environment which is dominated by pragmatism? More fundamentally, do the actors within the system wish to effect reforms which may contain the potential to undermine their present position within the bargaining process? In terms of research this argues for a

careful examination of the suggested reforms, an assessment of
their acceptability to the actors and their potential outcome. In
order that this can be undertaken it is important to commence
investigation into the *dynamic* of collective bargaining. Hitherto
examinations of health sector industrial relations have been
carried out largely by official inquiries, sponsored by government or governmental agencies. Moreover these have generally
been occasioned by untypical events, e.g. strikes, the demands
of incomes policy, etc. As such these inquiries tend to be post
facto, and their underlying aim has often been to provide a
'politically' feasible solution to a perceived problem: the provision of a temporary modus vivendi for the parties involved.
A principal requirement is for studies concerned with the day-
to-day conduct of industrial relations in the health sector. Until
such time as there is data on what constitutes 'typical' issues
and concerns for the actors, the basis for making assertions
about health sector labour relations will remain on unfirm
ground.

REFERENCES AND NOTES

1 Goldthorpe, J.H. (1978), Industrial Relations in Great
  Britain: A Critique of Reformism, in Tom Clarke and Laurie
  Clements, 'Trade Unions under Capitalism', Fontana, p.186.
2 Lord McCarthy (1976), 'Making Whitley Work', Department of
  Health and Social Security.
3 ACAS (1978), 'Royal Commission on the National Health
  Service: ACAS Evidence', ACAS.
4 Eberlee, T. (1900), Objectives of the Federal Government
  in Charting the Course, in F. Bairstow (ed.), 'The Direction of Labour Policy in Canada', McGill University,
  pp.13-21; US Department of Labour (1979), 'Public Sector
  Policies'; (1979), Department of Health and Social Security.
5 Lord McCarthy, 'Making Whitley Work'.
6 Barbash, (1980), 'Positive Collective Bargaining: Theory
  and Practice', University of Wisconsin, mimeo.
7 Barbash, ibid.
8 A social survey was conducted by Sethi during 1972-4, as
  part of his doctoral dissertation in which a sample of
  hospital administrators and trade union negotiators in
  selected hospital regions in Canada and UK. About 20 per
  cent of the general hospitals were visited by the researcher
  in Canada and UK (Ontario and Quebec in Canada, and six
  hospital regions in Manchester, Metropolitan London,
  Birmingham and Manchester). An average of three management representatives were interviewed in both large and
  small hospitals in Quebec and Ontario. Management respondents in England included group secretaries, hospital
  secretaries, and management representatives of the Whitley
  Councils. The staff sides in Quebec and Ontario included

representatives of the union and professional associations. The staff sides of the Whitley Councils in the UK included union officials, shop stewards and representatives of the professional associations. A total of 586 people were interviewed, in both countries, out of which 240 represented the management sides and 346 union sides. Sethi, A.S. (1974), A Framework for the Study of Hospital Labour Relations in Canada and the United Kingdom, PhD thesis, University of Manchester.

9 US Department of Health - Federal Mediation and Conciliation Service (1974), 'Impact of the 1974 Health Care Amendments to the NLRA on Collective Bargaining in the Health Care Industry', pp.431-3.

10 Stuart J. Dimmock, Participation or Control? The Workers' Involvement in Management, in K. Barnard and K. Lee (1977), 'Conflicts in the National Health Service', Croom Helm.

Contributors

George Adams – Chairman, Ontario Labour Relations Board, Toronto, Canada.

Dr S.D. Anderman – Reader in Law and Chairman of the School of Law, University of Warwick, Coventry, England.

John H. Angel – Solicitor and Industrial Relations Consultant, London, England.

Dr Thomas A. Barocci – Professor of Industrial Relations, Massachusetts Institute of Technology, Alfred P. Sloan School of Management, Cambridge, Mass., USA.

Dr David Beatty – Associate Professor, Faculty of Law, University of Toronto, Toronto, Canada.

Dr Michael Carpenter – Research Fellow, School of Industrial and Business Studies, University of Warwick, Coventry, England.

S.J. Dimmock – Lecturer in Industrial Relations, Nuffield Centre for Health Services Studies, University of Leeds, Leeds, England.

Dr Morley Gunderson – Associate Professor, Centre for Industrial Relations, University of Toronto, Toronto, Canada.

Lynn H. Harnden – Barrister and Solicitor, Gowling & Henderson, Ottawa, Canada.

Dr I.B. Helburn – Associate Professor, Department of Management, University of Texas at Austin, Austin, Texas, USA.

W.P. Kelly – Senior Assistant Deputy Minister, Federal Mediation & Conciliation Service, Labour Canada, Ottawa, Canada.

Dr Marvin J. Levine – Professor, College of Business & Management, University of Maryland, College Park, Md, USA.

R. Mailly – Lecturer in Labour Law, Nuffield Centre for Health Services Studies, University of Leeds, Leeds, England.

Dr T. Charles McKinney – Professor, School of Business and Public Administration, Health Services Administration Department, Howard University, Washington, D.C., USA.

Dr E. Moran – Executive Director, Ontario Medical Association, Toronto, Canada.

Dr Frank Reid – Associate Professor of Economics, at the Centre for Industrial Relations and Department of Political Economy, University of Toronto, Toronto, Canada.

Mrs Glenna Rowsell – in charge of Labour Relations, Canadian Nurses Association, Ottawa, Canada.

Dr Richard Santos – Professor, Department of Economics, University of Texas at Austin, Austin, Texas, USA.

Ms Cathy Schoen – Director of Economic Analysis, Service

Employees International Union, Washington, D.C., USA.
Dr Norman A. Solomon – Assistant Professor of Industrial Relations, Faculty of Management, McGill University, Montreal, Canada.
Dr A.S. Sethi – Associate Professor, Master's Programme in Health Administration, Faculty of Administration, University of Ottawa, Ottawa, Canada.
Richard H. Stansel – Director of Personnel Administration, Ottawa Civic Hospital, Ottawa, Canada.
Dr Charles Steinberg – Professor of Industrial Relations, Faculty of Management, McGill University, Montreal, Canada.
Dr A.V. Subbarao – Associate Professor, Faculty of Administration, University of Ottawa, Ottawa, Canada.
Randall Sykes – Senior Research Officer, Canadian Union of Public Employees, Ottawa, Canada.

Index

Abbreviations: C – Canada; UK – United Kingdom; US – United States

Advisory, Conciliation and Arbitration Service (UK) 149–50, 151, 152, 160, 289, 298–9, 360–1
Alberta 45–6, 100–1, 191–3
American Federation of State, County and Municipal Employees 65–6, 72, 219, 220–1
American Medical Association 239–40
American Nurses Association 68–9, 196, 197, 198–9
Anti-Inflation Board (C) 313–16, 316–19, 320–2
Arbitration 279–82, 287–8, 296–8
Association of Scientific, Technical and Managerial Staffs (UK) 76, 77, 201

Boards 276–9, 292
British Columbia 45, 209, 269–70, 291, 296–8; collective bargaining 174, 191, 210; Hospital Association 210–11; legislation 98–100, 269–70, 291, 295–6; Nurses Association 190, 191, 192
British Medical Association 151, 245–53 passim

California 196, 199
Canada: anti-inflation programme 313–16; arbitration 265, 290–2; bargaining 43–50, 174–7, 180–6, 190–6, 208–16, 235–6; collective agreements 306–9; compensative increases 317; conflict resolution 260–8; controls 316–23; dispute resolution 264; federal jurisdiction 97–8; incomes policy 304–24; inflation 305–6, 311, 313; Labour Code 98, 264, 268; mediator 264–5; nurses 44, 192; physicians 233–8, 319, 320; strikes 215, 230; unemployment 305–6, 309–11, 313; unions 43–5; wage settlements 311–12; wages and price changes 320–2
Canadian Nurses Association 190
Canadian Union of Operating Engineers 45, 174, 229

Canadian Union of Public Employees 44, 49–51, 74, 176, 208–9, 318–19
Carter Administration 347, 348, 350
Central Arbitration Committee (UK) 149
Centralisation 180–9
Civil Rights Act 1964 (US) 164
Civil Service Act 1960 (C) 97–8
Civil Service Pay Research Unit (UK) 178
Civil Service Reform Act 1978 (US) 128–9, 134, 293, 345
Collective bargaining 146–57, 151–7, 174, 177–8, 180–6, 187–9, 191, 210, 224–8, 358–64
College of General Practitioners (UK) 248
Committee of Inquiry into Pay etc. of Nurses and Midwives (UK) 333–4
Confederation of Health Service Employees (UK) 75–84 passim, 86, 88, 221, 231, 333
Confederation of National Trade Unions (C) 43–4
Connecticut 132, 199
Consumer Price Index (US) 343
Contracts of Employment Act 1963 (UK) 157, 158
Cost control commissions (US) 351
Council on Wage and Price Stability (US) 344, 347, 348
Counter Inflation Acts 1972, 1973 (UK) 332–3
Crown employees (UK) 157–8

Doctors and Dentists Review Body (UK) 247–50, 328, 334

Emergency Powers Acts 1920, 1964 (UK) 142
Employment Act 1980 (UK) 87, 139, 143, 156
Employment Appeal Tribunal (UK) 153–4
Employment Protection Acts 1975, 1978 (UK) 140, 148–52, 289
Equal Pay Act 1970 (UK) 157

Federal Mediation and Conciliation

Service: C 263-4; US 278-9, 293, 345

Federal Service Impasses Panel (US) 128, 293

General and Municipal Workers' Union (UK) 221, 231

General Nursing Council (UK) 87, 200

Halsbury Committee (UK) 179, 203, 295

Health and Safety at Work Act 1974 (UK) 154-5

Health Services Act 1976 (UK) 251

Hospital Consultants' and Specialists' Associations (UK) 252

Hospital Cost Containment Act 1977 (US) 349

Hospital Insurance and Diagnostic Services Act 1957 (C) 228

Hospital Labour Disputes Arbitration Acts 1965, 1970 (Ontario) 174-5, 211, 269, 291

Illinois 130-1

Incomes policy: C 304-24; UK 325, 341, US 342-57

Industrial Court (UK) 146-7, 148

Industrial Disputes Tribunal (UK) 147, 159-61

Industrial Relations Act 1971 (UK) 84, 140, 142, 156, 252

Industrial Relations and Disputes Investigation Act 1948 (C) 97

International Union of Operating Engineers (C) 45, 174, 228, 229

Iowa 293

Junior Hospital Doctors' Association (UK) 251, 252, 253

Labor Relations Act 1970 (Ontario) 269, 273

Landrum-Griffin Act 1959 (US) 118-19

McCarthy Report (UK) 179, 360, 362

Manitoba 44, 46-7, 102, 174, 193-4

Massachusetts 132, 279

Med-Arb 265-7, 268, 281

Mediation 273-6, 288

Medicaid 240, 349

Medical Care Act 1966 (C) 228

Medical Practitioners' Union (UK) 77, 245

Medicare 240, 349

Michigan 132, 134, 281

Minnesota 131, 217, 296

Monopsony 33-4

Montana 132-3

National and Local Government Officers Association (UK) 76, 82, 83, 88

National Arbitration Tribunal (UK) 147

National Board for Prices and Incomes (UK) 223, 327, 330-2

National Federation of Social Affairs (C) 53

National Health Service (UK) 74, 141-6, 180; incomes policy 327-36; junior doctors 250-1; private practice 250, 251

National Health Service Act 1946 (UK) 325

National Labor Relations Board (US) 60, 117, 120-1, 123, 124-5, 177, 196, 240, 292; and Taft Hartley Amendment Act 133, 135; v. Yoshiva University 242

National Union of General and Municipal Workers (UK) 76, 77

National Union of Hospital and Health Care Employees (US) 66-8, 124, 219

National Union of Public Employees (UK) 75-84 *passim*, 221

Nebraska 296

Negotiations 270-3

Nevada 293

New Brunswick 48, 106, 192, 195-6, 214

Newfoundland 49, 109-10, 192, 194-5, 297

New York 131, 177, 217, 218, 296, 297

Nova Scotia 48-9, 106-7, 192

Nurses Act 1943 (UK) 200

Nurses' Guild (US) 196

Nurses, Midwives and Health Visitors Act 1978 (UK) 202

Ontario 47, 175-6, 177, 185, 186, 212, 229, 295, 297; arbitration 290-1, 296; bargaining 174-7, 183, 194, 211-13, 229-30; Hospital Association 175-6; legislation 102-4, 269; Nurses' Association 175, 176, 190-2, 194

Oregon 132

Pennsylvania 131

Physicians, collective bargaining by: C 233-8; UK 244-53; US 238-44

Prince Edward Island 48, 107-9, 192, 194, 209, 291

Professional Standards Review Organizations (US) 344

Professions Supplementary to Medicine Act 1960 (UK) 202

Public Service Employment Act 1966 (C) 98

Public Service Labor Relations Act 1968 (New Brunswick) 214, 270
Public Service Staff Relations Act 1967 (C) 98, 135, 291, 292

Quebec 44, 47-8, 195, 213, 270; legislation 104-6, 291

Redundancy Payments Act 1965 (UK) 157
Regional Hospital Consultant and Specialists' Association (UK) 245, 251, 252
Register of Medical Auxilaries (UK) 200
Remuneration and Conditions of Service Regulations (UK) 148
Royal College of Midwives (UK) 200
Royal College of Nursing (UK) 77, 86, 88, 151, 200, 333
Royal Commission on Doctors and Dentists Remuneration (UK) 247-8
Royal Commission on Trade Unions and Employers Associations (Donovan Commission) (UK) 152, 159

San Francisco-Oakland 177, 218
Saskatchewan 46, 101-2, 192, 193, 270, 314
Service Employees International Union: C 44, 51, 63-4, 72, 174, 176, 228; US 219
Sex Discrimination Act 1965 (UK) 157
Spens Committee (UK) 246
Standing Commission on Pay Comparability (Clegg Commission) (UK) 88, 227, 290, 295, 335-8 *passim*
Steward, union 152-4, 155, 224, 225, 226

Taft-Hartley Act 1947 (US) 116-17, 118, 177; Amendment Act 1974 119-22, 133-4, 134-5, 217, 242-3, 270, 345, 360
Terms and Conditions of Employment Act 1959 (UK) 148
Trade union 151-5, 155-7, 167, 183-4,
185; *see also individual unions*
Trade Union and Labour Relations Acts 1974, 1976 (UK) 139, 142, 143, 151, 156, 252
Trade Unions Act 1944 (Saskatchewan) 270
Transport and General Workers' Union (UK) 76, 231

United Kingdom: ancillary staff 221-8, 335; arbitration 146-50, 288-90; centralisation 180-1; collective bargaining 146-57, 221-8, 199-205; collective labour law and industrial action 141-6; conciliation 146-50; contracts 158-9; discrimination 164-5; incomes policy 325-36; individual employment law 157-65; maternity rights 162-4; redundancy 161-2; strikes 135; unfair dismissal 159-61; union growth 75-8
United States: arbitration 292-8, 351; bargaining units 122-3; collective bargaining 146-57, 177-8, 180-6, 199-205, 221-8, 345; cost control programmes 348-9, 353; incomes policies 342-57, interns 239, 242-3; inflation 342-4; labour movement structure 58-63; price level increase 342; unionism 57-63

Voluntary Effort Progam (US) 349

Wage changes, supply responsiveness 34-5
Wagner Act 1935 (US) 97, 113-18, 177, 240, 241, 345
Whitley Councils (UK) 75-6, 135, 162-3, 178-80, 200-2, 327-9; administration and clerical 329; ancillary workers 328; doctors 246, 247, 327-8; nurses 327, 328-9, 330
Wisconsin 129-39, 131-2, 134, 279, 293